THE MAN-NOT

THE MAN-NOT

RACE, CLASS, GENRE, AND THE DILEMMAS
OF BLACK MANHOOD

TOMMY J. CURRY

TEMPLE UNIVERSITY PRESS
Philadelphia • Rome • Tokyo

TEMPLE UNIVERSITY PRESS
Philadelphia, Pennsylvania 19122
www.temple.edu/tempress

Copyright © 2017 by Temple University—Of The Commonwealth System of
    Higher Education
All rights reserved
Published 2017

Library of Congress Cataloging-in-Publication Data

Names: Curry, Tommy J., 1979– author.
Title: The man-not : race, class, genre, and the dilemmas of black manhood /
    Tommy J. Curry.
Description: Philadelphia : Temple University Press, 2017. | Includes
    bibliographical references and index.
Identifiers: LCCN 2016049920 (print) | LCCN 2017010224 (ebook) | ISBN
    9781439914878 (ebook) | ISBN 9781439914854 (hardback : alk. paper) | ISBN
    9781439914861 (paper : alk. paper)
Subjects: LCSH: African American men. | African American men—Race identity.
    | BISAC: SOCIAL SCIENCE / Ethnic Studies / African American Studies. |
    SOCIAL SCIENCE / Men's Studies.
Classification: LCC E185.86 (ebook) | LCC E185.86 .C986 2017 (print) | DDC
    305.38/896073—dc23
LC record available at https://lccn.loc.gov/2016049920

♾ The paper used in this publication meets the requirements of the American
National Standard for Information Sciences—Permanence of Paper for Printed
Library Materials, ANSI Z39.48-1992

Printed in the United States of America

9 8 7 6 5 4 3 2 1

This book is dedicated to my parents,

Mr. Tommy James Curry and Mrs. Shirley Mae Curry.

"It's the one thing they can't take from you."

Contents

THE MAN-NOT

Introduction

Toward a Genre Study of
Black Male Death and Dying

Addressing the Caricatures
that Serve as Theory in the Study
of Black Males

I SEE DEAD BLACK MALE BODIES, Black men and boys, in the streets. Dead Niggers made into YouTube sensations. I see their executions on the Internet: the corpses of Trayvon Martin, Michael Brown, little Tamir Rice cycled for eternity. I hear Jordan Davis's music and Sean Bell's vows. I feel Black male death all around me and I am scared—scared that one day I will be forced to not speak. They shame me when I speak about Black men and boys. They threaten me with the names of white men. I hear: patriarch, sexist, misogynist as they condemn me for identifying the murderers and lynch mobs of Black males. They wear hoods with disciplinary embroidery whispering *Nigger* under their breaths. These Black and white faces stand guard at the gates of the academy, and I fear they will make me be still; they will kill me. They will force me to remain silent. I write this knowing that my words will not outpace the bullet of another gun transforming living flesh into rotting meat. I know as I write this that another Black man or boy will die. I know as I think about their deaths, the end of their lives is coming to be. This America makes corpses of Black males. It is simply the reality of our day that Black males die. This death, however, is shunned, cast out of the halls of the university, and avoided at all costs by disciplines. This reality has not transformed any of the decadent theories that tie Black manhood to the caricatures of the 1970s. Black men are thought to be latent rapists—the Black Macho of old—violent patriarchs, a privileged Black male, craving the moment he is allowed to achieve the masculinity of whites. These mythologies, of decades long gone, remain the morality of disciplines and the political foundation from which racist caricatures become revered concepts.

I write this book from a twenty-first century in which Black men and boys are still being lynched in America. Otis Byrd was found hanging from a tree on March 20, 2015, in Port Gibson, Mississippi,[1] and Lennon Lacy's seventeen-year-old body was found on August 29, 2014, hanging from a children's swing set in Bladenboro, North Carolina.[2] I write from a twenty-first century in which Black men such as Matthew Ajibade are hit in their genitals with a Taser and beaten to death.[3] I write to you from a twenty-first century where a Black man named Kevin Campbell, a father stopped for driving on a suspended license, was confined to a cage for hours and anally sodomized by a Detroit police officer.[4] I write to you from a world where an innocent Black man can be deprived of decades from his life and convicted of rape because his face came to a woman in a dream as her rapist.[5] This is the precariousness that has come to define what Black men and boys endure as life. I write this book to give voice to the Black male coerced into silence: his experiences denied within disciplines and his realities refused by theory.

Theory is a fickle thing. The proliferation of discourses around sexuality over the past several decades has done little to clarify the relation between socially constructed gender categories (such as race and sex) and the biological bodies that possess them. Likewise, despite decades of debate, the category of masculinity remains indeterminate and somewhat vacuous, referenced almost solely by one's genitalia.[6] The appearance of more complex theoretical advancements articulated by the crest of race, class, and gender has come to conceal rather than reveal significant and empirical aspects of Black (sexual) life. Imposing analytic categories on bodies as substitutable for depicting actual social or historical relations obscures both the quotidian and the repetitive phenomena that materialize as various social stratifications. It is not uncommon for (complex) theories of masculinity to stand in stark contradiction to the actually observable positions of the groups they aim to reference.

Whereas masculinities studies outside the United States have begun the arduous task of assessing the presumed linkage among maleness, patriarchy, and domination, feminist theory in the United States has come to emphasize masculinity as primarily patriarchal and to claim those masculinities that do not coincide with this dominant gender hierarchy for itself—as progressive and feminist-inspired.[7] These masculinity scholars from Europe and its past colonies have insisted on the difference between hegemonic and non-hegemonic masculinities and argued for a more accurate account of (white) men that "further facilitates the discovery and identification of "equality masculinities: those that legitimate an egalitarian relationship between men and women, between masculinity and femininity, and among men."[8] They insist:

> Gendered power relations are dynamic, unstable and ambiguous, and dominant forms of masculinity do not always legitimize patriarchy. Therefore the question of men's patriarchal oppression of women must

remain an open empirical and contextual question. Gender and masculinity researchers therefore need to develop theoretical frameworks
that can grasp changes, complexities, ambivalences, ruptures and resistance.[9]

While the male descendants of colonizers are recognized for the naturally occurring varieties of masculinities within their group, this insistence on
multiple masculinities has often been denied to Black men who are the descendants of slaves. Theories concerning Black masculinity revolve around
a fixed political idea in the United States that is deemed progressive by the
extent to which it is sufficiently feminist and deemed patriarchal by the extent to which it is not. Unlike in mainstream masculinity scholarship, there
have been few efforts to verify non-hegemonic Black masculinities sociologically or conceptually separate from the already established norms in gender studies. Black males, who are stereotyped as hyper-masculine and violent
throughout society, are intuitively marked as patriarchal within theory. Instead of being similarly disrupted by the critiques of hegemonic masculinity's
failure to account for the class and cultural diversity within white masculinities, hyper-masculinity is proposed as the phylogenic marker of Black maleness. Consequently, Black males are thought to be the exemplifications of
white (bourgeois) masculinity's pathological excess. In other words, the toxic
abnormality of a hegemonic white masculinity becomes the conceptual norm
for Black men and boys.

Black males are often theorized as defective. As the gender theorist Arthur F.
Saint-Aubin explains, "Even when [B]lack men are the ostensible subjects
(they are, in fact, objects) of workshops, special journals editions, etc., they
are still marginalized theoretically and compared to a norm by which they are
usually judged lacking."[10] Because Black men are not subjects of—or in—
theories emanating from their own experience, they are often conceptualized
as the threats others fear them to be. This fear has been used to legitimize
thinking of Black males as degraded and deficient men who compensate for
their lack of manhood through deviance and violence. As the social scientists
Andrea G. Hunter and James Earl Davis explain, "Studies of Black women
emphasize how out of oppression a unique definition of womanhood was
forged, one in which adversity gave rise to strength. However, the discourse
around men and oppression focuses on the stripping away of manhood. It is
a perspective that casts Black men as victims and ignores their capacity to
define themselves under difficult circumstances."[11] This paradigm is far too
prevalent to not warrant remark. Racist accounts of Black males depict them
as lesser males who are lazy, unintelligent, aggressive, and violent toward
women and children and who abandon their families physically and cannot
provide for them economically, while nonetheless requiring coercive legal and
extralegal sanctions to control their hyper-masculinity and predatory inclina-

tions. Racism against Black men often results in their emasculation, criminalization, and death. Black men have not only survived but developed rich
analyses of this oppression under the capitalist ethno-patriarchal regime we
call white supremacy. However, their thoughts are not spoken of as positive
programs capable of actually addressing their suffering. The concepts emerging from Black male experience are often described as pathological coping
mechanisms fixated on Black males' achieving their manhood at any cost,
rather than liberatory ideas applicable to all Blacks.

Consequently, Black men's experiences of racism are framed as one-
dimensional, narrow, and devoid of any analyses that understand the horrors
of sexual violence. Such claims, however, severely underestimate the complexity of Black male subjugation under racist social systems and within periods of colonialization. As early as Calvin Hernton's *Sex and Racism in
America,* there has been a realization that "racial hatred is carnal hatred . . .
sexualized hatred"[12]—a phallicism or process that criminalizes Black males as
sexual threats like the rapist, while simultaneously constituting them as the
carnal excesses and fetishes of the white libido. Racism is a complex nexus, a
cognitive architecture used to invent, reimagine, and evolve the presumed
political, social, economic, sexual, and psychological superiority of the white
races in society, while materializing the imagined inferiority and hastening
the death of inferior races. Said differently, racism is the manifestation of the
social processes and concurrent logics that facilitate the death and dying of
racially subjugated peoples.

At the center of this complexity, the regenerative arc, so to speak, of this
ideology is the caricature of racialized men as threats to the social and biological reproduction of white order. Simply put, "One of the motivations behind European-American racism—as discerned for example in certain racial
myths and stereotypes, in certain civil and criminal statutes regarding miscegenation and rape, and in the history of racial brutality like lynching—is a
fear of [B]lack male sexuality and a need to control [B]lack masculinity."[13] For
the idea of an all-powerful white male figure to achieve cultural institution-
alization and buy-in from the masses, "the dominant culture needs its 'nigger
boys,' its ugly inferior, its 'other' in order to construct itself as superior and
beautiful 'men.'"[14] The Black male—the Nigger—was constructed as the white
race's antipodal monstrosity, a sexual threat to the very foundation of white
civilization if its savagery was not repressed. These speciations from the ideal
(white) male type are examples of the *testeric* condition that plagues Black
maleness generally in the United States.[15] Because *testeria* emerges from the
disjunctive isolation Black maleness has from the normative maleness that is
represented as white, the *testeric,* or the cool poser, or the eunuch manifests
the repression of the social order corporeally—in his flesh—as Pavlovian
peculiarities to stave off death. The death of Black males is meant to prevent
his reproduction, and impede his ability to reproduce. This is the boundary

between the abject and the corpse the Black male inhabits. It is the peculiar genre Black males occupy and the place from which their perspectives emanate.

The Man-Not as a Philosophical Grounding for a Genre Study of Black Male Death and Dying

Black male death and suffering is thought to be generic, captured solely by the category of race. Race, however, is not an efficacious category of analysis under our present intersectional and poststructural arrangement. Race is a category under constant disciplinary surveillance, exposing it to a seemingly infinite number of attacks for being overdetermined and essentialist and therefore in need of any combination of experimental antiessentialist solutions. This dispersion/deconstruction/dismissal of the race category has concrete consequences for Black males attempting to situate and describe their experience and history, because race has been the only category offered by disciplines through which Black men can theoretically articulate their experience. Consequently, Black males find themselves articulating their concerns through alien theories rooted in this displacement. Because race is accepted as socially constructed, all cultural and experiential products from a racial perspective remain suspect. Race consciousness is problematized and rejected prima facia as narrow and masculine, while gender, as Oyèrónké Oyewùmì reminds us, remains inextricably tied to biological notions of the female despite the performative and cultural-situatedness of the term.[16] Black and female allows for standpoints, histories, and experiences that serve to ground (gender) theory, while Black and male is taken to be the historical perspective that must be disowned to free these other-gendered, not-male voices.

It is routinely insisted that race and gender are socially constructed and illusory. Yet it is only race that is displaced, while gender, *being synonymous with female*, is centered as the dominant theoretical voice of Black subjectivity and vulnerability—a centering technique that depends on the sustaining anthropological assumptions of white gender categories, not those disfigured within the negation of Black(ness)—the nonhuman/nonbeing matrices authored within chattel slavery and colonialism. Gender becomes the symbolic representation of bodies—their intent—while race simply acts as a modifier and operates to overdetermine or lessen the power position of *maleness*. Consequently, gender studies becomes discourses about women, where racialized men are interpreted by the lack of power they have compared with real (white) men. Black men simply do not exist as viable social subjects or reflective entities, given their disfigurement within the established gender order. Rooting gender within the biological confines of the female body makes thinking about gender synonymous with thinking about women—the *who and what they re-*

late to. In this bio-mythos, the female is taken to be the taxonomic origin of gender(ed) knowledge and history, where that which is defined as *not female* can only be outside and barred from creating gender theory.

Because *maleness* has come to be understood as synonymous with power and patriarchy, and racially codified as white, it has no similar existential content for the Black male, who in an anti-Black world is denied maleness and is ascribed as feminine in relation to white masculinity. If whiteness is masculine in relation to Blackness, then Blackness becomes relationally de-fined as not masculine and feminine, because it lacks the power of white masculinity. Thus, Black maleness is, in fact, a de-gendered negation of white maleness that is feminine because of its subordinate position to white mascu-linity, but *not female*, because Black maleness lacks a specific gender coordi-nate that corresponds to either white maleness or white femaleness—and, as shown later, relates to the white female primarily as rapist. Maria Lugones similarly emphasizes the anachronism of attributing gender to the colonized and enslaved bodies we now think of through the frameworks of Black mas-culinity and Black femininity. As she remarks, "Under the imposed gender frame work [of colonial modernity] the bourgeois white Europeans were civilized; they were fully human. The hierarchical dichotomy as a mark of the human also became a normative tool to damn the colonized. The behavior of the colonized and their personalities/souls were judged as bestial and thus non-gendered, promiscuous, sexual and sinful."[17] The colonized/racialized subject was denied gender precisely to define the boundaries between the content of the human and the deficit of those racially speciated. This is not to say there was no sexual differentiation between bodies and the roles assigned to them. Rather, it highlights that "colonized people become male and female. Males became not-human-as-not-men and colonized females became not-human-as-not-women."[18] The Black man, deprived not only of an identity but also a history and existence that differs from his brute negation, experiences the world as a *Man-Not.*

Man-Not(ness) is a term used to express the specific genre category of the Black male. *Genre* differs from *gender* by this distance Black males share with Western man a priori and, by consequence, patriarchy. Whereas gender as-serts that historical and social orders, defined by the biologic marker of sex, are in fact synonymous with the historical and sociological location of Black males, genre expresses how the register of nonbeing distorts the categories founded upon white anthropology or that of the human. Popular categories of analysis such as class, gender, and even race suppose a universal human template upon which they imprint. But what is the applicability of human categories on the nonhuman? The Black male is negated not from an origin of (human) being, but from nihility. Frantz Fanon's reflections on objecthood and nonbeing are not simply descriptions of negation; they are not terms of proxemics but terms of register. Nonbeing expresses the condition of Black male being—the nihility from which it is birthed. Away from the bourgeois order of kind expressed by man, genre is specific to the kind, the type of existence expressed by the Black male. For Sylvia Wynter, *genre* indicates the disruption of the order founded on European MAN and WOMAN, which is expressed by the term of gender. The contact of Europe with non-Europeans reordered the gender schema, because "the primary code of difference now became that between 'men' and 'natives,' with the traditional 'male' and 'female' distinctions now coming to play a secondary—if none the less powerful—reinforcing role within the system of symbolic representations."[19] Insofar as Blackness expresses the indeterminacy of being as nonbeing, gender too is reformulated. This is why Wynter coined the word *genre* to replace *gender*. She writes, "'genre' and 'gender' come from the same root. They mean 'kind.' . . . [W]hat I am suggesting is that 'gender' has always been a function of the instituting of 'kind.'"[20]

The Man-Not grows from the incongruity I observed between what theory claims to explain and the *actual* existence of Black men and boys—an *actual* reality that remains excluded from its purview. Simply stated, analyzing Black males as the Man-Not is a theoretical formulation that attempts to capture the reality of Black maleness in an anti-Black world. Because it is rooted in the colonial formulation of sex designation, not gender, the Man-Not recognizes that racial maleness is not coextensive with or synonymous to the formulations of masculinity, or patriarchy, offered by white reality. The Man-Not is the denial not only of Black manhood but also of the possibility to be anything but animal, the savage beast, outside the civilizational accounts of gender. To suggest that Black males are, in fact, gendered patriarchs is an erasure of the actual facts of anti-Black existence and a substitution of the white anthropological template at the core of negating Black (male) existence as its end. Michael Brown's death, like that of Vonderitt Myers, Oscar Grant, John Crawford, Jordan Davis, Alton Sterling, Philandro Castile, and Stephen Watts, represents the accumulation of an intellectual failure to grasp the complexities and the motivations implicated within the genocidal logics of American racism beyond the categories of modern taxonomy. The Negrophobia that drove white America to endorse lynching as a technology of murder is the same anxiety and fear that now allow the white public to endorse the murder of Black men and boys as justifiable homicides. Black males are often killed by police officers because the officers claim they fear for their lives—that Black men have life-threatening weapons or guns. This phobia is a normalized and institutional program used to justify police violence, ostracism, and incarceration; it is a fear that is given so much weight in individual cases precisely because it is a fear that both white America and many nonwhite Americans share. The vulnerability of Black men and boys lies in this consensus, and it is one that extends beyond the borders of white psychopathology. It is an American maxim propagated through the mass media and the assumptions of liberal progressive gender politics and internalized by the populations—Black, white, male, or female—that consume these mythologies and images.

In academic philosophy, there has yet to be a text that deals specifically with the history and theorization of Black males. While there are accounts of Black men and boys throughout the social sciences, mostly focused on the obstacles facing this group, the discipline of philosophy has made no such efforts to investigate Black maleness beyond its alleged privileged position to that of the Black woman or its undesirability (hyper-masculinity, [Black] Nationalism, and so on). Heavily influenced by intersectional feminist accounts of race and gender, Black men are thought to exemplify a privileged *disadvantaged* status that obscures our viewing of gender when their reality or subjectivity is centered. Rooted in an idealist calculus, Black men are conceptualized as empowered by their male identity such that any asymmetry between intraracial groups, where Black men, for example, are more visible or more represented than Black women, is attributed to patriarchy. This book aims for a closer interdisciplinary examination of this gender(ed) claim. Using history, sociology, and a range of social science findings, this book argues that Black men and boys are, in fact, *disadvantaged* because of their maleness. Taking the Black male experience seriously shows that what is now called gender is cumulative, not causal, and while certain problems may accumulate around male or female bodies, they are not isolated to those bodies or their histories. Hence, instead of being protected by patriarchy, Black men and boys are revealed to be its greatest victims under closer examination.

This book is not predetermined; it is not merely an articulation of a foregone conclusion. It was not written as the imposition of a theory onto Black males—as objects of study—in which the desired conclusion was decided before the research into Black men and boys as complex subjects even began. This book *theorizes Black male life* in the United States: its dying and the reality of its death. In other words, this text aims not only to use theory to draw tenable conclusions from the actual data on intimate partner violence, homicide, and incarceration as it pertains to Black men and boys but also to use data to inform the abstract themes that, according to gender theorists, explain Black males' social reality. Far too often, Black males are projected into academic projects as the stereotypes individuals perceive them as rather than how they actually exist in the world. This book was written to overwhelm the silence imposed on Black males through negative racial caricatures that become absolved of their moral offensiveness once they are called gender theory. Ideas of Black men as abusers of women and children, rapists, and power-hungry deviants run rampant throughout the academy and inform what is intuitively expressed as academic (gender) theory. Is there sufficient evidence, however, to ground these theories?

While there is tacit agreement among American institutions (courts, prisons, the press, and so forth) that Black males' deaths and the individuals responsible for these murders will be ideologically supported in their rationalizations and financially rewarded for their actions,[21] this is not the full scope of Black male vulnerability. Black males also endure societal discrimination and social ostracism because of their maleness. In his personal life, the discrimination targeting the Black male in the workforce often results in his unemployment, which only confirms that he is undesirable and unwanted as a colleague or peer within universities, corporations, and many blue-collar occupations. He is assumed to be a deviant, so his history of trauma and physical or sexual abuse at the hands of men or women, which precipitates many of his interpersonal conflicts as an adult, is denied. He is interpreted as a violent and abusive individual in need of criminal sanction rather than as a victim in need of treatment and compassion. This book is concerned with the sociological, historical, and ontological weight of Black manhood. It explores how the myth of the super-predator is codified within the disciplinary proliferation of theories about Black masculinity and makes it seemingly impossible to conceptualize the Black male as a victim and disadvantaged when compared with other groups. This book shows how theory and stereotype converge throughout the multiple exegeses offered to analyze the external conditions and internal motivations of Black men and boys. Academic theory uses the same pathological explanations of Black male deviance, violence, and abuse that continue to haunt Black males and justify their murder in society. To advance theory, the vulnerability of the Black male is denied, and his disadvantage is obscured from a full viewing by scholars and the public. He is thought of only as a perpetrator, never a victim.

The Man-Not was thought of as a corrective of sorts, as a concept of Black males that could challenge the historical and theoretical accounts of Black men and boys that have proliferated throughout disciplines and are taken as gospel in academic research. This book is the first philosophical exploration of the oppression of the Black male that aims to synthesize the multiple findings and research concerning his condition across disciplines. Rather than simply reproduce sociological findings highlighting his societal disadvantage, I create a theory and operational paradigm by which we can understand the intellectual, historical, and sexual diversity of Black men. While such an exploration will never capture the full experience of Black male homosexuality any more than the Black male's heterosexual experience or his denied and condemned polyamory, The Man-Not is an attempt to reflectively engage the conditions that dictate the formation of Black male sexualities and the historical vulnerabilities that obscure our viewing of them as actual realities of Black manhood. This is a reflection not on "identities" but, rather, the historical material—the problems and experiences—that contour how Black men have come to define themselves. This is a book to challenge how we think of and perceive the conditions that actually affect all Black males and why we choose to see some things but deny others.

Black Masculinity as Buck Studies: Documenting the Links between Hegemonic Masculinity and the Reality of Black Males

The mimetic thesis, or the idea that Black males seek to emulate and ulti-mately realize themselves as patriarchs next to white men, has been a central feature of Black feminist ideology since the penning of Michele Wallace's *The Black Macho and the Myth of the Superwoman* in the late 1970s. The emer-gence of the Buck—the mythological heterosexual Black male figure that emerged from slavery—as the basis of Black male political aspiration in the twentieth century has been a central feature of Black masculinity studies for the past four decades. Wallace's text reduced the complexities of political eco-nomics, racism, history, and class mobility to the genital level. She maintained that Black men had internalized the white man's obsession with his penis. As she said, "[w]hite men were perversely obsessed with the [B]lack man's geni-tals but the obsession turned out to be a communicable disease and in the sixties [B]lack men came down with high fevers."[22] More than simply offering one perspective of the Black Power era, Wallace's text created a bridge be-tween white patriarchy and Black male political aspirations that allowed the racially specific accounts of white patriarchal power isolated to white feminist theories of dominance or hegemony to extend to Black males. The Black Ma-cho, the "male chauvinist that was frequently cruel, narcissistic, and short-sighted," was birthed by Black men accepting the sexual primitivism of the Black male presupposed by whites.[23] The Black man of the 1960s lost himself in the image of this brute, according to Wallace, making "himself a living testament to the white man's failures."[24] He suffered poverty, deprivation, and unhappiness "because his [B]lack perspective, like the white perspective, sup-ported the notion that manhood is more valuable than anything else."[25] Wal-lace makes a distinction between an organic and a mimetic Black manhood: "As long as [the Black man] was able to hold onto his own [B]lack-centered definition of manhood, his sense of himself was not endangered." The longer the Black male stayed in this country, the more "he would get the [B]lack and white perspectives confused."[26]

Largely influenced by the adoption of Freudian psychoanalysis and the idea of Black male assimilation into American society, contemporary Black gender frames continue to understand Black masculinity as striving to fulfill its oedipal drive toward the father right of white masculinity. Under this par-adigm, Black males are reduced to their phallic aspirations for selfhood and seek to dominate others to compensate for their subjugation. Gender theo-rists in the 1990s asserted that phallocentrism, patriarchy, and Black males' *lacking* (be it of power, recognition, or a symbolic phallus) were a viable in-terpretive frame through which Black maleness could be understood. Even today, Black males are depicted as the absence of themselves for one another, having few attributes worth emulating. Their lack of Black fathers, their lack of power in America, their lack of employment, their lack of manhood—all sociological phenomena—become the markers of their incompleteness, demonstrations of their definitional-ontological failures as Black males rather than proof of their subordinated male status and existence in a completely different register of sexuality. Black males are not only defined by this lack; they are also thought to be complete only when they stand side by side with white men. Consequently, Black masculinity is theorized through this psychoanalytic (unconscious) yearning for the world of the white man, his power, and his possessions, which often include the white woman.

By disregarding the historical examples of Black male resistance to white supremacy, as well as the traditional expectations of hegemonic masculinity supported even by Black women at the anthropological level as Christian, capitalist, homophobic, and so forth, the Black male is attached to patriarchy at a biological level, such that every action of self-defense, politics, or love becomes an exercise of his attempt to realize the patriarchy denied to him. Aaronette M. White summarizes this position in Black gender frames quite well:

> Though most African American men do not experience the same level of power as most [w]hite American men, patriarchy produces pecking orders across different groups of men and within different subgroups of men. Each subgroup of men defines manhood in ways that conform to the economic and social possibilities of that group. However, even marginalized men (e.g., poor men of color) accept the system because they benefit from the "patriarchal dividend," which is the advantage men in general gain from the overall subordination of women, particularly the women in their subgroup.[27]

Accounts similar to White's thinking can be found throughout Black masculinity literature,[28] but the evidence that subordinated masculinity is of the same species as hegemonic masculinity such that it can be of the kind that obtains this ideal is sorely lacking. To substantiate the view that Black men benefit from patriarchy despite their inferior social, economic, and racial status, White appeals to Raewyn Connell's first edition of *Masculinities* as evidence for the claim that Black men would be rewarded in a patriarchal society as men.[29] This grounding of patriarchy in Black male interest and his desire to be, or be like, the white male is suspicious. It suggests that while Black men can articulate themselves as oppressed subjects to myriad structures and ideologies, from racism to classism, imperialism to colonization, and religion to atheism, gender remains unknown to them despite their role and history as subordinated men positioned outside the masculinity of ruling-class whites in the United States.

The lure of white patriarchy is a common trope used to explain the mimetic urge of Black males, but why do we find no assumption of this imitative character in Black feminist accounts of Black womanhood, despite the vast historical works demonstrating the internalization of various Victorian gender ideals and social Darwinist theories, as well as their support for patriarchy as the basis of racial uplift during the nineteenth century? Black men and women have been subjected to the same cultural, ethnological, and anthropological theories rooted in racial evolution, yet only Black males are thought to have internalized these historical views to such an extent that their sociological realities have been transformed into Black masculine ontology. While much of Black feminism historically has appealed to democratic reform and continued integration into institutions, or to protection and recognition by the law (attempts to codify Black female vulnerability into societal institutions so that rape, domestic abuse, and discrimination are understood as violence to a living, breathing person), these appeals are recognized as calls for progressive change rather than a desire for the positionality and power of white womanhood, despite appeals to the same concepts and apparatuses that historically have sustained white women's (and men's, for that matter) economic and political power. There is no scholarship asserting that Sojourner Truth's "Ain't I a Woman?" proves that she aspires to the powers, recognition, and status of white women denied to her, but a litany that criticizes Black men for the slightest similarity to white thought or rhetoric concerning manhood.

Are only Black males envious of the position of the dominant classes? Take, for example, Truth's famous condemnation of Black men getting the right to vote, which has been quoted for years as evidence of the historical concern Black women have had about Black male political advancement:

> There is a great stir about colored men getting their rights, but not a word about the colored women; and if colored men get their rights, and not colored women theirs, you see the colored men will be masters over the women, and it will be just as bad as it was before. So I am for keeping the thing going while things are stirring; because if we wait till it is still, it will take a great while to get it going again. [w]hite women are a great deal smarter, and know more than colored women, while colored women do not know scarcely anything. They go out washing, which is about as high as a colored woman gets, and their men go about idle.[30]

Truth believed Black men were more brutal than the white men who orchestrated slavery and Black women were less intelligent than the white women who ruled over them. The historian Paula Giddings explains that "the difficult circumstances of [Truth's] life gave her a distorted view of [w]hites and Blacks."[31] Consequently, says Giddings, Truth shares a sentiment of Black men eerily similar to that of Elizabeth C. Stanton, who believed that "it would be better for a Black woman to be the slave of an educated [w]hite man than of a degraded, ignorant, [B]lack one."[32] If Truth's quote remains a reminder of the danger Black male politics has posed since the mid-nineteenth century, then why are we not also suspicious of the allure white womanhood could have over Black women?

Think of Stokely Carmichael's statement, "The only position for women in the SNCC is prone," for instance.[33] This sentence has become not only representative of him or of the ideology of the organization he represented but also evidence of Black males' patriarchal political inclination throughout the centuries.[34] Mary King, a member of Student Nonviolent Coordinating Committee (SNCC) and the author of *Freedom Song: A Personal Story of the 1960s Civil Rights Movement,* offers a vastly different account of this oft-cited statement. Carmichael's comment pertained to a position paper circulated for the November 1964 Waveland meeting of the SNCC written by Mary King and Casey Hayden. The position paper spoke to the assumption of male leadership and the role of male and female workers of SNCC. The position papers were meant to get the leadership to think about foundational questions: "'What is SNCC[?]' 'What do we organize[?]' 'Where do we organize[?]'"[35] The position paper on women asked the representatives to think about the role women played in the SNCC's leadership and decision-making structure. Specifically, the paper asked members to "consider why it is in SNCC that women who are competent, qualified, and experienced are automatically assigned to the 'female' kinds of jobs such as: typing, desk work, telephone work, filing, library work, cooking, and the assistant kind of administrative work but rarely the executive kind."[36]

King fondly accounts that Carmichael made fun of everything that crossed his agile mind, and this position paper was no different. When he came to the not-so-anonymous women's paper in the meeting, King recounts, "Looking straight at me, he grinned broadly and shouted, 'What is the position of women in SNCC?' Answering himself, he responded, 'The position of women in SNCC is prone!'"[37] According to King, the now infamous statement by Carmichael was a joke. She remembers that "Stokely threw back his head and roared outrageously with laughter. We all collapsed with hilarity. . . . It drew us all closer together, because, even in that moment, he was poking fun at his own attitudes."[38] Instead of describing Carmichael as some raging patriarchal maniac, King says, "Casey and I felt, and continue to feel, that Stokely was one of the most responsive men at the time that our anonymous paper appeared in 1964."[39] Several years later, Hayden confirmed King's recollection of events in SNCC. Even in 2010, Hayden remembered the SNCC as a "womanist, nurturing, and familial" organization. In fact, Hayden went as far as to state, "Women's culture and [B]lack culture merg[ed] for me in the southern freedom movement, especially in SNCC, free of constraints and the values of white patriarchy."[40]

What is it that essentially ties Black manhood—its aspirations, ideals, and perceptions—to random statements or jokes made by Black males to sexism and misogyny? What makes an individual's comments come to be understood as the historical consciousness of most, if not all, Black males? How does one Black man's thoughts in the 1960s come to represent the consciousness of them all, or even a majority of them, throughout time? Despite the prevalence of arguments to this effect, Black women were subjected to the sexist and misandrist ideas of the times no less often than Black men were. This is not an issue of masculinity or femininity as much as it is an issue of the assumptions of their day. Gender differences between Black men and women simply did not produce clear delineations of thought and attitudes throughout history. In fact, this is a position articulated by Wallace herself. She explains, "Black women would define their femininity (or their liberation, which was not, however, a movement) in terms of their lack of these same superficial masculine characteristics precisely because the myth of their inferiority, the [B]lack female stereotype, had always portrayed them as oversexed, physically strong and warlike."[41] Wallace actually argues that the Black Macho is only one side of the gender dynamic created by integration: "In the process of assimilation, integration and accommodation, [B]lacks had taken on the culture and values of whites in regard to sexuality and gender. This did more than make it inevitable that [B]lack men would be sexist or misogynistic: it also made inevitable [B]lack women's completely dysfunctional self-hatred." Yet there is not one exploration of this self-hatred taken on by Black women under the same conditions that allegedly created the Black Macho.[42] The Superwoman, literally the second half of the title to her book, has not generated any discussion in academic gender theory or Black feminism, despite the claim that, if we accept the Black Macho thesis, Black women aspire to the very same end.

Feminist-inspired theories of Black masculinity establish their legitimacy by racially profiling Black males. These theories assert a priori that Black males, as a group, are aspiring patriarchs, then surveil the individual behavior of Black men in society or, throughout a narrowly selected corpus of literatures accepted by disciplines, as evidence of that defect. This approach ignores the actual conditions and violence in American society that affect Black males and completely disregards the presence of the very same behaviors in other groups. Simply put, Black men appear to be explained by gender theory because they are the group most targeted by it. These accounts symbolically biologize Black maleness as the cause of seemingly endless pathologies that are actually expressed by any number of individuals regardless of their race or gender who find themselves in similar economic or political conditions. Contemporary thinking about patriarchy condemns Black male violence as an instrument of domination, while absolving Black women immersed in the same circumstances who display the same violent behaviors. It has simply become an accepted conceptual practice to construct Black males as malicious because their *excess masculinity* necessitates the domination of others, while women, regardless of multiple examples of violence, are constructed as ultimately good-intentioned and nonviolent because they are feminine.

Hegemonic Masculinity Theory and the Construction of the Black Male Threat: The Problem with Asserting Connell's Theory as Applicable to Black Males

The melding together of hegemonic masculinity theory and Wallace's account of the Black Macho within contemporary gender discourses is stunning. Sex role theory is heavily dependent on the political economy between men and women founded on the nuclear family in patriarchal societies, so it seems obvious that Wallace is not presenting the Black Macho as a sex role historically solidified by the relation between Black men and women within nuclear families. Wallace's rendering of history and slavery maintains that Black men and women have been denied the roles of white society because Black men and women were prevented from marrying and accepts that there was a Black manhood before the 1960s that was not Macho-istic. Wallace suggests that white masculinity was an ideal that Black men strived to attain, given their greater societal opportunities after civil rights. Allegedly, this newfound access to power led Black men to not only internalize white Americans' perverse hyper-sexual stereotypes of Black masculinity but also desire these sexual taboos politically for themselves.

Hegemonic masculinity theory resonates with many of the claims introduced by Wallace because Connell's first articulation of hegemonic masculinity was interpreted by scholars in the West as the aspiration toward which all masculinities tended. Hegemonic masculinity was a theory developed by Raewyn Connell in the 1980s. Connell's first work, *Ruling Class, Ruling Culture*, was a dense study of the Australian ruling class and its conflicts with the working-class population.[43] It is unsurprising, then, given Connell's interest in class theory, that Antonio Gramsci's theory of hegemony had some appeal to her evolving thinking about gender. As originally introduced, Connell conceptualized hegemonic masculinity as "a single structural fact, the global dominance of men over women."[44] Hegemonic masculinity asserts itself as a heterosexual practice that seeks to dominate women and subordinated masculinities that challenge its definition, such as that of homosexuality.[45] Connell does suggest that Western imperialism and colonialism fundamentally change the configuration of masculinity and femininity in relation to Blacks, but this thesis is not fully explored in this earlier work or introduced as a reason that some racialized or impoverished men might not seek to emulate the hegemonic masculine ideal in a given society.[46] Connell is very specific in her deployment of Gramsci's idea of hegemony in this regard:

In the concept of hegemonic masculinity, "hegemony" means (as in Gramsci's analyses of class relations in Italy from which the term is borrowed) a social ascendancy achieved in a play of social forces that extends beyond contests of brute power into the organization of private life and cultural processes. Ascendancy of one group of men over another achieved at the point of a gun, or by the threat of unemployment, is not hegemony. Ascendancy which is embedded in religious doctrine and practice, mass media content, wage structures, the design of housing, welfare/taxation policies and so forth, is.[47]

As a normative aspiration, hegemonic masculinity depends on socializing members of a given patriarchal society to an ideal form. Connell is very clear that "the cultural ideal (or ideals) of masculinity need not correspond at all closely to the actual personalities of the majority of men. Indeed the winning of hegemony often involves the creation of models of masculinity which are quite specifically fantasy figures."[48] Because hegemonic masculinity is held at the ideological level, there is no need for it to conflict with the emphasized femininity of the society—in fact, they would complement each other.[49] Connell's theory asserts that society is always in a "state of play"—dynamic, struggling, and meeting challenges against ideology with reification and new ideological rationalizations to support the desirability of the asserted hegemony. Institutions, individuals, and social forces are in constant interaction within the hegemonic masculine culture. There is no stasis or fixity in this account.

Connell's subsequent work, *Masculinities*, begins with a historical and theoretical conscience that is not readily apparent in *Gender and Power*. From the outset, Connell is clear that some societies simply do not have the concept of masculinity, much less an ideology of hegemonic masculinity. It simply is not universal. Connell also recognizes that "'masculinity' does not exist except in contrast with femininity. A culture which does not treat women and men as bearers of polarized character types, at least in principle, does not have a concept of masculinity in the sense of modern European/American culture."[50] Because it is a gender relation in society, masculinity is subject to social forces like any other relational phenomena. Connell outlines a three-tier model to understand the dynamics of masculinity. The first is power, or what is usually referred to as patriarchy or the subordination of women and dominance of men in Western/European societies. The second is labor, which includes not only wages but also the gendered division of wealth and work in these societies. Last but not least is cathexis or sexual desire. Extending her Freudian inclinations from *Gender and Power*, Connell asserts that the "practices that shape and realize desire are thus an aspect of the gender order."[51] As with her reading of Sigmund Freud in her first book, Connell is fascinated by Freud's explication of the "psychical and the social."[52] The motivations that drive how one constructs and participates in the external through the permission of one's internal is central in *Masculinities*. In 2002, Connell created a fourth category, symbolization, to capture what is sometimes referred to as performances of identity or the meanings conveyed by individuals through speech, dress, and behavior to assert their gender meanings.[53]

Unlike the assertions of many scholars who continue to use masculinity theory, Connell does not have a fixation on a specific politics as the solution to hegemonic masculinity and structures of patriarchy. As she concedes, "The formulation in *Gender and Power* attempted to locate all masculinities (and all femininities) in terms of a single pattern of power, the 'global dominance' of men over women. While this was useful at the time in preventing the idea of multiple masculinities from collapsing into an array of competing lifestyles, it is now clearly inadequate to our understanding of relations among groups of men and forms of masculinity and of women's relations with dominant masculinities."[54] In sharp contrast to the biologism operating within the premises of American gender theorists, previously highlighted by Oyewùmí's criticism of feminist gender analysis, Connell recognizes that "dominance in gender relations involves an interplay of costs and benefits, challenges to hegemonic masculinity arise from the 'protest masculinities' of marginalized ethnic groups, and bourgeois women may appropriate aspects of hegemonic masculinity in constructing corporate or professional careers."[55] Although Connell concedes that masculinity has established particular ways of using male bodies for work, there is no specific biological causality in which subordinated and subjugated masculinities necessarily aspire to embody hegemonic masculinity, any more than women of the dominant classes would seek to use that hegemony or emphasized femininity for their own interests. Perhaps more interesting, there is no suggesting that any one politic—feminist or otherwise—remedies the societal instantiations of hegemonic masculinity.

To escape the colonial paradigms of gender established on first world taxonomies, Connell herself has called for a shift away from Western concepts of gender altogether. This shift centers masculinities of the global South founded in anti-colonial struggle as radical departures from patriarchy. Connell maintains that formulations of Black and Indigenous masculinities birthed in conflict with colonialism and the imperial ruling class are non-hegemonic and offer models of resistance to patriarchy.[56] Such developments in Connell's thinking, which place Black men and other racialized males outside the purview of hegemonic masculinity, have been disregarded in American gender theories, which still rely on her much earlier formulations of hegemonic masculinity as well as a version of Wallace's theory of Black male assimilation into dominant white cultural norms. In short, Connell's theory excludes racialized males from the hegemonic masculinity paradigm, but in the United States the dominance of Wallace's assimilationist account of Black masculinity makes Black men de facto patriarchs.

In the United States, Robert Staples's decades-long work on Black masculinity and the Black family has been reduced to his debate with Audre Lorde
and Michele Wallace in *Black Scholar* in 1979.[57] Connell, however, recognizes
Staples's work as a serious challenge to hegemonic masculinity theory as originally proposed alongside James Messerschmidt's work on working-class masculinities.[58] Connell's use of hegemony is meant to explain how "gender
relations underscored the achievement of hegemonic masculinity largely
through cultural ascendancy—discursive persuasion—encouraging all to consent to, coalesce around, and embody such unequal gender relations."[59] For
Black males who were racially and sexually excluded from the ruling class,
such aspirations were unrealizable. The early work of Black women working
on gender and Marxism in the United States made such delineations abun-
dantly clear. Extending Angela Davis's argument in "Reflections on the Black
Woman's Role in the Community of Slaves" concerning the "objective equality
between Black men and women," from slavery to the Civil Rights era,[60] Gloria
Joseph, a Marxist Black feminist, argued that "the documented history of Black
women and men in the area of labor thus reveals that the peculiar institution
of slavery played a curious role in bringing about equality among Black men
and women as opposed to the inequality that was fostered among white wom-
en and men."[61] Because Black males (in terms of class position and a caste
position as racialized laborers) are structurally excluded from the ruling class,
serious thought was given in the late 1970s and early 1980s to their gender
orientation and whether or not they could even participate in the historical
and economic system of white patriarchy.

Remember: Connell has been developing her theory of gender and hegemonic masculinity since 1982. Her preliminary theories were based on her
initial study of Australian high school boys from ruling-class and working-
class families and the class aspirations reflected in the curriculum of these
schools.[62] It is a commonly articulated position with the advent of standpoint
epistemology that gender theories demand specificity to their subjects. It is
often assumed that works by Black women theorists entail some visceral so-
cial-historical-cultural connection to Black women, for example. In the case of
heterosexual Black men, however, there is a belief that their intentions and
motives can be adequately captured by generic theories of masculinity formulated on male children in colonial societies and upper-class settler culture. The
asserted closeness that Black males, among the poorest, most uneducated, and
most isolated (unassimilated) members of American society, are thought to
have to hegemonic masculinity and white patriarchy is evidence not of their
actual power or aspirations for (white) male domination, but of the extent to
which theorists and scholars have internalized the negative stereotypes about
Black males as hyper-masculine, violent, and dangerous. Instead of being specific inquiries into the attitudes, history, and destiny of Black men, theories
concerning Black masculinity are merely an attempt to read Black men into

the legacy established by white masculinity and condemn their political or economic aspirations that do not share the political motifs of liberal (Black) feminism as patriarchal. Under current disciplinary perspectives, Black males are denied the courtesy extended to other males throughout the world: the ability to organically formulate and practice non-patriarchal forms of manhood that are not dependent on feminist political norms.

Challenging the Caricature of the Hegemonic Black Male: The Sociological Findings of Black Male Gender Attitudes

Despite the mountains of empirical and conceptual ventures identifying and defining multiple notions of manhood and boyhood among Black males that dislodge the essentialist thesis asserted by Wallace, much of gender theory remains dedicated to the paradigm asserting Black heterosexual masculinity as the Buck or Black Macho caricature. Whereas mainstream (white) theories of patriarchy are debated and nuanced so that the theory (like Connell's) can be tested with empirical research, assertions about Black masculinity are taken as fact, to be complete and, moreover, incontrovertible. Posing challenges to prevailing theories maintaining that Black men are sexist, patriarchal, and set on domination are met with moral condemnation, while introducing material history to challenge the historiography maintaining that Black men pursued Civil Rights and Black Power to gain the right to dominate women and have sexual access to white women is classified as apologetics and summarily dismissed as "cape-ing for Black men." In a very real sense, theory mirrors the cultural and social context of its origin, and like the society from which it springs, academic (gender) theory is accepted as true because it rationalizes the accepted stereotypes of Black males held by the general public. There is a comfort found in theory that is not offered by public opinion, a correctness of sorts married to the word, despite it being no better founded than personal anecdote or experience. Black masculinity theory gains acceptance through an ideological rigidity that equates any disputing of the claim that Black men are patriarchs and sexist to a denial that sexism and patriarchy exist in Black communities. It is actually quite simple to hold that Black men are not patriarchs but are socialized to accept sexism, just as easy as it is to posit that in a racist society where Black males are criminalized and systematically impoverished, Black men and women are taught to pathologize that population. Nuance need not constitute denial.

Staples's *Black Masculinity: The Black Male's Role in American Society*, although rarely cited today in gender theory, is widely acknowledged as being among the first empirically driven analyses of Black males in American society. It shares this distinction with Lawrence E. Gary's anthology *Black Men*, which was published by Sage in 1981.[63] Contrary to the long-standing mythology that all race scholarship during the 1960s and 1970s was dedicated to the plight of the Black male, it became evident in the late 1970s that social scientists knew very little empirically about Black men and boys. Given the proliferation of texts about Black women and girls in the early 1970s, such as Joyce Ladner's *Tomorrow's Tomorrow*, La Francis Rodgers-Rose's *The Black Woman*, and *The Black Macho and the Myth of the Superwoman*, Gary noted, "Although these publications have added considerably to our knowledge of Black women and their families, to some extent they have created the impression in the minds of many people that the Black community functions primarily as a matriarchal family system. In fact, so little attention has been given to Black men as fathers and husbands that they have been referred to as the 'phantom of American family studies.'"[64] Early depictions of Black males in the social science literature caricaturized them as "street-corner men, pimps, deserters, criminals, hustlers, or ineffective family figureheads."[65] These depictions were not research; rather, they were myths used to explain the specific racial, sexual, and economic position under which Black males suffer as the product of their own cultural deficiencies. Black males were defined as problems, threats. They were "projected as psychologically impotent and castrated, dependent, incredulous, nebulous, irresponsible, and suspicious,"[66] and thereby responsible for their own lowly position in society.

Staples took a different approach in his study of Black men and boys in American society. He held that "institutional racism and its machinations shape the expression of [B]lack masculinity" in America and that this reality cannot be discounted in seeking to understand both the Black male's subjective experiences of manhood and the objective consequences of being both Black and male.[67] The historical circumstances of Black males in America gave rise to fundamentally different notions of manhood from those of white males: "In the case of [B]lack men, their subordination as a racial minority has more than cancelled out their advantages as male in the larger society." Staples insisted that this precarious position meant that "any understanding of their experience will have to come from an analysis of the complex problems they face as [B]lacks and as men."[68] Staples named this the dual dilemma. To many readers, this idea sounds like contemporary theories such as intersectionality in that it suggests that every subject is both raced and sexed. However, this idea was initially published in 1978 in the *Journal of Social Issues*, a full decade before the term *intersectionality* was developed.[69] Staples maintained that Black men had few privileges in America, except in relation to Black women, in that Black men had higher incomes than Black women in the 1970s. Staples does attend to the wit of history. In an era that witnessed the "bourgeoning of [B]lack nationalism with its attendant elevation of the [B]lack male to his rightful and historical role as head of the [B]lack family and community,"[70] it was women—mostly white women—who gained political and economic ascendency from the Civil Rights Movement.

Staples maintains that the economic and political isolation of Black men and boys gave them more egalitarian views of sex. It is generally conceded that Black men do not have the power to enact patriarchy to the extent that white men do, but this structural limitation is rarely connected to or thought of as a reason that Black men would formulate altogether different notions of manhood that resist gender hierarchies not only in the home but also in the larger society. Black men are by far the most liberal sex-race grouping in America. "They start dating earlier . . . , have the most liberal sexual attitudes, and are most inclined to have non-marital sex without commitment."[71] Within the institution of marriage, Black men are more involved than other males in doing housework, tending to children, and sharing decision making with their female counterparts.[72] Recent studies actually show that Black fathers are more involved with their children than men of other races, even when they are not married or living with the mother,[73] and they practice social fathering to the Black community at large in recognition of the structural violence that robs Black families and children of Black men's presence generally.[74]

Black men are not mimetic in the sense that they simply base their life aspirations or behavior on the precepts established by the larger white society. The sociologists Anthony Lemelle Jr. and Juan Battle show that in the Black community, "homophobia and homosexuality are equally stigmatized identities," and it is religious participation as well as one's gender, rather than masculinity itself, that indicate the likelihood that Black men or women will be homophobic and express homo-negativity.[75] Black males' attitudes concerning sex, love, marriage, and manhood itself differ largely from those of whites. What Black men do—how they actually behave—is more of a sociological than a philosophical point, but it is precisely how Black men and boys live out these perspectives in societies that gives their experience of themselves and the world theoretical import.

Academic theory has a passion for Black male mimeticism—so much so that it is analytic, a property of Black maleness itself. This position is little more than a myth disproved by the attitudinal studies on Black men since the mid-1980s. In reality, thirty years' worth of data validates Staples's analysis in the 1970s that Black males simply do not share the same definitions or hold the same cultural expectations as white men in America. Black males are socialized to understand manhood in the context of their vulnerability, the dangers their assertiveness and competitiveness are perceived to have in the larger society. Black men define manhood based not on their ability to dominate others but, rather, on their vulnerability to America's racist misandrist regimes. Claude Franklin writes, "Many Black male youth also learn that a lacuna exists between those traits of dominance and competitiveness internalized and their exhibition in the larger society. They are very much aware of the high rate of Black male unemployment, Black male underrepresentation in high-paying, high-prestige occupations, and the generally inferior status of Black males in

American society." It is only within Black subculture or interpersonal relationships that Black males can even express a "masculine" role, so their idea of
Black manhood is quite distant from that of the dominant white society.[76]

In fact, some studies have found that Black males' conceptualization of
manhood does not include any reference to the ideas of white masculinity.
Andrea G. Hunter and James E. Davis's "Constructing Gender: An Exploration
of Afro-American Men's Conceptualization of Manhood" asked one question
to a group of Black men in New York: "What do you think it means to be a
man?" The answers and clusters of ideas revealed that "discussions of masculinity were absent from men's definitions of manhood."[77] Hunter and James
explained that this difference in Black male perceptions of masculinity and
manhood possibly reflects a cultural awareness of the differences between the
physical sexual man and the social man, a distinction first introduced in Nathan and Julia Hare's *Bringing the Black Boy to Manhood* in 1985. The Hares
maintain that Black boys understand the social man as "a moral and jural
condition which extends, or should, far beyond the trappings and execution of
uncommitted sexuality."[78] Whereas masculinity was thought of as a reflection
of the dominant culture (aggression, power, and so on), for Black males "manhood emerged as a multidimensional construct that defines being a man in
terms of the self, a man's relationship and responsibility to family, and a world-
view or existential philosophy."[79] Manhood was the idea Black men used to
frame how they thought of themselves outside the ills and stereotypes of mainstream society and allowed a distinction between what they saw as masculine
(white) behavior and the behavior of a Black man. As Hunter and Davis explain, "Although masculinity may be a part of being a man, it is not the foundation on which manhood rests."[80]

The long disproven racist stereotype that holds Black men to be misogynist
and natural threats to women remains the starting point for many conversations concerning Black males. Contrary to these ascriptions, Black men and
boys have consistently demonstrated that their subordinate (racial) male position has made them more aware of sexual oppression and gender inequality.
In 1983, Noel A. Cazenave asked if all Black men suffer from the *double bind,*
or being expected to fulfill traditional masculine roles while being denied
manhood because of their race. His study found middle-class Black men,
those Black males thought to embrace the ideals of hegemonic masculinity
most readily, to have more progressive gender attitudes than white men; to
"approve of nontraditional roles for women, women's issues, and egalitarian
marital relationships[;] and [to] believe that men can learn a great deal from
the way women act that can be incorporated into their own behavior."[81] In
1989, Ruby Lee Gooley's study of race and gender consciousness among Black
Americans found that "the mean race and gender consciousness levels of Black
women are more similar to the mean levels for Black men" than to those for
white women.[82] While the early 1990s marked the popularization of intersec-

tionality and the presumed gender consciousness of Black bodies based on their biological designation as male or female, multiple empirical studies confirmed the findings of the previous decade maintaining that Black men were certainly more aware of, if not more conscious of, gender inequality than other men and women.

For instance, in 1995 Kathleen Blee and Ann Tickamyer's "Racial Differences in Men's Attitudes about Women's Gender Roles" used National Longitudinal Survey cohorts from 1960 to 1981 to test the attitudes and racial concepts of gender between white men and Black men. Although the study used data collected as long as thirty years before Hunter and Davis's study, it found that "African American and [w]hite men differ in their attitudes about women's gender roles, that beliefs about gender roles change across time, and that individual status and life course processes influence gender role attitudes."[83] Because Black males are socialized to see women as earners in the home, they have far more equitable ideas of women's labor than white males and see Black women as co-workers needed for the economic survival of the whole. These attitudinal differences are not simply isolated to how Black men see Black women; they reflect a much deeper understanding of how sexual oppression operates in relation to racism. Andrea Hunter and Sherrill Seller's "Feminist Attitudes among African American Women and Men," published in 1998, attempted to respond to assertions about Black men's beliefs about gender with empirical findings. They were very perceptive in noting, "Despite the body of work on African American women and feminist thought, there have been few empirical investigations or theoretical discussions of feminist ideology or consciousness among Black men."[84] Hunter and Sellers's study sought to measure three issues they believed were central to feminism: "(1) recognition and critique of gender inequality, (2) egalitarian gender roles, and (3) political activism for the rights of women."[85] Similar to previous studies, Hunter and Sellers's study found that "African American women and men . . . tended to have similar positions on the feminist issues examined."[86] In addition, Hunter and Sellers observed, "African American men are often cast as having few positive proactive adaptive strategies to handle the 'crisis' associated with a diminished primary provider role." Their analyses show that Black men's experiences with police brutality and unemployment "may facilitate a recognition of the importance of both women and men inside and outside the home, particularly in difficult times. Hence, one response to a threatened male breadwinner role is a shift in gender role attitudes."[87]

Evelyn Simien's *Black Feminist Voices in Politics* uses the National Black Election Studies, the National Black Politics Study, and her own National Black Feminist Study to document the broad support Black men have for women's issues. Simien's work dispels the common mythology insisting that Black feminist commitments are fundamentally tied to a Black and female identity. According to Simien, "[B]lack women and men recognize that the problems of racism, poverty, and sexual discrimination are all linked together; [B]lack feminists are beneficial to the [B]lack community; [B]lack women should share equally in the political leadership; [B]lack women should take on a more prominent role in the [B]lack church; and the overwhelming majority of respondents ([B]lack men and women) felt they share a common fate with [B]lack women."[88] What is perhaps the most controversial aspect of Simien's work is that her studies have found that "[B]lack men are equally and, in some cases, more likely than [B]lack women to support [B]lack feminism."[89] In a subsequent article—"A Black Gender Gap?"—Simien updates her findings, concluding that Black men and women share the idea of intersecting oppressions and linked fates. Simien writes, "The present study provides additional evidence to support the claim that African American men have truly progressed in their thinking about traditional gender roles and have supported [B]lack feminist tenets for longer than many realize. African American women are similarly supportive of [B]lack feminist tenets, but to a lesser extent than African American men."[90]

Several years later, Catherine Harnois used Simien's National Black Feminist Study to test Patricia Hill Collins's theory of standpoint epistemology. According to Collins, a Black woman's standpoint is defined as "those experiences and ideas shared by African American women that provide a unique angle of vision on self, community, and society."[91] Harnois's work, like Simien's, found that Black men are as likely—and in many cases, more likely—to support the values (such as the interconnectedness of race, class, and gender) and political behavior traditionally thought to belong solely to a Black feminist orientation.[92] Harnois found that Black men are supportive of Black women's leadership roles in politics and have supported gender equality more wholeheartedly than any other group of men and more than some women.[93] Contrary to the purported correctness of standpoint epistemology, gender simply does not control the political sentiment or limit the social consciousness of Black males. Black men experience the world alongside Black women; they, like Black women, are abused because of their race and sex, yet theory holds that because they are not women, their awareness of gender inequality cannot be due to their maleness. So while Black women's gender progressivism originates in their outsider position, it is suggested that Black men's progressive gender attitudes cannot originate from theirs. These are ideological assertions based on the imagined history of (Black) maleness as privileged and normative rather than an account of the particular disadvantages that make racialized maleness an outsider positionality in white patriarchal societies, and the possible origin of a Black male genre theory. Because of their peculiar subordinate racial/sexual position, Black males are able to understand the complexities of social life much better than the academic theories allegedly designed for the same end.

Today, the deployment of contemporary gender theories, such as intersectionality and hegemonic masculinity, assume long disproven myths concerning Black male socialization and political aspiration. Many of the aforementioned empirical studies sought to test the attitudes and worldviews of Black males as a way to address the historical caricatures of Black men as jealous aspirants craving white male power and dominion. These empirical studies capture what has long been denied to Black males in theory: a reflective capacity. Because of their marginalization and oppression, Black men have developed a separate historical consciousness of manhood that is quite distinct from that of (white) masculinity. Instead of facilitating an exclusive cognizance of their own oppression in terms of race, Black males have explained their oppression consistently formulated in terms sensitive to their peculiar sexual oppression—their particular vulnerabilities as Black males who are unemployed, hunted, and discriminated against. Black men feel empathy for women's sexual oppression beyond the presumed racial register because they experience the world as economically, sexually, and politically endangered. In other words, Black males are empathetic because the economic and political obstacles they face are simultaneously experienced in the world as racial and sexual vulnerabilities.

Despite these findings, many scholars, both Black and white, male and female, will continue to assert that generally Black males are sexist, misogynist, and patriarchal. These stereotypes not only function to condemn and dehumanize Black males, but they also give communality to the self-selected academic class who find intellectual and political unity in pathologizing them. When these long disproven stereotypes are given the label of theory, the racist generalizations offer the illusion of specialization to the Black men and women building their careers as experts on Black masculinity and protects whites against charges of racism, since their hatred and fear of, and discrimination against, Black males can be rationalized as theoretical advance. Unsurprisingly, the very same efforts that are morally praised as decentering Black men (the denial of their death and poverty, the ridiculing of panels on these topics, the denial of venues for publication) in the academy are condemned as racist when practiced in society. Like the racist rationalizations that justify stop and frisk, racial profiling, and Black male death, Black masculinity studies constructs Black men as a threat to women and others, codifies such constructions through theory, and legitimizes the discrimination and isolation of Black males throughout the academy based on the alleged *physical* danger they pose through their mere presence and supposed *spatial* threat they pose to others through their opinions.

The Need for a Black Male Historiography:
Resisting the Mimetic Imposition on Black Male History

The biological reduction of Black masculinity to its sexual assignment of "male," largely built on the vacating of the historical peculiarity of race and the consciousness Black men have gained through centuries of racist colonial oppression, allows all sorts of evils to be ahistorically ascribed to the aspirations of Black manhood. The lack of rigorous study and non-fictive exploration of the Black male's particular historical consciousness enables disciplines and theorists to erase the specific ontogeny of Black manhood throughout the centuries, preferring his "perceived" sexual designation as male to serve as the foundation of his historical and contemporary psychology. This essentialism, this biologically determined percipience, is never questioned as currently applied to Black males, despite a history in which the "feminization of colonized men seems rather a gesture of humiliation attributing to them sexual passivity under the threat of rape."[94] Whereas Black women are argued to have developed a historical consciousness and various strategies to deal with their marginality and sexual oppression, Black men—even when shown to have been victims of rape, economic marginality, medical experimentation, cannibalism, and castration—are denied the capacity to engage reflectively and respond to these realities. Canonical gender theory asserts that Black males' only answer to their victimization, even when at the hands of (white) patriarchy, is, in fact, (white) patriarchy. How can one historically study Black males who are denied humanity, Man-Nots, in a way that is not confined to colonial notions of gender?

Chapter 1, "On Mimesis and Men," aims to break the historiography of gender theory that maintains that the end of slavery marks the beginning of Blacks' assimilation of bourgeois European gender norms as the path toward freedom. It shows that within nineteenth- and twentieth-century Blackness there was a retreat from many of the foundational modes of gender in the West. As a historiography of Black males, Chapter 1 articulates the breaks in the assumptions that Black and male(d) bodies simply aspire to patriarchy. A tradition of Black manhood is erected on the foundations of ethnology that was anti-imperial, anticolonial, and, consequently, not patriarchal. Over the past decade, several works dedicated to exposing the colonial origin of gender have problematized our casting of gender, the theoretical deployments of the masculine and feminine, on Black bodies. Darieck Scott's *Extravagant Abjection: Blackness, Power, and Sexuality in the African American Literary Imagination* aims to capture the conditions of Blackness and the intuitive capacities of the Black abject prior to gender. For Scott, the abject marks "gender in a state of relative undifferentiation, gender as (however momentarily) not-yet-defined."[95] The abject denies gender differentiation within Blackness. This depravation imposed on bodies by Blackness "needs to show itself as not-masculine. But this does not mean that it is necessarily feminine, or only feminine, merely that it cannot be narrated except as the negation of what it exceeds or overruns."[96] Scott marks an indeterminate being expressed as a negation, or lacuna, of gender itself.

Abdul JanMohamed's conceptualization of racialized sexuality aims to ground a similar point regarding the formation of the gender concept within the history of racist violence in the United States. JanMohamed writes, "Within the confines of United States slave and Jim Crow societies, racialized sexuality exists at the point where the virtual powerlessness of certain subjects intersects with the massive prohibitive power of various state and civil apparatuses, power that, it must be emphasized, is always underwritten by the actual or potential use of massive coercive violence."[97] Within repressive structures such as slavery or Jim Crow, Black sexuality is configured in relation to the asymmetric power imposed by white bourgeois sexual mores. The Black body, constrained by impending death, is unable to express a normative sexuality that is not shackled to the asymmetry between Blackness and whiteness. The contingency of Black sexuality, defined by the relation and will of the white subject in relation to which it is positioned, requires conceptualizing the sexuality of virtually powerless groups within a register that is completely different from the foundation of gender that is traditionally offered and is merely the anthropological template of bourgeois white culture. For Black males, this nexus of negation is peculiarly affixed to their near-zero degree of social conceptualization as flesh and death, their transition to meat.[98]

Contra Hortense Spillers's distinction between body and flesh as the poles of the captive and liberated subject,[99] where flesh is prior to the (gendered) rules of the body that erase the herstory of violence committed on African female flesh beyond rape, JanMohamed suggests that insensate flesh, or meat, is an impending threat that conditions Black maleness to accept castration as the "bareness of bare life" itself.[100] Racialized castration is the force of maturation that transform boys into men in JanMohamed's reading of Richard Wright's accounts of Black masculinity. JanMohamed writes:

> Racialized castration . . . is not really concerned with managing the principle of substitutive equivalence on the register or *signification or the Symbolic* as such, but rather on the register of political power and control. And it is on this register that racism attempts to negate the principle of substitutive equivalence between one citizen and another (in their capacity as citizens) by erecting a barrier on the basis of racial identity. And it is precisely the erecting of this barrier through the act of castration that constitutes the profoundly phallic and sexualized character of the racial border. In this context, a [B]lack "boy" can become a "man" only by understanding and "accepting" the prevailing structure of sexualized racial difference, which is to say, by accepting his social castration, failing which he will have to face the possibility of his literal castration.[101]

The threat of castration and the impending fatal force of death share in the origination of Black manhood in the United States. Blackness distorts gender, making it inoperative on Black bodies. This historical distortion consequently makes the extension of the gender category inapplicable to the condition of Blackness and those sexed bodies within wretchedness or abjection. As the literary theorist Greg Thomas explains, "There is no universal man socialized in opposition to a universal woman, or vice versa; there is a white man and a white woman specied over and against Black African 'slaves,' who may be described as male and female."[102] We are not studying MEN when speaking of Black males; we are studying negations of *(white)* MAN itself. Chapter 1 argues that theory must be able to explain the historical moments concerning the creation of race and the denial of gender for Blacks in the nineteenth century.

Chapter 2, "Lost in a Kiss?" takes up the question of mimesis from the opposite end of the spectrum—through the analysis of a convicted rapist and nationalist named Eldridge Cleaver. In many academic circles, Eldridge Cleaver is the quintessential Black Macho. He is the rapist, the Buck, and the narcissistic terror of Black women at large. But what if he was something else? What if Cleaver reveals that he was not simply a rapist but a theorist of the erotics that preceded rape, the homoerotic production of Black men as convicts, the nameless Black male flesh that is sacrificed to the prison-industrial complex? He was convicted of rape in 1958 and freed from prison for that crime in December 1966. It was after his release that he met Huey P. Newton and Bobby Seale, who had founded the Black Panther Party on October 15 of that year. Cleaver's book *Soul on Ice* was not published until 1968, the same year he began teaching at the University of California, Berkeley. There is no justification for Cleaver's use of rape, but as scholars we can try to understand his motivation and the pathologies involved in his decisions. To understand Cleaver, we must resist the present-day inclination to insinuate that his rape conviction, his time in the Black Panther Party, and his intellectual works were synonymous or simultaneous.

"Lost in a Kiss?" gives some context to the sexual violence Black men historically experienced at the hands of white women and, in effect, white patriarchy during Jim Crow and well into the 1960s. By situating the rape of Black men historically, I show that the convict-criminal is a category endemic to Black maleness that makes Black males vulnerable to repetitive sexual repression, violence, and rape. Today, incarceration is thought of as a racist monument, a historically racist institution. Rarely is the prison thought of as a formative institution that produces specific kinds of beings, Black male beings, in society. As a consequence, prison rape is thought to be simply the function of male attempts to dominate other men and not a means of producing these kinds of selves in the world through sexualization. Cleaver, however, argues for a very different conceptualization of rape in prison. Cleaver argues that Black male sexuality is thought to be parasitically attached to the quest of

Black male politics and resistance against white supremacy. Cleaver traces the obsession with the criminalization of Black male sexuality to slave revolts such as that of Nat Turner. Referring to William Styron's depiction of Nat Turner as the inevitable rapist of Emmeline Turner in *The Confessions of Nat Turner*,[103] Cleaver asks, "Why do you think that white boy who wrote a book about Nat Turner turned Nat Turner into a freak? The basic lie of his book was about who Nat Turner wanted to fuck[;] Nat Turner killed white people, white bitches. And he killed for [B]lack people, for [B]lack bitches. So who do you think he related to fucking?"[104] Who the Black man is thought to lust after is the libidinal motivation behind all of his political acts—his defining impulse is thought to be rape; he pursues politics simply to gain the opportunity to rape more. To conquer Black men and dissuade them from resisting white males, the prison was constructed as a homoerotic arena of surveillance and corporealization. The political resistance of the Black male is criminalized as the extension of his brutish nature to rationalize this market. To contain his resistance, society creates notions of criminality affixed to the capacity of his Black phallus. It produces him as undifferentiated Black phallic flesh, able to be used or killed at the whim of white men and women. There are not individual Black men or boys; there is only the Black male. The prison simply stores these Black male bodies for later use.

Black Male Vulnerability as a Foundation: Evaluating the Political Economy of Black Male Erasures from Theory

Black male vulnerability is the term I use to capture the disadvantages that Black males endure compared with other groups; the erasure of Black males' actual lived experience from theory; and the violence and death Black males suffer in society. The term is not meant simply to express the material disadvantages Black males face due to incarceration, unemployment, police brutality, homicide, domestic and sexual abuse throughout society, or their victimhood. The term is also meant to express the vulnerable condition—the sheer fungibility—of the Black male as a living terror able to be killed, raped, or dehumanized at any moment, given the disposition of those who encounter him. Black male vulnerability is an attempt to capture the Black male's perpetual susceptibility to the will of others, how he has no resistance to the imposition of others' fears and anxieties on him. Despite the contemporary intersectional, feminist, and liberal-progressive framings of gender hierarchies that maintain that Black men have some privilege based on their maleness, Black men and boys lag behind on practically every population indicator, from education and income to health and mortality.

Classrooms are hostile environments for young Black boys.[105] They are often thought of as lazy, disruptive, and in need of the most discipline.[106] Teachers routinely assert that Black boys are less intelligent than whites and Black girls and treat them less favorably as a result.[107] Some scholars have even shown that parents have taken up the view that Black boys are less academically gifted than Black girls. These lower parental expectations for Black boys academically leads to not only less parental involvement in their education but also less reward or encouragement for their academic success.[108] The negative experiences Black boys endure from kindergarten through twelfth grade have very real consequences for college and beyond. Since the dawn of the twenty-first century, Black men have received fewer than 40 percent of the associate, professional, and doctoral degrees awarded to Black Americans.[109] The consequence of Black males earning fewer bachelor's and doctoral degrees is reflected in the number of Black male professors at Title IV institutions throughout the country. According to the most recent report by the American Association of University Professors, there are roughly 48,000 Black male and about 70,000 Black female professors at Title IV colleges or universities in the United States.[110] Black female professors outnumber Black male professors by a little more than 20,000. In contrast to the history of white Americans in higher education, Black men have always been outnumbered by their female counterparts in college enrollment and degree attainment. As the demographer Anne McDaniel explains, "The historical trend in college completion for [B]lacks is not marked by the reversal of a gender gap that once favored males, as it is for whites, but rather entails a longstanding female advantage."[111]

Similarly, the economist Rhonda Sharpe notes, "Since 2000, Black women earned twice as many associate's, bachelor's and master's degrees as [B]lack men and nearly twice as many professional and doctorate degrees."[112] The growth of Black women in the university has allowed them, as a group, to attain tenure-track employment at rates comparable that of their non-Black counterparts over the past two decades,[113] while Black males are still trying to gain sustainable access to colleges and universities at the baccalaureate level.[114] This historical advantage of Black women in education, first remarked on by W.E.B. DuBois in 1927, brings attention to a stark race-sex inequality disregarded by many, if not most, scholars working on race and gender.[115] If this gender gap in education continues, warns Wilma Henry, "by 2097, all of the baccalaureate degrees earned by African Americans will be bestowed on African American women."[116] The smaller number of Black males pursuing college as a first choice drives many into labor-intensive blue-collar occupations. While these jobs will offer some economic independence compared with those years spent in college, Black males in these blue-collar occupations rarely climb the economic ladder into the middle class. This lack of class mobility for Black males carries the risk of poverty and unemployment.

Incarceration has also had a devastating impact on Black males' lifelong economic prospects. At the end of 2009, an estimated 841,000 Black men and

64,800 Black women were in state or federal prisons and local jails.[117] According to the Bureau of Justice report on prisoners, "On December 31, 2014, [B]lack males had higher imprisonment rates than prisoners of other races or Hispanic origin within every age group."[118] The economists Derek Neal and Armin Rick found that "the growth of incarceration rates among [B]lack men in recent decades combined with the sharp drop in [B]lack employment rates during the Great Recession have left most [B]lack men in a position relative to white men that is really no better than the position they occupied only a few years after the Civil Rights Act of 1965."[119] The impact of incarceration is not simply rooted in the removal of these Black males from society. Incarceration also marks Black men for years after they are released, making employment and basic sustenance nearly impossible. Evelyn Patterson and Christopher Wildeman's recent study "Mass Imprisonment and the Life Course Revisited" found that imprisonment has even more devastating effects on Black males' economic condition and quality of life than previously thought, since incarceration robs Black males of disproportionately more years that they are capable of working. Patterson and Wildeman conclude, "The total amount of time [B]lack men on average spend marked—not in prison but an ex-prisoner and felon—is far larger (at 11.14 years, corresponding to roughly 27 percent of their working lives). . . . [T]his means that [B]lack men spend on average 31 percent—roughly one-third—of their working lives either locked in a state prison or struggling to overcome the negative outcomes that result from their marked status."[120] As Becky Pettit argues, "High rates of incarceration among [B]lack men—and [B]lack men with low levels of education in particular— have profound implications for accounts of their social standing and that of their children, families, and communities where they live prior to and following incarceration."[121] Incarceration, then, is more than simply an institution; it is a socially invigorated stigma that marks poor, uneducated Black males throughout their lives and is far too often related to their impending deaths. But what if society is so dangerous for Black men and boys that prison, despite its deleterious consequences, is preferable? Evelyn Patterson's "Incarcerating Death: Mortality in U.S. State Correctional Facilities, 1985–1998," points out that Black men are actually safer in prison than in American society. She writes, "For [B]lack males at every age, death rates were higher for the population outside of prison compared with their same-race counterparts in prison."[122] What are scholars to make of this paradoxical social reality?

Historically, the prison has been explained as an institution that deprives the criminal of freedom. Incarceration is thereby linked to slavery and America's history of racism by the extent to which Black men are criminalized and then made into prisoners, but rarely do these analyses explore the sexual aspects of imprisonment. As with our notions of racism, and even American slavery, Black males are imagined only in terms of their confrontation with white male power, never in terms of their vulnerability to rape or sexual violence at the hands of white men and women. Regardless of race, we live in a culture that denies the vulnerability of men to rape generally. Rape, when it does happen to men, is thought to be perpetrated only by other men. Women are never thought of as rapists or as perpetrators of sexual violence. As Lara Stemple, Andrew Flores, and Ilan Meyer explain, "Stereotypes about women, which reflect gender and heterosexist biases, include the notion that women are nurturing, submissive help mates to men. The idea that women can be sexually manipulative, dominant, and even violent runs counter to these stereotypes. Yet studies have documented female perpetrated acts that span a wide spectrum of sexual abuse, which include even severe harms such as nonconsensual oral sex, vaginal and anal penetration with a finger or object, and intercourse."[123] Female perpetration of sexual violence does not occur in a vacuum. Female perpetrators are aware of the innocence attributed to femininity and consequently the protection being female offers them from being seen as perpetrators of sexual violence, especially in cases involving imprisoned Black males.

Even with the change of the definition of rape by the Federal Bureau of Investigation (FBI) from "the carnal knowledge of a female forcibly and against her will" to "the penetration, no matter how slight, of the vagina or anus with any body part or object, or oral penetration by a sex organ of another person, without the consent of the victim," there has been little change in the public's perception of male rape.[124] As Stemple and Meyer explain, "Although the new definition reflects a more inclusive understanding of sexual victimization, it appears to still focus on the penetration of the victim, which excludes victims who were made to penetrate."[125] Despite the change in the actual law, data collection still operates on the idea that males are perpetrators rather than victims of rape. Because male victims "who are made to penetrate" are classified under sexual victimization in FBI reports, the actual number of nonconsensual sex acts forced on males is not classified as rape. This means that the number of males who are actually raped remains invisible not only to the public but also to scholars reporting the data. Despite their prevalence, female perpetrators of rape remain unrecognized and undertheorized.[126]

According to Stemple and Meyer, the "12-month prevalence estimates of sexual victimization show that male victimization is underrepresented when victim penetration is the only form of nonconsensual sex included in the definition of rape. The number of women who have been raped (1,270,000) is nearly equivalent to the number of men who were 'made to penetrate' (1,267,000)." The authors continue:

This striking finding—that men and women reported similar rates of nonconsensual sex in a 12-month period—might have made for a newsworthy finding. Instead, the [Centers for Disease Control's] public presentation of these data emphasized female sexual victimization, thereby (perhaps inadvertently) confirming gender stereotypes about victimization. For example, in the first headline of the fact sheet aiming to summarize the [National Intimate Partner and Sexual Violence Survey's] findings the CDC asserted, "Women are disproportionally affected by sexual violence." Similarly, the fact sheet's first bullet point stated, "1.3 million women were raped during the year preceding the survey." Because of the prioritization of rape, the fact sheet failed to note that a similar number of men reported nonconsensual sex (they were "made to penetrate").[127]

Such definitions serve as the cultural foundation for how we understand rape generally throughout society, but perhaps even more consequential is the role these definitions play in the disregard for rape in prisons. This heteronormative lens, which limits rape and the desire to rape to the power of men over women, has severely overdetermined how scholars have come to understand incarceration and blinded many to the history of sexual violence and rape that occurs within the prison.

Prisons are routinely excluded from household crime surveys.[128] Thus, prisoners, who are frequently victimized by staff and other prisoners, are not considered in various publicly reported measures of rape and sexual coercion. Currently, "prison rape discourse focuses almost exclusively on sexual abuse perpetrated by men."[129] The popular notion is that prisoners rape prisoners, when in reality significant numbers of staff, both male and female, are reported to rape inmates. The dominant perception is that male staff rape female inmates; in reality, however, we find varying expressions of rape that are not only homosexual but also heterosexual and perpetrated by women. Even when the Bureau of Justice Statistics found that 69 percent of male prisoners report sexual misconduct by female perpetrators, the impact and trauma caused by such victimization is de-emphasized and made to conform with traditional gendered assumptions about sex—specifically, who can be the victim in forced sexual interactions.[130] This denial is particularly worrisome for our knowledge of incarceration and its effects on Black males. As Kim Buchanan explains, "The notion that [B]lack male criminals—stigmatized inside and outside prison as hyper-masculine rapists—might be sexually abused by law-enforcing women contravenes every intuition race and gender stereotypes have to offer."[131] As such, scholars are blind to white men's homoerotic coercion of Black men and willfully deny that Black males are victims of white women's sexual power and violence within the prison.

Multiple social scientists are alerting scholars to the incompleteness of information we have about Black males to understand their disadvantages in health, income, and mortality because of policing and incarceration. Meanwhile, scholars in English, women's and gender studies, and various assortments of liberal arts assert not only that we have enough knowledge about Black men to justify not studying them but also that our present knowledge of Black males is complete and uncontestable. These scholars hold that Black men have an enduring ontological advantage over Black women because they are male, despite the aforementioned disadvantages they have in relation not only to whites but to Black women, as well. These realities—facts, so to speak—are unmoving to theorists, since a moral right(eous)ness is asserted in de-emphasizing Black male vulnerability. Chapter 3, "The Political Economy of Niggerdom," examines this phenomenon as a function of political economy, although it may be the case that the erasure of Black males from disciplines may be the function of somewhat metaphysical rather than ideological structures of thought. While an analysis of the super-predator, domestic and sexual violence, and the presumption of Black males as only perpetrators, and not victims, of violence may expose the limitations of academic scholarship, the consequence of such an examination may entail confronting the reality that Black maleness is cemented semiotically, and thereby ontologically, as a category of death and disregard within the symbolic order of America.

The Death of Black Men: The Race-Sex Nexus of Black Male Existence

In not being MAN, there is a negation of the humanity and personhood of the Black male. Man-Not-ness names the vulnerability that Black men and boys have to having their selves substituted/determined by the fears and desires of other individuals. The Black male stands in relation to others as always vulnerable because his personhood, who he actually is to himself, is not only denied but also negated by society. Social contact is perilous, as the nature of the Black male is overdetermined by the encounter he has with other individuals or the power others have to define him when they encounter his body. He is denied sociality because every encounter a Black male has with others holds the potential for accusation. In a racist society, the Black male body has a logic all its own. Merely seeing the body of the Black male differentiates it from that of a white man (humanity) and separates it in kind from the phylogeny of the human. The Black male is defined by this distance to MAN, his nature being replaced with that of the brute and savage; he is made into horror. He literally is met with death, the effect of disposability and fungibility, because in the minds of others who see him, he represents death—he is imagined to be their greatest fear, in need of extermination. This terror is not solely racial antipathy; it also includes a very real sexual appetency.

The lust—the libidinal desire—for the Black male's body that serves as the motivation behind his condemnation and death is not altogether new. Frantz Fanon argued in *Black Skin, [w]hite Masks* that the "Negrophobic woman is in fact nothing but a putative sexual partner—just as the Negrophobic man is a repressed homosexual."[132] Fanon is clear that the substance of his analysis is not the Negro in general but specifically the Black male, since he refers to the homoerotic nature of the white man's desire for Black men. This is important for understanding the implication of Fanon's assertion that, "in relation to the Negro, everything takes place on the genital level."[133] This sexual dimension of violence is therefore a substantial intervention into our categorical assumptions about "race." Fanon is arguing that in racism toward the Black male, there is a psychosexual oppression, a death-driving fear that stimulates the sexual desires of white men and women. Or, as Fanon says, "When a white man hates [B]lack men, is he not yielding to a feeling of impotence or of a sexual inferiority? Since his ideal is an infinite virility, is there not a phenomenon of diminution in relation to the Negro, who is viewed as a penis symbol? Is the lynching of the Negro not a sexual revenge? We know how much of sexuality there is in all cruelties, tortures, beatings."[134] The satyriasis that motivates what Black males are substituted for in the minds of white men has consistently received less attention than it perhaps has deserved. While the nymphomania of the white woman is suggested as the basis of her heterosexual obsession with the Black phallus, the homoerotic manifestations of anti-Black racism—the disgust toward but lust for the Black male body—are rarely theorized as fundamentally linked to the violence Black men and boys suffer.

Chapter 4, "Eschatological Dilemmas," diagnoses the satyriasis that manifests as the homoerotic for a more accurate diagnosis of this problem—the drives and erotic motivations behind white society's desire for Black male death. What needs are satisfied by killing the Black male—looking upon his corpse? Black men are rarely thought of beyond their dead bodies. What makes them that, the corpse, is relatively unknown. The cause of their death is thought to simply be racism, and rarely proceeds beyond literally stating this. The process by which Black male life is lost is inconsequential to theory, so to speak. This chapter names this problem, but when confronting academic theory's current preference for speaking of Black men only as their corpses, we are forced to engage the very real and unshakable bias the numerous deaths of Black men and boys imprint on our conceptualizations of the *Black male*. Because he is literally absent/non-existent/dead, he is not thought to need new theoretical accounts. In short, his existence is thought to be fully accounted for within our preexisting theories, despite the incompatibility these theories have with his actual life and his specific embodying of Black manhood.

Death seems to seek out the Black body indiscernible as (hu)man. The death of Black men and boys has become so normalized in our society that it is expected. It is part of the social order of policing, white vigilantism, and the presumed outcome of a Black man's involvement with whites, specifically white women. The dead Black male body is so common that we are not shocked by seeing it lying in a pool of blood like Michael Brown or found hanging from trees like Frederick Jermaine Carter.[135] Black male death, despite its horror and gruesomeness, is tolerated within America. Whereas the violation of other bodies is thought to be too unsightly to be seen, the dead bodies of Black males are circulated, shared, and memed with little hesitation. Many in our society accepted this reality as a norm, but what effect does death have on the lives, the mental concept of the self, that Black males formulate in this violent world? How do Black males regard the future in a world that is so limited by the present?

To be a Black male is to live in constant fear of being accused of some offense against another. Black men live in a world where any accusation against them is thought to be evidence of their guilt. Imagine a world in which any individual, who can be thought of as a victim of a Black male, has the power to define him as a criminal. This is the world many Black males find themselves imprisoned within, too often defined by the accusations of others against them rather than their actual character. Take the case of David Owens: In 2012, he was stopped by police officers as he returned home from a long day working at New York's flagship Macy's store. The officers demanded his identification, then began arresting him. Despite multiple pleas, the officers refused to tell David Owens why he was being arrested—that is, until they walked him to a "hysterical and possibly intoxicated white woman," who identified him as the "Black man with a hoodie" who stole her backpack.[136] Although he had no previous criminal record, a time clock receipt showed he was at work, and he provided the phone number of his supervisor to corroborate his story, he was arrested and served six weeks imprisoned at Rikers Island.[137]

In some cases, Black men are locked away without trial. Two years earlier, Kalief Browder was arrested for allegedly stealing a backpack. He was imprisoned at Rikers Island for three years without trial. For more than two years, Browder was held in solitary confinement. Although he was a minor, he was routinely brutalized, beaten, and starved by guards.[138] Browder emerged from prison a broken man and suicidal. He made his first failed attempt at suicide in November 2013; his second, in June 2015, was successful.[139] What possibilities exist for a Black man treated as a non-person, as a Blackened thing robbed of moral character? What possibility for life do Black males have when they are reduced to their bodies and determined to be little more than the fear elicited in others? Chapter 5, "In the Fiat of Dreams," tries to make sense of this problem. Our present conceptualization of Black maleness lacks an account of the vulnerability the Black male has in relation with others. As a phobogenic entity, the Black male is liable for the anxiety other individuals experience, whether they are white or Black, male or female. He is culpable for the violence these groups imagine, for their delusions as if they are actual. This shared neurosis often leads to the rationalization of Black male death in America.

In April 2015, the *New York Times* ran a story reporting that 1.5 million Black men were missing (in a comparison with Black women age twenty-five to fifty-four) from daily life due to death and incarceration.[140] This report resurrected charges that America is deliberately and indiscriminately enacting a program of genocide against Black men and boys,[141] but what it did not include was that Black males between eighteen and twenty-four suffer homicide victimization rates double those of Black men age twenty-five to thirty-four.[142] Imagine being a young Black male and knowing that you belong to a group where in your prime-age years—years usually associated with thriving and growth—you may not survive. How does one feel knowing that homicide and imprisonment define the transition from boyhood to manhood? The violence that Black males suffer at the hands of police, the prison-industrial complex, and other Black Americans in impoverished neighborhoods creates an extraordinary psychological burden that is too often ignored in academic literature. Society continues to pretend that, because it remains so normalized or inconsequential in the minds of others, the death of Black men has no effect on the mental health of Black males generally. Black boys are committing suicide at rates much higher than in previous decades and than their Black female counterparts,[143] while poor and unemployed adult Black men consistently report higher numbers of daily encounters with racism and depression than Black women.[144]

Witnessing other bodies who look like you slaughtered in streets; seeing young Black boys executed and broadcast for the world to see; observing the continuing extinguishing of the life, the people, that are Black and male have real consequences. The present theories offered to explain Black male identity, such as intersectionality, have no explanation for the grotesque—for the disproportionate death and dying of the Black male, the display of his corpse. Chapter 5 theorizes Black males as subordinate males in a white patriarchal society targeted for their racialized sexual relation to white males. By historicizing the increased rates of suicide among Black males, as well as their selective targeting in America, I seek a new formulation of ethics to promote a true understanding of the conditions antecedent to their death. I argue that rather than the rhetoric(s) of shaming that focus(es) on Black males as problems, deviants within society, we need a paradigmatic analysis of the world the Black male endures, a viewing of the world that exposes its brutish reality and effects on Black males, even if this realization comes at the expense of the cherished hope many theorists insist should serve as the foundation of inquiry into race. I suggest that anti-ethical thought is the only way for scholars and activists to move toward a more accurate study of Black men and boys, because it is only in the recognition of the incompatibility between Black (male) life and the supposed civility of American society that we truly understand how institutions, policies, and dehumanization function to concretize the caste status of Black men and boys and, by consequence, the larger Black community.

On Mimesis and Men

Toward a Historiography of the Man-Not;
or, the Ethnological Origins of the Primal Rapist

To hell with the "[w]hite Man's Burden!"
To hell with Kipling's verse!
The Black Man demands our attention:
His condition is growing worse.
Why lose sleep over his burden?
All mortals have their share,
The [B]lack man's growing hardships
Are more than he can bear.[1]

BLACK MEN enter our theoretical purview through the stereotypes and anxieties produced within our own time, so the historical milieu from which they actually emerge and in which they live is thought ultimately to be irrelevant to the production of theory. The academic theorist fears the Black males represented in our present day, so it is easy to rationalize these phobias, which interpret Black men as patriarchal, violent, and indifferent to the suffering of others, as method. Making one's phobias a historically salient feature of the world lends objectivity to the subjective, so establishing these stereotypes as antecedents legitimizes Black masculinity as theory rather than as theorists' pathology. Why do our imaginings of Black males from slavery to the present day begin with these associations? Despite their origins in America beginning alongside the Black female slave, Black males are thought to reproduce and desire rather than resist and disown the (white) patriarchy of American empire. But what account or reading of history justifies this perspective? What motivates the scholar to interpret all political activity by Black men as their attempts to mimic the white male patriarch, instead of their efforts to redefine, re-create, and reconfigure Black manhood? The demand to recognize race and gender as central to Black women's historical struggles was accompanied by the power not only to define the Black female subject but also to insist on her motivations and her aims. The Black male subject, however, has no such power. Scholars investigating Black manhood are not only denied the ability to assert that Black males do not, in fact, conform to white masculinity but also condemned for suggesting that Black men do not, in fact, aim for this semblance, given their distance from gender/MAN/human. Under the current paradigm, Black males are theorized as only mimetic entities, incapable of reflectively challenging white patriarchal social roles.

Oyèrónké Oyewùmì's *The Invention of Women* problematized how the biological body functions in the epistemology, and consequently the historiography, of gender throughout the West.[2] While Oyewùmì's rendering of Yoruba culture has been both acclaimed and criticized, her analysis of gender has served as a crucial intervention into feminist analyses presuming not only that social position but also social consciousness can be indicated by demarcating that which is masculine/male and feminine/female.[3] Oyewùmì suggests that present conceptualizations of gender, although heralded as social-constructionist analysis, are in fact biological interpretations of reality in which "social identities are all interpreted through the prism of heritability." This body reasoning makes biological determinism the "filter through which all knowledge about society is run."[4] The body is the focal point of understanding the "other," or that which is external to the self. It establishes knowledge about others through intuitions, somatological impressions connected with how one associates meaning with the biological form, the flesh of others. Said differently, the biological body tells one not only how to differentiate selves but also the intentionality of the other's flesh. In her identification of the oscillation between the biological and the social, Oyewùmì observes that "social construction and biological determinism have been two sides of the same coin." She continues, "The centrality of the body: two bodies on display, two sexes, two categories persistently viewed—one in relation to the other . . . is about the unwavering elaboration of the body as the site and cause of differences and hierarchies in society." Bodies become conceptual deployments within our explanations of social relations and the historical origins of inequality, instruments thought to capture complex and historical dynamics by one reference point elevated above the inexplicability of the material world. As Oyewùmì writes, "So long as the issue is difference and social hierarchy, then the body is constantly positioned, posed, exposed, and reexposed as their cause."[5] The body marks a peculiar conceptual space dictating not only how one thinks about reality but also what one perceives as the relations that constitute reality. Within this configuration, the Black male is used as a caricature of opposition to that which is Black, female, and feminist.

Contrary to the dogmas of Black masculinity, Black manhood was a dynamic historical character that not only recognized the importance of Black women to the racial project, an idea that simply was not controversial under nineteenth-century ethnology, but also challenged white patriarchy's various manifestations as systems of economic oppression, programs of colonial imperialism, and doctrines of racial evolution. Our current studies of Black men primarily focus on politics, meaning that Black men are judged by the extent to which they included Black women in organizations or leadership positions in the nineteenth and twentieth centuries. Rooted in the identitarian logics of our present day, which concede knowledge about gender to the perspectives voiced by the bodies marked by gender, Black men who lived centuries ago are held to post-integrationist standards of intersectional theories developed in the 1980s. Under this paradigm, Black men are deemed sexist or non-sexist, patriarchal or progressive, by the extent to which they mirror the attitudes of Black women of their own time, not by their actual thoughts about white patriarchy and its systemic reverberations throughout the centuries.

Whereas the purity and virtue of the nineteenth-century Victorian white woman was dislodged by historicizing her position and participation within a racialized and capitalist American empire, today the myth of moral infallibility has been reestablished by our twenty-first-century practice of combining race and gender categories such that the Black woman has now replaced her nineteenth-century predecessor as the transcendent feminine idol unaffected by her historical epoch. Today, race and (female) sex establish the limit of the gender concept. Gender conceptually centers patriarchy as both origin and problem, while race indicates the degree to which subjects may exercise masculine power. In other words, the distinction between the man and the woman emerges when one conceptualizes systems of relation, inequities throughout history, and asymmetry between bodies as the problem of gender itself. Anything and anyone that stands in relation to (outside) woman/gender now becomes condemnable for *not being* woman/gendered/female. As such, even those who are raced and excluded from white patriarchy historically become (analytically) patriarchal because they are designated to be *man* and thereby defined outside of *woman*.

Overdetermined by the essentialism tying the biological marker of male to that which is patriarchal, current theories of gender assert that Black males exist in a world of false consciousness that obstructs their ability to understand their position within patriarchal structures. Robbed of their historical vulnerability to rape, castration, and death due to "the mark of maleness," Black male figures are judged not by the rigor and depth of their understandings concerning patriarchy but by the extent to which they mirror the scholarly interpretation of the women in their day. This chapter argues that the Black male stands outside this (gender) origin, not because of his race, but because of his maleness. Because the Black male is often defined by a categorical redundancy of "him as male," his sexual difference, his genre, is usually obscured from sight.

He is thought to be like the white male because he is biologically male. The notion of a different historical consciousness, or development of manliness, is thought to be conceptually impossible and without historical substantiation, not because there is no actual evidence, but because the proof is imperceptible under the present categorical assortment of knowledge. This historicization of the Black male does not solidify another race/gender standpoint. In actual point of fact, there is no oppression that is "unique," in the sense that oppression happens to only one group of people within history. The study of the Black male shows that certain kinds of violence accumulate around certain bodies, and these are the discoveries of his specificity revealed by study. Closer attention to Black males throughout history shows that patriarchy is not an insular and gender-opposing system that protects all men while subjugating all women. Patriarchy stands appositionally to femininity as a self-regenerative system (both ideologically and biologically). It depends on white womanhood to enact its domestic terrorism and global imperialism. Patriarchy depends on white femininity for its propagation. Just as "MAN" and his expression of masculinity have meaning within Western patriarchal logics, so, too, are the female and her feminism the representation of the wombs that birth the masculinity of this order. Patriarchy evolved to protect white womanhood because white womanhood is not only the foundation on which empire is built but also the nascence of the expendable white male surplus needed for imperial conquest. She births MAN, so the white woman is given a peculiar power under white supremacy. This reality is excluded from theory in an effort to maintain the essential category of the woman as morally good and subjectively vulnerable and in need of recognition and preference in discourse.

In fact, it was the newly won freedom of Black men that launched the theorization of our modern concept of gender. Their freedom inspired ethnologists and feminists to give accounts of *femininity* that were vulnerable to male violence. It was ultimately the threat of Black male citizenship that gave substance to our current concept of gender in whites.[6] Under nineteenth-century ethnological schemes, Black men and women were of a different evolutionary stock of beings. Gender did not exist because of their Blackness. This racial (gender) ontology, thought to be apparent in nature and observable by science, could not produce men and women like those of white civilization, and it is from here—that place in history—that Black men strove against the imperial reach of white masculinity and white femininity. This chapter indicts the idea that Black men were gendered throughout history in such a way that they could share in the fruits of patriarchy. By articulating the vulnerability Black men have faced at the hands of white civilization—the sexual, economic, and racial exploitation they have suffered at the hands of white men and women—it becomes easier to see that the violence Black males have suffered exceeds the disciplinary category of masculinity. The

Black male was defined outside of the world; understanding why and how he engaged this negation should amend our present investments in gender.

Part of the Family: The Modality of the Enslaved

In the 1830s the domestication of American slavery marked a decisive shift from the previous century's idea of the natural slave unfit for liberty to the slave as the undeveloped savage in need of civilization and improvement.[7] G.W.F. Hegel's commentary on the Negro and Africa actually serves as a grounding of the ethnology used in America regarding enslaved Africans. Hegel writes, "In Negro life the characteristic point is the fact that consciousness has not yet attained to the realization of any substantial objective existence—as, for example, God, or Law—in which the interest of man's volition is involved and in which he realizes his own being." Hegel believed that Africans had no notion of the other or a higher power outside their own existence. He thereby concludes that "the Negro . . . exhibits the natural man in his completely wild and untamed state."[8] Because the slave was thought to have no knowledge of his selfhood, or the human soul, the Negro was thought to be completely sensual. For this race, "Human flesh is but an object of sense—mere flesh"; it holds no meaning beyond its perception.[9] The sensual, savage Negro was trapped in the natural condition of being, a stage of "absolute and thorough injustice." The Negro was thought to have no spiritual or reflective consciousness of *its* existence, so slavery was a means of developing the Negro. Hegel is adamant that "slavery is itself a phase of advance from the merely isolated sensual existence—a phase of education—a mode of becoming participant in a higher morality and the culture connected with it." While Hegel believed that "slavery is in and for itself injustice, for the essence of humanity is freedom," the Negro is the exception, "for this man must be matured."[10]

Hegel's depiction of the Negro was not the rambling of a simple racist posing as a philosopher. Hegel's *Lectures on the Philosophy of World History* spanned the years 1822–1831 and reflected the most authoritative ethnological thinking of the nineteenth century.[11] These lectures overlapped Hegel's revisions to his *Encyclopedia of Philosophical Sciences* and conveyed what was considered the world's most advanced thinking as to the nature of the African. The description of the African as sensuous and not beyond the raw state of nature was not isolated to the colonial apologetics of Europeans. In the United States, the sensual nature of the Negro was used to justify the modernization of the American slave institution. Thomas Jefferson expressed a similar view in 1779, in his "Notes on Virginia," saying of the Negro, "In general, their existence appears to participate more of sensation than reflection. To this must be ascribed their disposition to sleep when abstracted from their diversions, and unemployed in labour. An animal whose body is at rest, and who does not reflect, must be disposed to sleep of course."[12] Although Jefferson's statement was made in the second half of the eighteenth century, George Stroud's *Sketch of the Law Relating to Slavery* in 1856 showed that Jefferson's idea of the Negro was widely cited in support of American slavery within numerous states in the nineteenth century.[13]

The sensual nature of the slave, his lack of reflective capacities, required both order and education for *his* improvement. To remedy these defects in Negro character, American slavery underwent an evolution. As the historian Willie Lee Rose explains, "In the nineteenth century, the phrase 'domestic institution' came to mean slavery idealized, slavery translated into a fundamental and idealized Victorian institution, the family." The domestication of slavery was not simply political. It introduced philosophical architecture or an order of Man on the backs of enslaved African peoples. As Rose continues, "Proslavery philosophers intended to suggest a benign institution that encouraged between masters and slaves the qualities so much admired in the Victorian family: cheerful obedience and gratitude on the part of children (read slaves), and paternalistic wisdom, protection, and discipline on the part of the father (read master)."[14] Whereas the eighteenth-century justifications for slavery rested on the confinement of Africans to the realm of the nonhuman, nineteenth-century laws "restricting chattels' movement and eliminating their education indicate [B]lacks were categorized as a special and different kind of humanity, as lesser humans in a dependency assumed to be perpetual. In earlier, harsher times, they had been seen as luckless, unfortunate barbarians. Now they were to be treated as children expected never to grow up."[15] As the noted ethnologist John H. Van Evrie and pro-slavery propagandist explained:

> The great foundation principle, the subordination or "slavery" of this negro element was universal, and for two hundred years and upwards unquestioned in a single instance on this continent, or indeed any other . . . for like the relations of the sexes, of parents and children, etc., [slavery] was inherent, pre-existing, and sprung spontaneously from the necessities of human society. The white man was superior—the negro was inferior—and in juxtaposition, society could only exist, and can only exist, by placing them in natural relation to each other, or by the social subordination, or so-called slavery of the negro.[16]

The Negro's moral cultivation depended on the advances of the white civilization according to nineteenth-century ethnologists. Slavery was merely an expression of the universal racial order that was based on not only scientific theories of racial inferiority but also the belief that the organization of the state and broader society should be modeled on the patriarchal hierarchy of the family.

This history adds to Angela Davis's claim that "if Black women were hardly women in the accepted sense, the slave system also discouraged male supremacy in Black men." Given the absolute power of the slave master, Davis is correct that "the promotion of male supremacy among the slaves might have prompted a dangerous rupture in the chain of command,"[17] but even more threatening was that Black manhood, if achieved within the institution of slavery, threatened the very chain of being established on the Victorian family model. Slavery absolutely denied Blacks a gender; they were beasts of burden. As Rose writes, "While the plantation community was a patriarchy and the planter's family a matriarchy, the domesticity in the enslaved cabin at the quarters was, ironically, about as close an approximation to equality of the sexes as the nineteenth century provided." Because of slavery an "androgynous world was born, weirdly enough, not of freedom, but bondage."[18] The African was labor, the corporealization of Blackness. *It* was not afforded the distinctions founded on white bodies; nor was *it* delineated by gender as masculine or feminine.

The order of American slavery established on the domestic realm of the family was thought to be at the foundation of America as a nation and, as illustrated shortly, as an empire. As C. G. Memminger noted in 1851:

> In the Hebrew polity, we have the Family as the basis and origin of all government. The individual is only known as one of a Family. His duties and rights are measured by his position there. If he is the father, he commands; if the son, he obeys. In the one case he provides and gives; in the other, he takes and receives. Inequality and dependence prevail throughout; all benefit or all suffer from the good or evil of each. . . . A few moments' reflection will show that Southern Society, in common with that of the most stable Governments known to history, rests upon this Family or Hebrew basis. . . . The Slave Institution at the South, increases the tendency to dignify the family. Each planter is, in fact, a Patriarch—his position compels him to be a ruler in his household. From early youth, his children and servants look up to him as the head, and obedience and subordination become important elements of education. Where so many depend upon one will, Society necessarily assumes the Hebrew form. Domestic relations become those which are most prized—each family recognises its duty, and its members feel a responsibility for its discharge; The Fifth Commandment becomes the foundation of Society. The State is looked to only as the ultimate head in external relations, while all internal duties, such as support, education, and the relative duties of individuals, are left to domestic regulation.[19]

In our poststructuralist moment, patriarchy would seem obviously to reso-
nate with Memminger's account. There is a white male "father" who orders
and controls enslaved Africans who are thought to be children, and this is the
basis of both government and nation. The intuitive (ahistorical) "critical" reaction is far too deterministic to be useful in our attempts to grasp the reality
of Memminger's claim. The domestication of slavery was not solely determined by white male power. The institution itself gave rise to different spheres
of influence. Africans needed not only to be controlled but also to be improved and educated. The white father enforced law and order, but it is the
white (imperial) mother who dictated societal morality and education. These
modalities introduced patriarchy as the platform from which the civilizing
power of the white woman was displayed. This account offers a much needed
complexity to the presumed asymmetrical relations between white men and
women and the enslaved. Beyond mere "politics" or "identity," the position of
whites within slavery was indicative of established orders of being endemic
to the institution. Enslaved Africans were oppressed by both white men and
white women. Different qualities were thought to be advanced by their servitude to each.

Contrary to the presumed passivity of the white woman, where her day-
to-day abuse of slaves is denied and thought to have been violence committed
only by white men, the white woman was charged with the managing and
punishing of slaves as she saw fit. While the home was certainly ordered toward patriarchy in which white men "expected to be obeyed by women, children and slaves," the white woman "showed unusual power within that
domain." Because she reared children, the white woman was thought to "set
the standards for behavior."[20] In the South, this power over the moral realm
motivated white womanhood to differentiate itself from manhood. It was an
ideal she "sought diligently to live up to the prescriptions." As an English visitor remarked concerning the order of a slaveowner's North Carolina home,
"The legislative and executive powers of the house belong to the mistress, the
master has nothing to do with administration; he is a monument of uxorious-
ness and passive endurance."[21] The power of administration was the white
woman's primary relationship to slaves. As the historian Ann Firor Scott
writes, "The mistress had to dispense justice, settle small personal feuds, and
cajole those who did not want to work."[22] Despite her erasure, the southern
white woman's work was to extend the order of the home beyond its physical
architecture and into the world. The plantation was just the frontier it most
immediately bordered.

In 1853, Horace Mann, the famous antislave education reformer, wrote
that the charge of woman is "the empire of Home,—that most important of
empires, and the parent of all empires and emperors."[23] The academic construct of woman is ontologically set against that of man; by effect, the maladies, such as racism, empire, imperialism, and nationalism, are thought to

originate from masculinity. Theorists assert this a priori opposition as an
analogous rationale to assert that the rise of woman (her rights, writings, and
criticisms of society) throughout the mid-1800s was, in fact, set against patriarchy. The historical record shows that feminism encouraged rather than opposed white male rule. The historian Mary P. Ryan argues, "The 1850s saw two
icons—the isolated home and the imperial mother—installed at the center of
popular discourse."[24] On the one hand, "the idea of woman's moral superiority, inherent in her characterization as pure, loving, and protected from the
temptations of the world,"[25] was thought to define the home (which was isolated from the industrial and violent white male world of politics) and served
as the foundation of her feminism. On the other, "the moral power of women
was transported in one great, mythical leap from the fireside circle to the vast
expanses of national life, from family to society, from isolated home to mother's empire." Conceptually, imperial isolation is a contradiction of terms, but
it formed the sociological basis of both the political isolation and the political
power the white woman was given throughout the 1800s. The moral and civilizational superiority of the white woman served as the basis from which
white women asserted their rights as "women" over and against those of savages, particularly racialized and savage men. As Ryan writes, "Glorifying the
female in her home confinement, precluded a feminist critique of gender
asymmetry,"[26] because the moral superiority of the white woman over the
white man was rooted in her isolation from the world. Although Ryan never
connects the "empire of the mother" to the growing empire of the United
States, her text attempts to push against the historical narration of women as
simply repressed and misled by domesticity. As she writes, "With motherhood
as its symbolic crown and the home the functional center of their empire
women did, in fact, command a critical social position."[27]

The literary scholar Amy Kaplan's article "Manifest Domesticity" is critical
of Ryan's inability to see how the rise of white motherhood within the isolated
home was used as a metric to establish the barbarism of foreign/alien/racial-
ized people and justify colonialism. Kaplan claims that Ryan's *Empire of the
Mother* "employs empire as a metaphor framing her analysis; yet she never
links this pervasive imperial metaphor to the contemporaneous geopolitical
movement of imperial expansion or to the discourse of Manifest Destiny."[28]
Kaplan maintains that Ryan's blind spot "stems from the way that the ideology
of separate spheres has shaped scholarship; until recently it has been assumed
that nationalism and foreign policy lay outside the concern and participation
of women."[29] The term *domestic* "has a double meaning that not only links the
familial household to the nation but also imagines both in opposition to everything outside the geographic and conceptual border of the home."[30] The
white mother, her empire, begins in the home but takes that which is outside
of the home as the racialized other, the uncivilized world that needs modernization and improvement. This historical inclination of patriarchy toward ter-

ritorial expansion and Manifest Destiny has also been well documented by
Amy Greensberg, but for her it is primarily male dominance—masculinity's
nationalist fervor—that implicates womanhood. While Greensberg showed
that "westward expansion proved that domesticity and Manifest Destiny could
be mutually reinforcing,"[31] womanhood is imagined to be culpable only for
erroneously believing in the ideas of imperialism, not acting on them, since
most white women were thought to be confined to the home.

In Ryan's view, the home is isolated from the industrial and political impetus of Manifest Destiny and colonial imperialism. Those motivations belong to
the character of white masculinity. Kaplan maintains that Ryan's view of the
home breaks down when domesticity is interrogated not as mutually reinforcing but as mutually constituting Western empire. Kaplan argues that "domesticity can be viewed as an anchor, a feminine counterforce to the male activity of
territorial conquest."[32] In this sense white womanhood was a source of the colonial logics that made that which is outside the home foreign and that which
is foreign a threat to all that was domestic. There was power in the empire of
the home that cannot be adequately captured within the popular historical narration of the home as oppressive and the white woman's position as comparable
to that of the Black slave. Throughout the mid-nineteenth century, white wom-
en enthusiastically embraced what Kaplan calls imperial domesticity. These
women understood that "by withdrawing from direct agency in the male arena
of commerce and politics, woman's sphere can be represented by both women
and men as a more potent agent for national expansion." The modalities asserted within the domestic sphere, the order of white man, woman, and child,
operated as a metric to judge the racialized *other* as uncivilized and thereby able
to be subjugated. Rather than domesticity operating as the limit of white womanhood, Kaplan shows, "The outward reach of domesticity . . . enables the in-
terior functioning of the home."[33] The white home of the 1860s forward not
only was used to gauge the civilization of all other races but also was necessary
to the settler project itself. As the historian Margaret Jacobs explains, "[The
home] was an essential means of establishing dominance in the new settlement.
Settler colonies thus relied on the mobilization of white women, who were
charged with making and keeping the home, as key figures in promoting settlement."[34] According to white women's rights activists of the time, this made
white women indispensable to the West's civilizing missions abroad.

Those Who Can Be Colonized: Ethnology as the Foundation of Black Sensuality and the Black Male Rapist

The chain of being established on the (white) family was not isolated to the
political economy of nineteenth-century American slavery. It was, in fact,
scientific and the cornerstone of modern ethnology. The American Ethno-

logical Society was founded in 1842, only months apart from the Ethnological Society of London,[35] but "modern ethnology," whose approaches had benefited from Charles Darwin's *Origin of the Species* after 1859, is distinguished from these earlier incarnations in its use of evolution to explain the divergences among races. A. H. Keane's *Ethnology: Fundamental Ethnical Problems; the Primary Ethnical Groups* claims that ethnology proceeded through a comparative method of racial groups to determine "the absolute and relative value of racial criteria: miscegenation; the origin and evolution of articulate speech and its value as a test of race; the influence of the environment on the evolution of human varieties, on their pursuits, temperament, religious views, grades of culture; the evolution of the family, clan, tribe and nation."[36] The nineteenth-century psychologist, historian, and philosopher Wilhelm Dilthey (who also held Hegel's Chair of Philosophy at the University of Berlin) wrote that "ethnology describes the natural articulation of the human race and the resulting distribution of human life over the face of the earth in light of its physical characteristics. This ethnology thus investigates how the human race, on the basis of family ties and kinship, is naturally grouped into concentric spheres measured by degree of kinship, i.e., how in each narrower sphere, along with closer ties, new common characteristics appear."[37]

Because ethnology focused on the relations races shared, racial contact was explained within white gender hierarchies ordered to a familial hierarchy led by the patriarch. Arthur de Gobineau's *The Inequality of the Human Races* (1854) is an instructive example of this hierarchy in practice. While his text is considered one of the most illustrious racist political treatises of the nineteenth century, it is useful to remember that it appeared during the same decade as the discourse of imperial domesticity and reflected the order imposed on the African as savage but childlike and feminine. Gobineau believed that "every human activity, moral or intellectual, has its original source in one or [the] other of these two currents, 'male' or 'female;' and only the races which have one of these elements in abundance (without, of course, being quite destitute of the other) can reach, in their social life, a satisfactory stage of culture, and so attain to civilization."[38] Civilization is founded on the masculine or feminine principle operating to build a republic. Gobineau insisted that "institutions . . . invented and molded by a race of men make the race what it is. They are effects, not causes."[39] Unlike our twenty-first-century theories of social constructionism, Gobineau held that the creations of our society emanate from the inner personality and substance of races: "The male nations look principally for material well-being, the female nations are more taken up with the needs of the imagination."[40] The superiority of the German stock is birthed from the generational accumulation of blood from male races, while degenerate European races of the South are accepting more feminine blood. This is the foundation from which philosophy and poetry, language

and literature, grow. The mark of race's male and female principle is so re-
markable that Gobineau actually argues:

> If a degraded people, at the lowest rung of the racial ladder, with as
> little significance for the "male" as for the "female" progress of man-
> kind, could possibly have invented a language of philosophic depth, of
> aesthetic beauty and flexibility, rich in characteristic forms and precise
> idioms, fitted alike to express the sublimities of religion, the graces of
> poetry, the accuracy of physical and political science—such a people
> would certainly possess an utterly useless talent, that of inventing and
> perfecting an instrument which their mental capacity would be too
> weak to turn to any account.[41]

Following the ethnological order that establishes Africans as ungendered,
Gobineau made the lack of civilization synonymous with the temperament of
the race. Because savage races lacked the distinctions of gender, Africans
could not appreciate the creations that are birthed from the gendered tem-
peraments of the masculine and feminine, such as truth, God, and poetry. As
with the concomitant logic of the patriarchal home, the patriarchal race was
ordered such that white men and women could civilize and improve the savage races. As Jules Michelet writes, "Africa is woman; her races are feminine."[42]
The designation of a race as feminine was not to suggest that the feminine race
was, in fact, gendered but that the feminine race held an inferior relation to
the patriarchal Anglo-Saxon race and possessed a sensual constitution. They
were feminine because they were to be ruled by the masculine race of white
men and women.

Ethnological theory created a stark divide between the Black race and the
white race. Because all Black people are of the feminine-savage races, Black
men and women could not partake in the same "genders" of a dominant masculine race. The nineteenth-century ideas of race and gender (if such a term
can even apply to Africans) were the result of complete differences in the kinds
of evolutionary species between racial groups. Evolution meant that every race
would have different gendered kinds within its group, if it developed to actually grasp civilization. Nonwhite/savage/primitive groups were denied altogether the specific race-gender distinctions that whites had because such
distinctions were *specific to*, the exclusive mark of, the civilized white races. In
this sense, there were no categories or universals that captured the shared historical experiences between these groups. Commenting on nineteenth-century sexual delineations within racial taxonomies in *Imperial Leather: Race,
Gender, and Sexuality in the Colonial Contest*, Anne McClintock argues:

> Racial stigmata were systematically, if often contradictorily, drawn on
> to elaborate minute shadings of difference in which social hierarchies

of race, class and gender overlapped each other in a three-dimension-
al graph of comparison. The rhetoric of *race* was used to invent distinctions between what we would now call classes. At the same time,
the rhetoric of *gender* was used to make increasingly refined distinctions among the different races. The white race was figured as the
male of the species and the [B]lack race as the female. Similarly, the
rhetoric of *class* was used to inscribe minute and subtle distinctions
between other races. The Zulu male was regarded as the "gentleman"
of the [B]lack race, but was seen to display features typical of females
of the white race.[43]

While this may seem contradictory to our twenty-first-century ideas, it is
crucial to understand the differences between nineteenth-century ethnology
and the schemas of our present day. According to the European ethnologies
that served as the basis of the nineteenth-century account of race, gender
simply did not exist *within* the Negro race. Blacks were primitive and as such
had not yet evolved to the level of civilization necessary to warrant distinctions between men and women. As purely sensual beings, they had no reflective sensibilities that could grasp the purpose of gender roles, which was to
ground civilization, much less the morality of femininity or burdens of masculinity according to nineteenth-century racial sciences.
    Ethnological science had a peculiar effect on studies of Black males. Con-
sistent with McClintock's historical schema, nineteenth-century ethnologists
categorized the Negro male as the racial instantiation of what was known in
the white race as female. For example, Franz I. Pruner-Bey suggested that "the
[B]lack man is to white man what woman is to man in general, a loving being
and being of pleasure,"[44] while Carl Vogt held that "the grown-up Negro par-
takes, as regards his intellectual faculties, of the nature of the female child,
and the senile white. He manifests a propensity for pleasure, music, dancing,
physical enjoyments, and conversation, while his inconstancy of impressions
and of all the feelings are those of a child."[45] Despite the alleged lack of reflective capacity and the notable feminine character of Black males, ethnologists
interpreted the sensuality of the Black male as uncontrollable, insatiable, and
dangerous. In other words, the supposed childlike mentality of Black males
did not stop ethnologists from developing scientific theories that inevitably
would claim that Black males were biologically predisposed to rape.
    During the U.S. Civil War, Black male savageness and pre-rationality was
so solidified within the mind of nineteenth-century ethnologists that Black
soldiers were studied in the nude to ascertain their masculine attributes. As
the historian Melissa Stein explains, "Secondary sex characteristics like body
and facial hair were of keen interest to white scientists during and after the
Civil War."[46] Van Evrie explained, "The intellect—the mental strength—the
moral beauty, all the qualities of the inner being, as well as those outward at-

tributes tangible to the sense, harmonize perfectly with the growth of the beard, and when that has reached its full development, it is both the signal and the proof of mature manhood."[47] Van Evrie claimed that the Caucasian was the only bearded race, and the male beard "symbolizes our highest conception of manhood—it is the outward evidence of mature development—of complete growth, mental as well as physical—of strength, wisdom and manly grace."[48] Because the Negro male had very little facial hair, "except a little tuft on the chin and sometimes on the upper lip," he did not exhibit the physiological characteristics of manhood and, by effect, was disqualified from social manhood rights and citizenship. The Union was so firmly committed to these markers of manhood that in 1863 it commissioned the Sanitary Commission to measure "the most important physical dimensions and personal characteristics of the diverse male bodies to who their work afforded access."[49] Physicians were to "observe the colored troopers when unclothed and record their pilosity on a scale from one to ten, with ten representing the maximum which he had ever seen or should see in a white man."[50]

After the Civil War, ethnological theories arguing for the natural defect in Black males proliferated. With the end of slavery, many scientists argued the Black male's innate inclination to rape was freed. As the sexologist G. Frank Lydston claimed:

> When all inhibitions of a high order have been removed by sexual excitement, I fail to see any difference from a physical standpoint between the sexual furor of the negro and that which prevails among the lower animals in certain instances and at certain periods. . . . [James] Kiernan, in the *Journal of Nervous and Mental Diseases* in 1885, called attention to a fact which is very pertinent to our present inquiry—namely, that the furor sexualis in the negro resembles similar sexual attacks in the bull and elephant, and the running amuck of the Malay race. This furor sexualis has been especially frequent among the Negroes in States cursed by carpet-bag statesmanship, in which frequent changes in the social and commercial status of the Negro race have occurred.[51]

While enslaved, the Negro was subjugated by the law and the punishment of the whip. According to the Texan physician F. E. Daniel, during slavery "there was no perversion of the sexual sense. The males did not desire the white women, nor dream of ravishing the white children. . . . [F]reed from these restraints . . . and despite torture and certain death staring him in the face, the rape fiend, the negro sadist, wreaks his vengeance and spite on some innocent child and gratifies, in that unnatural manner, his abominable lust."[52] Slavery, instead of being justified as a political institution, was the juridical containment of Black male savagery—a condition under freedom that would lead to the ravishing of white women and the moral regression of the Black race. During the late 1800s, the sexuality of Black males became the dominant social problem of the post-slave society.

The sensual nature attributed to Blacks depicted the whole race as irrational and childlike, but it peculiarly made the Black male a sexual deviant and aggressor. This was his nature. The onset of puberty regressed the Negro male's intellect and empowered his primal sexual lust. According to the turn-of-the-century physician William Lee Howard:

> It is a fact observed by those who are in a position to study the negro that with the advent of puberty all intellectual development ceases; even the "sound memory," which is the cause of much apparent precociousness, seems to be submerged by the growth and activity of sensuality. With the advent of puberty the Negro shows his genesic instincts to be the controlling factor of his life. These take hold of his religion, control his thoughts, and govern his actions. In the increase of rape on white women we see the explosion of a long train of antecedent preparation. The attacks on defenseless white women are evidences of racial instincts that are about as amenable to ethical culture as is the inherent odor of the race. It is this sexual question that is the barrier which keeps the philanthropist and moralist from realizing that the phylogenies of the Caucasian and African races are divergent, almost antithetical, and that it is gross folly to attempt to educate both on the same basis. When education will reduce the large size of the Negro's penis as well as bring about the sensitiveness of the terminal fibers which exist in the Caucasian, then will it also be able to prevent the African's birthright to sexual madness and excess—from the Caucasian's view-point.[53]

The size of his Black penis indicated to ethnologists that the Negro was ruled by that appendage, unaffected by religion, morality, or reason. Because progressive methods were thought to be incompatible with his nature, his savagery was often characterized as a medical disorder in need of punitive surgical procedures such as castration.[54] The sexual insatiability of the Black male was established as scientific fact, and rape became married to his character.

By the turn of the century, social Darwinism had made a lasting impact on the ethnological considerations of race across the world. Because the African male was thought to be irrational and barbarous, he was not a patriarch and therefore unfit to rule or govern himself. The Black male was thought of as that *thing* that is to be ruled. He could not be improved through education or religion because his sexual instincts overwhelmed the higher facilities to which ethics or reason would appeal. Whereas the white male was rational and ordered, the African male was sensual and violent and in need of a patriarchal ruler to make him obey the laws of civilization. In the nineteenth century, the Black male was thought to be a threat not only to white women but to all women, Black as well as white. Colonialism was often justified as an effort to save the savage women from their brute males. As Louise Newman writes, "For over a century, Westerners had presumed that primitive women were overworked, sexually abused, or otherwise badly treated by men of their cultures."[55] Like Newman, Gail Bederman argues that "savage (that is, nonwhite) races . . . had not yet evolved pronounced sexual differences—and, to some extent, this was precisely what made them savage. Savage men had never evolved the chivalrous instinct to protect their women and children but instead forced their women into exhausting drudgery, cultivating the fields, tending the fires, carrying heavy burdens. Overworked savage women had never evolved the refined delicacy of civilized women."[56] Judging from this model of the home founded on patriarchy's projection of the empire of the mother, "most social Darwinists located primitive societies at an earlier stage of development than civilized societies and often measured a society's relative position in the hierarchy of primitive-to-civilized nations by woman's 'status' or 'condition.'"[57] The Black/African male was identified as an abuser of the primitive woman, and colonialism was rationalized as an attempt to save her from her savage male counterpart.

Within the evolutionary schemas of ethnology, the distinctions within racial groups constituted differences in *kind*—one could be rank and file or upper class—but these were fundamental evolutionary distinctions among Blacks, not labels taken on as indicative of the shared conditions of individuals within the race or across different races. Blacks and other savage races could not be compared with whites on the basis of presumed universal categories such as masculinity and femininity; they could only be "recapitulated," to paraphrase the work of Granville Stanley Hall. Recapitulation theory claimed that evolved races pass through the stages of primitivism as they mature from childhood to adulthood. Ontogeny prevented the primitive races from possessing the qualities of the civilized race. Within this account, a physiologically mature adult Black male would be thought of as the moral and intellectual equivalent of a white child.[58] Because the racial designations were always inferior, it was thought that the ontogeny of the white race could serve as the scale of the development for the inferior races. Our present-day understandings simply reduce these ethnological distinctions and evolutionary beliefs to "political" beliefs and erroneous racist ideology, where in reality these were scientific doctrines accepted by both Black and white thinkers and produced any number of positions about race, manhood, womanhood, and racial uplift. In nineteenth-century terms, the Black race was savage and did not have genders. There were sexual differences between males and females within the Negro race, but in relation to the white race the Negro was feminine. The only evolutionary distinction that mattered between Black males and females emerged after puberty, whereby the *feminine* Black male was transformed into the *Black male rapist*, and this transformation was especially relevant for white women's rights activists.

The Sexual Inversion: The Primal Rapist as Feminism's Foundational Ethnology

The white woman was an essential component of the colonial endeavor. Her presence in the colony not only accentuated racial and gendered lines but also determined the spatial arrangement of the geography she occupied. Whereas anthropologists such as Ann L. Stoler have shown that "European women were not only the bearers of racist beliefs, but hardline operatives who put them in place . . . fostering new racial antagonisms, formerly muted by sexual access,"[59] the position and power of white women in the American colony has not been thoroughly explored. This is not to overlook the work by historians such as Allison Sneider, Margaret Jacobs, and Louise Newman, who have established that the quest for women's rights, and what is generally understood as feminism, is more properly understood as a complement to the imperial-patriarchal endeavor rather than a challenge to it.[60] Early women's rights activists' arguments against disenfranchisement and patriarchy insisted that white women "were effective civilizers, every bit the equals of white men because of a shared evolutionary history."[61] From Elizabeth Cady Stanton to Charlotte Gilman, there was an insistence that the [w]hite Woman's Burden entitled her to rule alongside white men at home, as in the case of the ballot or abroad as the colonizer. From this historical viewing of white women's relation to "natives" and Blacks, feminism is patriarchy—or, more accurately, its perfection.

Despite these literatures, this history of white women's violence and gendered racial dominance has had little effect on disciplinary conceptualizations of white women's rights or the gendered power white women had over Black men after emancipation. The vulnerability the white woman exhibited toward the racialized (male) *other* established her moral superiority to the savage brute who would threaten her piety. The anthropologist Abouali Farmanfarmaian writes that white womanhood "could only be, and indeed was, sanctified in contrast to a transgressive other, namely, the native rapist and the promiscuous native woman."[62] Within this context, white women established themselves as racially—hence, morally and intellectually—superior to newly enfranchised Black men by perpetuating the idea that their virtuous womanhood was, in fact, the target of his savagery.[63] Created as vulnerable to the Black rapist, the white woman was able to justify all sorts of punitive sexual acts against free Black men that indicated not only that they were unfit for freedom in the republic but also that their demise was necessary for the entrance of white women into the public square of governance. Suffragettes used their position within patriarchy as civilized, masculine white women to enforce violence and death against the newly enfranchised barbarous male. In this political contest, the entrance of the white woman into the (perilous) public from the (protected) home required white men to make the political space safe, or to execute the white woman's primary social threat: the Black male *rapist*. In America, lynching was the violence of choice.

Lynching for the crime of rape was a political and racial rallying point for white men and white women. In a similar vein, Grace Elizabeth Hale observes that lynching was not only about the emasculation of Black males but also about the masculinization of white women. Lynching empowered white women to stand above the now unsexed (castrated) Black male as a patriarch and more man-like master who has conquered the savage Black male beast. Explaining the participation of white women in lynching, Hale writes:

> [w]hite women often participated as announcers of the upcoming event, as spectators, and as gatherers of wood and other fuel. They directed the actions of large numbers of white men by alleging rape, attempted rape, or even an attempted stare, and by demanding tortures and egging mobs on. In one case, a woman even stood on the car and yelled "roast the nigger" when it seemed the mob might show mercy. Not just the white man was empowered when the Black man was literally and symbolically deprived of his masculinity. The lynching narrative moved white women towards masculinity even as it subtly shifted white men away from maleness, embodied in the Black beast, that they were trying to capture through castration.[64]

Current theoretical practices suggest that the reach of patriarchy immobilized white women such that they were not perpetrators of violence, only blind to their whiteness and exclusive in the pursuit of their racial interests. Among theorists, white women are imagined throughout history as passive and inactive, absent from history and thereby absolved of the violence committed against Blacks throughout history. Consequently, the violence white women committed against Black men—specifically, their participation in lynching—has been thought not to exist.

At the turn of the century, white women activists supported lynching and proliferated the Black rapist mythology throughout feminist literature. The most ironic example is the feminist Rebecca Latimer Felton. She began her political career as an advocate for Black women in the 1880s. She began her antirape activism on behalf of a fifteen-year-old Black girl named Adaline Maddox, who was sentenced to five years of hard labor for stealing fifty cents.[65] Felton found that the treatment of young Black women in the convict lease system was horrifying. They were raped by the white guards, forced to have interracial children, and shackled day and night.[66] By 1897, Felton's anti-rape activism had taken a decidedly anti-Black turn. Instead of recognizing the connection the myth of the Black rapist had to the Jezebel myths affecting Black woman, Felton embraced the criminalization and extralegal murder of Black males. She wrote, "If it takes lynching to protect women's dearest possession from drunken, ravening human beasts, then I say lynch a thousand a week if it becomes necessary."[67] This racist and misandrist ideology defined not only white perceptions of Black men but also public policy toward them. The rapist was a symbol of the race problem and an obstacle to white women's political power.

In 1898, however, Charlotte Gilman argued in *Women and Economics: A Study of the Economic Relation between Men and Women as a Factor of Social Evolution* for a concept of the Black rapist as the birth of evil in the world.[68] This exceedingly racist text begins with a "Proem" that tells a creation story of humanity. Humanity begins with "two-fold man." Two-fold man actually refers to both the primitive man and the primitive woman, who lack gender distinctions because they are savage. "Primitive man and his female were animals, like other animals," Gilman explains. "They were strong, fierce, lively beasts; and she was as nimble and ferocious as he, save for the added belligerence of the males in their sexual competition."[69] Two-fold man was "born equal; they were comrades."[70] Consciousness came to primal man and woman slowly. Through consciousness they learned about pain, and about pleasure, and he learned about woman. As they labored together in the forests, he learned about rape. He learned that "he will have her when he pleases."[71] Gilman believed that "the origin of woman's subjection and the sexuo-economic relationship was the development of the primitive rapist."[72] Like the other women of her time, Gilman equated the primitive man with the Negro male. She understood the meaning associated with Black male sexuality and, like her predecessors, depicted him as anathema to white civilization and the white womanhood at the center of it. Gilman's text demonstrates that the idea of Blacks as ungendered, savage, and primitive still formed the intellectual and progressive milieu of the twentieth century.

Even progressive feminists such as Jane Addams were convinced of the myth of the Black rapist. In "Respect for Law," Addams argued that southern lynching often "rises to unspeakable atrocities" and "is complicated by race animosity." Nonetheless, she wrote that "brutality begets brutality, and proceeding from the theory that the Negro is undeveloped and therefore must be treated in this primitive fashion, is to forget that the immature pay little attention to statements but quickly imitate all they see. The under-developed are never helped by such methods."[73] The dawn of the twentieth century birthed a feminist activism that used the myth of the Black male rapist as a bridge between white women's moral capacities and a more visible political presence and engagement with societal problems. The Black male was most often the problem feminists chose to address.

While white women were framing women's rights as resistance against the primal Negro rapist, Archibald H. Grimke argued, in "The Sex Question and Race Segregation," that white women were still actively raping and sexually assaulting Black men throughout the South during Jim Crow. After describing how white men would seduce and rape the Black women, Grimke said, "But there is another aspect to this side of the subject which must not be entirely ignored, and that is the existence in a few instances of illicit relations between some white women and some colored men in the South. That such relations have existed in the past, and do actually exist there at the present time, there is absolutely no doubt whatever."[74] Grimke explains there have always been white women who have conducted secret sexual relationships with Black men as a means of satisfying their lust:

> For it is a fact hardly less curious, if not so strange, that there are men who while they would not think of marrying into a class beneath them would nevertheless live readily enough in a state of concubinage with women of that class. And in this upper class there are women, not many, it is true, who would do the same thing. They care enough for the men in the class beneath them to enter into illicit relations in secret with them, but not enough to enter into licit relations with these same men in the open, in the gaze of a scornful and horrified world. Has it ever been seriously considered that like father may occasionally produce like daughter in the South? And that such moral lapses by a few white women of that section may be accounted for in part at least by that mysterious law of atavism? The sons are like their fathers in respect to their fondness for colored women, why may not one daughter in, say, ten thousand, resemble those fathers in that same shameful, though not altogether unnatural respect? Do not such instances, few and far between at present though they may be, furnish matter for thoughtful people of the South regardless of sex, race, or color?[75]

It was well known that white women pursued and coerced Black men into sexual relationships, but any insult to a white woman's advances, as well as any surrender to her demands, could be considered rape.

The writings and activism of early feminists helped make the fear America had of the Black rapist the dominant political ideology of Jim Crow. Through the symbolism of the Black rapist, feminism garnered popular support in its narrative of white female vulnerability to rape. By casting the primitive Black male as their natural enemy, feminists of the nineteenth century provided ideological fuel to the murderous lust white men expressed toward Black male bodies. The primal rapist inverted the male-female hierarchy and confined Black men to the modality of the slave, even after emancipation. In other words, the myth of the Black rapist allowed white women to exercise their sexual power over Black men through illicit sexual relations and rape and to further white men's justification to murder and lynch Black men in an attempt to garner political power and deny political rights to Blacks in the United States. Contrary to the distant and extricated position from which white womanhood is usually theorized, excluded from the formulation of racism and sexual violence, an attentive, historically informed theorization of Black males illuminates the calculated efforts white women took to make their sexual vulnerability the rallying point of white-supremacist violence against Black people through the nineteenth century and early twentieth century. History suggests that instead of simply competing within an American political field for rights, Black men were, in fact, excluded from American politics by the violence specific to their sexual representations as Black and male, an existence that permitted lynching, rape, and execution to prevent the Black male's rise as a citizen in the American public.

They Were All Patriarchal: Challenging the Mimetic Thesis, Given the Status of the Black Home in Racial Uplift Ideology

Twenty-five years ago, Beverly Guy-Sheftall published her doctoral dissertation as *Daughters of Sorrow: Attitudes toward Black Women, 1880–1925*. Guy-Sheftall's study was an attempt to explore the "attitudes between 1880 and 1920 that have been frequently expressed about [B]lack women by whites, male and female, and by [B]lack males."[76] Gender is definitive in Guy-Sheftall's work; she assigns convergence and divergence around this axis, noting "the points at which these attitudes intersect and diverge."[77] Acknowledging that "the scholarship on [B]lack male attitudes toward [B]lack women is woefully inadequate, especially for the period between 1880 [and] 1920,"[78] Guy-Sheftall had to rely on the only two sources available at the time: Lawrence Friedman's *The [w]hite Savage: Racial Fantasies in the Postbellum South* (1970) and Rosalyn Terborg-Penn's "Black Male Perspectives on the Nineteenth-Century Black Woman" (1978). Friedman argues that Black men were committed to Victorian standards of womanhood and the home. He writes:

> Clearly, white Southern racists and [B]lack activists looked at women in similar terms. Both viewed the female as a second sex with distinctly limited privileges. But the parallel ran even closer. Since antebellum days, Southern planters idolized the white woman as a jewel of the universe, adorning her in finery and speaking of her as a near goddess. . . . By the turn of the century, as articulate Negro activists

busied themselves on the racial front, many thought in the same
terms. . . . Both claimed guardianship over their women; both elevated the female above the state of mortals. Southern males, white and
[B]lack, were therefore participating in the dehumanization of wom-
en. . . . Hence, the effort to fortify racial pride through exaltation of
pure womanhood was likely as disastrous for the [B]lack race as for
the white.[79]

Following Friedman, Guy-Sheftall argues that Black men, "like their white
male counterparts, were reluctant to challenge accepted notions of True
Womanhood," and Black men's commitment to the Victorian notions of
womanhood inhibited Black women from developing their full potential.[80]
Ultimately, Guy-Sheftall concludes that Black men internalized "some of the
culture's notions about sex roles. Because they are male, [B]lack men believe
that they should protect their women from the evils of the world and that
[B]lack women, because of their sex, should assume the major responsibility
for the moral stature of the race."[81] On this view, Black men took on Victorian ideas of manhood and womanhood in an effort to establish the patriarchal order of whites among newly freed Blacks. bell hooks extends Guy-
Sheftall's analysis by arguing, "Most 19th-century [B]lack men were not ad-
vocating equal rights for women. . . . They wanted to be recognized as 'men,'
as patriarchs . . . [and] could not assume this position if [B]lack women were
not willing to conform to prevailing sexist gender norms."[82] This exclusion
was not solely political, but also intellectual, as many "Race Men" such as
W.E.B. DuBois failed to "imagine [B]lack women as intellectuals and race
leaders."[83]

Over the past several decades, these criticisms of nineteenth-century
Black male thinkers have largely been accepted without question. The ar-
chaic gender norms of nineteenth-century America generally offend the
sensibilities of most twenty-first-century scholars, so there has been an automatic condemnation of Black male ideas that parallel what are thought to be
white patriarchal norms. This disposition has moved from what was the actual state of gender in Black communities in the nineteenth century to what
scholars two hundred years later may think about those arrangements. This
is to say that, given the popular acceptance of these criticisms, there is a surprising omission in Guy-Sheftall's study, and in such literature more generally, concerning how Black women thought of themselves in relation the
gender norms of their day. Did Black women *desire* to be placed within the
home and call for the protection of Black men?

Nineteenth-century ethnology made the home the foundation of racial
uplift ideology. It was a racial project that required racial manhood and ladylike womanhood to drive political progress. Although rarely acknowledged,
evolution was endorsed by many, if not most, well-known Black women

thinkers as the scientific justification behind racial uplift. The historian Louise Newman explains:

> As the personal and political struggles of Anna Julia Cooper, Ida B. Wells, and Mary Church Terrell suggest, civilization, racial progress, and woman's protection within the home were interconnected in ways that made it impossible for [B]lack women to repudiate altogether the prevailing ideologies of the cult of domesticity and true womanhood. Like their white counterparts, [B]lack women reformers also used evolutionist discourses of civilization to justify their own social activism. They asserted their duty to "elevate" and "uplift" the masses of [B]lack women, upholding the values of domesticity, chastity, temperance, and piety that the white middle classes considered to be evidence of a civilized race.[84]

The home was key to Black Christian middle-class men and women in the 1880s. Anna Julia Cooper was one of the most adamant champions of establishing the home on traditional Victorian "gender roles." In her essay "Womanhood: A Vital Element in the Regeneration and Progress of a Race" (1886), Cooper argues:

> The late Martin R. Delany, who was an unadulterated [B]lack man, used to say when honors of state fell upon him, that when he entered the council of kings the [B]lack race entered with him; meaning, I suppose, that there was no discounting his race identity and attributing his achievements to some admixture of Saxon blood. But our present record of eminent men, when placed beside the actual status of the race in America to-day, proves that no man can represent the race. Whatever the attainments of the individual may be, unless his home has moved on *pari passu*, he can never be regarded as identical with or representative of the whole. Not by pointing to sun-bathed mountain tops do we prove that Phoebus warms the valleys. We must point to homes, average homes, homes of the rank and file of horny handed toiling men and women of the South (where the masses are) lighted and cheered by the good, the beautiful, and the true,—then and not till then will the whole plateau be lifted into the sunlight. Only the BLACK WOMAN can say "when and where I enter, in the quiet, undisputed dignity of my womanhood, without violence and without suing or special patronage, then and there the whole Negro race enters with me."[85]

Cooper is not arguing that, because of their race and sex identity, Black women can usher in the race. Quite to the contrary: She is actually saying that the race can advance only on equal footing with the homes of the rank and file of the race. We must not look to the elite (sunbathed mountaintops) to see that the reason and truth of Apollo (Phoebus is his Latin naming) has reached the masses (the valleys below). The masses must be lifted up. Because homes are reflective of the status held by the women of the race, then women must be civilized to achieve true racial uplift. This is why Cooper insists that the average homes of working-class men and women must be advanced *pari passu*, or on equal footing with the most exceptional of the race.

In the nineteenth century, "gender" distinctions between men and women, the status of the home, and the condition of a race's women indicated a race's evolutionary stage. Cooper explicitly endorses such a view. Cooper begins "Womanhood" by reflecting on the differences between the idea of the home in the United States and in countries of the East. She begins with so-called Oriental countries, which she claims have confined women to "ignorance, infamy and complete stagnation." She then moves to the Muslim. Cooper writes, "Mahomet makes no account of woman whatever in his polity." Because the Koran was a "product and not a growth" of Arab civilization, it paid no attention to the status of the home. As she writes, "The Arab was a nomad. Home to him meant his present camping place." Cooper argues that it is the Muslim god who ordains such a view. Whereas the Christian god "makes and sanctifies the home," Mahomet made the home a "transient bauble to be toyed with so long as it gave pleasure and then to be thrown aside for a new one."[86] Cooper saves her most caustic remarks for the Turk. She quotes an unnamed writer stating, "The private life of the Turk is the vilest of the vile, unprogressive, unambitious, and inconceivably low." While Turkey has produced great men, and brilliant minds, "men skilled in all the intricacies of diplomacy and statesmanship; men who could grapple with the deep problems of empire and manipulate the subtle agencies which checkmate kings," these minds "were not the normal outgrowth of a healthy trunk. . . . There is a worm at the core! The home life is impure!" Cooper turns with pleasure to the examples of Europe and America from the effete and immobile civilizations of the East. While the Eastern nations are slowing decaying, the West is synonymous with "all that is progressive, elevating and inspiring."[87] "On what basis does this hope for American civilization rest?" Cooper asks. "Can anyone doubt that it is chiefly on the homelife and on the influence of good women in those homes?"[88] Cooper's question is not rhetorical; it conveys her view on the matter:

> Now after our appeal to history comparing nations destitute of this force and so destitute also of the principle of progress, with other nations among whom the influence of woman is prominent coupled with a brisk, progressive, satisfying civilization—if in addition we find this strong presumptive evidence corroborated by reason and experi-

ence, we may conclude that these two equally varying concomitants are linked as cause and effect; in other words, that the position of woman in society determines the vital elements of its regeneration and progress. Now that this is so on a priori grounds all must admit. And this is not because woman is better or stronger or wiser than man, but from the nature of the case, because it is she who must first form the man by directing the earliest impulses of his character.[89]

Cooper demonstrates that it is not only Black men who fundamentally believe it is the charge of the woman to dictate the morality of man. Cooper indicates that this fact is a priori, meaning that morality (character) is synonymous with the concept of the woman herself.

"The male may bring, as an exotic, a foreign graft, say of a civilization, to a new people. But what then?"[90] Alexander Crummell's answer is womanhood: "If you want the civilization of a people to reach the very best elements of their being, and then, having reached them, there to abide, as an indigenous principle, you must imbue the womanhood of that people with all its elements and qualities. Any movement which passes by the female sex is an ephemeral thing. Without them, no true nationality, patriotism, religion, cultivation, family life, or true social status is a possibility."[91] Like Crummell, Cooper understood that racial development is dependent on the status of the woman; she says that "the position of woman in society determines the vital elements of its regeneration and progress."[92] In fact, this view was widely held even among the Black women social scientists of the late 1800s.

In her keynote address at the woman's meeting of the Atlanta Sociological Laboratory in 1897. Lucy Laney announced, "Motherhood, honored by our blessed Master, is the crown of womanhood. This gives her not only interest in the home and society but also authority. She should be interested in the welfare of her own and her neighbors' children. To woman has been committed the responsibility of making the laws of society, making environments for children." The making of the "laws of society" connoted the woman not as singular subject but as creator of society through the home: As Laney said, "The chief joy of home is mother."[93] Similarly, Olivia Davidson claimed, "We cannot too seriously consider the question of the moral uplifting of our women, for it is of national importance to us. It is with our women that the purity and safety of our families rest, and what the families are, the race will be."[94] The historian Michele Mitchell argues that "reform activists who labored on behalf of the race were imbued with politicized missions to change the habits, environments, morals, and lives of African Americans. [These] activists . . . took it upon themselves to convince their sisters and brothers that progressive individuals behaved in certain ways, that proper homes had strong patriarchs, pure mothers, and children schooled in race pride."[95] Contrary to the claims of Guy-Sheftall and hooks, patriarchy and established gender roles were an uplift program endorsed by both Black men and women. Current Black feminist historiography starts from an ahistorical claim: that gender created difference between Black men and women in the nineteenth century, while class, religious, and racial sentiments were similar. This a priori distinction between male and female gender is what grounds the opposition between nineteenth-century Black men and women, not their actual circumstance.

For Cooper, no tension emerges between the manhood and womanhood of the race; in fact, they necessitate and depend on each other. The fundamental nature of womanhood was to develop in the race a patriarchal manhood capable of protecting the Black woman and Black home. "The race is just twenty-one years removed from the conception and experience of chattel, just at the age of ruddy manhood," remarks Cooper.[96] To make the race more (*masculine*) civilized, mothers and the development of homes were fundamental. Cooper was clear on this point: "A stream cannot rise higher than its source. The atmosphere of homes is no rarer and purer and sweeter than are the mothers in those homes. A race is but a total of families. The nation is the aggregate of its homes. As the whole is sum of all its parts, so the character of the parts will determine the characteristics of the whole. These are all axioms and so evident that it seems gratuitous to remark it."[97] To build homes, the race needs men to protect the ladylike character of the Black woman. Black women need "men who can let their interest and gallantry extend outside the circle of their aesthetic appreciation; men who can be a father, a protector, a brother, a friend to every weak, struggling unshielded girl."[98] The Black woman in the South needs chivalry, regardless of her station. It is the protection of her honor and sexuality by Black men from the lower classes of white men that the colored girl of the South needs. Cooper observes that the Black girls in the South are "often without a father . . . or stronger brother to espouse their cause and defend their honor with his life's blood."[99] As husband, as father, by name, Cooper calls for Black men to take up their manhood to advance the cause of the race and womanhood. In calling for Black men to protect, she is laying claim to a schema of racial advancement that demands the division of sex roles (gender) and the protection of weaker women.

As the historian Glenda Gilmore observes, "By admonishing men to fulfill their potentials, Cooper executed an end run around patriarchy. Ideal patriarchy should not limit women; it only did so when the man in question was stunted. In fact, men could take women's striving as a useful early warning sign to encourage them to exercise patriarchy more strenuously. If women were gaining in the race of life, men should run faster."[100] The historian Crystal Feimster has argued that "[Cooper's] call for the protection and elevation of [B]lack womanhood stressed both the advancement of British civilization and a Christian manhood that sought to honor and protect all women. Cooper called on [B]lack men to do their part to ensure the safety of [B]lack womanhood."[101] Given the condemnation of nineteenth-century patriarchy,

Gilmore questions the legitimacy of the term, given what Cooper demands. Gilmore maintains that "Cooper never addressed the problem that her reasoning created—that is, if patriarchy ceases to limit women is it still patriarchy?—by calling the hand of the patriarch."[102] Following the evolutionist trends of the day resolves Gilmore's question, for Louise Newman argues that "Black women's desire for and advocacy of bourgeois respectability, which mandated conformity to the norms of patriarchy, was not so much evidence of their class conservatism, however, as it was of their commitment to taking responsibility for racial uplift."[103] Is patriarchy oppressive when it is a demand of Black women or only when it is an aspiration of Black men?

Cooper describes Alexander Crummell's "The Black Woman in the South" as a work penned by "Moses and the Prophets." Cooper actually claims she owes her thinking about Black womanhood to the correctness of Crummell's previous work. She writes, "Nor . . . could it have been intended that I should apply the position when taken and proven, to the needs and responsibility of the women of our race in the South. For is it not written, 'Cursed is he that cometh after the King?' and has not the King already preceded me in 'The Black Woman in the South.'"[104] Despite the influence Crummell's "The Black Woman of the South" had on Cooper's "Womanhood," it is Cooper's work alone that is thought to stand out as exceptional in its regard for Black womanhood.[105] Given that feminists praise Cooper's contributions to intersectionality and gender theory, it seems clear that Crummell's maleness erases his reflection on Black womanhood in favor of Cooper's, despite the essays making the same recommendations and assumptions concerning Black womanhood. Crummell recognized Black women's precarious position. He writes, "The fine domesticities which give the charm to family life, and which, by the refinement and delicacy of womanhood, preserve the civilization of nations, have not come to her. She has still the rude, coarse labor of men."[106] Because the home life of the Black woman was not secure and safe, it afforded her neither protection from white men nor the luxuries of feminine delicacies.[107]

Crummell believed that Christian women of intelligence and piety, well trained in domestic economy, should go to the South "to show and teach them the ways and habits of thrift, economy, neatness, and order; to gather them into Mothers' Meetings and sewing schools; and by both lectures and talks guide these women and their daughters into the modes and habits of clean and orderly housekeeping."[108] He calls for a domestic revolution that extends racial uplift to the masses, a revolution "raising up women to be the helpers of poor men, the rank and file of [B]lack society, all through the rural districts of the South."[109] Cooper does not disagree. She is supportive of Christianizing the Black women of the South; in fact, she insists that "the idea of the radical amelioration of womankind, reverence for woman as woman regardless of rank, wealth, or culture, was to come from that rich and bounteous fountain from which flow all our liberal and universal ideas—the Gospel of

Jesus Christ."[110] The only difference in their proposals is the emphasis Cooper places on Black male protection of Black women as necessary to the thriving of the home. Despite these similarities, *gender* insists that an a priori opposition must exist between the sexes. Even when Black men and women endorse the same idea, gender theory imposes difference and defect where Black male endorsements of Victorian ideals are described as patriarchal and Black female endorsements of the very same ideals are deemed progressive.

Escaping savagery and ascending into the civilization modeled on white middle-class values was thought to cultivate white respect for Black humanity. It was widely believed that white society would be able to recognize civilization among the notable Black classes, regardless of race. This assumption was the grounding for much of the activism Black intellectuals, journalists, and poets undertook in the late 1800s. Mitchell explains that "concerns for sexual purity, child rearing, habits of cleanliness and self-improvement enabled club women and race men to promote certain modes of behavior to instruct their brothers and sisters on how to attain a range of ideas."[111] For Black Americans, who saw themselves as the Best men and women of the race, there was a demand that their class, their distance from poor uneducated Blacks, convey the quality of their manhood and womanhood. Because class denoted intraracial divisions, those who had elevated—the upper class—took responsibility for improving the (uncivilized) rank and file. Gilmore states, "Because of their own embrace of Victorian manners and morals, middle-class Black men and women worried constantly about poor [B]lack people's public activities."[112] Contrary to popular Black feminist historiographies, racial uplift was a concerted effort between race men and women to create specialized gender roles within the race that required "racial solidarity with [B]lack men (rather than criticism of them) . . . as well as acceptance of patriarchal authority."[113]

Racial uplift ideology had a missionary quality with regard to the rank and file. As Kevin K. Gaines argues in *Uplifting the Race: Black Leadership, Politics, and Culture in the Twentieth Century*, racial uplift actually describes "a [B]lack middle class ideology, rather than a [B]lack middle class."[114] Gaines continues, "It was precisely as an argument for [B]lack humanity through evolutionary class differentiation that the [B]lack intelligentsia replicated the dehumanizing logic of racism. . . . [H]owever problematic, the bourgeois cultural values that came to stand for intra-racial class differences—social purity, thrift, chastity, and the patriarchal family—affirmed their sense of status and entitlement to citizenship."[115] For the contemporary scholar, this means that the meanings commonly attached to gender or Black patriarchy/masculinity/femininity are, in fact, class ideologies, not the actual state of gender (which could only possibly be possessed by Black elites) among Blacks in the nineteenth century. If these were debates occurring within aspiring Black middle classes and imposed by the Black middle class on the rank and file, what is the basis of the assertion that Black men believed in sexual roles similar to those of white men? The current feminist historiography can be maintained only if the histories of the poor laboring class of Black folks in the nineteenth century are made irrelevant to theory. It has become common practice to emphasize the gender differences between subjects and bodies, especially with regard to male bodies. However, class position and class aspiration remain unexamined to the scholar. Crummell is readily seen as male, but the shared middle-class aspirations between him and Cooper are invisible.

The Black Man's Burden: Black Male Resistance and the Mother Right

Something peculiar happens when the Black male is historically reconstructed. Instead of observing Black male activity throughout the centuries as the product of reflective human beings, Black male resistance is theorized as an accumulation of defects. Historical analysis is reduced to the choosing of random examples sometimes centuries apart showing that individual Black men excluded or held "traditional white views" of Black women. This is part of an effort to show nineteenth-century Black men to be synonymous with the Black Macho of the twentieth century. Every political organization led or created by Black males is thought to be nationalist and, by definition, to exclude Black women. The evidence for this conclusion is not based on any actual survey of the political organizations Black men have founded; rather, it is constructed on the basis of the American Negro Academy's all-male leadership.[116] The role Black women played in the National Negro Conventions, the Afro-American League, the Atlanta Sociological Laboratory, and the Negro Society for Historical Research are thought to be irrelevant to any understanding of Black male political aspirations and behaviors.[117] This imposed opposition is analytic; no amount of evidence seems able to disprove the overarching ontological relationship that Black maleness is thought to have to (anti)Black femaleness, regardless of the century in question.

Black women historians have certainly made the case that nineteenth-century Black men were not simply mimetic beings attempting to re-create white patriarchy. Rosalyn Terborg-Penn, for example, argues that the lack of antisuffrage organizations among Black men, their support for the education of, and their political organizing with Black women indicate that nineteenth-century Black men "expressed an egalitarian view of the relationship between [B]lack men and women."[118] Terborg-Penn's claim is quite similar to Paula Giddings's argument that "all Black women abolitionists (and most of the leading Black male abolitionists) were feminists," despite their prioritization of race over what is now called gender.[119] Elsa Barkley Brown considered the effect the right to vote had on gender relations and found that Black men thought of the right to vote as a racial right, where church forums empowered Black women to decide the direction of the vote alongside Black men.[120] Even

Black women at the dawn of the twentieth century, such as Gertrude Mossell, noted that "the men of the race, in most instances, have been generous, doing all in their power to allow the women of the race to rise with them."[121] Almost a decade ago, Martha S. Jones, speaking to Black men's relationship to Black women's public activism, said that "readers may be particularly struck by the prominence of male allies . . . men who spoke, and often acted, in support of women's claims for rights and public authority" and insisted that "their presence complicates previous understandings of African American feminism."[122] Despite these examples and challenges, Black gender theory, specifically the historiography of Black men, has not budged.

While it is important to understand the relationships between Black men and women throughout history, this relationship itself should not act as the measure of Black men's awareness of or participation in patriarchy and its resulting sex roles. In other words, Black men's "gender consciousness" has been studied only by the extent to which it conforms to twentieth-century ideas of women's liberation in the form of gender inclusivity and mirrors Black women's attitudes in the 1800s. This tells us nothing about how Black males historically thought of Black manhood, only how we judge their disagreement with contemporary political ideology. For example, Black men's supposed embracing of Black Nationalism is claimed to be gendered and patriarchal, while their simultaneous rejection of imperialism, which is widely understood to be the international projection of ethnocentric nationalism and masculinity, is relegated solely to racial concerns.[123] There is no actual rationale for such divisions; they are simply intuitions asserted to maintain theoretical coherence. Imperialism exceeds the limits of this paradigm, so it is discarded as excess and relegated to the category of race in an effort to maintain the narrative of gender. Imperialism and colonialism have always involved deeply sexualized narratives and the creation of a racialized male other who terrorizes the nation, family, and women of empire.[124] Such narratives specifically concerned the Black male, and they highlight why Black men's rejection of imperialism, the Black Man's Burden, is central to our understanding of Black males' sexual consciousness and their particular historical genre.

The projection of white masculinity globally was not simply about male dominance. It was an expression of the familial hierarchy that demarcated the boundaries of the white race. Rudyard Kipling's poem "The [w]hite Man's Burden" was an example of this racial claim. Kipling proclaimed the white man's yearning for domination and imperial conquest. Nations such as Cuba, the Philippines, and Puerto Rico were uncharted territories filled with Black bodies for labor and sexual conquest. Kipling urged the white race to "send forth ye best breed, go send your sons to exile."[125] The idea of the [w]hite Man's Burden conveyed the racial demands of white superiority. As the literary theorist Patrick Brantlinger writes, Kipling "clearly believed that the white race was charged with the responsibility of civilizing—or trying to civilize—

all of the dark, supposedly backward races of the world."[126] The [w]hite Man's Burden was both a projection of whiteness and a projection of white maleness. It was a duty aimed at establishing the white race as the master of the darker races the world over through the order of civilization, an order established on the patriarchal rule of the family.[127] Black males, whether they were intellectuals, soldiers, or workers, rejected this decadent imposition of white male rule.[128] Because they were depicted as primal and unformed men, Black men understood what the [w]hite Man's Burden meant for the darker races. The savageness of the male figure—the dark rapist—accompanied the rationalizations for imperialism.

Black men responded in great opposition to the exportation of white patriarchy. As a direct response to Kipling's call, Dr. J. H. Magee founded the Black Man's Burden Association in 1899.[129] Other Black men wrote "Black Men's Burden" poetry mocking Kipling's imperial call. The Reverend H. T. Johnson, editor of the *Christian Recorder*, held that Black manhood stood in fundamental opposition to that of the white man. The Black Man's Burden was a conceptualization of the dark race's humanity that recognized the vulnerability and suffering of the world. It was a concept of empathy with those who were victims of colonization. "Pile on the Black man's burden," wrote Johnson. "'Tis nearest at your door. / Why heed long bleeding Cuba. / Or dark Hawaii's shore? / Hail ye your fearless armies, / which menace feeble folks."[130] The Black man is burdened to live within the world created by Kipling's call. The burden of the Black man is that he knows of the death and misery that accompanies white civilization. It is, in fact, barbarism, since every problem—Black, Brown or Red—is sealed "with bullets blood or death."[131] J. Dallas Bowser's "Take Up the Black Man's Burden" similarly linked the condition of the Black male in America with that of darker races the world over: "The haughty Anglo-Saxon was savage and untaught— / A thousand years of freedom, a wonderous change has wrought. / Take up the Black Man's burden, Black men of every clime. / What though your cross be heavy, your sun but darkly shine. / Stoop with a freeman's ardor, lift high a freeman's head. / Stand with a freeman's firmness, March with a freeman's tread."[132] Black men stood with the darker races for freedom, for the ability to determine their own civilization and escape the tyranny of the whites. They demanded to be self-determined.

Like X-Ray's poem that introduces this chapter, Hubert Harrison's "The Black Man's Burden," fundamentally opposed the "providence . . . placed upon the white man's shoulders."[133] Harrison suggests that there is a fundamental opposition between the order of the white man and the political rights and sexual propriety of the Black male. In Georgia, an amendment was proposed suggesting that "colored men should be allowed to vote only if two chaste white women would swear that they would trust them in the dark!" Identifying the primal rapist myth underlying such a proposal, Harrison said that it is either by "force or fraud . . . that the great bulk of Negroes of America are political pariahs today."[134] The white man imposes inferiority on the darker races by dissolving the distinction between the labor and the people who labor. The imperial pursuit does not bring civilization or freedom; it deprives the colonized of humanity. Harrison writes, "When a group has been reduced to serfdom, political and economic, its social status becomes fixed by fact."[135] American Negroes are deprived of their work, but also their lives by lynching. America is the example of what the [w]hite Man's Burden brings; it is, as Harrison says, "a horrid mockery."[136] The poetry and writings ignited by Kipling's insistence for imperial conquest offer evidence of a fundamental break between the notions of white manliness and Black manhood at the close of the nineteenth century. Black men did not stop here, however, in their attack on patriarchy.

At the dawn of the twentieth century, some Black men embraced African matriarchy as the preferred evolutionary schema to European patriarchy. For example, according to Edward Blyden, Jean Finot's *Race Prejudice* showed "in all the essentials of real manhood, physical, intellectual and moral—the Negro is not inferior to any other section of the human race and progress under conditions similar to those which have contributed to the development of the more advanced portions of mankind."[137] Finot argued that there are "no inferior or superior races, but only races living outside or within the influences of culture."[138] Blyden saw that Finot's work upset the ethnological origin of civilization. He understood that Africans could, in fact, have or, more appropriately, be matriarchal—a (feminine) race—and still grasp onto civilization. Whereas Finot saw the assimilation of traits as proof of the equality of races, Blyden insisted that it is Africa that looks down on the civilization of Europe. As he says of the civilized Africans, "They have grasped the principle underlying the European social and economic order and reject them as not equal to their own."[139] Lauding the Bundo Society, the ancient order of women that served as a school for African mothers, as the foundation of African society, Blyden defends the African family's emphasis on motherhood as civilized.

DuBois was even more explicit. Like Harrison, he maintained that the patriarchal racial evolution of Europe created the economic and, by effect, cultural debasement not only of the women of the darker races but also of the African mother idea. The power produced by the exploitation of the body of the Black male as labor/slave commented on by DuBois in *The Negro* (1915) is in tandem with the regeneration of his labor from his mother's womb, which is commented on in "The Damnation of Woman."[140] DuBois argues, "The father and his worship is Asia; Europe is the precocious, self-centered, forward striving child; but the land of the mother is and was Africa."[141] DuBois deliberately addresses the Bachofen *mythos* at the root of the West's supposition of African inferiority—the mother right—which suggests that as a stage of racial development, the matriarchal is inferior to the Apollonian.[142] This is a direct challenge to Cooper's invoking of Phoebus, or patriarchal reason. DuBois writes, "Nor does this all seem to be solely a survival of the historic matriarchate through which all nations pass—it appears to be more than this—as if the great Black race in passing up the steps of human culture gave the world, not only the Iron Age, the cultivation of the soil, and the domestication of animals, but also, in peculiar emphasis, the mother idea."[143] DuBois is so committed to this idea that he argues, "When Toussaint [Louverture] and [Henry] Christophe founded their kingdom in Haiti, it was based on old African tribal ties and beneath it was the mother-idea."[144] The Black race creates the world—its politics and history—around the cultivation of this matriarchal presence. It is matriarchy, not Black imitation of the patriarchal order of family, nation, and empire, that leads to Black liberation for DuBois.[145]

The Black Man's Burden was deployed against the divine right of white men and women to rule non-European societies. It was an attack on the sexual order of white supremacy. Black men understood that the order of the white family, presumed to be the structure of civilization itself, was false. They conceptualized the possibility of families ordered on the mother, stateless societies, and economic conditions that did not require the reduction of the darker races to labor, and looked to Africa for her mother-right. As DuBois explains, the self-realization of the Negro race in the early twentieth century "was not simply for their rights as men, but for the ideals of the greater world in which they live: the emancipation of women, universal peace, democratic government, the socialization of wealth and human brotherhood."[146] Black males rejected the *gender* of white civilization by refuting the evolutionary claim whites had to racial superiority. Rejecting the Victorian order of the family, projected as the relation the nation has to civilization, radically ruptures the standard of civilization deployed by white supremacism. Black men created the polemics allowing the darker races to create culturally relative orders of being and indicted domestic slavery as the ethnological basis of Blackness. Unlike present discourses, which presume that the category of woman can be corrupted only by whiteness, Black men have shown that womanhood itself depends on the colonized other: the savage Black male rapist. Robbing Black men of their historical sensibilities because such understandings do not conform to the categorical meanings imposed on their time reeks of caricature.

Conclusion

Throughout the literatures of the nineteenth and twentieth centuries, patriarchy has placed the Black male in direct opposition to white womanhood and, consequently, in opposition to the white family, nation, and empire. His very existence not only threatens the reproduction and hierarchal order of family but also exposes patriarchy as a system fundamentally dedicated to its reproduction and thereby the power and status of the white woman over racialized others. The Black rapist is the societal manifestation of this logic. The Black male is defined as a rapist, a primal beast, to mark him as unsuitable, permanently excluded from civilized society. Violence defines the border of the Black male's relationship with/in the United States. He is anathema to, because he threatens, the order founded on white patriarchy. Contrary to current theories, which presuppose a mimetic relationship between Black men and white men in which the Black male has undergone a nearly complete assimilation of the ideological and material (economic, political) structures of patriarchy, the history of Black males in the United States tells of vast political and anthropological distance from white male power. Black men simply do not desire it.

In *Negroes with Guns* (1962), Robert F. Williams identifies this very same relationship among white womanhood, racial segregation, and Ku Klux Klan violence in the Jim Crow South. Williams holds that white womanhood is the rationalization deployed by white patriarchy to justify its murderous logics toward Black males. The white woman was the justification offered to the white public for the terrorism launched against the Black community. Lynching, the castration of Black men, was offered as recompense for being Black and male, raced and rapist. Williams offers a powerful illustration of this claim:

> People have asked why a racist would take his wife into a riot-torn community like ours on that Sunday. But this is nothing new to those who know the nature of Klan raiding. Many Southern racists consider white women a form of insulation because of the old tradition that a Negro is supposed to be intimidated by a white woman and will not dare to offend her. [w]hite women are taken along on Klan raids so that if anything develops into a fight it will appear that the Negro attacked a woman and the Klansman will of course be her protector.[147]

Williams's understanding of the relationship that white womanhood has to white-supremacist violence motivated Eldridge Cleaver to articulate the symbolic relationship white womanhood holds next to the Black man. Cleaver was a great admirer of *Negroes with Guns*. As Kathleen Cleaver recalls, "I saw it when I first came out to the Bay area in July of 1967 in Eldridge Cleaver's apartment. He had a whole case full of them, and he was handing them out. And anybody that came into the Black Panther Party had to get a copy of *Negroes with Guns*, they had to read it and we had to discuss it."[148] The next chapter investigates the impact of Eldridge Cleaver's unpublished manuscript, *The Book of Lives,* alongside *Soul on Ice*, the book originally titled *[w]hite Woman/Black Man.*

Lost in a Kiss?

The Sexual Victimization of the Black Male during Jim Crow Read through Eldridge Cleaver's The Book of Lives *and* Soul on Ice

I'm perfectly aware that I'm in prison, that I'm a Negro, that I've been a rapist, and that I have a Higher Uneducation. I never know what significance I'm supposed to attach to these factors. But I have my suspicion that, because of these aspects of my character, "free-nor-mal-educated" people rather expect me to be more reserved, penitent, remorseful, and not too quick to shoot off my mouth on certain sub-jects. But I let them down, disappoint them, make them gape at me in a sort of stupor, as if they're thinking: You've got your nerve! Don't you realize that you owe a debt to society?[1]

D ESPITE HIS IMPACT on the development of Black Power and American Civil Rights organizations in the 1960s to 1970s, Eldridge Cleaver's in-sights and works have been reduced to the ramblings of a self-admitted rapist. The identity politics of today and the hegemonic force of disciplines have made Cleaver into an archetype of the Black Panther Party and the pre-sumed entelechy of Black men over the past six decades. Taken to be the moral position of all progressive scholars, these mythologies have persisted without challenge and with little attention to the erasure of the sexualized violence of Jim Crow and American segregation that Cleaver and other Black writers, such as James Baldwin and Richard Wright, were reacting against. In our ideations, Cleaver simply appears as a rapist; he had no history, no trau-ma, no socialization or oppression that could make him such. He emerges from history as Black phallic negativity, the symbol of the Black male's lack, and is codified as the representation of all Black masculine politics—the Black

Macho. There is no denying that Eldridge Cleaver was a criminal. He was twice convicted, once on drug charges in 1953 for the possession of marijuana and again in 1958 for rape with the intent to murder; later, he fled in exile after an assured conviction for a shootout with the police.[2] Existentially, one could regard Cleaver as a torn subject, a traumatized individual, or a psychopath. However, none of these labels—standing in for any number of deviant dispositions in the minds of scholars—fully captures the relevance and theoretical significance of Cleaver's reflections on the events unfolding before his very eyes during the Black struggle for Civil Rights in America.

Cleaver's insights into anti-Black violence and death, capitalism, government surveillance, and the global reach of white supremacy are indispensable components of an intellectual account of the emergence of these systems from the 1950s to the present, yet his voice is absent because his life and body are unacceptable to the disciplinary position of a theorist. He is a criminal, alleged murderer, and rapist; he is not the stuff of which academic theory is made. Cleaver is solely defined by the horrors described and admitted in the opening pages of his classic *Soul on Ice* (1968). Most scholars ready to dismiss Cleaver for his homophobia, misogyny, and sexism—all arguments filtered through the lens of Michele Wallace's reading of his work and the psychoanalytic disposition in *Black Macho and the Myth of Superwoman*—have done little work to complicate this interpretation or even look for more in the writings of Cleaver or the Black Panthers to question it. In fact, as the emerging focus of academics has turned more toward the writings of prison intellectuals in an effort to address the ever-expanding prison-industrial complex, Black male political prisoners have been largely ignored or erased as part of the moral penance decentering Black men in disciplines altogether. Many of these discussions concerning the role of the political prisoner, the Black revolutionary, and the prison-industrial complex as a continuation of (neo)slavery occur without any attention to the sexualized violence used to target Black males or any need to center the Black male's experience of imprisonment from slavery to Jim Crow within these discussions. Most discussions of the prison-industrial complex are praised simply for venturing into the topic such that it can be considered under (public) discussion. The prison-industrial complex is not rigorously analyzed as an institution with a historical libidinal obsession toward Black male flesh. Analyses of the prison are praised simply for condemning it as a kind of neoslavery—without the benefit of a historiographic reorientation toward the period of slavery continued by the ongoing murder and imprisonment of Black people, especially young Black men.

In an unpublished manuscript entitled *The Book of Lives*, Cleaver analyzes the cultivation of the homosexual revolutionary cause from inside the prison. He is quite candid and open about his own homosexuality and challenges one to think about Black manhood beyond our popular politics claimed on the basis of identity histories. He insists that the reader recognize the specific societal and historical vulnerability of Black men. This text is a prelude to *Soul on Ice* and resonates with his account of the Black male as the Supermasculine Menial; it is a fantastic analysis, however, that stops short of the escape the Black male has from the objectification of the white imagination—the creative phobic engine of the white maniac. Cleaver captures death while announcing the white woman's culpability and her role in the rape-murder and fetishization of Black men in the process. Cleaver writes to flee being a convict; he writes to become man/human. His work is offensive precisely because he diagnoses the psycho-juridical trauma of gender that keeps the Black man "out of harmony with the system that is oppressing him."[3]

Reflections on Cleaver's Homosexuality and Its Clash with Black Macho Ideology

In the essay "Eldridge Cleaver: He Is No James Baldwin" (1973), Huey P. Newton recalled a dinner he had shared with Baldwin in 1967. Having been invited by Baldwin, Newton chose Cleaver to be his guest. "When we arrived," according to Newton, "Cleaver and Baldwin walked into each other, and the giant six foot three inch Cleaver bent down and engaged in a long passionate French kiss with the tiny (barely five feet) Baldwin." Newton was shocked, saying later, "I did not understand then but now realize that Baldwin ('The Native Son'), who had neither written nor uttered a word in response to Cleaver's acid literary criticism . . . , exposed Cleaver's internal contradiction and tragic flaw; in effect, he said 'If a woman kissed Cleaver she would be kissing another woman, and if a man kissed Cleaver, he would be kissing a man.'"[4] Contrary to popular belief, *Soul on Ice* was not the un-doubtable bible and spiritual manual of the Black Panther Party. In fact, the text, especially its view of masculinity, was debated within the party.[5] Newton argued that the text ultimately showed the projection and reach of Cleaver's self-hatred, a self-hatred Cleaver projects on Baldwin that is more accurately a reflection of Cleaver's own repressed sexuality.[6] As Newton notes, "Yes, Baldwin is a homosexual, but he is not a depraved madman." Baldwin was an open homosexual; Cleaver repressed his homosexuality. "The problems, difficulties, and internal conflict that Cleaver has with himself—because he is engaged in a denial of his own homosexuality—is projected onto an eternal self (Baldwin) in order to defend his own threatened ego."[7]

Although Newton's essay has been included in anthologies for more than a decade, no serious scholarly attention to Cleaver's homosexuality has surfaced. For some, Susan Brownmiller's view that "Cleaver's thought pattern and the ideological construct he used to justify his career as a rapist . . . reflects a strain of thinking among Black male intellectuals and writers that became quite fashionable in the late 1960's" is all that needs to be said about this era, and about Black male productions on sexuality.[8] Similarly, Black feminist renderings of Cleaver, such as that found in Wallace's *Black Macho and the Myth of the Superwoman*, depict Cleaver to be LeRoi Jones's "other half," "an even more effective voice for Black Macho."[9] Like Brownmiller, Wallace believes that Cleaver "did a lot to politicize sexuality in the Black Movement"[10]—the problem, of course, in her view being that Cleaver politicized the Black Macho, or the latent historical Black rapist identity.

Black Macho and the Myth of the Superwoman centers the sexual lust the Black male has for the white woman as the driving force behind his quest for civil rights. In Wallace's view, some Black men wanted white women simply because they were hostile to Black women, while others believed that "white women gave them money and made them feel like men." This attraction was not fleeting but epochal for Wallace. As she remarks, "Some white women were quite blunt: They wanted [B]lack cock because it was the best cock there was."[11] This sexual order ushered in by the Civil Rights Movement, given the new economy of sexual competition created by the Black man's access to the white woman and new political power, led Black people to imitate America's standard of the family and focus on heterosexual relationships between Black men and women. This realization situated on an allegedly new sexual opportunity for Black men also revealed the material disadvantage of Black masculinity. Wallace notes, "The Americanized [B]lack man's reaction to his inability to earn enough to support his family, his impotence, his lack of concrete power, was to vent his resentment on the person in this society who could do least about it—his woman. His problem was that she was not a woman. She, in turn, looked at the American ideal of manhood and took the only safe course her own fermenting rage and frustration could allow her. Her problem was that he was not a man." As Wallace saw it, as "[B]lacks began to lean more and more toward Americanization . . . [they internalized] self-hatred."[12]

The Black man, however, took a peculiar devolution for Wallace. As the Black man internalized the Americanized version of himself, he began to embrace the sexual caricature of the Buck as a way to compensate for his economic and political emasculation. Before its resuscitation by Black men in the 1970s, Wallace insisted that the Buck made his last appearance in *The Birth of a Nation*. According to Wallace, "The Buck is the only [B]lack stereotype that is sexual. He is brutal, violent, virile, tough, strong—and finds white women especially appealing."[13] Wallace concedes, "The Ku Klux Klan, the lynch mob, and Jim Crow legislators said their task was to prevent the [B]lack man from violating sacred womanhood. In pursuit of this mission, thousands of [B]lack men were lynched, murdered, degraded, their homes destroyed."[14] Wallace maintains that instead of inspiring disgust or even fear of white womanhood, this historical brutality only reinforced "the notion of the [B]lack man's access to white women as a prerequisite of his freedom."[15]

In fact, it was this dynamic that "shaped the minds of both those white women who came south as part of the Civil Rights Movement and the [B]lack men who met them."[16] Wallace, like Thomas Dixon Jr.'s *The Clansman*, is arguing that Black men pursue civil and political rights to gain sexual access to white women; like early twentieth-century "Buck" fiction, she imagines that Black male political power is motivated by the sexual capture of white women. Later in the chapter, we see that this is the exact opposite of what Cleaver intends.

The Black male activists of this time became representations of this sultry imago. Stokely Carmichael was "the nightmare America had been dreading— the [B]lack man seizing his manhood, the [B]lack man as sexual, virile, strong, tough, and dangerous."[17] Martin Luther King Jr., the opposing mentor of Black Power's militancy, is described by Wallace as "a glaring impossibility—a dream of masculine softness and beauty, an almost feminine man."[18] Malcolm X was seen as "virile, strong, and generated a powerful, fearsome presence . . . [who] had spat in the faces of the white woman and white man."[19] While King's murder proliferated the rationalizations for militancy and a Black Macho posture, it was Malcolm's death that killed "the chance for a [B]lack patriarchy" and launched the fixation of a then imprisoned Cleaver with obtaining his manhood.[20] Cleaver, inspired by the hyper-sexualization of the cool/hip Black male activist depicted in the writings of Norman Mailer, was a more effective Black Macho than even LeRoi Jones. Reading *Black Dada Nihilismus* as a political program, Wallace notes that Cleaver, "as a former rapist," had a similar revolutionary sentiment. According to Wallace, like Jones, Cleaver's "raping was not a crime against women but a political act."[21] As Wallace sees it, "[B]lack women and white women were victims of America's history and . . . the white man was a victim of his own Frankenstein monster."[22] This hyper-Macho-ism, then, depends on a rampant hyper-heterosexualism, in Wallace's view, a tendency appositionally described as homophobia. She continues:

> If one is to take Cleaver at his word, the [B]lack homosexual is counterrevolutionary (1) because he's being fucked and (2) because he's being fucked by the white man. By so doing he reduces himself to the status of our [B]lack grandmothers who, as everyone knows, were fucked by white men all the time.
>
> However, it would follow that if a [B]lack man were doing the fucking and the one being fucked were a white man, the [B]lack male homosexual would be just as good a revolutionary as a [B]lack heterosexual male, if not a better one. Black Macho would have to lead you to this conclusion. If whom you fuck indicates your power, then obviously the greatest power would be gained by fucking a white man first, a [B]lack man second, a white woman third, and a [B]lack woman not at all. The most important rule is that nobody fucks you.[23]

Wallace presents Black men as culturally and psychically committed to the Black Macho mythology. Black men, in both their heterosexual and homosexual variety, are anti-Black woman because she is the one who does not get "fucked." It is these impressions and representations of Black males, more than half a century later, that are made synonymous with Black masculinity. In this view, Black males have lacked reflection and, unlike their Black female counterparts, only assimilated the caricatures of white society rather than resisted them.[24]

As Jared Sexton remarks in "Race, Sexuality, and Political Struggle: Reading *Soul on Ice*," "In many ways [Wallace's] efforts in that now canonical Black feminist text provide a sort of interpretive framework for much more popular and academic opinion on the movement in general, the Black Panthers more specifically, and Cleaver in particular, up to the present."[25] Despite Wallace's substantial revision and recanting of *The Black Macho* in the introduction to the 1990 Verso edition of her text—along the lines of many of the substantial criticisms such as Paula Giddings's "The Lessons of History Will Shape the 1980s—*Black Macho and the Myth of the Superwoman* Won't," Alison Edwards's "Rape, Racism and the [w]hite Women's Movement," and Maulana Karenga's "On Wallace's Myth: Wading through Troubled Waters"—the Black Macho idea continues to haunt any engagements with Cleaver's *Soul on Ice*. Regarding Cleaver as a figure and thinker, Sexton correctly states that Black Macho ideology "wards against the critical interpretation (versus mere rejection or avoidance) of his thought prior to his exile in 1968."[26]

Regardless of its large-scale acceptance as a serious analysis of the Black Power Movement and the political tendencies of Black men from the 1960s forward, *Black Macho and the Myth of the Superwoman* is little more than the impressionistic renderings of a young Black woman observing the events of the Civil Rights Movement offered to her by mainstream media.[27] Over a decade later, Wallace admitted that her view of Black men was rooted in her traumatic experiences with her father and stepfather. As she says about her interaction with Black men generally, "I expected and found hostility, anger, competition, violence, dishonesty, misogyny and ignorance. These experiences had a lot to do with my 'theories' about [B]lack men and [B]lack male/female relationships as a [B]lack feminist." While many contemporary gender scholars would celebrate such an epistemology, Wallace's view rarely rises above our more accepted notions of the stereotype. As she admits, "I am not saying that there aren't some [B]lack men out there who are mean to women. . . . What I am saying is that I was not actually aware then that there was any other kind of man."[28] Wallace saw Black men as the unvarying trauma of her childhood and incapable of loving Black women. Wallace actually concedes this point, saying, "There are many [B]lack men who love [B]lack women, and vice versa, although I didn't know it at the time I wrote *Black Macho*."[29]

Wallace created a narrative offering America a view of Black masculinity—its political strivings—rooted in America's fear of Black male militancy and miscegenation. Wallace offered white America a reason to hate Black men; she gave them an auto-ethnography of the torture she suffered at the hands of Black men and called it "theory,"[30] a moniker that solidified her text as the creed all disciplinary interpretations of Black masculinity must honor decades later. Although this goes unmentioned by the various scholars who remain inspired by *Black Macho and the Myth of the Superwoman*, Wallace has admitted there is no actual evidence of the Black Macho idea she presented. In the 1990 introduction, she writes:

> If I had to do it over again, I would no longer maintain that Black Macho was the crucial factor in the destruction of the Black Power Movement, not because I no longer think it is true at least in some sense—and certainly it was true in the world I inhabited then—but because it was a claim that was impossible to substantiate at the level of sociological, historical or journalistic data. While it may be a valid interpretation of events to say that a brand of [B]lack male chauvinism contributed to the shortsightedness and failure of the Black Power Movement, there are other interpretations equally valid—for instance, that police and CIA repression were also factors in the demise of the movement. Moreover, from another perspective (although not necessarily my own) the Black Liberation Struggle can be viewed as never ending or beginning but rather waxing or waning, usually invisible to the dominant discourse, virtually since [B]lacks became slaves in the Americas.[31]

Wallace's hesitancy is conveyed only more sharply by her mother, Faith Ringgold. In *A Letter to My Daughter, Michele Wallace, in Response to Her Book, "Black Macho and the Myth of the Superwoman,"* Ringgold makes scathing indictments of Wallace's position. Ringgold writes, for example, that "the term [B]lack macho has no substantial reference to the [B]lack men who provided leadership in the [B]lack struggles of the 60s, many of whom lost their lives in order to make life better for all of us."[32] These ideas, insists Ringgold, emerge from her daughter's having "mixed cinema with life."[33] Ringgold asks her daughter how she could liken Black manhood to that of a psychopath or James Bond movie. "James Bond is a white man. And violent death is the theme that sells . . . in western culture. How can you attribute this phenomenon to so-called [B]lack macho? Open your history books and let us add up the score; so many for the [B]lack man, so many for white American. Who is the winner now?"[34] Throughout the text, Ringgold expresses disbelief and disappointment in her daughter's argument. Ringgold is adamant that her four-

teen-year-old daughter's revelation of the Black male in the 1960s simply was
not substantiated by facts or experience: "Michele, our family has lived for
three generations in a [B]lack community without knowing that the [B]lack
man is a psychopath. Where did you discover this about him?" Ringgold is
clear: a violent death is "America's concession to so called Black Macho's demand for his 'manhood,' and it is the only concession he can count on getting."[35] In a brief review of her mother's book, Wallace admits, "Almost nothing
I wrote in *Black Macho* would I repeat or continue to agree with now. I feel like
I have changed in every way possible and that I am always changing my opinions about such matters in particular. My mother's firmness and certainty continues to fascinate me."[36] Despite these admissions by Wallace herself, *The
Black Macho* remains an authoritative lens from which to view Black manhood
within the academy and throughout its various concentric publics.

   Because the Black Macho myth demands a heterosexual obsession with
"fucking" (white) women, there has been little discussion beyond the hyper-
hetero-masculinity allegedly embodied by Cleaver or a questioning of the
seemingly natural-necessary and inevitable homophobia to which the hetero-
Black male identity is committed. In fact, even Vincent Woodard's *The Delectable Negro* (2014), a book about the literal and figurative consumption of the
Black male body—the eating of the Black male, cannibalism sustained by the
homoerotic sexual urge of racism—merely mentions Cleaver's homosexuality and his review of Baldwin in *Soul on Ice* as a contradiction, given their
kiss.[37] In the introduction to *The Delectable Negro*, Woodard argues:

> Black gays in the late twentieth century found themselves in a double
> bind of history and memory, which had an unfortunate result: Black
> people equated their sexual identities with homosexual violation dat-
> ing back to slavery. . . . For example, Eldridge Cleaver associated anal
> sex between a white man and [B]lack man with a racial death wish
> extending back to slavery and with miscegenation. Cleaver conflated
> his contemporary understanding of the homosexual person with the
> particular and different ways in which homosexuality was thought of
> and configured in the context of slavery.[38]

Woodard did not have any knowledge of Cleaver's *The Book of Lives*, of course,
and thus chose to read Cleaver as fearful of thinking about homosexuality in
its fullness rather than as a Black male theorizing the economic and political
operation of homoeroticism in society and the prison. There is no second
thought to Cleaver's possible homosexuality and the genealogy that arises
from within the context of the Black gay man shackled to revolution and only
later problematized by the cosmopolitan identity thought to make up the
Black gay male experience in the 1960s. Woodard argues that "the inability to
creatively imagine homosexuality during slavery reflected a fundamental fear

within the [B]lack community of moving outside of the normative categories of masculinity, reproduction, pleasure, and family."[39]

Is this truly Cleaver's problem, given his reflection on the homoerotic and repressive nature of the prison and the stud farm? Cleaver configures sexuality as a matter not of identity but, rather, of historical social engineering—sexual desire is created in the subjugated and animated by subjugation. The white male retreating into the mind alienates the body by creating the Nigger brute as his antithesis. This brute is neither heterosexual nor homosexual; he is fungible, bending to the desire-fear of the white society that surrounds him. Woodard's view demands that we understand masculinity-reproduction-pleasure-family as teleological constituents of one another, that to some extent they entail the accompaniment of one another successively. Is this truly the case? Is it the case that the historical assemblage of what we call "Black and masculine" has avoided or not imagined the homosexual simply because it runs against the "imagined norm" of Black hyper-masculinity or super-heteronormativity? What are the texts and moments that offer the ontological caste of Black male heterosexuality while eliding the historical moments of Black male sexual vulnerability altogether, or debasing them to accidents of Black maleness, inconsequential to the overarching construct we take to be "Black masculinity"? Such a position emerges not from historical proof but, rather, from the imagined reality of excluding the reflections of Black men on their condition from slavery forward. It pretends that Black men did not comment on their own sexual vulnerability to white men and white women. Even worse, such a narrative asserts that even if we do read the experiences and reflections of Black men on their sexual victimization and the dynamics of white colonial erotics on their flesh, it would have no consequence for our current thinking about Black masculinity or gender more generally.

The Book of Lives and Cleaver's Homoerotics

Cleaver's unpublished manuscript is undated but reads as if it is a survey of his time in jail during the late 1950s. Cleaver's work is heavily autobiographical, placing him and his thoughts in direct contact with the personalities he creates to represent various aspects of Black male character during his time. Cleaver begins the book by describing his encounter with a character he comes to call Little Jesus. He says, "I first met Little Jesus in the Los Angeles County Jail, in which I was kept while going to trail in 1957."[40] This would suggest Cleaver is writing or reflecting on the problems in the text during his incarceration for rape. Cleaver describes Little Jesus somewhat strangely. He says he was charged with "assaulting a white woman with a knife, and snatching her purse," while nonetheless contending that Little Jesus had "the air of a Black bourgeois thrown in jail for the first time in his life."[41] Little Jesus was a Christian man, married with two little children. He declared his innocence, believing that as a Christian, he would be saved by God from the false accusation of assaulting a white woman. When challenged by the inmates as a fraud, he said that "he felt like Daniel in the lion's den, that we were all foul and corrupt, steeped in sin, that we were all damned to hell, and that we were going to burn for our blasphemous remarks against his father, Almighty God, and his Divine Son and Our Holy Savior, Jesus."[42]

Little Jesus refused to get out on bail. He was convinced that the trial would clear him from any wrongdoing—that, after seeing his family and hearing testimony from his minister that he was a "good" Black man, the jury would see that he was incapable of assaulting a white woman. According to Cleaver, such presentations mattered little to the outcome: "The white woman said that she had been walking down the street one afternoon, minding her own business and up popped this nigger—that little nigger sitting right there trying to look innocent now—snatched her purse, and in the process stabbed her in her arm with a long knife."[43] Little Jesus "produced witnesses who swore, on the Bible, that he had been attending a class at the church at the very time that this woman's purse was snatched,"[44] Cleaver writes and then adds, "Then he painted, for the jury, a picture of his life, rooted like a tree in the Baptist Church." Cleaver points out somewhat flippantly that Little Jesus presented a "model nigger that would make Booker T. Washington leap with joy in his grave if he could see it. A technically skilled, literate, voting, Christian nigger with a family."[45] Regardless, the majority of the jury voted not to convict him. His bail was reduced, and Little Jesus was let out. A year later, the district attorney took him to trial again, with the same evidence but a different jury, and convicted him.

Prison is a field of study for Cleaver in the unpublished manuscript, and Little Jesus is simply the first character of many who are inevitably trapped by the demands and laws of a racist society to protect white women at the expense of Black men—their lives and those of their families. What Cleaver rightly points out throughout the text is that the character of individual Black males is ultimately irrelevant to the overall machine that produces and fills the prison. This representation of Little Jesus, however, is simultaneously the fatalism of the world for a Black man and the path toward salvation Cleaver finds through his own journey and struggles with the world. As he did in his later reflections in *Soul on Ice*, Cleaver attempts to situate Blackness on the sexual foundations of white supremacy—or, more accurately, the need of white supremacy to sexually exploit the Black male body as nothing more than flesh. The Black man is defined by his corporeality. He is only the body, a confinement that denies reflectivity and his capacity of mind. Cleaver has visited this theme more popularly in the chapter "Allegory of the Black Eunuch," in *Soul on Ice*, asking readers whether they had ever "wondered why the white man genuinely applauds a [B]lack man who achieves excellence with his body in the field of sports, while he hates to see a [B]lack man achieve excellence with his brain? The mechanics of the myth demand that the Brain and the Body, like east and west, must never meet."[46] Cleaver maintains that the Black male body is reduced to flesh within a racist society; thus, the Black male becomes ontologically confined by the sexual order of society imagined by the white male. He is unable to simply "act" contrary to the ends assigned to him within this corporeal economy. It is through this condition, thriving on the physicality of the Black male, that the white-supremacist order makes the Black male disposable and determined-subjugated by the external forces of America's oppressive institutions. He—as body—has no natural resistance to the commands placed on his flesh as a prisoner, and it is this personification/representation of the Black male as dehumanized that Cleaver uses to demonstrate to the reader that the Black male is a criminal not simply in the prison but throughout his life in society. The realization that the Black male is not free and has no need for faith is a central feature in Cleaver's rendering of Little Jesus throughout *The Book of Lives*.

Little Jesus's faith did not waver upon his return to prison. Cleaver says, "When he walked up and down the Big Yard, Jesus was his Shepherd, and he had the aspect about him that he was waiting for a dazzling light to burst forth in the sky, and for strong angels, with invincible wings, to swoop down and carry him over the walls."[47] Resolved in his Christianity, Little Jesus "accepted the job and rehabilitation program that the prison officials set before him and braced himself, standing firmly on his faith in God, for the monotonous process of appeal to unfold."[48] Little Jesus is a character not of optimism but of that faith in deliverance Cleaver sees as being inextricably tied to the suffering of Black men in America. Despite all that is done, there is some resolve, an irrational and unfounded belief that systems, because of the force of God himself, will respond to the moral character of the oppressed. It is initially this faith that attracted Cleaver to Little Jesus.

One day, Richard, Little Jesus, received a letter from his wife. It said that she had "come to the conclusion that I cannot share a life of marriage with a Christian, no kind of Christian, even if less severer than you."[49] His faith seemed to be denied by his wife, who no longer wished to share his religion, and word came down that the Appeals Board had upheld his conviction. Little Jesus had little left to stand on. Cleaver says, "We stopped calling him Little Jesus, because we no longer understood what that might mean to him."[50] Slowly, Cleaver says, "I watched Little Jesus become a convict. The world that he had been into had failed him, had split half-in-two. It lay now in ruins around his feet. He began to relate to the fact that he was in prison, like everybody else."[51] This transformation in Little Jesus resonates with Cleaver's rejection of God in "On Becoming" in *Soul on Ice*. "Our atheism was pragmatic," he declares to the reader:

I had come to believe that there is no God; if there is, men do not know anything about him. Therefore, all religions were phony—which made all preachers and priests, in our eyes, fakers, including the ones scurrying around the prison who, curiously, could put in a good world for you with the Almighty Creator of the universe, but could not get anything down with the warden or parole board—they could usher you through the Pearly Gates after you were dead, but not through the prison gate while you were still alive and kicking.[52]

Cleaver himself was lost; he did not know how to interact with Little Jesus without his faith mediating (providing hope) to them both. Cleaver confesses, "If he was, indeed, an innocent man, and if at the same time he was really such a Christian, then I had right on the tier with me, just a few cells down, a nigger who righteously fitted the description of Job, with a chain of long suffering."[53] This vulnerability and the strength of Richard's belief attracted Cleaver to him. It is in this writing of the text that the reader sees that Cleaver is expressing not only admiration of and bewilderment in the character of Richard but also desire for him. When speaking to the physical appearance of Little Jesus, Cleaver describes him as a short man with smooth brown skin. Cleaver conveys to the reader that Little Jesus was attractive and had a "nice little smooth ass, that stood up and out just like the nice smooth, brown ass of a nice smooth brown girl."[54]

Cleaver was not the only one who noticed Little Jesus's ass. According to Cleaver, everyone checked out Richard's ass, but it was not until one night when they were standing naked in the shower line that he himself realized his lust for Little Jesus:

I was standing in a line next to the one Little Jesus was in, and a few places behind him in the line so that I got a full view of his ass. I realized at that moment that I wanted to fuck Little Jesus right in his sweet little holy ass. It was all I could do to keep from getting an erection.[55]

Cleaver understood the danger of his lust for Little Jesus. His desire for Richard was dangerous in the prison: "With all of the wee-wee and asshole games that go down in the shower line at San Quentin, it is not cool to be standing there with a hard on. It would be certain to be misunderstood, because everybody there would interpret it in their own way, according to what they saw in you or what they want you to be."[56] This is a powerful moment in *The Book of Lives*. Cleaver discloses to the reader both his homosexuality and his vulnerability in prison as a Black male. He shows to the reader the fungibility of the Black male self, its ability—or, rather, its lack thereof—to resist the desire and power of others to create in the Black male what they wish him to be. This vulnerability is vacating. It gives Cleaver reason for his lust for Little Jesus and shows it was not impulsive.

Cleaver's lust for Little Jesus entailed great risk. Cleaver worried that Little Jesus would reject his advances. He feared Little Jesus to some degree, saying, "Little Jesus showed signs that if he ever turned away from God, he was perfectly capable of killing somebody."[57] On the one hand, Cleaver confesses that he was hesitant to tell Little Jesus because he could become violent. On the other hand, Cleaver was personally unsure of what, exactly, he felt for Richard. As he remarks following his initial desire to "fuck Little Jesus," "I mean, did I specifically want to fuck Little Jesus, or was I just uptight, having had no pussy for a long time now, and just want to get down, to fuck, to come, in something other than my own hand, at night when I masturbated."[58] Cleaver hated masturbating in prison. He felt "contempt for the whole process and "deeply remorseful for having done it." This contempt was totalizing and brought about a "stark pain to the bottom of the roots of myself."[59]

We see here the problem of sexual desire that has developed for Cleaver both historically in his disavowal of homosexuality and in his denial of his lust for white women in *Soul on Ice*, his "symbolic representation of the forbidden tribe of women."[60] The prison made Cleaver into a convict. He experiences himself as the conduit of the sexual animus imposed on him as a rapist—the plaything of white society. As such, he is confused by his desire. "After remaining suspended in amazement for a spell," Cleaver intimates, "I wanted to fuck Little Jesus. After relating to that fact, I started trying to figure out how to do it."[61] Many readers will mistake Cleaver's lust for sex with another man as the provocation of the text; they will be overcome by it. While Cleaver's lust for Little Jesus certainly does change the heteronormative hyper-masculine framing of Cleaver's life and our present interpretations of his works, a more central point is being made about the relationship of Black male sexual repression—the fear and anxiety of it—and the manufacturing of the Black male body as a purely sexual object/product within the walls of the prison.

The prison to a large extent negates the concepts of agency that have now become established as the origin of individual action. Cleaver is a prisoner. What he is told he is and what he imagines himself to be require an interiorized fantasy, not a deliberate action toward a self-authored end. For Cleaver, he does not yet know what he is to be. He is a *fucking thing*. He is thought to be so from birth. So in this moment he doubts his desire and lust—this feeling he insinuates as care toward Richard—as merely his lust for pussy. His desire to fuck Little Jesus, then, cannot be interpreted as Cleaver being an active (agent) and Little Jesus being a passive object of his desire. The prison makes both Black men fucking things and in doing so robs them of humanity and their ability to recognize what it is they really are.

When Cleaver finally has the opportunity to have sex with Little Jesus, he does so under the surveillance of the prison. The Garden Chapel was the place where sex with men happened in Cleaver's story. The Garden Chapel was away from the physical cells of the prison but was nonetheless maintained by the officials of the prison as a space for men to have sex with other men. Cleaver knows that the Garden Chapel—the place marked out for the homoerotic— was nurtured by the prison itself. "The question of whether or not the Garden Chapel was bugged had been debated for years. If it was bugged, then it must have been very important to the prison officials. If they heard everything that was discussed in the Garden Chapel, if they had all that information, then I can understand how the walls of that prison have stood for so long."[62] Cleaver uses the chapel to illustrate the use of the sacred to maintain the sentience of the state. Even the place of faith, the boundary between the will of the flesh and the piety of the soul, is ruled by the white sexual order of society. The chapel shows the reader that Black male sexuality exists under the surveillance of the administrators.

The Prison and the Making of the Black Male as Convict

The prison is a coercive force constraining and reorganizing the very being of the Black men within its walls. Contrary to the assertion of the hyper-masculinity of prison, Black men lack the power to appeal to or access patri-archal masculinity in prison. In fact, it is their imprisonment that enables the anxiety that white society feels toward the Black male body to be internalized as the psychology of the Black male mind, as the newly created convict. Eleanor Novek's work on Black masculinity under incarceration reiterates this powerlessness of Black men within prison: "Masculine norms in prison are deeply affected by confinement, loss of autonomy, surveillance, rigid institutional rules and lack of resources."[63] The prison subsumes the Black male self only as penis and flesh. In *Soul on Ice*, Cleaver notes that "the penis, virility, is of the Body. It is not of the Brain. . . . [I]n the deal which the white man forced upon the [B]lack man, the [B]lack man was given the Body as his domain."[64] Toward the end of the 1960s, Cleaver had already worked out the role white administrators (in both society and prison) determined for the Black penis: It was the symbol of pure animalistic brute sexual force, the criminal rapist beast. This is the transformation Cleaver notes in *The Book of Lives*:

> In a society founded upon the ethic of reward and punishment, plea-sure and pain, profit and loss, the lives of those inside its prisons will be organized around pain and structured into the prison system will be forms intended to hurt. You are startled when you first feel this grasp, this constriction, holding you like a vice and the natural im-pulse is to flee. You turn and turn inside of yourself, like a rat scratch-ing inside a cage to get out, until you realize that you are trapped and

that though you are in pain you cannot move. So you sit there stoned, like the wall? You are becoming something else.[65]

This *becoming* highlighted by Cleaver has some very real parallels to the first chapter of *Soul on Ice*. In the original typewritten text of *The Book of Lives*, Cleaver writes, "You become something else," but then scratches out the type and changes it to "You are becoming something else." This process of change, substantiated later as the chapter title "On Becoming," dialectically marks an indeterminacy in his thinking about his sexuality and his suspension of any sort of normative value he places on it in the late 1950s while in prison. He notes, "Everyone who feels the grasp of a prison is changed, I won't say for better or for worse. We were all changing and we knew it, and we were terrified at what we might become, most of all because we didn't really know what it would be."[66] Here again there is an editorial mark in the text; initially it reads, "at what we were becoming," which suggests that there is a coercive determination, a fixity, that they all knew was coming because of their time within the prison. Cleaver writes:

> I could see around me, what was happening to others. But that didn't tell me much about me. I saw that Little Jesus was becoming more and more like a woman. He became more feminine in his gesture. There once was a rigidity in Little Jesus, as though deep down inside himself, somewhere, perhaps in the last outpost of the soul, he was resisting becoming a bitch. If so, then now he had lost that struggle. No one would have been surprised if Little Jesus started sprouting tits.[67]

Notice how Cleaver lacks a moral descriptor following his observation of the feminization and homosexual attraction of convicts as in *Soul on Ice*. Cleaver simply cannot say it is "better or worse," given the sexual repression of the society toward Black men. He makes no comments in this text that speak of homosexuality as aberrational. Throughout *The Book of Lives*, he explains it as a dynamic both cultivated by the prison and in some sense desired by the prisoner. In this sense, Cleaver aims to observe rather than moralize the condition of the Black male prisoner.

Despite Cleaver's confession to loving another man, many scholars and gender theorists will insist that this has no effect on our present readings. To some, Cleaver's description of Little Jesus will appear to be consistent with his homophobic criticisms of Baldwin in *Soul on Ice*. These scholars will no doubt maintain that Cleaver may have been a repressed homosexual, but he was still a homophobe. However, the careful scholar must attend to the meanings being corrected, scratched out, *revised* throughout the original text before simply insisting on the correctness of our present perspective. Cleaver actually says, "I could see around me, what it looked like others were becoming to me."

This suggests that he maintains the position he took upon recognizing his initial attraction to Little Jesus in the shower: that convicts have no will to resist the imposition of others on them. Little Jesus is seen as a woman because that is what Cleaver sees as representing his sexual attraction to Little Jesus as a man. This is also the fungibility Newton claimed is exposed by Baldwin's kiss: Cleaver's malleability to the will of others because he lives his life as the vessel of the convict. The convict was not simply the creation of the prison but the sociogenic production of the society that produced the prison and gave rise to that which we know as the prisoner. The convict is reactive—an empty self of rage. He has little faith in anything or anyone. As they did from Little Jesus, all love and social relationships retreat from the convict. Cleaver understands the convict as asocial—a lonely and abandoned entity. He writes, "Even our wives and lovers whose bed we've shared, with whom we have shared the tenderest moments and most delicate relations, leave us after a while, put us down, cut us clean aloose and treat us like they hate us." The convict internalizes this social isolation and reacts. He is distrustful of social sentiment and craves revenge—or, as Cleaver puts it, "All society shows the convict its ass and expects him to kiss it: the convict feels like kicking it or putting a bullet in it. A convict sees a man's fangs and claws and learns quickly to bare and unsheathe his own, for real and final."[68]

Eldridge Cleaver's Supermasculine Menial and Frantz Fanon's Phobogenic Object

In the introduction to the Rampart Books edition of *Soul on Ice*, Maxwell Geismar writes, "Cleaver's book has definite parallels with Fanon's *Black Skin, [w]hite Masks*." Geismar sees the similarity between Fanon's and Cleaver's work in their analysis of the problem of "identification as a [B]lack soul which has been 'colonized'—more subtly perhaps in the United States for some three hundred years, but perhaps even more persuasively—by an oppressive white society that projects its brief, narrow vision of life as eternal truth."[69] Unfortunately, the neglect of Cleaver as a figure has also resulted in an ignorance of the concerns Cleaver and Fanon share over the sexual configuration of colonialism and racism. Fanon argues that the white "Negrophobic man is a repressed homosexual."[70] Fanon recognizes that racism, the aversion the white male has to the Black man, is explained not solely by his hate for the Black male but also by his fear of, and desire for, him. Cleaver maintains that white male domination over the Black male is a sexual obsession with his Black virility. Following his reading of Charles Odier's *Anxiety and Magic Thinking* (1947), Fanon offers an analysis of the white man's subjective insecurity and fear of the Black man. Fanon insists that the "Negro is phobogenic," meaning that the Negro triggers a pre-rational fear in the mind of the white. This fear objectifies the Negro, overdetermining his being as the phantasm of the white mind. The objectified Black is "endowed with evil intentions and with all the attributes of a malefic power." The Negrophobic man, the white man fearful of his imagination of Blackness—of the Nigger—interprets the Black man as the embodiment of his forbidden sexual desire. This is why Fanon provokes the reader, asking, "In the majority of Negrophobic men has there been an attempt at rape? An attempt at fellatio?" Desire and terror share a synergistic fate with regard to the Black man; he inspires fear in the mind and lust in the loins of the white man. Fanon maintains, "If an extremely frightening object, such as a more or less imaginary attacker, arouses terror, this is also—for most often such cases are those of women—and especially a terror mixed with sexual revulsion."[71] The sexual revulsion of whites is not disgust; they are not repulsed by the thoughts of "fucking" a Black man. They are ashamed of their repressed sexuality that craves him—the immoral and shameful things his flesh allows.

Cleaver says, in an effort to rationalize the brutality of slavery, "The [B]lack [man] was seen as a mindless Supermasculine Menial. Forced to do the back-breaking work, he was conceived in terms of his ability to do such work—field nigger, etc."[72] The Supermasculine Menial is undifferentiated Black male flesh. It is all body and alienated from its mind. For the Supermasculine Menial, "The mind counts only insofar as it enables them to receive, understand, and carry out the will of the Omnipotent Administrators."[73] What is this will of the Omnipotent Administrator? What does the white man desire in a society and social order constructed on his sexual anxieties and fear of the Black male? Cleaver's answer: the body. In "The Primeval Mitosis," Cleaver argues, "The Omnipotent Administrator is launched on a perpetual search for his alienated body, for affirmation of his unstable masculinity." As an abstraction from the body, the white male becomes "a worshipper of physical prowess." There is a psychosis involved with his relation to the body. He seeks the power of being a physical body, but he nonetheless comes to "despise the body and everything associated with it." The white male's retreat to the mind is fear inspired. He fears the realization of his physical impotence next to the Black male. Since impotence is the negation of his white male body's power, an exposure of its fragility, he attempts to dominate the Black male in an effort to satisfy his need for "evidence of his virility." The Black male, the Supermasculine Menial, con-stitutes a very real threat, since it is his goal to overthrow the social system created by white men's sexual anxieties. The Black male is thought to be "a lesser breed than himself and his kind,"[74] so the very thought of being unsettled by such a creature is met with displays of unfathomable violence and cruelty to convey to Black men the impossibility of such a feat. Remember, for Cleaver the social order is sustained by the power to enforce the sexual anxiety of whites against Blacks, and given that "the police are the armed guardians of the social order," Blacks cannot be surprised by the level of violence waged

against their racial group generally and enforced against Black men specifically. The phobias generated by white anxiety are "weapon[s] in the struggle
between the Omnipotent Administrator and the Supermasculine Menial for
control of sexual sovereignty."[75] These fears whites have of Black men ignite
compliance from the white public and their consent for the death of the Black
male beast-rapist-criminal. It is this terror the Black male represents to the
white man that Cleaver, like Fanon, believes exhibits the white man's homoerotic obsession with Black male flesh:

> The Omnipotent Administrator cannot help but covertly, and perhaps
> in an extremely sublimated guise, envy the bodies and strength of the
> most alienated men beneath him—those furthest from the apex of
> administration—because the men most alienated from the mind,
> least diluted by the admixture of the mind, will be perceived as the
> most masculine manifestations of the Body: the Supermasculine Me-
> nials. (This is precisely the root, the fountainhead, of the homosexual-
> ity that is perennially associated with the Omnipotent Administrator.)[76]

Fear must be contained, managed. It is fear that demands the prison, since
the prison is constructed to cage the white man's Nigger. The prison is designed with his sexual obsession, the white man's homoeroticism, in mind. It
is a physical manifestation of the racist architecture the white race uses to
construct and punish the Black male for its desire of him. As a structure, it is
imagined to be a place for Black male bodies that expends their labor and or-
ganizes their brute sexuality for whites' viewing pleasure. Like slavery and
segregation, the prison is based on what Cleaver calls the "all-pervasive myth
which at one time classified the [B]lack man as a subhuman beast of burden."[77]

In "Caged and Celibate," Mumia Abu-Jamal says that the prison shackles
the sexuality of the inmate. Because the prison denies the convict sociality
and family, "imprisonment, with all it entails, is as much, if not more, an act
of state violence than the silent violence of poverty."[78] Imprisonment divests
convicts of their social self. It condemns all that makes the Black male believe
he could be a human being and aims to make him accept, at a psychological
level, that he belongs in the prison because he is a dangerous rapist and killer.
It makes the Black male believe that his sexual desire can be exercised safely
only within the walls of the prison, under the watchful eye of the white man,
who protects all others from the Black male's savagery. Abu-Jamal says, "It
should be no surprise that the prison is a hotbed of homosexuality, which, in
turn, is intricately linked to a system of dominance among men. Although all
prisons have rules which prohibit homosexual contact, it continues unabated,
fanned by bans against conjugal visitation and implicit administrative acceptance."[79] Sexuality as an expression of the convict's social existence (his possibility for love, connection with other men or women, an indication he is

desired as a man) is denied. Homosexual sex is encouraged under the pur-view of the prison. In a prison, the playpen of white hedonism, the Black convict is transfigured as a physical object used within the various matrices of power directed by white desire. He is labor—physical and sexual. He exists for the enjoyment and legitimation of the white ideas created to explain his existence. He is prisoner because he is criminal. He is anally penetrated be-cause he is lascivious. This, of course, is not to suggest that homosexuality is an aberration birthed by the prison; rather, it is an attempt to show that racial domination has involved, and continues to involve, the power of man over man, where the homoerotic is an inextricable aspect of racial psychology, power, and white men's desire to determine the Black male body's uses.

Cleaver maintains that the prison is able to sustain itself because it con-trols and regulates the sexuality of Black men. The white man creates the prison for his own viewing pleasure; it is an arena of sexual experimentation, hedonism, and power. The question is: to what extent does the Black male internalize the white male's racial schema? In a chapter from *The Book of Lives* entitled "Bitches," Cleaver argues that fucking is the central motivating force of societal repression and the unfounded obstacle in revolution:

> To reorganize society you have to reorganize fucking. If you reorga-nize society and don't reorganize fucking, it will lead to counter-revo-lution. The new style of fucking arises out of the struggle itself. Fucking itself is revolutionized, as much as eating and work. Every revolution has to take a position on fucking. In the past, every revolution has left fucking undealt with. They don't disturb it because the new regime is erected upon the sexual habits of those who support it. Slavery could not have lasted if there had not been niggers willing to fuck for the master on the stud farm. In fact, somewhere in every nigger's mind, those who were out there in the cotton fields, the men, there was the heavy dream of waking up one morning on a stud farm.[80]

American racism thrives because it is able to make Black men intuitively ac-cept their disposability. Black men are programed to desire "stud-hood." Dis-owned by society and inculcated with his position as laborer, the Black male learns to accept and valorize the body as his only mode of existence. He comes to crave recognition of his flesh; he demands attention to his triumph as a "fucking machine" and expects to be rewarded for successfully embody-ing the white man's Black flesh. This is the "sensitizing action" Fanon traces to the petrification of the Black male. The Black man without external self-validation, dependent on only the values of the white society, "stops behaving as an actional person."[81] Contrary to the paradigm of the active Buck offered by Wallace, Cleaver suggests that the stud is passive. Stated differently, where-as the Buck fucks for himself, the stud fucks for the master—he is sexualized for the benefit of a more powerful other—the white man. This inaction, the inability of the Black male to exist outside the definitions/desires of whites, makes him existentially dependent on the white other for his self-esteem. As Fanon argues, the Black man's goal in this condition is the white man, since it is only the white man who "can give him worth."[82] Despite the depravity of defining oneself based on the sexual fetishes of white men, the Black male is offered only this definition of himself.

This sexual objectification of Black maleness, and its production/engineering as *that which only fucks*, occupies a denounced aspect of Black manhood. It is assumed that the Black man simply desires the power to *fuck*, since *fucking* is the necessary condition for him *to be*. But this ontological requirement manifests as the sexual paranoia marking the societal vulnerability that, Cleaver argues, is caused in the Black male's relation to whites. In short, the sexualization of the Black male body by whites is not simply oppression but speciation, where the Black male shares no relation to the established categories of (white) gender, except as their possession. Anthony Lemelle Jr.'s reading of Cleaver's *Soul on Ice* results in a similar point. Lemelle argues, "Under the gaze of the 'real' (white) gendered male, [B]lack men are (en)gendered as (b)lacking the possession, executing historically through the processes of colonization, enslavement, and internal colonization the representation of the [B]lack male body as an object to be possessed. In the gaze of the white wo/man's eye, [B]lack men find the position of the running, dancing, jiving, and sexing buck who is 'good for nothing' but good sex."[83]

The Black male is not given the power of male domination in this white-supremacist society. Because his sexuality is determined to be a negation of (white) humanity, his sexuality is defined, thought to be exercised, only as an extension of his intent for ill and harm. Even rape is predetermined, because whether a Black man commits rape or not, he will always be seen, even in consensual sexual relations, to be a rapist. His mere presence intends rape, and the prison is built to house this inevitable act. The Black male is therefore vulnerable to racism and the rationalizations of a white-supremacist society that make him into a lustful raping beast because he has sexual desires. All sexual acts by Black men must be controlled, which means that the Black male, his dick, must be repressed. Under the guise of repressing his savage nature, white men and women are able to "fuck" the Black male into submission. He is now able to be raped, used for the sexual pleasure of the order, because his nature demands punishment for its sexual inclinations. As such, the Black male is never seen as the victim of sexual violence; he is seen only as its perpetrator. In reality, it is "fucking" that is left out of our scholarly accounts of American racism. It is unmentioned because despite all of our poststructuralist tools of interpretation and deconstruction, the mind of the Black intelligentsia cannot bear the weight of white society's deepest violation of its Puritanical virtue—its fetish with Black male flesh. Our contemporary accounts of racism dispel the homoerotic allure white men have for Black male flesh and the hedonistic eroticism the white woman holds for the Black phallus.

Soul on Ice and Cleaver's Diagnosis of [w]hite Womanhood

Few people know the story of Cleaver's *Soul on Ice*. The book was originally written as a prison manuscript inspired by Caryl Chessman's *The Kid Was a Killer*.[84] Cleaver wanted to write a book that would bring attention to his case and lawyers to his cause. The original title of the book was "[w]hite Woman, Black Man," and it was this provocation that kept his manuscript, allegedly full of a "racist history," from leaving the prison.[85] Cleaver concerns himself with the sociological vulnerability of Black men to the ontological femininity ascribed to white womanhood that inspires violence against the Black male. Under our present intersectional logics, white women are charged with racism primarily based on the historical exclusion of Black women from their women's rights efforts and their blindness to racism as a political agenda more generally. These narratives are largely elementary accounts of the active roles white women played in the establishment and maintenance of white supremacy and the use of violence against Black men. Cleaver is not blind to the racial abuses white women deliberately committed against Black men under protection of their alleged vulnerability to the Black male rapist. The white woman, or the Ultrafeminine, dominates through projection. Since the white woman embodies womanhood as "an image of frailty, weakness, helplessness, delicacy, daintiness,"[86] she is the idea white society is willing to protect physically at all costs. Insofar as other bodies are outside of this white female construct, they are subject to violence. The white woman is thereby defined as asexual, accessible only to the white male, but this is not her own sexual intentionality. The white woman resists the imposition of "virtue," not directly challenging the sexual mores of the white male who imposes asexuality on her, but exercising her sexual power over the Black male. Cleaver describes her white lust this way: "At the nth degree of the Ultrafeminine's scale of psychic lust stands the walking phallus symbol of the Supermasculine Menial. Though she may never have had a sexual encounter with a Supermasculine Menial; she is fully convinced that he can fulfill her physical need."[87] Cleaver's account has some historical warrant.

Historically, white women's sexual and political aspirations have been tied to an intricate, but ignored, exercise of racial and sexual violence against Black men. During slavery, white women used rape to dominate Black male slaves. These white women would coerce Black men into prolonged sexual relationships, routinely raping them for their own sexual pleasure. Enslaved mulatto men were of particular interest to white women. As Thomas Foster writes, "The sexual abuse of 'nearly white' men could enable white women to enact radical fantasies of domination over white men with the knowledge that their victim's body was legally [B]lack and enslaved, subject to the women's control."[88] If their sexual exploits were ever discovered, they would simply appeal to the racist calculus holding Black men to be rapists and white women to be too pure and white ever to sexually desire a Black male. While our present understanding of white womanhood sees white women as always sexually vulnerable to (predatory) Black men, within American slavery "white women of the planter class were certainly able to wield power over [B]lack men, although all white women could coerce enslaved [B]lack men given the legal and social setting in which they lived. Planter-class women might more easily and more believably have persuaded the community to view them as innocent victims of their sexual contact with [B]lack men."[89]

During Reconstruction, white women not only were presumed innocent in any possible contact they had with Black men; they were defined as such, regardless of their class position in society. Even when whites knew that the sex between a Black man and white woman was consensual—or, as in the case of Edward Coy, "rested upon a yearlong liaison with a white woman"[90]—the Black man had to be lynched for the protection of white womanhood nonetheless. Martha Hodes explains the rationale for this practice:

> To white Southerners who wished to preserve racial hierarchy in the absence of slavery, it was crucial that both elite and nonelite white women minded the boundaries of the color line and gave birth only to white children. Without slavery to differentiate [B]lacks from poor whites, it was equally important that the ideas about the purity of white women included poor white women. For to characterize all white women as pure had an important effect: it made sex between a [B]lack man and a white woman by definition rape, because a "pure" white woman, no matter how poor, could not possibly (in white minds) desire sex with a [B]lack man.[91]

Ironically, it was white women's activism around antirape activism and their championing of lynching (the Black male rapist) that propelled them to the center of twentieth-century American political life. Crystal N. Feimster observed that

> white women's participation as actors and audience at lynchings had opened up a wider space for them in public and commercial life. If they could lynch they could do anything. They had faced their worst fears. They had survived the Civil War and the violent politics of Reconstruction and Populism—coming out on the other side strong and confident in their ability to engage the racial and sexual politics of the New South. From demanding legal protection to participating in mob

violence, the new southern woman exercised all the privileges of white supremacy to demand women's rights.[92]

Within the mythology of white female vulnerability to the Black rapist, white women were able not only to exercise their sexual power over Black men through illicit sexual relations and rape but also to use Black men's sexual vulnerability as political capital with white men against Blacks more generally. As Kathleen Blee observes, the growth of white women's participation in lynching and their connection of such public and political demonstrations to women's rights also coincides with the national founding of Women Ku Klux Klan (WKKK) organizations in the 1920s.[93] Contrary to the distant and extricated position from which white womanhood is usually theorized, excluded from the formulation of racism and sexual violence, an attentive historical theorization illuminates the deliberate and calculated efforts of white women to make their experience and presence the rallying point of white-supremacist violence against Black people through the nineteenth and early twentieth centuries. So history suggests that instead of simply competing within an American political field for rights, Black men were, in fact, excluded from the political field of American politics by the violence specific to their sexual representations as Black and male, a position that permitted lynching, rape, and execution to prevent their rise in the public.

By the 1950s, white womanhood's innocence and sacredness had been codified in law. Two cases in particular accentuate the force white womanhood exerted on the lives of Black males, a paradoxical racist formulation allowing Black men to be raped without acknowledgment and persecuted as rapists even when knowingly innocent. The first is the now forgotten case of Willie McGee. On May 8, 1951, Willie McGee was electrocuted in Laurel, Mississippi, on a much disputed charge that he raped a white housewife named Williametta Hawkins. As Danielle McGuire argues, "McGee entered into a long sexual relationship with his white employer, Mrs. Williametta Hawkins, after she threatened to cry rape if he refused her flirtatious advances." Hawkins first propositioned McGee in 1942. It is important to remember that McGee was a Black male laborer in the Deep South in the 1940s. Jobs for Black men were few and far between, "so he was committed to taking odd jobs around her house" for his livelihood. McGee recalled, "I was waxing the floors and she showed a willingness to get familiar." But Hawkins used work to mask her demands for illicit relations. McGee recounted, "She frequently sent for me to do work which gave opportunities for intercourse."[94] McGee's wife learned of her husband's victimization firsthand, when Hawkins confronted both of them as they walked home from a movie theater, saying to Willie, "I got my car over here. Come on into my car with me."[95] McGee told Hawkins to go away—"I am with my wife"—to which Hawkins replied, "Don't fool with any Negro whores." McGee ultimately complied with Hawkins's demands, fearful of the violence Hawkins could bring to him and his family. His wife reportedly said to a friend, "People who don't know the South don't know what would happen if Willie told her no."[96] This illicit relationship shows that even when a Black man is coerced into sex with a white woman, he is incapable of being recognized as a victim of rape and sexual violence. This is just one of the many sexual vulnerabilities Black men endured at the hands of white women during Jim Crow.

The second case that problematizes the sexuality of a Black man in relation to a white woman was that of Mr. McQuirter. On February 17, 1953, a Black man was convicted of assault with intent to rape because he was on the same street as a white woman. According to *McQuirter v. State*, a Black man was found guilty of an "attempt to commit an assault with intent to rape." On the night of June 29, 1951, Mrs. Ted Allen testified, a Negro had said something unintelligible as she passed his truck parked in front of the Tiny Diner in Atmore, Alabama. Allen testified that this Negro male followed her down the street, eventually coming within two to three feet of her. A white officer, Clarence Bryars, stated that after his arrest, the Negro said that "he came to Atmore with the intention of getting him a white woman that night." McQuirter held a completely different story from Allen's. He denied following Allen or making "any gesture toward molesting her or the children" or "making any statements to the officers." Even though he had never been arrested and produced two witnesses who testified to his "good reputation for peace and quiet and for truth and veracity," he was convicted. What is important in *McQuirter* is not simply the racism of the conviction, given that the white woman was not harmed, but the intent assigned to McQuirter as a Black male who was simply on the same street as a white woman. The judge instructed the jury to consider the race of the accused next to that of the white woman: "In determining the question of intention the jury may consider social conditions and customs founded upon racial differences, such as that the prosecutrix was a white woman and defendant was a Negro man."[97]

In "The Unintentional Rapist," I. Bennett Caper argues that the law has always defined the Black male as a rapist and defended the presumption that in his contact with the white woman it is his intent to rape. In *McQuirter*, this assumption demonstrates that Black men are forever sexually vulnerable to any engagement with white womanhood. As Caper notes:

That McQuirter's walking alone on the same street as Mrs. Ted Allen, a white woman, was an encroachment upon her space, is also taken as a given. Even McQuirter, in his testimony, understood that the proper thing to do once he saw Mrs. Ted Allen was to turn around and wait until . . . they had gone. Space is racialized, and so is sex. By sex, I am not referring to gender here. I am referring to actual sex. It is not only the possibility of non-consensual sex that is being policed; what is also rendered illicit is even the possibility of interracial consensual sex. What is at risk is not just sexual intercourse, but its natural precursor, social intercourse.[98]

Under Jim Crow, a Black man is expected to know the social parameters overlaying white society's understanding of sexuality and to know that he is perceived as a threat to white female sexuality. Jim Crow was a sexual order that criminalized and lynched Black men for looking at white women for longer than thirty seconds. This crime, known as eye(ball) raping, cost Black males their lives and ensured they would cast their eyes and selves downward when in the presence of a white woman.[99] McQuirter is a demonstration of this draconian idea in practice. This case articulates the expectation that Black men would castrate themselves, remove themselves from sight, so that they might not offend or inspire the sexual anxiety and fear of white society. For the safety of white women and the calm of white men, the Black male had to shrink—refuse to be seen—to maintain social order.

What social life can Black men have under a regime dedicated to the protection of white womanhood? A Black man is a rapist even when he is not, so to speak. Consequently, Black masculinity is defined by the whim of white sexual anxiety. The rape of Willie McGee was not simply the white woman's external construction as pure and innocent of desire for Black men, but Hawkins's internalization of such a privilege—to want and take of Black men sexually without consequence. Instead of simply being passive witnesses to the unfolding of white supremacy, white women developed sexual agency within the allegedly repressive parameters of Victorian asexuality through their domination of Black males. By aligning their aspirations for political power alongside white patriarchy's need to stamp out Black manhood, white women were able to be recognized publicly as enforcers of the racial order in an effort to control the barbaric lasciviousness of Black men while using Black male bodies for their sexual pleasure under the protection of white-supremacist dogmas maintaining that no white woman could ever sexually desire a Black male. As such, the myth of the Black rapist was not only a racist fiction telling of a rampant Nigger-beast craving the flesh of white women but also a deliberately accepted mythology perpetuated by white women to conceal their violence and rape of Black men. With the level of sexual racism and misandry directed at Black men specifically, it should seem unbelievable that Black men did not think about or reflect on the level of sexual violence directed toward their flesh.

Contrary to popular interpretations and disciplinary mythologies concerning the writings of Black male intellectuals during the early twentieth century, Black men were extremely interested in and attentive to the sexualized violence of American racism and colonialism. Because the notion of gender offered to intellectuals dealing with racism and American slavery is presented almost exclusively through Black feminist historiography, there is little discussion of Black male contributions and reflections on rape, lynching, and sexual coercion before the 1970s. Black male scholars were trying to understand how the economic conditions of colonialism and the political institutions of American racism such as Jim Crow segregation made the Black body a sexual object for white fantasy. For example, in *[w]hite Man, Listen!* Richard Wright argues that "living in a waking dream, generations of emotionally impoverished colonial European whites wallowed in the quick gratification of greed, reveled in the cheap superiority of racial domination, slacked their sensual thirst in illicit sexuality, [ultimately] draining off the dammed-up libido that European(s) had condemned."[100] Remember, Frantz Fanon argues that for Blacks in the colonial situation, "everything takes place on a genital level."[101] Mere contact with the Black male "is enough to evoke anxiety. . . . For the sexual potency of the Negro is hallucinating." Fanon observes that "contact is at the same time the basic schematic type of initiating sexual action (touching, caresses—sexuality)."[102] The Black man is made into a sexual catalyst of a phobia evoking eros. His mere presence ignites the sexual paranoia of the white mind—phobic cravings and the anxiety caused by the fearful relation to the Black male—and drives the white to imagine its sexually terrifying fantasies as actual. This is why Calvin Hernton describes the white woman as a taboo and terror in the mind of Black boys growing up in the South. Hernton argues, "The taboo of the white woman eats into the psyche, erodes away a significant portion of boyhood sexual development, alters the total concept of masculinity, and creates in the [B]lack male a hidden ambivalence towards all women, [B]lack as well as white."[103]

For a Black male, his self-imposed distance from the threats imagined by whites—the extent to which he has internalized the anxiety of the white mind and adjusted his behavior accordingly—makes him respectable. He makes himself silent, the bearer of others' phobias, so that in conceding the legitimacy of others' perception of him, he behaves as an entity that can disown their impositions. This is why Hernton ultimately concludes that Black men must be asexual (perform racial castration) to survive their encounters with white women. "Because he must act like a eunuch when it comes to white women, there arises within the [B]lack man an undefined sense of dread and self-mutilation. Psychologically he experiences himself as castrated."[104] This is why Cleaver begins *Soul on Ice* with an attempt to break his obsession with the symbolic representation of the white woman—the Ogre. Because the Black man is sociogenically constructed to be psychically dependent on the form of white womanhood to be a man, he is lured into the cycles of failure brought about by his structural inability to ever have the white woman and the effects his obsession has on his love of the Black woman. Heteronormativity within this order depends on the aspiration of man to desire woman; since the Black man is not man, he is told that manhood is had through white womanhood.

This is why Cleaver decides to develop an "antagonistic, ruthless attitude toward white women." Cleaver begins to define the white woman through her historical substance rather than his idealizations in a short ode entitled "To a [w]hite Girl." In this brief poetic expression, Cleaver renames the white girl the "white witch, the symbol of rope and hanging tree, of the burning cross."[105] His hate for his oppressor—the white woman—is articulated in his rage against not only her flesh but also the definition of her as pure and innocent that he is forced at gunpoint (the police, the lynch mob, the prison, the white society) to accept of her.

The Black Male Is Not a Latent Rapist: A Concluding Sentiment against the Disciplinary Support of Black Macho Ideology

Cleaver's *The Book of Lives* provides a glimpse into the mind of a Black male: poor, uneducated, and oppressed by white men and women in a world with no gauge of morality or sentiment for Black male life. Throughout both texts—*The Book of Lives* and *Soul on Ice*—Cleaver asks readers to situate themselves in a world where Black men are lynched and castrated on the mere accusation of having offended a white woman. Any glance or acknowledgment of a white woman by a Black male, be he a man or a boy, in social spaces was taken to be the demonstration of his desire to rape her. The best-known narrative to this effect is the lynching and murder of Emmett Till in 1955. Cleaver challenges contemporary academics to imagine a world of no political options that recognize the plight of Blacks. What is to be done in the abyss of nonrecognition and death? Do we simply impose a morality on Cleaver and condemn him for not being a "better person" living in Jim Crow? This reaction, although supported throughout the academy, is simply reactionary. It offers very little engagement with what Cleaver is diagnosing as the pathologies of Black sexuality under white supremacy.

Many critics and scholars who condemn Eldridge Cleaver as a rapist simply ignore what it is that Cleaver is reacting against in *Soul on Ice*. Cleaver abruptly announces to the reader, "I became a rapist," but he does so only after his ode "To a [w]hite Girl." Cleaver's hate for the white woman consumed him, ultimately transforming him into the mythological beast of white legend. "To refine my technique and modus operandi, I started out by practicing on [B]lack girls in the ghetto—in the [B]lack ghetto where dark and vicious deeds appear not as aberrations or deviations from the norm, but as part of the sufficiency of the Evil of the day—and when I considered myself smooth enough, I crossed the tracks and sought out white prey," says Cleaver.[106] The now infamous passage concerning Cleaver's view of rape is a consequence of his acceptance of this dehumanizing myth:

> Rape was an insurrectionary act. It delighted me that I was defying
> and trampling upon the white man's law, upon his system of values,
> and I was defiling his women—and this point I believe, was the most
> satisfying to me because I was very resentful over the historical fact
> of how the white man has used the [B]lack woman. I felt I was getting
> revenge.[107]

As mentioned earlier, many feminist critics, such as Susan Brownmiller and
Michele Wallace, would come to accept that rape was simply the personality
of Black male intellectuals during the 1960s and 1970s. This narrative is constructed by connecting Cleaver to the provocation in *Black Dada Nihilismus*,
by Amiri Baraka (formerly known as LeRoi Jones): "Rape the white girls.
Rape their fathers. Cut their mothers' throats." Almost unilaterally, these critics have decided that Black men desire rape as a means of political expression
and power. Black men are not social and historical beings under this account,
which is to say that Black men are not reflective or reacting against what they
see as the historical denial of their rape at the hands of white men and wom-
en. They are simply brutes fixated on the "fucking" of the white woman. These
early feminist authors assert that Black men crave white women as their political end, despite its time-tested result—namely, death. Cleaver, however,
notes, "There are, of course, many young [B]lacks out there right now who
are slitting white throats and raping the white girl. They are not doing this
because they read LeRoi Jones' poetry, as some of his critics believe. Rather,
LeRoi Jones is expressing the funky facts of life."[108] Cleaver offers the reader a
realism that has yet to be surpassed. By the end of the section, he clarifies that
he does not endorse rape; instead, he tries to explain how the system creates
and punishes the Black male rapist.

Though brutal, Cleaver believes within the facts of anti-Black life that there
is the possibility of salvation. He urges the Black male to resist being consumed
by his hatred of the white woman and move toward an understanding of the
system and the underlying sexual ideology that defines the Black male as little
more than the inevitable rapist. When Cleaver returns to prison, he recognizes that his course of action, his alleged insurrectionism, was wrong. Becoming a rapist led him astray "not so much from the white man's law as from
being human, civilized." It was his realization of his own humanity that made
him say, "I could not approve the act of rape."[109] During his time in Folsom
Prison, Cleaver recognized "the price of hating other human beings is loving
oneself less."[110] He understood at a visceral level that when he argued for the
use of rape against white women, he was "in a frantic, wild, and completely
abandoned frame of mind."[111] Instead of simply being the sexualized construct
of the white imagination, Cleaver attempted to create an analytic of the sexualized dynamics that drove the Black male to become a raging body trapped by
the prison and exploited by society. The last chapter of *The Book of Lives* con-

cludes with an analysis of the social stratifications caused by fucking: "Fucking can make you rich and it can make you poor, It can also keep you rich and keep you poor, It can kill you directly, or cause you to get killed. It can give you new life and it can save your life. It can block you or assist you. It's a thing well hidden by society from sight, but it is in fact the starting point. Everything starts with fucking."[112]

After Cleaver regains his sense of humanity, he realizes that all social stratifications are rooted in the white race's attempt to distance itself from the threat of Black male sexuality. *Soul on Ice* is an attempt to analyze the sexual dynamics behind the targeting of Black men in American society. Cleaver is forced to witness the deaths of Black men in a world organized toward that very goal. Black men were executed for offending any sentiment of white society. Cleaver's reaction to the murder of Emmett Till offers some insight into his thinking about Black men's vulnerability to sexual violence under Jim Crow, but it is rare that white women are ever discussed as culpable for the murder of Black men. Usually, such conversations tend to absolve white women as justified in their fears, and by consequence, their racist actions are negated by what they perceive to be the imminent threat of rape. Whereas Cleaver holds firm to the idea that "Emmett Till . . . was murdered, for allegedly flirting with a white woman" and predestined for death because of the desire put into him by a white society that elevated the white woman to a status of perfection and beauty,[113] contemporary accounts of this event tend toward a moderate view of Brownmiller's original thinking on the matter, holding Till accountable for his alleged "intent."

Brownmiller interprets Till's "wolf-whistle" as more than an innocent dare among children; instead, she asserts that Emmett "Bobo" Till's whistle "was a deliberate insult just short of physical assault, a last reminder to Carolyn Bryant that this [B]lack boy, Till, had in mind to possess her." In the mind of this white woman, Susan Brownmiller, the whistle had made Till the moral equivalent of his murderer, J. W. Milam. Because a Black boy could even imagine and brag to his friends that he "had" a white woman up North, whites in the South demanded his death. As Milam recalled the night he murdered Till, "'He showed me the white gal's picture! Bragged o' what he'd done to her! What else could I do? No use letting him get no bigger!'"[114] While Angela Davis responded to Brownmiller's interpretation of the events, saying that "many of her arguments are unfortunately pervaded with racist ideas,"[115] which make her discussion of rape and race a pretentious apologetic for white women's interests and fears,[116] there is an implausibility to the conceptualization of a fourteen-year-old boy being able to rape a white woman in broad daylight in the Jim Crow South. In our effort to care for the threat to white womanhood, which continues to conceal itself in our contemporary anxieties over (interracial) rape, the Black male is imagined to be a superhuman beast capable of overriding the social and structural constraints that prevent his interaction with and access to white women in the South. For decades, scholars have continued to assert that Till's wanting of this white woman was, in fact, an actual threat. Historians such as Stephen J. Whitfield have defended the sympathy Brownmiller shares for Till while nonetheless offering ambiguity and credence to the alleged fear the white woman Carolyn Bryant, Till's alleged victim, suffered. Whitfield offers various narratives in which Till did not simply whistle at Bryant but grabbed her waist and asked her out on a date.[117]

As Simeon Wright, Till's cousin, recounts, "Bobo didn't ask her out for a date or call her baby."[118] He simply whistled at her. In both cases, however, there is the reality that sexual racism requires the death of Black males to protect white womanhood. The offense is the mere thought that as a Black male he could exist as able to speak to, much less touch, a white woman. After sixty-two years, Carolyn Bryant (Donham) now admits that she lied about her encounter with Emmett Till. In 1955, on the witness stand of the Tallahatchie County Courthouse, Bryant told the court that Till had forcefully grabbed her hand, asked her for a date, chased her, blocked her escape, clutched her waist, and told her of his previous sexual encounters with white women.[119] Bryant led the court to believe that she had barely escaped his hold. Her testimony was so convincing that one Mississippi newspaper insisted that "the case should never have been called the wolf whistle case, but an attempted rape case."[120] In her memoir, Bryant confesses that Till never grabbed her or uttered any sexual obscenity. She admits that she lied to the court, deliberately tailoring her testimony about Till to match the imagery of the Black rapist beast.[121]

Jim Crow shackled Black males to passivity in order to survive. The KKK and night riders were a daily part of Black life in Mississippi during the 1950s, so the idea that a Black boy (a child) could harm an (adult) white woman amid this repression is nonsense. One cannot ascertain Till's intention or what his whistle meant. Such a gesture is allowed to occupy the feminist imagination only because it is a racialized account of an allegedly more debased and savage masculinity placed in contrast to white womanhood, which is represented as ontologically pure and innocent. It simply is not the case that white women were innocent or ignorant of this societal arrangement called Jim Crow; they knew such a gesture would lead to Till's death. So the question, given the asymmetry between the Black boy and the white woman protected by the extralegal violence of Jim Crow, is: What was her intent and her desire to bring about the death of a Black boy who whistled? Even as a twelve-year-old child, Simeon Wright knew that segregation was enforced by violence:

> There were all sorts of other ways of keeping us in our place—impoverished, without power, and under their thumb. Basically, we were not free, could not choose our own destiny, and might as well have been

living in South Africa under the apartheid regime rather than America. . . . The violent system of Jim Crow laws was backed by the intimidation of the Ku Klux Klan, the White Citizens Council, and other vicious segregationist groups. Any [B]lack person brave enough to violate this system was immediately confronted by angry white men with murder on their minds.[122]

The white woman—or, rather, white womanhood—is the lynchpin of white supremacy. It is the representation of the order aimed to be sustained by the power and organization of society. Cleaver understood that Black manhood was engineered to be subservient to this will; consequently, the body of the Black male was both disposable to this social order and in violation of it.

While we as scholars, thinkers, or students can disagree with and rightfully condemn the reactionary rationalization of Cleaver's tending toward rape, we cannot, as either students of history or theorists, overlook his analysis of the society that raped Black men and then murdered them as rapists. To this day, Cleaver has been the only thinker brave enough to take on the taboo subject of white women's role in the racial and sexual violation of Black men. Rather than some crazed rapist, Cleaver shows himself to be a vulnerable man enraged by the denial of his desire for Little Jesus but aware of the white womanhood that made him and Richard convicts. Cleaver was among the first thinkers to explain how the homo-hetero-sexual binary cannot capture the dynamic erotics that fuel white desire for the death of Black men and boys. The history and practice of Black male sexual exploitation has shown itself to exceed the delineations marked by sex with men (homo) and sex with women (hetero) sexual identities of our times. The abuse of Black men shows that their suffering occurs within the manipulation of multiple aspects of sexuality. The Black male was raped by both white men and women; he is dehumanized by a violence that is inenarrable under our present categories used to describe sexual violence. The context of Cleaver's rage, and his resistance to our present order as part of the ideological rationalizations mandating his dismissal as theorist, must be analyzed alongside this limitation of our times. If the university remains dedicated to condemning him as a rapist, then it must also condemn the world of rape that gave rise to his reactionary insurrectionism. The sexual violence and rape of Black males is still an operating, but largely ignored, dynamic of American racism exercised against Black men and boys. The next chapter analyzes how the maleness of Black men and boys disadvantages them throughout American society and why the sexualization of Black males is obfuscated in our academic accounts of Black male oppression.

The Political Economy of Niggerdom

*Racist Misandry, Class Warfare, and the Disciplinary
Propagation of the Super-predator Mythology*

The case against Lil B [Michael Lewis] was really about, about accommodating a powerful racist political socioeconomic agenda that at once invented and condemned [B]lack boys as superpredators.[1]

THE SENSIBILITIES of the Black American intellectual concerning race have historically been cemented to their ascendency within empire. How one writes about race, offering hope for change in opposition to the totality of racism, and communicates an aspiration for the possibilities made available by American ideals such as freedom, justice, and equality has been the demarcation between what is called radical and what is called progressive. In "The Failure of the Negro Intellectual" (1973), E. Franklin Frazier describes Black intellectualization as the de-Niggerization of Black scholarship, a retreat from using Black experience as the foundation of theorizing the Blackness, or an "emptying of his [her] life of meaningful content and ridding him of all Negro identification."[2] The study of Black folk under the integrationist milieu shows the danger that Black intellectuals, this Black bourgeoisie, pose to our conceptualizations of, our thinking about, Blackness, which was described in Carter G. Woodson's *The Mis-education of the Negro* (1933). In trying to distort the content of Blackness to fit within the confines of disciplinary study, the study of Black folk by the academic class reflects the desire of Black intellectuals to be the beneficiaries of the anthropological history, and consequently the post-racial possibilities articulated through white humanity while desperately seeking to separate themselves, as a class, from the pathological representation(s) associated with the Nigger—that decadent racial connotation inhibiting the recognition of their spiritual transcendence to a more bourgeois class. Assimilating canonical knowledge(s), then, acts as the means by which life is grasped—revelation—pulling the Black intellectual away from the wretchedness sown into the flesh of Black people and the death of Niggers. It is here that he (the Black male, the Nigger) is avoided. As Frazier notes, "One is reminded of the words of Langston Hughes in *Ask Your Mama*, where he says that the African visitor finds that in the American social supermarket [B]lacks for sale range from intellectuals to entertainers. Thus, it appears that the price of the slow integration which the Negroes are experiencing must he bought at the price of abject conformity in thinking."[3]

The effect of racism is much more complicated than the blanket history of exclusion usually offered as the master narrative of slow, arduous progress in the academy. It is undeniably true that Black scholarship was denied entrance into the American university, while the scholarship and thought allowed in the academy was moderate and rewarded for taking integrationist stances far removed from the political and philosophical tone of the Black (Inter)Nationalist and anticolonial traditions thought to originate primarily in the masculinist rage of the Black male.[4] This historical problem by which the Black thinker is allowed to become an institutionally supported *Black intellectual* is not unlike the disciplinary constraints and erasures that are currently limiting the theoretical works surveyed and subjects taken up in current works on American racism dealing with Black men and boys. The Black male, his realities as both the Black man and the Black boy, is antithetical to the upward trajectory of the Black academic class. His existence is a stark reminder of the reality of racism and remains a contradiction to the mythology of racial progress held so dear by many a Black academic. Because Black maleness is pessimism—literally the foundation of the dissatisfaction and hopelessness in the order of anti-Blackness sustained by society and thought—the study of his actual being is shunned, erased for the convenience of maintaining a political narrative of racial advancement and equality able to be explained by less material and more intersectional/poststructural theoretical accounts. The theory and conceptualizations of the world originating from the life of the Black male are altogether ignored, and his death, which exposes the machinations of anti-Black racism peacefully coexisting among the symbols used to rationalize the story of racism's slow demise in America, are de-emphasized for the recognition of more ideal intersectional subjects.

The Black male is the victim of disciplinary circumstance. Our current orders of knowledge intuitively assert that masculinity remains invulnerable to the gendered violence(s) that appear(s) on first glance to be parasitic to the female body. This ontological assertion holding that sociological phenomena should be recognized as gendered only when women experience them has led to an ahistorical assertion—namely, that certain violence(s) continue to make women vulnerable, but since they are female violence(s), they are not experienced by males. The suffering of the Black male, however, stands in sharp contrast to this analytic calculus often deployed by academics. Because there is no attempt to reconcile his alleged theoretical privilege as a male with his material disadvantage as Black and male in this society, Black maleness is largely determined by the ahistorical synonymousness to white maleness more generally. There is no ontological-semiotic attempt to categorize the Black male's historical and sociological vulnerabilities within the "male" category. He is simply overdetermined and imperceptible within the multiple male configurations that name him. Under disciplinary arrangements of gender and sexuality, the unemployment and underemployment of the Black male; his lack of high school education and college matriculation; his disproportionate physical and sexual abuse at the hands of Black men and women, foster parents, and the police; and his disproportionate death and incarceration are obscured. Our understanding of gender makes the disparities under which racial males suffer ultimately irrelevant to the theories that account for Black maleness itself.

Rather than simply fight for the inclusion of Black males as "gendered" and, by consequence, affected by "gendered" violence, this chapter situates the vulnerability of Black males theoretically by analyzing the disciplinary obstructions to his study. How does one think of racist misandry—the particular hate of the Black male? What explains the erasure of Black male vulnerability within disciplines and the theories that emerge from them in the face of the proliferating facts of Black male demise? How enduring does sociological or historical disadvantage have to be, how severe, before it becomes encased within—referred to by—his peculiar location as Black and male? The conceptual exploration of Black male vulnerability—of his dehumanization economically, politically, and sexually—must confront *his* material reality, and that confrontation should bridge the gap between theory and facts.

The Violence of Poverty: Black Males and the Stigma of Criminality

It is no secret that the modernization of America's economy during the 1970s and 1980s had dire consequences for Black men.[5] The post–Civil Rights economic prospects for Black men, who traditionally had been blue-collar workers and laborers, were marked by poverty and growing unemployment in the second half of the twentieth century. As the economist Amadu Jacky Kaba observes, unlike their female counterparts, who have seen tremendous economic, political, and educational gains over the past several decades, Black men have not seen great strides in their mobility from poverty or comparable gains in education. In many ways, their position indicates only further social and political marginalization.[6] In the late 1970s, James B. Stewart and Joseph W. Scott observed that, because they are racialized men, Black males suffer from deliberate and institutional programs designed to remove them from society.

Stewart and Scott maintained that the institutional decimation of Black men through police violence and incarceration emerged from a political economy that deliberately confined young Black men to poverty, exploited Black males for cheap labor, and rationalized their death as a consequence of their deviance and undesirability in American society.[7] Unfortunately, the institutional decimation of Black males has continued uninterrupted for the past several decades. The consequences of this practice have been so severe that some authors have begun referring to poor Black male youth as "disconnected" and economically doomed, since "long-term disconnection correlates highly with low-income family backgrounds but also with poor future economic prospects—for the individuals themselves, their spouses or partners, their communities, and their children."[8] In short, Black males exist in a world of violence, predicated on a very tangible social exclusion whereby they become sanctioned by society, not participants within it.

Recent research finds that employers not only are less likely to hire Black men after they are incarcerated but also discriminate against Black men more generally because "the high rates of crime and incarceration among young [B]lack men are likely to reduce the employment prospects of those with no criminal background themselves. Employers frequently cannot distinguish accurately between those who do and do not have criminal backgrounds."[9] In fact, Black men with no criminal records and degrees are less likely be called back for interviews than white men with criminal records.[10] The strong cultural associations of Black males with criminality and danger allows employers to legitimize their racial biases as sound business sense. For many Blacks, job discrimination begins with the reading of their names, since a Black-sounding male name often results in being eliminated from the call-back pool.[11] Black males are severely burdened by their association with criminality. Black males with criminal records have little to no prospects for work, while Black men with degrees often receive little to no benefits from their credentials.[12] Black men who are rated equal in performance and qualification to their white counterparts are paid less, despite their productivity.[13] Even in those instances where Black boys find themselves reared in a viable middle-class family, they are much more likely to be victims of "downward mobility," or falling out of the middle class as adult Black men due to employment discrimination.[14]

Theorizations of Black men continue to focus on job discrimination and their (labor) exploitation without a serious consideration of Black males as undesirable workers. In liberal arts and humanities disciplines, the conversation about Black men's economic position is continually framed around income and wage differentials between men and women, with little attention given to Black males' employability or the stereotypes applied to the Black male worker. The assumptions about Black men in the workplace are largely derivative of the patriarchal thesis deployed by second wave feminism, which holds that Black men have more power, authority, and economic standing than their female counterparts in professional occupations.[15] Overwhelmingly, Black men as a group are blue-collar workers; however, for the few who occupy the (white) skilled labor sectors of America, assumptions of male privilege and power have followed.[16] Historically, Black men often fare worse than Black women in professional and skilled employment settings because of the different stereotypes applied to Black males and the level of education between the groups.[17] Black men are often associated with such negative stereotypes that any assertive act of speech or demonstration of leadership is thought to be threatening. In these (professional executive) environments, Black men are penalized for exhibiting agentic characteristics (assertiveness, self-confidence, conviction), while Black women are not.[18] This penalty is so severe that a disarming mechanism (e.g., a baby face, humor)—a skill or quirk that allays the threats that whites perceive Black males to pose to them—is recommended for Black men.[19] Even in middle- to top-tier jobs, criminality and racist myths follow Black men to boardrooms. Class and education simply do not protect Black men from the racist stereotypes attached to their lower-class counterparts.

For Black men, work—or, more accurately, the denial of work—is a sexually specific refusal. The denial of work cannot be articulated as a common sociological or economic phenomenon; it is not simply a class problem. While unemployment can and does affect all racial groups in America, the Black male is deprived of work as a means to sustain both the prison and his status at the bottom of the economic hierarchy. Unable to compete for jobs with their white counterparts or obtain jobs like their Black female counterparts, many Black men turn to illegal activities as a means of economic sustenance and survival, inevitably placing them in contact with the criminal justice system, the police state, and the prison-industrial complex. The relationship among poverty, incarceration, and Black male vulnerability is not abstract. In Portsmouth, Virginia, a young Black man named Jamycheal Mitchell, who was poor and had a history of mental problems, was arrested for stealing "a bottle of Mountain Dew, a Snickers bar and a Zebra Cake worth a total of $5 from a 7-Eleven." He was incarcerated for four months without trial. On August 21, 2015, he was found dead from starvation. His body was "extremely emaciated and practically had no muscle mass left" when it was found.[20] Poverty creates conditions that make young, uneducated, and unemployed Black males into scavengers. They are forced to live or die by chance. It is this peculiar reality where criminality, the denial of work, poverty, and Black maleness push Black men and boys toward the prison and ultimately toward death at the hands of the police or of other Black males forced to scavenge for survival. The system that excludes Black males from work and life is creating logics of death that are sustained and accepted by both Black and white members of society. We turn from the poor; we do not theorize about them. We acknowledge their position and, like the aristocrats of old, express some regret for their station in life. This class bias from which Black people generally, but Black males particularly, are observed is saturated with condemnation, not earnestness or understanding.

Unprepared and lacking options for employment, many Black men turn to illegal activities as a means of economic sustenance. Participating in criminal activities in an effort to survive within a society that will not educate, hire, or train Black men and boys inevitably places these young Black males in contact with the criminal justice system and the ever-expanding prison-industrial complex. Following the institutional decimation of Black men pointed out in Stewart and Scott's work on the relationship between prisons and poverty, Michelle Alexander's *The New Jim Crow: Mass Incarceration in the Age of Colorblindness* (2010) argues that "mass incarceration . . . is the most damaging manifestation of the backlash against the Civil Rights Movement."[21] Mass incarceration destroys Black families, removes fathers from homes, and makes Black men, both literally and figuratively, a disenfranchised and unemployed under-caste. According to Alexander, the prison-industrial complex targets Black men: "Our criminal-justice system has for decades been infected with a mind-set that views [B]lack boys and men in particular as a problem to be dealt with, managed and controlled. This mind-set has fueled a brutal war on drugs, a get-tough movement and a prison-building boom unprecedented in world history."[22] This largely overlooked aspect of incarceration, which both *feeds* and *feeds off of* the poverty of Black men, remains descriptive in most scholarly works dealing with Black males. The War on Drugs as well as policies legitimizing racial profiling and illegal search and seizure on Black male bodies have legitimized not only the surveillance itself but also public fears of Black males. Black males who come in contact with the criminal justice system are stained by the crest of the state. Black men are not only dehumanized as prisoners, but their lives are forever affected as criminals. This grim reality is proof of not only racism but also the consequences of the peculiar sexual violence and caricatures that have come to represent Black males as deviants and rapists in this society. As Devah Pager points out:

> At any given time, roughly 12 percent of all young [B]lack men between the ages of twenty-five and twenty-nine are behind bars, compared to less than 2 percent of white men in the same age group; roughly a third are under criminal justice supervision. Over the course of a lifetime, nearly one in three young [B]lack men—and well over half of young [B]lack high school dropouts—will spend some time in prison. According to these estimates, young [B]lack men are more likely to go to prison than to attend college, serve in the military, or, in the case of high school dropouts, be in the labor market. Prison

is no longer a rare or extreme event among our nation's most marginalized groups. Rather it has now become a normal and anticipated
marker in the transition to adulthood.[23]

The closeness young Black men have to prison is rarely thought of as a
peculiar kind of sexual violence. Eldridge Cleaver and Black male political
prisoners like him boldly announced the realities of incarceration, but very
little understanding remains of the effects of incarceration on Black males and
its relation to their specific sexual disadvantages in society. While Black men
and boys are spoken about with an eye to the seeming inevitability of their
status as criminals and, eventually, prisoners, contemporary theory pays no
attention to the endless ways in which imprisonment and policing are a kind
of sexual violence initiated by the objectification and surveilling of the Black
male body. Poor young Black men are thought to be thugs and in need of correction. Many Black men who are not imprisoned or dead still live their lives
controlled by the state. Young Black men who are on probation not only endure the economic consequences of their conviction but also are reminded
daily of their unfreedom by the state. Victor Rios argues, "When a young
person is on probation, he is left with few rights; he can be stopped and
searched for no reason, and can be arrested for noncriminal transgressions
such as hanging out with his friends or walking in the wrong part of the
neighborhood."[24]

The over-representation of young Black men in prison limits the ability
of scientists, clinicians, and doctors to gain valuable information about their
health. Becky Pettit believes this is an epistemological problem with real political and policy consequences. By not seeing Black men who are incarcerated, the study of Black men is deprived by a collective blindness that "hinders
the establishment of social facts, conceals inequality, and undermines the
foundation of social science research, including that used in the design and
evaluation of social policy."[25] Similarly, Emily Wang has argued that incarceration makes the tracking of Black males' health problems especially difficult. Her findings suggest that "the high rates of incarceration of [B]lack men
during the past three decades may have accounted for up to 65 percent of the
loss to follow-up among [B]lack men" in clinical studies. Because incarceration affects Black men disproportionately, we know significantly less about
their health outcomes than about those of white men and women or of Black
women.[26]

Perhaps the greatest irony of these realities is while the sociologists, de-
mographers, and criminologists issue warnings about the ignorance we share
in not knowing enough about the actual conditions and life chances of Black
males, scholars in the liberal arts insist we know far too much already and
should research their suffering less. Under the current gender regime, these
Black males—their lives—now absent from society remain simultaneously

unpresented and erased in theory. Gender theorists insist that we know about them intuitively, so we need no account of their subjectivity in theory beyond the problems (Black masculinity) they present for other identities. Such intuition is in reality merely the rationalization of ignorance. We claim to see and know what cannot yet *actually* be known, because we understand Black males as negative entities we wish to avoid. There is simply not enough information about the Black males vacated from society through death or prison to know all of what theory claims. The prison, like death, prevents our ability to observe and study Black men and boys as they live. This blindness of Black male life means that as scholars and observers we fail to perceive the extent of Black male disadvantage and vulnerability. We turn from evidence simply because we trust the allure of a construct like Black masculinity to do the work of evidence. The story of Black men's failures or personal narratives of their violent behavior stand in for facts about Black men. Consequently, our understanding of the actual conditions of Black men rarely rises above this level.

Little Niggers: Elaine Brown's Analysis of the Super-predator Mythology

The concrete flux of anti-Blackness, those material dynamics of social pressure and anti-Black rage that animate policy, police-state violence, and white vigilantism are doctrinaire societal obsessions convinced of their desire for the death of Black men. The plexus of white supremacism in American society is not a simple naming or practicing of animus against Blacks. The lifeline, blood, and sustenance of white supremacy is the psychical complacency and Negrophobia that all people in America have of the Nigger, that wretched poor Black child—she who mothers them and he who multiples. Despite the democratic prose of equality, the reality is that addressing the social inequities as they affect Black men and boys requires real structural, psychological, economic, and legal change. As Toby Jenkins remarks:

> The challenge reflects a social oxymoron: seeking to advance the status of a population that the larger society has systematically oppressed. On one hand, society espouses rhetoric of concern and desire to elevate Black males, but on the other hand, society practices a policy of oppression, prejudice, and disregard. Put differently, the experience of the Black man in America seems to be one in which he is called "mister" but is treated with a "niggardly" regard. And the result is the positioning of Black males at the lower rungs of society and their experiencing underachievement in almost all aspects of life.[27]

From this oxymoronic state springs contradictory thinking about race and racism that asserts the sociological conditions, the external environmental problems in poor Black urban spaces, as evidence of a more fundamental and inheritable cultural disposition toward deviance, criminality, and murder. This is the milieu from which Little B (Michael Lewis) springs. Lewis is known to most as "an out-of-control thug who killed a man at 13."[28] In 1997, he was arrested for killing Darrell Woods in front of his two children and wife. While many activists continue to maintain Lewis's innocence, the issue in which this work is particularly interested is more about the stereotypes of Black men and the Black community used to justify the wrath of the state and public sentiment used to convict Lewis. The sexualized racist narrative surrounding Little B adamantly asserted that he killed Woods to "prove his toughness, his manhood."[29] Because Lewis was a Black boy, his journey to manhood was dictated by fulfilling his savage instinct to kill.

In the mind of the public, Little B's childhood (the life of a Black boy) represented the evilness of Black manhood made manifest. There was no exemption from the public; there was no sympathy for him as a child, because ultimately he was not a child or even a human. At his core, he was a Nigger. Little B was the result of the pathology of the Nigger, let loose, the warning white America has heralded since slavery: If you give these Blacks freedom, they will turn into beasts. Little B was the symbolic proof to the white imagination that a Nigger, even a Nigger child, must be ruled. Commenting on the repetitiveness of the *Atlanta Journal Constitution*'s describing Little B (a child) as evil, Elaine Brown realized that the term was meant to express a phobia, "some sort of primal fear of the beast within . . . as though Little B were a mythical wolf-boy."[30] An editorial in that newspaper argued that Little B was a young killer and that "many of these young killers are living outside the bounds of normal social interaction, tiny thugs who kill at the slightest insult—or sometimes without any provocation."[31] But the *Atlanta Journal Constitution* simply reproduced the decades-long symbolism that marries "young Black males" to "criminals." Melissa Harris Barlow's monumental study "Race and the Problem of Crime in 'Time' and 'Newsweek' Cover Stories, 1946 to 1995" argues that "crime began to be racialized in the current form in the 1960s, when criminals began to be equated with 'young [B]lack males.'"[32] As a reaction to the push from the Black community for civil and political rights, a national campaign was launched by a cover story in *Newsweek* in March 1965 that sought to make crime generally synonymous with Black men specifically. The ideological work done to solidify the connection between crime and the "young Black male" in the mid-1960s defined the discourse about race for decades to come and marked "an important dimension of the shift from traditional to modern, symbolic racism." This modern racism, fixated on the criminality of the "young Black male," facilitated the "public consent for the extreme levels of coercive control applied to a substantial proportion of the African American population."[33] It is here that we see the levels of violence that spell death and ruin for Blacks in America being justified as sanctions against Black communities in an effort to control both the deviant impulse and the birth of young Black males.

The ideology that started as a reaction to the political and economic mobilization quickly became a core belief of American society, eventually seeking to be validated by various conjectures in the social sciences. In 1995, John DiIulio coined the term "super-predator" to describe the burgeoning crime wave due to young Black males. In "The Coming of the Super-predators," he argued that a crime wave was coming and that, "while the trouble will be greatest in [B]lack inner-city neighborhoods, other places are also certain to have burgeoning youth-crime problems that will spill over into upscale central-city districts, inner-ring suburbs, and even the rural heartland."[34] DiIulio meshed the myths of scientific racism with a post–Civil Rights America focused on culture and environment to persuade a twentieth-century American public that this was really not about race but about the cultural failures and moral poverty of poor urban communities. According to DiIulio, "Moral poverty is the poverty of being without loving, capable, responsible adults who teach you right from wrong. It is the poverty of being without parents and other authorities who habituate you to feel joy at others' joy, pain at others' pain, happiness when you do right, remorse when you do wrong." At the extremity of moral poverty, however, DiIulio presents Blackness, unnamed but visible through the imagery of a problem people identified by the raw concepts of their social condition. He says, "In the extreme, moral poverty is the poverty of growing up surrounded by deviant, delinquent, and criminal adults in abusive, violence-ridden, fatherless, Godless, and jobless settings."[35] Despite attempts to pitch this theory as "nonracial" and "scientific," DiIulio ultimately identifies his target—the young Black male—and warns, "Not only is the number of young [B]lack criminals likely to surge, but also the [B]lack crime rate, both [B]lack-on-[B]lack and [B]lack-on-white, is increasing, so that as many as half of these juvenile super-predators could be young [B]lack males."[36]

DiIulio's attack on Black men and boys is foundationally based in the view that "all that's left of the [B]lack community in some pockets of urban America is deviant, delinquent and criminal adults surrounded by severely abused and neglected children, virtually all of whom were born out of wedlock."[37] Like the analysis offered by Angela Davis concerning the myth of the Black rapist, these theories show how the stereotypes of Black men and boys as predators are symbiotic to the racist sexual mythology concerning Black women and girls, both of which pathologize the whole Black community.[38] Just as DiIulio depicts Black men and boys as "stone cold predators," he depicts the Black mother—and, by extension, the Black community—as neglectful and dangerous, since "the abject moral poverty that creates super-predators begins very early in life in homes where unconditional love is nowhere but unmerciful abuse is common."[39] This theme of Black pathology gets scientific language toward the end of 1996 in the book *Body Count: Moral Poverty and How to*

Win America's War against Crime and Drugs, which argues that Black urban spaces are best understood as "criminogenic communities," or "places where the social forces that create predatory criminals are far more numerous than the social forces that create decent, law-abiding citizens." The problem, according to DiIulio and his co-authors, is that "most inner city children grow up surrounded by teenagers and adults who are themselves deviant, delinquent, or criminal."[40] Although DiIulio rejected his super-predator thesis years later, the language and imagery of the Black super-predator remains imprinted on the nation's collective psyche, as does the violent mythology of the Black communities from which these Black men and boys come.[41]

Internalized Vulnerabilities: Black Male Vulnerability among Other Blacks

While there can be no denial of the prevalence and destruction caused by white violence against Black men and boys, it is not the only dynamic that threatens Black male life. In Black communities, Black men and boys are also victims of domestic and sexual abuse at rates far higher than those for their white male counterparts. Black males are thought to be too dangerous to actually be victims of domestic and sexual violence. While conversations concerning police brutality or racism are common, albeit misunderstood, there is rarely any attention to the ways in which sexual and domestic violence affect Black men in their own communities. The hyper-masculine stereotypes of Black males make it almost unfathomable for many onlookers to see Black men and boys as victims of women's violence or rage. And in those few instances that such conversations become somewhat possible, they are mischaracterized as an irrelevant phenomenon that ultimately deflects from the prevalence of female domestic and sexual abuse. In reality, Black men and boys suffer physical and sexual abuse from men and women within their communities. This fact remains unacknowledged in current academic disciplines governed by the calculus of identity, since any centering of the Black male, even when addressing his specific experiences and dynamics of trauma, are deemed to be unjustified. He is simply the wrong body, thought to be undeserving of the position as subject/*subject*. Typical of the ways in which Black men are overdetermined by the corpse—the dead Black male body—conversations concerning abuse of Black males have been erased altogether under current theorizations of Black masculinity. In other words, the only oppression Black males can have is the death caused by racism. Since domestic and sexual violence exceed the limits of this conceptual boundary, it is not seen; it is thought to be nonexistent and irrelevant to our current understandings of Black men and boys.

Historically, Black men have been well represented as victims of both intimate partner violence (IPV) and intimate partner homicide (IPH) in government reports since the 1970s.[42] Regarding IPH, "Among [B]lacks the gender ratio was below 1.0 prior to the mid-1980s, as fewer [B]lack females than [B]lack males were murdered by intimate partners; by the mid-1990s, the ratio reached 1.5 [B]lack female victims for every [B]lack male."[43] In fact, "Between 1976 and 1989 more [B]lack men were killed by their wives than [B]lack women were killed by their husbands. After 1990 the order was reversed, and the murder rate among [B]lack wives and ex-wives was higher than that among [B]lack husbands and ex-husbands."[44] Overall, Black communities endure higher rates of IPV than white communities, as both Black men and Black women are more likely to experience domestic violence than their white counterparts. Reporting for the U.S. Department of Justice, Callie Rennison and Sarah Welchans observed that "[B]lacks were victimized by intimate partners at significantly higher rates than persons of any other race between 1993 and 1998. Black females experienced intimate partner violence at a rate 35% higher than that of white females, and about 2½ times the rate of women of other races. Black males experienced intimate partner violence at a rate about 62% higher than that of white males and about 2½ times the rate of men of other races."[45] The National Intimate Partner and Sexual Violence Survey (2010) makes a similar case for considering Black men as victims of IPV. According to the report, while an estimated 40.9 percent of Black women, or roughly 6 million Black women, will experience some form of IPV in their lifetime, 36.8 percent, or about 4.6 million, Black men will, as well.[46]

The historical patterns of Black male victimization and death are often left out of the narratives concerning the nature of domestic violence to sustain the almost exclusive focus currently held by gender theorists on women as victims and men as perpetrators. Contrary to contemporary theory, which insists on masculinity as the sole cause of domestic abuse, IPV and IPH in the Black community, like that in the white community, is heavily correlated with the concentration of poverty in these areas.[47] In reality, Black men and women are subject to this kind of violence; it is not simply patriarchal, as if it were perpetrated exclusively by males. Intimate partner violence is an extension of the violence found in neglected communities, which enters homes through the psychology and interpersonal relationships of men and women affected by economic, political, and various other environmental traumas.

Efforts to center Black male victims in discussions of IPV are often cast as erasure of the real victims of domestic abuse: women. Often, attempts to discuss the suffering of Black males, whether they are husbands, boyfriends, or children, are dismissed as irrelevant to the more important issue of Black women's victimization by men. Among scholars, male and female, a belief exists that if a Black man is attacked by a Black woman, he deserves it, or because he is male, it is his obligation to de-escalate female aggression toward him, even if it means he is physically or verbally assaulted in the process. These reactions are the outgrowth of a deeply held conviction that men are the perpetrators, not the victims, of domestic violence. In liberal arts disciplines, domestic violence is thought of almost exclusively as patriarchal violence. In fact, bell hooks has argued that the term *domestic violence* should be replaced with *patriarchal violence*, because it "continually reminds the listener that violence in the home is linked to sexism and sexist thinking, to male domination."[48] Often the humanities appeal to intuitive observations and personal experience to supplant empirical study and evidence as in the social sciences. The effect of such appeals, however, in the case of underreported or unpopular phenomena can contribute to the further marginality and invisibility of social practices. Academic fields continue to discount the rates and consequences of domestic abuse and violence on the psychology and personhood of Black males, simply because the epistemic traditions of these disciplines allow evidence to be discounted for personal experience.

Under this schema, if the speaker has not seen Black men or boys abused, then there is a case for suggesting Black men and boys are not abused or that they are not abused to an extent that is significant enough to warrant discussion as a social problem similar in magnitude to the abuse of women. These conversations function as an extension of disciplinary politics rather than the prevalence of IPV and IPH throughout society. It is common for domestic violence to be used as evidence for establishing patriarchy as the political dividing line between Black men and women, as well for Black women's need of feminist politics concerned with their particular vulnerability due to their race and gender.[49] Very little discussion of race and IPV deals with the mental, economic, or environmental causes of these conflicts or the populations identified by the National Crime Victimization Survey's qualitative reports of abuse. These discourses assume that ending domestic violence (against women) is a matter of eliminating toxic masculinities and patriarchy instead of ameliorating the conditions in which these populations find themselves or improving their access to mental health or substance abuse treatment.

Intimate partner violence and homicide and sexual violence against Black men and boys offer evidence that our understanding of the oppression of Black males also has an ideological dimension that is internalized not only by the larger white society but also by members of their own racial group. These internalized vulnerabilities, so to speak, make Black men potential victims of all those who engage them. Because society dehumanizes Black men and boys, constructing them as invulnerable to offense, individuals recognize that there is little punishment for taking violent action against this group. Internalizing Black male vulnerabilities is not about individuals simply believing stereotypes about Black males; it is about how individuals are socialized to understand that society's conceptualization of Black males as criminal and savage empowers anyone to act against Black men and boys without fear of punishment. Internalizing the vulnerable social positions of populations, as in the case of Black men, offers individuals a providential rationale for committing violence or acting against individuals from groups that society thinks of as evil in the flesh. The pervasiveness of misandric myths about Black men has allowed stereotypes and antipathies to be internalized throughout the society without question. Within the consciousness of individuals, internalized vulnerability exists as an almost intuitive knowledge of the fungibility of Black males in society, so that the social or personal relation or contact an individual has with a Black male offers a level of power over *that* Black male body. Since Black males can never be victims, other individuals—even other Blacks and minorities—have the power to abuse, exploit, or rape them without fear of sanction. In other words, the dehumanization of Black men and boys generally by society gives individuals explicit permission to dehumanize them, as well. In this sense, perpetrators of violence against Black males are not guilty of any crimes at all. They are simply participating in the subjugation of nonhuman things that have no moral status or empathy in the larger society, especially in the case of personal or intimate partner violence.

Duluth No More: The Ideology and Politics behind the Patriarchal Thesis

In *Education Groups for Men Who Batter: The Duluth Model*, Ellen Pence and Michael Paymar (the inventors of the model) argue that treating men who batter their partners is "not a neutral endeavor." In the Duluth program, "Each facilitator conducts a group within a community, a program, and a personal philosophical framework that either supports a man's process of change toward non-violence, or reinforces his dominance over the woman he batters." Theory "guides practice," say Pence and Paymar, and their theory is simple: "Men are culturally prepared for their role of master of the home even though they must enforce the 'right' to exercise this role. They are socialized to be dominant and women to be submissive."[50] The Duluth model holds that men need not intend to batter women; it is an automatic, almost unconscious response, part of the programing men are taught in "their families of origins and through their experiences in a culture that teaches men to dominate."[51] Many clinicians and psychologists, however, adamantly disagree with this model. For example, Donald Dutton has argued that "intervention systems like the Duluth model were focused on confronting sexist attitudes or male entitlement. The problem was there that there was no evidence that batterers had sexist attitudes."[52] In addition, Kenneth Corvo, a professor of social work, maintains, "In spite of strong and consistent clinical and etiological linkages, the Duluth model views substance abuse as almost irrelevant in the perpetration of domestic violence."[53] While gender scholars in the humanities have continued to insist that there is an intuitive link between domestic violence and patriarchy, clinicians have offered study after study demonstrating that there is little clinical or etiological evidence to support the claim that domes-

tic abuse is solely the province of patriarchy or that men abuse women because of psychological or psychoanalytic disposition toward domination.
Histories of previous abuse, addiction, and mental health are so highly correlated to incidents of partner violence that it is negligent to ignore these
factors in incidents of IPV.[54] In fact, the noted psychologist Denise Hines
maintains that it is precisely these factors (previous abuse, drug and substance
abuse, and mental health) that explain the almost symmetrical rates of abuse
perpetrated by women against men in the general population.[55]

Perhaps the greatest irony concerning the Duluth model is that one of the
founders, Ellen Pence, admitted that the weakness of the program was that it
lacked clinical findings to support the theory that patriarchy was the cause of
domestic abuse. In the subsequent article "Some Thoughts on Philosophy,"
Pence explains, "Although the DAIP [Domestic Abuse Intervention Pro-
grams] staff has argued against using causal explanations that require practitioners to assume a fairly universal psychological makeup among batterers
(i.e., stress or anger control problems), we have developed some of our own
truisms that also reduce complex social relationships to slogans. One was the
notion that batterers use violence, coercion, and intimidation to control their
partners." As Pence says, "He does it for power, he does it for control, he does
it because he can—these were advocacy jingles that, in our opinion, said just
about all there was to say."[56] Pence conveys that these jingles supplanted the
need or search for evidence: "By determining that the need or desire for power was the motivating force behind battering, we created a conceptual framework that, in fact, did not fit the lived experience of many of the men and
women we were working with. Like those we were criticizing, we reduced our
analysis to a psychological universal truism."[57] Despite the incongruity of
their theory to the lives and actual motivations of abusers, Pence and Paymar
successfully established a male psychologism that would come to establish the
motivation men had for abuse and define women as the sole victims of this
kind of violence. According to Pence, the Duluth model was never meant to
explain the actual cases or circumstances of domestic violence. It was about
imposing the ideological stance of the model and its staff, and that meant
ignoring violence between same-sex couples and violence committed by
women against men. Cases of domestic abuse that did not fit their theory
were simply dismissed as irrelevant to the ideological commitments of the
Duluth project. Pence explains:

> It was the cases themselves that created the chink in each of our theo-
> retical suits of armor. Speaking for myself, I found that many of the
> men I interviewed did not seem to articulate a desire for power over
> their partner. Although I relentlessly took every opportunity to point
> out to men in the groups that they were so motivated and merely in
> denial, the fact that few men ever articulated such a desire went un-

noticed by me and many of my coworkers. Eventually, we realized that we were finding what we had already predetermined to find. The DAIP staff were interpreting what men seemed to expect or feel entitled to as a desire. When we had to start explaining women's violence toward their partners, lesbian violence, and the violence of men who did not like what they were doing, we were brought back to our original undeveloped thinking that the violence is rooted in how social relationships (e.g., marriage) and the rights people feel entitled to within them are socially, not privately, constructed.[58]

Pence admits that ideology rather than careful empirical studies formed the philosophical foundation of the Duluth paradigm. "We all engaged in ideological practices and claimed them to be neutral observations," writes Pence.[59] In its earliest formulation, Duluth was solely committed to the criminalization of male perpetrators, even while realizing that the criminal justice system did not effectively change the social norms that were most responsible for IPV.[60] Pence's comments on Duluth's paradigm have had little effect on how liberal arts disciplines account for IPV and IPH. The deliberate exclusion of violence committed by women against men and children by Pence and early gender theorists following her model has been moralized away as anti-woman or victim blaming rather than a serious challenge to how one conceptualizes violence within the home or intimate relationships. Ultimately, the validity and soundness of the theory has seemed to be irrelevant to its adoption in the humanities as an explanatory model of male aggression and Black males' compensatory motivations for violence.

The premises of this model have sustained decades of work and legitimized assumptions thought to explain IPV in Black communities. Contrary to the dominant view of domestic abuse in the Black community articulated by authors such as bell hooks and Kimberlé Crenshaw, who maintain the validity of the patriarchal thesis (Duluth model),[61] multiple social scientists, social workers, and psychologists have shown that the causes of IPV and IPH cannot be culturally universalized to the Black community. For example, Carolyn West, a noted Black feminist psychologist, argues that IPV "victimization and perpetration can involve men and women of every race/ethnicity, age, socioeconomic status, sexual orientation, and relationship status, including married, cohabiting, and dating couples."[62] In this view, domestic violence is an outgrowth of conflict between people in which either or both can be perpetrators and victims simultaneously. This view of domestic violence is particularly sensitive to the ways that previous research has built theories and claims from the study of only white heterosexual couples and sought to universalize such findings across all groups. Because of the large number of whites reporting incidents of abuse and constituting the subjects of research, many researchers have thought it legitimate not only to generalize their findings to all groups but also to focus primarily on the unilateral aspects of IPV. However, when one evaluates the rates of IPV among Black, Asian, Hispanic, and Indigenous men and women, "few gender differences in rates of physical and psychological aggression [are] found."[63]

Bidirectional Abuse and Intimate Partner Violence against Black Men

In sharp contrast to the white community, in Black communities IPV was found to be exceptionally defined by bidirectionality. Various studies have found that Black cosmologies of womanhood, vulnerability of females, and violence differ greatly from those of whites.[64] While unilateral violence occurred at higher rates among Black males and females than in the white population, in Black households "mutual violence was most frequently reported. The rate of self-reported bidirectional IPV (61%) was 2 times that of unidirectional female-to-male partner violence (FMPV; 31%) and about 6 times higher than unidirectional male-to-female partner violence (MFPV; 8%)."[65] As the epidemiologist Niki Palmetto clarifies, "A bidirectional violent relationship signifies that both partners perpetrate violence in a given relationship (not necessarily within each violent episode)."[66] In Black communities, there is no fixed perpetrator or victim: Black men and women can be both simultaneously and often are.[67] In this sense, bidirectionality signals that Black IPV is rooted in mutual victimization and violence; these patterns consequently socialize men, women, and children into cycles of mutual conflict in which perpetrators cannot be clearly marked. As the epidemiologist Raul Caetano, the public health scholar Suhasini Mikler, and the clinical psychologist Craig Field remark, "The influence of Black ethnicity on the occurrence of bidirectional partner violence appears to be independent of education, income, employment status, drinking, alcohol problems, and history of violence in the family of origin."[68] While we know that the aforementioned environmental stressors increase the probability of IPV, something else is operating in the Black community that particularizes intimate violence as bidirectional.

A major obstacle to the recognition of Black male victims of IPV and IPH is the stereotype that Black men who are the intimate partners of Black women are most responsible for their deaths. The most publicly debated example of this racist myth occurred in 2009 surrounding a speech on domestic violence by Attorney-General Eric H. Holder Jr. In the speech, Holder claimed, "Disturbingly, intimate partner homicide is the leading cause of death for African-American women ages 15 to 45."[69] In his defense, Holder did not pull this statistic out of thin air; the claim that IPH was the leading cause of death for Black women—and, by implication, that Black men made up the vast majority of perpetrators—was commonly made in peer-reviewed domestic violence literature and government reports, including the *National Institute of Justice Journal*, throughout the 2000s.[70] Ultimately, however, the claimed statistic could not be verified as fact and consequently was revised and excised from several reports and publications as an error.[71] The 2003 issue of the *National Institute of Justice Journal* was revised on March 11, 2014, to say, "Homicide . . . is a leading cause of death in the United States among young African American women aged 15 to 45 years,"[72] and the Department of Justice website now includes a disclaimer and explanatory note to Holder's speech that reads:

> These remarks, as originally delivered in 2009, cited a statistic naming intimate partner homicide as the leading cause of death for African-American women ages 15 to 45. This statistic was drawn from a range of reputable sources, including a 2003 study by the National Institute of Justice. However, recent figures indicate other causes of death—including cancer and heart disease—outrank intimate partner homicide for this age group.[73]

It is one thing to point out the mistakes of peer-reviewed articles regarding misrepresentation of facts or errors of citations in government reports, but the life of this statistic concerning the implied danger Black men pose to Black women is a different species of concern.

Holder's claim about IPH was believable because, when it was stated as a gender proposition, it disarmed the resistance many social scientists and scholars felt toward racist stereotypes of Black men as dangerous and violent and allowed them ultimately to accept it as fact. This fantastic statistic took on a life of its own and gained facticity based on a consensus among academics and the public that Black men are, in fact, violent and thereby real threats to the women in their communities. It is easily shown via a cursory examination of the Centers for Disease Control's reports that IPV simply could not be the leading cause of death of Black women. Intimate partner homicide is a subset of homicides committed in a given year. From 1998 to 2013, homicide ranked second to unintentional injuries for young Black women age fifteen to twenty-four, while Black women within the average age of marriage (twenty-four to forty-four) were less likely to die from homicide generally. Among Black women age twenty-four to forty-four, homicide ranged from the fourth to seventh most likely cause of death; thus, contrary to the idea that Black men are dangerous as spouses and intimate partners, the threat of homicide as a leading cause of death diminished among Black women in this age group.[74]

Black female perpetrators of domestic violence are not uncommon in the Black community. This should come as no surprise, given that male victims of domestic violence are not as rare as gender theorists usually assert.[75] Various community studies and self-reporting surveys indicate some agreement between Black men and women regarding the rates of IPV perpetrated by females.[76] We see headlines of such occurrences constantly across various media platforms, but we do not respond because we are culturally conditioned not to see or sympathize with Black male victims of such abuse. On July 31, 2015, Alexis Stanton was charged with assault after pouring hot grits on a man and then beating him with a bat.[77] On August 6, 2015, Barvetta Singletary, an aide to President Barack Obama, shot at her boyfriend with his own gun for allegedly having an affair.[78] Most notably, the singer Ray J was beaten by his girlfriend Princess Love, sustaining a torn ligament, fractured ribs, and a busted lip.[79] On September 29, 2015, Natalie Chase Robinson was arrested for throwing bleach in her boyfriend's face, covering him with alcohol, and setting him on fire.[80] When Black males are victimized by women, society and even Black academics, male and female, take the incidents to be comical. Despite the moralizations condemning domestic violence throughout society, there is a failure to see women as perpetrators. However, to truly address domestic violence, scholars and practitioners must come to recognize that "women's violence needs to be understood as a part of the picture of domestic violence as it may be a key aspect of more effective prevention and intervention strategies for IPV."[81]

Like his victimization at the hands of the larger white society, the Black male's victimization by women is explained away by suggesting that Black males are so dangerous and violent that they could not possibly be victims or that they deserve the violence imposed on them. Case studies and statistics offering proof of Black male victims of bidirectional abuse or abuse perpetrated unilaterally by females in the Black community are often explained away by appealing to the obviousness of Black male aggression and violence toward Black women. Routinely, the revelation of Black women as perpetrators of domestic violence against Black men is met with the retort that women attack or kill Black men in self-defense. While authors have proposed this explanation for higher rates of bidirectionality within various literatures, it has never been confirmed as true among female abusers.[82] Not knowing the reason behind certain phenomena is not a reason for theorists to retreat into racist stereotypes about Black males' violent disposition toward women.[83] This bias among gender theorists not only erases Black male suffering and death at the hands of intimate partners but also erroneously establishes patterns of thinking suggesting that "despite the overrepresentation of African American male victims of domestic violence and female-perpetrated homicides . . . males alone are responsible for intimate violence and are not themselves harmed by abuse."[84] While nothing could be farther from the truth when considering the actual rates of Black male victims of IPV and IPH, Black masculinity theories often lack such substance regarding Black males.

What currently passes as theory not only ignores the prevalence of bidirectionality in the Black community but also suggests that Black male victims are morally irrelevant to our understanding and condemnation of IPV. Current explanations of the role race plays in IPV systematically erase the numbers of Black male victims in the mind of the theorist. Conceptualized as contradictions to the intuitive gender hierarchies established by our understanding of the masculine as perpetrating and the feminine as victimized, Black male victims of IPV and IPH are said to either not exist or not matter to the discussion at hand. This conceptualization of Black males is dehumanizing, because it insists that their suffering does not deserve to occupy a moment of our consideration as something real. Black males are told they can only be perpetrators of violence and remain unseen by gender theory as anything more, since their reality requires the recognition of female perpetrators. Ignoring their pain and suffering simply because they are Black men, or because they are abused by Black women, solidifies the racist regime of society in theory. These racist logics maintain that the Black male can only be criminal, only danger, only threat—he cannot be human, vulnerable, or victim, especially to a (Black) woman.

Liberal arts scholars need to understand domestic violence in the Black community as more than proof of a predetermined biocentric theory of Black male pathology. Multiple clinicians and public health scholars have concluded that decades of research into domestic violence in the Black community "provides no support for a conclusion that African Americans have an inherent biological or cultural propensity for violence; rather, the stressors and oppressive systemic forces that disproportionately affect African Americans place them at greater risk for domestic violence."[85] As such, there is no evidentiary basis to insist that Black maleness, or toxic masculinity, is causally related to the high incidence of domestic violence among Blacks. Domestic abuse is a problem of conflict that risks the death and injury of Black men, women, and children. Just as IPV perpetrated by males is associated with injury or death, so, too, must we confront the prevalence and danger of violence perpetrated by females. Male victims of female-perpetrated violence suffer from physical injury and disfigurement, depression, anxiety, and, in some cases, death, just as their female counterparts do.[86] Furthermore, domestic violence in the home creates a nexus of trauma that leads to concrete harm against *both men and women* and socializes young Black boys and girls into similar patterns of intimate violence as adults.[87] As West remarks, "Exposure to childhood violence in the form of being the victim of child physical abuse or witnessing domestic violence in the family of origin also has been associated with higher rates of IPV among Hispanic and African American men, women, and couples."[88] We can no longer conceptualize IPV as perpetrated solely by males in the Black community.[89] We need theoretical frames that engage IPV bidirectionally and ecologically to better understand this phenomenon and its consequences among Blacks.

Not Wanted and Not Cared For: Sexual Abuse and
the Rape of Young Black Boys

Heavily related to the environmental causes of intimate partner violence are the problems of sexual violence and the rape of Black boys in our communities. The poverty, criminalization, and unwantedness of Black boys combine to create staggering realities around their sexual vulnerability and invisibility.[90] As Nikitta Foston notes, "A major reason for the increasing rates of sexual abuse in Black America is that young Black boys are indiscriminately arrested at an early age and sent to local or state facilities where they are routinely raped or assaulted. Sexual assault, violence and abuse occur so often in group home settings and foster homes, and rehabilitative centers, simply because you don't have the quality of care or the necessary supervision."[91] This abuse is not isolated to male or female perpetrators. Black boys are at risk with both.[92] The trepidation toward associating sexual abuse and rape with homosexuality in the Black community must be engaged just as much as our cultural stigma asserting that women cannot be rapists. Black boys being penetrated and being forced to penetrate are both legally defined as rape.[93]

Black boys find themselves overrepresented and the most unwanted in foster care.[94] Though Blacks are generally less desirable than whites, Black girls are twice as likely to receive an application for adoption as Black boys.[95] This unwantedness makes Black boys especially vulnerable to multiple unsupervised interactions with adults and homes that increase their vulnerability to sexual abuse and rape. Despite biases that may hold that Black males "can't be raped" or are not severely affected by rape and sexual molestation, the reality is that all abuse has very real consequences. On August 8, 2014, Melinda Gaffney, a thirty-year-old Black woman, shot and killed Terrance Forks, the sixteen-year-old father of her child.[96] Not only was the case not widely reported, but Forks also was not thought of in any account as a victim of statutory rape or sexual assault, even though, at sixteen, he was a minor. The young Terrance Forks is thought of only as a dead Black boy, not the victim of sexual assault. "Even abuse at the hands of a woman, experts say, can have a negative impact on a young Black man's sexuality in adulthood," writes Foston. "Although a boy's early experimentation with a woman has often been referred to as a 'rite of passage,' it can complicate his psychological perception of impotence if he is unable to perform."[97] The lack of attention to and knowledge of male victims of sexual abuse and rape makes the recognition of serious mental health issues such as anxiety, depression, and antisocial behavior more difficult to recognize in Black males burdened by the racist stigmas that hold them to be sociopathic entities, regardless of their specific traumatic histories.

The sexual assault of Black boys and the ways this particular violence toward them conditions their socialization and maturation is practically nonexistent within academic literature generally and is rarely mentioned with any degree of empirical certainty in Black masculinity literature.[98] Perhaps this should come as no surprise, since, Shirley Salmon-Davis and Larry E. Davis write, Black boys who have been sexually abused "have been understudied, underreported, and underresponded to."[99] Black boys experience sexual abuse largely in isolation. They rarely have access to professional resources or social networks that understand and can speak to the reality of male victims of sexual assault and rape. The young boys experience feelings of loss, alienation, and fear of removal by the state if the abuse is reported.[100] Abandonment, anger, neglect, distrust, and depression are all realities for young victims of sexual violence. This is only exacerbated by the lack of other Black males in Black communities in whom young Black boys can confide: "Given the high percentage of female headed families in the African American community, not having a reliable confidant is a reality for many African American boys. . . . In this sense, an African American boy's perception of a female caretaker's failure to acknowledge this issue may contribute further to his feelings of rage and depression."[101]

Throughout Black celebrity culture, we often see Black men confessing that their first sexual experiences were, in fact, statutory rape,[102] yet such revelations create no impetus to study or acknowledge Black male rape. Lil' Wayne, for instance, maintains that he lost his virginity at eleven to a fourteen-year-old.[103] Chris Brown's confession of being raped at age eight by a much older teenage girl drew similar indifference.[104] Black boys are forced to suffer the stigma and psychological trauma of rape alone. While many learn to explain it away as a rite of passage, the trauma does not simply disappear. While it is acknowledged that homosexuality and, by effect, male-on-male rape of young Black boys may be an uncomfortable topic to broach, the discussion of female perpetration of rape against Black males is engaged as an impossibility.[105] The hyper-masculinity of the Black male brute resonates in the minds of observers and theorists as a denial of his sexual victimization and rape by women. The idea many hold is that a Black male could never be overpowered or abused by any woman—he is a lil' Buck. He craves sex; he is the aggressor—the rapist. This overdetermined envisioning of the Black boy makes even his empirical suffering (his stories, the actual facts of the matter) imperceptible to the general public and academic audiences alike.

There is a lack of shelters and services for men generally, but because of the stereotypes that view Black males as only perpetrators of domestic and sexual violence, Black men and boys are left without treatment for their trauma or amelioration of the mental anguish caused by abuse.[106] It is this untreated and unacknowledged history of sexual trauma that manifests itself as violence against intimates later in life.[107] Many academics not only ignore but also defend this invisibility by suggesting that focusing on male victims—specifically, Black male victims—of rape takes our attention away from the realities of female rape victims. In general, the denial of Black male victimization within disciplines is thought to be necessary to the advancement of a gender-progressive view of racism. This paradigm is not about progressivism toward gender but about the aversion to studying Black men and boys throughout the humanist sciences. The documented cases of sexual coercion and abuse of Black males in the social sciences should serve as evidence for thinking about these realities anew throughout the humanist sciences.[108]

The New Racism: The Black Academic Class and the Political Economics of Black Male Erasure

The Condemnation of Little B (2002) launches an attack on the academic and bourgeois economic interests of intellectuals, state officials, and politicians. Following the economic analyses articulated by thinkers such as Huey P. Newton, Malcolm X, and Harold Cruse, Elaine Brown argues that twenty-first-century development of racism built around the prison-industrial complex and the sacrificing of young Black men and boys to the corporate Leviathan remains ignored even in radical leftist and academic progressive movements.[109] Brown builds her analysis from Malcolm X's account of the modernization of the slave plantation as a symbol of the slave culture and economic modes of production that have survived and modernized to accommodate the racist capitalist culture of the twenty-first century. X's analysis of the plantation economy in the United States made Black intellectuals, as well as white liberals, uncomfortable, because unlike the Marxist-Leninist left that aimed to subsume racial class division as part of the ideology of the bourgeoisie, X's analysis particularized the class aspirations and divisions within Black society as remnants of the slave culture's hold on the Black mind. Following Malcolm X's schema of white supremacy and economics in the United States, Brown argues for understanding the class hierarchies between poor working-class Blacks and educated and middle-class Blacks as a function of white sociopolitical organization:

> Blacks not only remained in the same oppressive relationship to the new industrial economic structure as under slavery, but also remained trapped in the same inferior role in the social and cultural scheme under American apartheid. Now the field Slaves were the [B]lack masses, sharecropping or cleaning the factories of an urbanized America, cordoned off in their southern shanty towns or new northern ghettos. The House Slave now owned a funeral home or barbershop or catering business or, having miraculously managed an education at one of the land-grant or turn-of-the-century colleges built for [B]lacks, was a teacher, a doctor, or a lawyer, mostly attending other [B]lacks. Though he was, like the post-emancipation Field Slave, suffering un-

der social segregation and discrimination, the industrial House Slave often harbored the mentality of the old House slave, particularly in fear and hatred of the Field Slave and in obsequiousness toward the Master.[110]

The racial progress the Black race has enjoyed after the Civil Rights era is merely symbolic. The legislation and opportunities offered to "Black people" did not extend down to the bottom. In fact, in Brown's view, the economic mobility and opportunities for education offered to Blacks ultimately splintered the Black community more sharply, placing working-class Black folk, the poor urban folk, outside of the purview of "racial achievement," allowing more powerful Blacks to legitimate the racist stereotypes of the lower classes without remorse. Brown argues:

> Too many [B]lacks who had come to occupy places of power in the American scheme, no matter how limited, no matter how vicarious, were beginning to feel no obligation to align themselves with the struggle of the [B]lack masses, were doing nothing for the [B]lack community, and doing nothing with impunity, were doing nothing to use their limited power to elevate the Race. Now, they seemed to rise guiltless above the underclass, even renouncing their ties to the [B]lack underclass.[111]

Unlike those whose schemas simply want to identify anti-Blackness in the asymmetries between white life and Black life throughout the various concentric spheres of American society, Woodson, Frazier, and W.E.B. DuBois assert that attention must be called to the categories/means/views of study. Within these various planes of social existence, the various ideological foundations of life and death, be it as subject or object, as worker or owner, as man or women, or as citizen or criminal, Blackness—or, more appropriately perhaps, anti-Blackness—functions as the origin of these dynamics. The Black bourgeoisie is not proof of the Marxist logic that holds class to be the superseding principle determining the racial. Rather, the Black intellectual class is a political manifestation of the power anti-Blackness holds on the minds and lives of Blacks escaping death, so that even with economic mobility, and relatively little power, the Black elite, the Black subject, the Black desiring to be citizen runs, flees, from the ontology of being the Nigger, the sanctioned beast, the super-predator magnetized toward death. This is the foundation of twenty-first-century racism—the new racism described by Brown as focusing on the death and dying of young Black men and boys.

The new racism that Brown refers to places anti-Blackness within the changing political economy of America as deliberately growing empire. Brown contends that with "America's new economic shift to a base of high-

speed technological production, America's new Masters . . . have fashioned a
new domestic social Darwinist agenda justifying the continued exploitation
of the poor, especially those eternally poor [B]lack masses."[112] In this dichoto-
mous struggle for survival, the new age racist seeks to "forge [B]lacks into a
viable market by forcing those millions of ghettoized [B]lacks back to their
'natural' role as cheap labor, so as to supply them with an income in order to
build up the [B]lack consumer market." The new age house slave, the Black
bourgeoisie, anyone who has "elevated to the house on the back of [B]lack
struggle, finds his significance in his ability and willingness to serve the New
Age Racist agenda . . . his very livelihood is dependent on his willingness to
do even more than his historical counterpart."[113] This political/cultural economy of anti-Black currency rooted in the distancing of the Black bourgeoisie
from poor urban Black folk is a neoliberalist calculus, the *homo economicus*,
choosing freedom from the burden of having the darkest soul, the material
poverty of those Niggers, even though such an act commits the lower classes
of Black people to be the cheap labor of the white-supremacist society through
the eradication of the freedoms gained through Civil Rights—condemning
Black males to corporate imprisonment and, ultimately, physical death. This
is the Negrophobia of the Black intellectual class, the phobia of being the
corpse, the example, the overproduced, in the eyes of the societal managerial
structure.

This critique was previously raised at the beginning of the 1960s. Reacting
to the seemingly unmovable racist organization of America and the fixed-class
stratification of the Black working class, DuBois argued that "a class structure
began to arise within the Negro group which produced haves and have nots,
and tended to encourage more successful Negroes to join the forces of mo-
nopoly and exploitation, and help victimize their own lower classes."[114] As with
the analysis offered by Frazier's "Failure of the Negro Intellectual," which originally appeared in *Black World* in 1962, two years after DuBois's "Socialism and
the American Negro," DuBois saw the splintering off of a Black racial class that
saw themselves as intermediaries between the Black working folk and the
white power structure. This socialization at both the level of pure economic
interest and, as Frazier points out, in the ideas deployed in studying the Black
working class create inaccuracies and lack of interest in improving the actual
conditions of most Black people. Frazier warned that the class of our intellectuals and the originators of the theories we use to understand the Black masses "think very much the same as white Americans, even concerning Negroes."[115]
Frazier accuses this class of mistaking the economic interest they have in maintaining their social position as the desirable economic arrangement, despite
the suffering, poverty, and death, occurring within the masses of Black folk. In
refusing to start with the colonial situation and slavery and preferring instead
to urge moral calls for equality ensuring "the superficial aspects of the material standard of living among Negroes and the extent to which they enjoy

civil rights," the Black intellectual is "remiss in his grasp of the condition and fate of American Negroes."[116] This is a problem of disciplinary knowledge: how we come to know, continue to study, and normatively suggest the end for Black folk as objects/pieces of our visions as Black academics/intellectuals. The Black male, that violent dirty Nigger, that criminal, is thought to be the source of Black poverty and criminality. The Black intellectual does not see the condition of Black men as capable of being remedied or vindicated through sociological study and social reform. The Black male is thought simply to be impervious to cultivation and, as Brown suggests in her analysis of the super-predator myth, deserving of death, incarceration, and ostracism. The erasure of Black men and boys from thought is ultimately a methodological problem of "how we come to know of the Black male" and "how we *think* the Nigger."

From Boys to Men: The Need to Study Black Men and Boys beyond the Confines of Black Masculinity

Far too often, Black men and boys are recognized only as summaries of raw sociological data: idle collateral, figureless subjects vacated in person and defined by number. These Black males are thought to be little more than the numbers indicating that Black males are social problems: on the street, inevitably dead, or permanently locked away. Black males are not imagined as living human beings. They are merely thought to be particular expressions of group phenomena—individual examples of a problem population that are the criminals, deviants, and dangers that plague society. Their lives are not seen, because death is normal for them; he is—they are—disposable. The Black male who escapes death but is held within the prison is no more visible. Because we do not understand the actual realities of Black males, we conceptualize them as they are imagined—ruled by stereotypes masquerading as theory—and remain trapped by the narratives of Black males as problems. Instead of being viewers invested in the complexities of Black male life, theorists embrace the racist caricatures of Black men as concepts. Consequently, Black males are written into gender theory as the dangers the academic theorists fear—the stereotypes by which Black men and boys are represented within society.

Anti-Black racism, the urban landscape that is its architecture, and the brutality of the police state all operate to confine Black men to poverty and various cycles of abuse and death. It is often thought that the academic scholar, the theorist, rises above the sociological realities, such as poverty, death, and criminality, that surround the Black male. Far too often, scholars studying Black males ignore the extent to which these social phenomena are made synonymous with the very concept of Black men and boys and are subsequently also interiorized in the mind of the theorist. Our current theorization of Black males mirrors this social reality instead of challenging it. Even in theory, Black males become the origins of social problems rather than victims of them. Ontologically, Black men are made synonymous with social evil. Sociologically, they are conceptualized as simply expressing this nature through deviance.

Current theory only perpetuates this absence of Black men in thought. Their representation as problems and dangers deserving of death, incapable of the complexities given by life, lies behind our present descriptions of them as violent patriarchs set on domination and self-destruction. Black males desperately need new ideas to account for the violence (economic, political, and industrial) that turns Black men and boys into corpses. Currently, Black maleness is conceptually confined by its social result—Black Death—rather than life, sociality. These patterns of perception, of collapsing death into the undesirability of thinking about the Black male, sustain the disciplinary disposition toward Black men generally and show little possibility that these people/humans/lives can be thought of in the minds of most as more than the cessation of their existence.

For young Black boys, maleness in a white-supremacist society is fraught with difficulty and the all-too-likely outcome of death. Even when they become men, this racialized masculinity is not thought to result in a recognizable intellectual maturity and social standing of a citizen; rather, the masculinity imposed on these Black male bodies is known only through its uncontrollable excess, its lack of maturation, where any and all transgressions (no matter how small or idiosyncratic) are understood to be demonstrations of the more primitive and uncivilized aspects of a not-yet-evolved savagery. Black males are deprived of ontogeny—they are seen as they will forever be. As Geoffrey Canada, president of the Harlem Children's Zone, remarks concerning Black boys, "The image of the male as strong is mixed with the image of male as violent. Male as virile gets confused with male as promiscuous. Male as adventurous equals male as reckless. Male as intelligent often gets mixed with male as arrogant, racist, and sexist. . . . Boys find themselves pulled and tugged by forces beyond their control as they make the confusing and sometimes perilous trip to manhood."[117] The milieu from which manhood springs is saturated with racist caricatures that all seem to legitimate the fear Americans have of Black men. The images and perception of Black men as dangerous to society, women, and themselves ultimately creates a pattern of thinking that allows the seeming inevitability of death for the young Black male to be justified. If one truly wishes to understand the relationship between anti-Black racism and Black male sexuality, Black manhood cannot continue to be understood by its lack or the extent to which the racism imposed on the lives of Black men and boys simply prevents them from being capable of structurally asserting and emulating the ideal of white male patriarchy. In reality, the effect of anti-Blackness on Black males is epistemic in that it denatures how Black manhood is seen. Anti-Blackness creates a schema of social terror that substitutes the deviancy white males occupy in society, their pathology, as the nature of Black males. A more correct analysis of Black manhood must focus on the vulnerability of the Black male, not the decontextualized assertion that his biological sex equals power, privilege, or a lust for domination. An understanding of racism and chauvinism shows that the oppression of the Black male (his barring from work, his incarceration, and death) is rooted in an imposition of a deadly masculine caricature—a barbarism that justifies multiple genocidal logics and encourages racist misandry, or hatred of Black men, throughout this society and the disciplines birthed from it.

The Black male is not born a patriarchal male. He is raced and sexed peculiarly, configured as barbaric and savage, imagined to be a violent animal, not a human being. His mere existence ignites the Negrophobia taken to be the agreed-on justification for his death. This fear, or cultural intuition, expressed toward Black males calls on this society to support the imposition of death on these bodies and offer consent for the rationalizations the police state presents to the public as its justification for killing the Black beast, the rapist, the criminal, and the thug. The young Black male's death, the death of Black boys, is merely an extension of this logic, the need to destroy the Black beast cub before it matures into full pathology. The Black boy, that child, is seen as the potential to be the Nigger-beast. This anti-Black dynamic that specifically affects the Black boy has been referred to by Elaine Brown as a new kind of racism, a racism built on the anti-Black mythology of America's Black males as super-predators. The super-predator mythology not only acts to legitimize the violence responsible for the deaths of Black males but also inculcates the rationalization that, given what Black males actually are, Black male death is necessary and an indispensable strategy for the safety and security of American society. Overlooking the genocidal disposition of America toward Black males presents an incomplete diagnosis of the impetus behind the levels of violence and sanctions imposed on Black communities (Black women, Black families) in an effort to control the lives of young Black males.[118]

The stigma of criminality plagues Black males throughout their lives and specifically affects their ability to obtain work. This active discrimination confines Black men, those with criminal records as well as those without criminal offenses, to poverty and economic insecurity. Throughout liberal arts disciplines, which tend to prioritize experience and positionality over sociological data and empiricism, it is common practice to point selectively to wage disparity between Black men and women or appeal to the idea of Black male privilege to de-emphasize the consequences of Black male unemployment and disadvantage.[119] In stark contrast to our academic configurations of race, class, and gender, various sociological studies show that Black males are more economically disadvantaged than other groups. This knowledge should inspire scholars to study the conditions and the effects of those conditions on the larger communities to which these Black men belong rather than retreat into identity politics. The exclusion of Black men from the gender category results in a singular analysis that confines all of their disadvantages to racism. Because racism is shared not only by their female counterparts but also by various ethnic and religious groups that have become racialized, Black males' oppression is thought of as a general phenomenon common to all disadvantaged populations. No racialized group is more criminalized, killed by homicide, or isolated from society as Black males. This is readily apparent when one surveys the empirical evidence on mortality, unemployment, incarceration, and education. However, in liberal arts disciplines, such evidence is not enough, as empirical work is disregarded in favor of ideology and rarely has an effect on theory.

The super-predator is a powerful mythologization of Black men and boys wherein violence and the death of this monstrosity is considered the only solution to its existence. More than a decade ago, the noted critical race theorist Angela Harris argued that "gender violence does not produce only female victims; indeed, since most victims of violent crime are male, it may be that more men than women suffer from gender violence. This does not mean that the traditional feminist focus on violence against women is wrong; the gender system operates precisely to disempower women as a class. But this recognition should not obscure the fact that hierarchies of race, class, sexual orientation, and gender itself also mark out groups of men as vulnerable to the violence of other men."[120] Police brutality, the establishing of dominance with force, sexual penetration, and, in some cases, death have defined a specific sexual relationship between the dominant white male group and the powerless Black male group in America. Many police officers reduce Blacks to the status of savages. As with the nineteenth-century edict of the [w]hite Man's Burden, "Police officers in poor urban minority neighborhoods may come to see themselves as law enforcers in a community of savages, as outposts of the law in a jungle."[121]

The gendered racism directed toward Black males is apparent in the disparity in police killings in this country. While no official database records police shootings,[122] several activist groups began compiling and documenting fatal police shootings by race, gender, and age over the past several years. In all reports, Black males are found to be the largest race/sex victims of fatal police shootings. The first public study of police shooting undertaken by Operation Ghetto Storm in 2012 reported 313 Black victims of fatal police encounters; 290 of those killed were Black men, and 23 were Black women.[123] Mapping Police Violence undertook a similar study in 2014 and found 304 fatal police encounters that year; 292 of the victims were Black men, and 12 were Black women.[124] In 2015, the *Washington Post* began a national online database recording fatal police shootings across the United States in real time.

By the end of 2015, the *Washington Post* reported, 248 Black males and 10 Black females had been killed by police in the United States.[125] By the end of 2016, the *Washington Post* reported that 233 Black Americans had been shot and killed by police. Black men were 222 of those killed.[126]

American society not only is generally dangerous for Black men but also uses fatal force to limit the number of Black men in the population and control their political dissent. Police killings specifically target Black males under the language of social welfare to limit the political will this group can exert within the democratic system.[127] In other words, police violence is an extra-juridical activity that is determined to be *necessary* by the law, because these deaths are *necessary* to maintain the white racial interests the law represents to the majority white population of the United States. These killings are legitimate to whites because the police offer the American public evidence of Black male criminality as the rationale for the killings. The American public, secure in its racist-sexual tropes of Black male criminality and danger, consents to the police as executioners-murderers of Black males, because this public is now convinced that the death of Black men and boys is *necessary* for their protection and the security of society. It is this racial consensus among white citizens, American legal institutions, and the police that circumscribes the perilousness of the world Black males inhabit.

In this world, Black males are not men at all; they are sexualized as animal and nonhuman. Black men and boys are thought to be primitives gazing on the white man as *Man*. The white *Man* then coerces the Black (male) savage into accepting his order, in which Black males are made *Not-Man* through violence and death. The primitiveness imposed on the Black male robs him of the potential to ever be innocent. In being defined as savage, he is imagined to be outside civil society. Civilization has escaped him. He is not simply othered but made nonexistent, reconfigured as white masculinity sees fit to justify his subjugation or extermination. He is created by the society and accepted by citizens as a threat to their very existence. He is policed so that order can be maintained. The super-predator myth is simply the outgrowth of this rationalization, a shared justification—one accepted by the society at large—to legitimate his execution and death. This is not simply a racial issue in the sense that it is *only* members of white society who see the Black male as a danger; it is a problem of how poor Black men and boys are defined in this society and how that definition is assimilated and used by all groups and classes distant from the conditions that confine the poor Black male within it.

The criminalization of Black men and boys makes it difficult to believe that they can ever actually be victims of violence. Even childhood cannot protect young Black boys from the genocidal logics of American society. As the psychologist Phillip A. Goff remarks, "Black boys are seen as more culpable for their actions (i.e., less innocent) within a criminal justice context than are their peers of other races." Because Black boys are actually perceived as older and, hence, more culpable for their behavior, there is an implicit dehumanization that "not only predicts racially disparate perceptions of Black boys but also predicts racially disparate police violence toward Black children in real-world settings."[128] Police often imagine the Black boy—a child—to be physically threatening, the manifestation of the savagery thought to be inherent in his Black maleness, a violent beast and predator. The association of Black males with animals—specifically, apes and monkeys—diminishes our sympathy for their humanity; they are caricatures that increase not only the propensity for, but also the acceptance of, greater levels of violence directed toward them. Goff's implicit bias research has explained that the association between the Negro and the ape is not simply an abstract and detached stereotype. Rather, it is a historical trope used to justify the dehumanization of Black people, "a method by which individuals and social groups are targeted for cruelty, social degradation, and state-sanctioned violence."[129] Black male death and dying is the result of this engineered societal program, and the machinations of this apparatus obscure and in many cases deny our ability to see the lives of Black men and boys as worthwhile.

Little B is simply one example of the anti-Black misandry that targets Black men and boys as violent predators. There are verifiably hundreds of thousands more. Even today, the super-predator myth persists, materializing itself in the justification for killing Black men and boys in broad daylight and before the American public. Black males are never victims; rather, they are violence personified. Michael Brown ran through bullets to assault Darren Wilson. Michael Brown was seen only as rage. He was dehumanized before his murder as nothing more than the violent Black male he was thought to be—cast as a superhuman threat to white life.[130] Darren Wilson described himself as a victim of a mythological creature, an overpowering super-predator. He saw himself in a life-and-death battle with an evil entity, and white society legitimized his paranoia as fact.[131] Unlike the assumed psychoanalytic and symbolic references to anti-Blackness that find their way into academic accounts of Black death and anti-Blackness, the death of Black men and boys is concrete and real. It needs no translation, because dead bodies are lying in streets covered with blood and the perceptible declension of Black male flesh. It is obvious, but just as the death of the Black male is material, any accounting for the conditions that make his life an impossibility within the walls of the academy is suspiciously absent. Theory cannot imagine him as he is. His corpse is the spectacle that draws whites into conversation with the Black scholar. Without this white attention, Black scholarship cannot seem to find him, because his life is not a subject that brings disciplinary reward. His death when whites are watching or when the world notices—now, that is a completely different matter, because every Black scholar is an expert on anti-Black death and the dangers the Black male faces. His death remains public and commonly accepted as part of the world. It is seen every day by Black academics, with little reflection in their work or theories. The scholarship of many Black theorists regards the death of the Black male without a thought of sympathy. His death is simply ignored while those who demand his life occupy a central place in our thinking and more fundamentally in our theory are condemned as privileging Black male victims above all others.

The study of Black men and boys must begin with new assumptions about them that appeal to a new audience. The present academic class—Black and white—has internalized the same pathological depictions of poor Black males that the larger society has. This internalization of hatred for lower-class Black men—this racist misandry that links criminality, rape, and domination to a presumed savageness—justifies the disciplinary chauvinism against studying them. In other words, the Black academic class, like the Black middle and upper classes to which they aspire, are able to make a distinction between themselves and Niggers through the physical distance and moral condemnation of the lower Black male group. This condemnation of the heterosexual Black male—the super-predator—allows these classes to find commonality with the larger white infrastructure that supports their labor in the academy.

Conclusion

The sexually specific reality in which Black men find themselves relating to criminality, education, and work shows that the gender category needs to be thought of not as causal but as focal. In other words, instead of thinking of gender as a category that bodies possess that causes unique disadvantages specific to the category, it would be more accurate to think of what is called gender as the peculiar position many groups have that involves their sexual designation and the societal perceptions of such designations that condition the propensity for disadvantage. Theoretical accounts of sexual disadvantage between groups, or what is currently referred to as gender inequities, would more accurately refer to the accumulation of disadvantage and violence around these groups, not the idea that such violence or disadvantage is unique to, or exclusively possessed by, said group. It is empirically true that Black women also suffer from unemployment and job discrimination, but a different bias affects the Black male. This is not a question of denying that both suffer unemployment. It is a question of understanding why Black males seem to be affected differently and disproportionately compared with their female counterparts and a question of why Black females seem to be affected differently and disproportionately compared with other populations. This is the point of study: to understand the world and the reality faced by the groups under investigation.

Because we do not understand the actual, we conceptualize the imagined and remain trapped by the lullaby of Black masculinity as an all-explaining construct instead of letting the evidence before us disclose the complexities of

Black male life. The territories of anti-Blackness, the urban landscape, the feudal geography of the police state—all operate to confine Black men to such poverty and cycles of abuse and death that theorization is desperately needed to account for the violence (economic, political, industrial) that turns Black men and boys into corpses. Black masculinity is conceptually confined by its social result—Black death—rather than life. Black masculinity reduces all Black males to a disposition, an ahistorical character, to demonstrate their power and abuse their contemporaries. So in theory, Black males are simply the less powerful casualties of the violent world they intimately sustain. These patterns of perception, of collapsing death into the undesirability of thinking about the Black male, sustains the disciplinary disposition toward Black men generally and shows little possibility that these people/humans/lives can be thought of as more than the cessation of their existence in most people's minds. How we think of, theorize, Black male death is the primary concern of the next chapter.

Eschatological Dilemmas

*Anti-Black Male Death, Rape, and the Inability to Perceive
Black Males' Sexual Vulnerability under Racism*

A N EERINESS HAUNTS THE GRAMMAR of philosophical discourse on racism
that predicates ethical problems and our moral disposition toward Black
death: necromancy, which is the result of the death imposed on Black
male life, and the Black academic class's Negrophobia, or their fear of being
seen as those Black males marked for death. Necromancy is as much the result
of white racist compulsion—the manifestation of the anti-Black phantasm
lurking within the mind of the academic that vacates Black male life to an
absence upon the impressing of pen to page, which is coterminous with his
impending Black male deaths in society—as it is a problem of thought, whereby the thinking about, the speaking of, Black people as (living) human beings
aspiring toward ends in the world is made impossible by the obsession white
thought has for the Black corpses it creates through rituals of white violence.
To write about Black men's experience of and challenges to racism is to engage
in a reflection that is their anticipation of death. Theorizing about Black males
involves an existential hesitancy that is grateful for not being that Nigger that
is to be killed or doomed. The phronesis of the professor-thinker-theorist cultivates distance from that doomed Blackness that is associated with Niggers.
The writing that emerges from the racist appetency of reason seeks to displace
the realities of Black men and boys in an effort to preserve the illusions of
freedom, democracy, citizenship, and personhood. This thinking, in which the
deaths seen in the mutilated bodies of Black men captured by the state and
murdered by white vigilantes are in the background of our discourse about
racism, insists on the need for Blackness to be reimagined as more social—an
urging that demands the feminization/queering/pluralization of Black subjec-

tivity more generally toward a viable living. Instead of inspiring a focused acuity into the nature of white supremacy, these dead men and boys are, in fact, charged with limiting and obscuring our attempts to "get at racism" and are dismissed as fostering an unproductive nihilism. Because subjects live, aspiring toward futurity, the Black male, who is defined by death and dying, is outside subjectivization and morally condemned as an inappropriate source of theorizing about the world. The persistence of Black male death in society is behind this disregard/disgust toward Black male life, as well as the brutality of ignoring Black males' present plight as a subject of study in the academy.

The suffering of Black men and boys and, ultimately, their physical death breeds fear among Black academics. The fear of being mistaken for those Niggers marked for death motivates them to run away from, not write about, these Black men and boys. This fear is the origin of this disciplinary pathology; the genesis of their Negrophobia is the imperiled existence of Black males in society—a necrophobia. Death conditions how Black people, and especially how Black intellectuals, approach the social reality before them. Death is not simply the finality of some Black lives. Death-murder-violence socializes how Black people think about the very possibility of life—who is fit for it and, by effect, who constrains/overdetermines which subjects are chosen to be the representatives through which Black life is seen, thought, and written about in text. Every belief in a civil, social, democratic society is involved in denying the severity of Black males' suffering because the acceptance of their realities ridicules the conditions and beliefs that one can muster to hope for an improved America. To sustain the normative force of ethics, democracy, and civility, the Black male must be made inconsequential to how theory is formulated. If his condition, both his material circumstances and his death, is regarded as the consequence of Black male obsolescence, then the Black academic becomes culpable for his marginalization and (un)thought-ness. For the theorist, the Black male has no meaning beyond his physical death. His erasure is a problem that is only compounded by his unpopularity as a topic of academic study and ultimately renders his nonbeing without remedy.

Today, Black intellectuals write and assimilate Blackness into the categories of disciplines to escape death—real physical death—and attempt to distance themselves from this death through class mobility and social recognition. The Black academic class is an aspiring middle class able to observe the dying of poor working-class Black folk from a distance. In this sense, Blackness is written out of the academic enterprise generally and forced into conceptual expressions of convergence and canonical imitation, while Black maleness is ignored altogether and erased specifically, thought of only as pathological, the platform from which other gendered discourses form in reaction. In spite of the world before us, where young Black boys—children—are murdered by the state and other white vigilantes for their potential and propensity to become

Black men, academic writing, the research that writing aims to convey, remains categorically indifferent to the contradictions that Black maleness holds in a white-supremacist state that not only denies "manhood" to Black men and boys but also imposes patriarchy on them as seemingly endless and unfettered violence. This patriarchal violence enacted against Black men and boys is not only wielded by white men and women but also actively enforced by the state. To resist the hegemony of these studies, writing about Black males is not enough. There must be a reformulating of the terms describing the (sexual) vulnerability the racialized male endures under patriarchy.

Despite the failure of gender scholars to empirically substantiate the claim that the maleness of Black men and boys confers privilege within a patriarchal society, intersectionality remains committed to asserting that Black male vulnerability is predominately due to race, not sex. While Black men suffer disproportionately more from police violence, incarceration, unemployment, and undereducation than whites and Black women, none of their disadvantage is thought to originate from being both racialized as Black and biologized as male. In this way, gender theory denies Black males the ability to be subjects of study or subjects that offer insights into the sexual racism they experience at the hands of white patriarchy. Liberal arts disciplines and scholars often condemn as patriarchal and disadvantageous to the study of the Black woman any research that focuses on Black male experience. This erasure of the Black male from philosophical and conceptual study is not the result of ignorance or a failure to attend; rather, it is part of a deliberate effort to displace and eliminate our knowledge of the realities that facilitate the death of Black men and the violence against Black boys. This casting away of the Black male is applauded by scholars and rewarded by disciplines, because such disregard maintains the division between disciplinary knowledge and the "problem people" observed—the poor violent Black males understood solely as objects of study who, ultimately, deserve our moral condemnation.

Necromancy: The Crisis of Speaking to the Dead

What does death look like to a Black man? Is it a loving farewell of a life lived well or the regret, the anger he feels for having been allowed to suffer without end from the irremovable Blackness that has stained his flesh? Does a Black man anguish over not being spared from his life, envious of W.E.B. DuBois's first born? DuBois's reflection on the "Passing of the First Born" in *The Souls of Black Folk* offers some insight into the care and affective relationships Black men share with one another through death. While DuBois celebrated the birth of his son, he feared what life meant for a Negro boy. In recounting the moments after his son's birth, he remarks, "In the Land of the Color-line I saw, as it fell across my baby, the shadow of the Veil."[1] Within the Veil, he stood "a

Negro and a Negro's son."[2] A mere ten days after the birth, DuBois saw the Shadow of Death come for his child. The fear of losing his baby, of losing his little boy, was quickly replaced with a small but growing joy. As he says:

> All that day and all that night there sat an awful gladness in my heart,—nay, blame me not if I see the world thus darkly through the Veil,—and my soul whispers ever to me, saying, "Not dead, not dead, but escaped; not bond, but free." No bitter meanness now shall sicken his baby heart till it die a living death, no taunt shall madden his happy boyhood. Fool that I was to think or wish that this little soul should grow choked and deformed within the Veil![3]

Death came to rescue DuBois's young boy. It saved him from a life within the Veil, within the space of deformation of one's self. Death was an escape from the tragedy of living as a Negro boy. There was something terrible to be avoided in experiencing the world that DuBois felt needed to be celebrated. It was his emancipation from a living death.

The repetitive deaths of Black men, accepting their burdens of life, speak to one another with death as the medium of their exchange. Imagine what it means to see this life from the eyes of a Black boy, anxious and afraid of a youthful death—doubtful that he could live long enough to be a Black man? Is it possible even to contemplate these ends, and if Black male life is this death, this capture within nonbeing, constantly confronted with its end, what does it mean, what can it mean, to speak to Black men or write about the Black male, as *living*? How does thought, thinking of Black men, deal with this reality? If he had a choice to live, would DuBois's son choose it? As a Black boy, could he choose life?

The repetitive deaths of Black men are thought to be inconsequential to how we frame the life and study of this ever-expiring subject. The demography of death and dying represented by homicide rates, suicide, incarceration, poverty, unemployment, and the educational status of this group is thought to be irrelevant in comparison to political identity projects within the academy. Black maleness is continually marked by de-emphasis. To cope with the loss of their sociality, Black men memorialized one another's deaths as escapes from the dehumanization of life. The death of the Black male is ignored so that he does not overshadow allegedly more important and deserving subjects. And his corpse—the result of a life gone, a murder that resulted from state violence or societal neglect—is framed as/interpreted as/judged not worthy of note. He is destined to be interpreted by the mother he left, the state he fled, and the world by which he was hated. He is no author. In 1903, DuBois feared that a Black boy's life was condemnation. He knew that the tragedies of life might allow one to exist physically as a living organism but impaled the spirit—the very soul—of the Black male. DuBois writes to his son in death as a proleptic vision of the life he will one day enjoy when he, too, dies and escapes the veil.

Black male scholars who dare to speak about and study Black men and boys as theory-producing subjects, beyond their dead corpses, are despised by the academy. Their insistence on studying material violence, the complex sexual history of brutalization that presents the Black male as a victim of rape and sexual racism, is met with disdain and accusations of essentialism, misogyny, and nationalist ideology. Thus, any study of Black men and boys is relegated solely to the empirical, where their failures and death can be assigned numerical value. The Black male is forced into a repetitive stasis—his death, incarceration, and poverty described as part of the centuries-long problem of Blackness. Described sociologically as the Nigger, himself indistinguishable from the conditions of his wretchedness, he is denied the capacity of being a thinking subject. It is asserted that the Black male has no place in conceptual thought, since starting with the Black male as a thinking subject—as *demanding thought*—runs counter to his place in the background of other subjects' thinking. He is to be problematized and deconstructed but never presented as a subject through which we can or should see the world. In short, the neglect of Black men and boys is asserted to be a moral necessity where the scholar is forced to ignore the horror of conditions surrounding the Black male to think more abstractly about the lives of others. To choose to write on Black males is to accept that you and they are in conversation with death.

What do we make of this problem of how we think? How do we write about, or anticipate the existence of, death-bound entities? Our formulations of ethics, normative values, and presentist accounts all presume that *life* is the basic condition necessary to conceptualize individuals who represent groups or populations as subjects of thought. The philosopher thinks of ethics, how a rational being ought to act, with the utmost faith in the immediate existence of that individual. But what if that individual resists being thought of because he belongs to a particular group? The being of Black men cannot be comprehended accurately in the abstract, because Black men are constrained and excoriated by the categories used to actually *think* of them.

The routine accounts of racism predicated on whites' aversion to Black skin fail to capture the fullness of this generalizable white-supremacist predilection, because the Black male's sexual vulnerability is excised from history. It is not known to most, and even then not as constitutive of the violence the Black male undergoes. Because the Black male is thought to be empowered by his maleness and the nuance and care needed to understand his peculiarity are consequently neglected, the Black male has been the most ignored subject in the attempt to pluralize identities intersectionally. Seemingly, feminists can use intersectionality to study Black and white women and white men in the dawning field of masculinity studies, while Black men and boys fall victim to a moral moratorium insisting that they can be studied only as mimetic subjects always in danger of perpetuating and participating in patri-

archy. Robbed of reflective affect, Black masculinity is reduced to a hegemonic identity, the still imposing relic of Black males' political activism in the
Black Power and Civil Rights movements. This hyper-masculinity is then
read backward, casting every Black male figure in history as the archetype for
the coming Black masculine rage of the 1960s. To date, practically no work
has been done to establish the genealogy of racialized death and sexual violence against Black men as the basis of understanding Black masculinity or
the normative endeavors of the Black male. Current scholarship on Black
males focuses unjustifiably on one frame of inquiry—namely, the problema-
tizing and reformation of Black masculinity toward more feminist ends.
While Black men are said to have "a gender," they are thought to be disadvantaged solely on the basis of their race. Their deaths are argued to be a consequence of racism, not of their maleness, since maleness under the present
intersectional calculus supposedly gives them an advantage over women and
is thought to be an entitlement of the power of patriarchy.

Although white European colonial people gained the power to impose
male domination through genocide and slavery, today Black men, the victims
of the white settlers' genocidal rage, are thought to be partners in patriarchy's
continuing trajectory. This kind of analysis asserts that gender unites all men
through a shared masculinity, without explaining how nonwhite men maintain patriarchal desire to dominate across a society torn apart by race and In-
digeneity and factionalized by class, religion, and sexuality. Patriarchy, a
system of white male domination that uses racism, capitalism, militarism, and
sexual violence to subjugate the multiple others created as degradations of
Western man, has been made possible only through the particular colonial
violence and neocolonial economies of white nations and white supremacism.
While many gender scholars adamantly insist that gender is socially constructed, its substance and meaning filled in by history, culture, and context, contemporary academic accounts of patriarchy rhetorically gesture toward social
constructionism but offer little more than biologism—accounts of patriarchy
that simply assert that all men, regardless of their race and history of victimization within white empire, pose a patriarchal threat due to their biological designation as male.

Gender theorists currently do not hesitate to "epidermalize" the Black male,
chaining his very being to his flawed body, his corpse in death, and morally
condemning him using the racist dogmas of Kantian physiognomy, in which
one's character allegedly can be intuited from the phenotypes of the body. The
Black male is recognized only to be problematized and condemned. He is thereby defined in prolepsis, as the already present pathology of his obsessive mimetic lust to be the white manic, regardless of his actual aversion toward white
supremacy and his inability to acquire the power and consciousness necessary
to reproduce the world as the white father/state/empire. These analyses impose
a stillness of mind on the Black male, a pathological dependence asserting that,

regardless of knowing the origin of his murder at the hands of the white manic, his own Black death ultimately means nothing to him at all.

Black Man's Dying: The Racist Sexualization of the Black Male in America

Sexual violence against Black men and boys has remained a routine, and historically denied, aspect of anti-Black racism. In our everyday lives, Black men are publicly assaulted and exposed to the sexual coercion of the police state. Despite the violence that defines their lives under racism, their stories and these public displays of racism's sexual components remain an unapproachable area of study under our current disciplinary arrangement of knowledge—specifically, the gender category itself. On January 7, 2014, Darrin Manning, a sixteen-year-old Black boy, was castrated by a female police officer who found him suspicious. Manning was a child, a straight-A student; he was searched and patted down, then his testicles were squeezed by this woman of the state so hard that they ruptured with an audible pop.[4] This is not as uncommon as one might think. Young Black males are constantly subjected to sexual assault and coercion in their daily encounters with the state, in the seclusion created on public streets through police interrogation, and under the aegis of now unconstitutional surveillance practices known as "stop and frisk."[5] On August 9, 1997, Abner Louima, a Haitian man, was sexually assaulted by Officer Justin Volpe in a Brooklyn police station. Louima was arrested for allegedly striking Volpe in a crowd. Once transported to the police station, Louima was forced into a bathroom, where Volpe grabbed his testicles, kicked him in the groin, and then anally penetrated him with a bathroom plunger. Showing no remorse—or, rather, showing the sexual etiquette of the police state toward Black men—he paraded the plunger around the station as proof of his conquest.[6]

As Carlyle Van Thompson explains, "Although fully horrific, Abner Louima's experience highlights the construction of racial difference as a threat to white masculinity, to which ritualistic violence has been an extreme response."[7] Van Thompson is clear: "The raping and sexual torture-mutilation of Black men is not a new phenomenon."[8] The violence Louima suffered was not isolated to the specific event created by the specific individual (Volpe). The violence he suffered was an imposition of a white's will on his Black male flesh. For centuries, racism has materialized through racist erotics imposed on Black flesh. The power white society maintains over Black bodies can be recognized in the defenselessness the Black male body shows in the face of the determined racial narratives whites use to defend the murder, rape, and sodomy of Black males for the pleasure of the state and society. Racism is this fungibility, the ease by which the Black male body is able to be disfigured and castrated without resistance—mutilated into the mold of the particular white fantasy. Racism is the condition, the property of the flesh, that makes it possible for Volpe to so easily translate his desire into a reality on the flesh of Abner Louima. Louima is not a man to Volpe; his Black manhood is not male to him, a Man-Not-ness that is easily disregarded. In short, "Although Louima's genitals were left intact after this savage assault, he may never think about his Black body, his sexuality, and his masculinity the same way. Thus, America's white-supremacist culture sucks up the shadows of Black men, leaving them invisible to the dominant society and often to themselves."[9]

The sexual violence against and rape of Black men is not isolated to the most spectacular incidents of our recollection. Black men live under the constant threat of rape and sodomization from police. On August 28, 2004, Coprez Coffie was stopped by Officer Scott Korhonen and Officer Gerald Lodwich. In an effort to find drugs, Korhonen stuck a screwdriver in Coffie's anus.[10] Even when white officers assault other nonwhite people, there is an association with the sexual violence committed by the police with Black men. Angel Perez was raped to make him submit to being an informant. In October 2012, the Chicago police anally penetrated him with a pistol, with one officer yelling, "I hear that a big [B]lack nigger dick feels like a gun up your ass."[11] The sexual violence of the police is not isolated to the act of sodomy. The fear that white men have had of the Black rapist, the mythical beast conjured within the white imagination to justify lynching, also serves as justification for violence against Black men. On September 16, 2013, the white state replied to a 911 call by a white woman fearful of a Black man, Jonathan Ferrell, who was injured and bleeding from a car accident and simply seeking help. The woman's fear led to Ferrell's execution by the white men of the state.[12] Mere contact with the police is an opportunity for Black males to be sexually assaulted. In 2013, Andre Little was hit in the scrotum with a Taser by Officer Kristopher Tong for refusing to move to a different train platform.[13] On December 20, 2015, a thirty-three-year-old Black man named Corey Green was attacked by police. He underwent surgery to restore blood to his testicles after a "cop stomped on his groin with a boot, crushing his scrotum."[14] These are not isolated violations of Black men; we often think of Black males being victims of racism and *only* in the most extreme circumstance being sexually violated. This is, in fact, racism as it affects *all* Black males; sexual violence/rape is the imprint of racism on the flesh of the Black male in America.

My analysis is not meant to convey to the reader that the rape of Black men occurs only at the hands of the state. For many Black men and boys, white vigilantes, everyday white citizens, become their potential rapists or murderers. The death of Trayvon Martin has been discussed by intellectuals, media pundits, criminal justice experts, and social justice activists exclusively as a narrative of race-based violence. While it is nonetheless true that Martin's death has served as a grim reminder of anti-Black violence, there has not been one article, blog, or public conversation dealing with the possibility of

Martin being sexually assaulted by George Zimmerman, despite Rachel Jeantel's announcing to the American public that she told Trayvon Martin that
Zimmerman could have been a pedophile.[15] On January 10, 2013, two young
Black men were strangled by four white assailants in Joliet, Illinois. Two white
women and two white men killed Eric Glover and Terrance Rankin, surfed
on top of their bodies, and then had a threesome on their corpses.[16] This
story received little national coverage and to this day remains untouched by
the literature or problematized as a racist act of sexual violence against Black
men. Even when Black males are raped and killed by white men, as in the case
of the murder of Dione Payne, rape charges are rarely sought against the
white perpetrator.[17] Despite testimony from an eyewitness describing how
Payne was beaten, robbed, and anally penetrated with a rod by Michael Watson, there was no conviction for, or even acknowledgment of, Payne's rape.[18]
Black males, even as children, are denied the capacity to be seen as sexual
victims. Racism, taken only to be the hatred of one's skin color, erases the
sexual vulnerability that Black males historically have endured at the hands
of white men and women. In short, the erotic nature of Black male death is
denied to maintain the stability of our disciplinary categories. Academics,
scholars, and policy makers find comfort in alienating the homoeroticism
and sexual fetishization of Black male flesh. In doing so, racism remains an
accident among civilized societies rather than the barbaric sexual lust whites
have for the anal penetration and castration of the Black male body.

Under our intersectional norms, Black male death is viewed as generic. It
is normal—a routine and repetitive occurrence. Categorically, it is simple: a
base property of "race" denied subjective-gendered-sexual uniqueness. Politically, Black men's and boys' deaths have been morally condemned as heinous
acts of racism but dealt with as little more, rarely thought to need or be worthy
of subjective theoretical explanation. Such disciplinary/intersectional logic(s)
erase(s) the full lives and experiences of these Black men and boys as people
and reduce(s) our understanding of them to their deaths. In the mind of the
Black intellectual, the academy, these Black men and boys represent numbers,
the examples with which to start the conversation, not the loss of a full person,
a productive human. Let me be clear: This erasure that accepts the normalcy
of Black male death simultaneously accepts the racist disposability of Black
male life. Our present theories used to analyze the racial oppression of Black
men, the act of theoretical interpretation, leave Black men to be understood
primarily by their dying and, in consequence, allow their deaths to be weighed
against other political interests or more ideal subjects. Dehumanization finds
its extremity in making the lives of the oppressed inconsequential; it is not
being able to think of the Black male beyond his corpse that is the real result
of racism's dehumanization. Racism "thingifies" Black life, and the reduction
of Black men and boys to the event of their dying leaves the aim of racism—accepting the racially oppressed as not human, nothing lost—unquestioned.

Making the suffering of Black men and boys a second thought—weighing it as less valuable because it is so common, saying, "Maybe he should not have died, but . . ."—is not a statement affirming the lives of Black males. The deaths of Black men and the lack of a category, or the empathy, to understand the fullness of their suffering in a racist society empower others to interpret their lives for them, which has the effect of lessening them in death. Because Black men die, and because Black men are decentered as the normative subject of thinking, there is a collective forgetting that collapses our understanding of them to their corpses and not their life's activity. We do not know what these Black men "were," or what these boys wanted to "be." We confine them to "our example of racism," or "yet another one."

The killing of Black males has always involved an erotic obsession with their Black flesh. It stimulates the lust of whites, their appetite for scarred and lifeless Black male flesh. The reality unfolding outside the academy, in the actual world, where Black men and boys are being executed has shown no regard toward the intersectional morality of the university or the gender reductionism of disciplines that continue to excise the experiences and deny the horrors inflicted on Black men and boys for the sake of theory. This is why the actual deaths of Black men and boys shown to us publicly are found consistently to exceed the categorical limits imposed on Black masculinity through the category of "race" and denied under the category of gender. The categorical abstractions of race, class, and gender used to analyze (and, most worryingly, decide what is perceived or able to be interpreted concerning) Black masculinity deny the sexual motivation behind racist violence against Black males. Even worse, these categories mythologize an a priori theory of gender rooted in the relationship of (white) maleness to (white) femaleness and assert through analogy that any asymmetry between Black males and females is ontological. What follows from this asserted calculus is that Black men are benefactors of a sociologically established privilege given to them through their maleness by a historically (white) patriarchy. Through moralization, Black masculinity is de-emphasized, found guilty of some conceptual offense, even when the observer is tasked with examining the fleeting lives and seemingly inevitable deaths of Black men. Current gender theory demands that the observer impose erroneous historical mythologies to justify the hierarchy between the male and the female demanded by theory. This forces scholars, students, and the public to offer superficial analyses of Black male death, because our current theories are capable of only narrow racial accounts of the vulnerability from which Black men and boys suffer; our theories deny that anti-Blackness involves racist erotics that peculiarly affect Black male bodies, consequently triggering the murderous predilection of whites.

The Black male is thought to be a shadow of sorts, a transmutable horror formed in the mirage of the onlooker's most dreadful thoughts. This nightmarish creature that we call the Black man is found throughout the Western world. Legend asserts that the Black male transforms into the worst fears of his onlookers upon their recognition of him; he is known as death-rape-murder to all but himself. James Baldwin once said, "To be an American Negro male is also to be a kind of walking phallic symbol: which means that one pays, in one's own personality, for the sexual insecurity of others."[19] To be Black and male, then, is to have one's social genesis, the body through which one is recognized, rooted in caricature, its transfiguration as a phobic entity— a living *sciaphobia*. The white man's fear of Black men does not impede his excitement or the stiffening of his penis in his murderous encounters with Black men and boys. The body is the site of understanding the *being* and *intent* of the thing in Western epistemology. The primacy of sight, the focus on the visual entity, has been the basis of Western thought since Immanuel Kant's racial geography and use of physiognomy to perceive the interiority of man from exterior facial and phenotypical features.[20] Under these (racial) deductions, the recognition of racial and sexual difference demands that an intent be assigned to the body perceived by the white observer. In the case of Black men, these logics create phobias to rationalize the killing and use of those bodies. Under this somatic epistemology, recognition is as prevalent as phobia in the knowing of others, especially racialized male others.

Baldwin's Analysis of [w]hite Men's Homoerotic Lust for Black Men's Death

The phobic obsession white men have for the castrated corpse of the Black male body is illustrated to great effect in James Baldwin's "Going to Meet the Man." The opening lines of Baldwin's short story transport the reader into the bedroom of Jesse, an impotent sheriff, frustrated by his inability to "fuck" his white wife. Baldwin intentionally shows the reader the intimacy between a white man and a white woman to demonstrate how the Black male is the sexual aspiration of whites; they want to fuck like him, or be fucked by him. The Black phallus sexually arouses them. The white man wants to possess it, while the white woman yearns to be penetrated by it. Despite Jesse's best efforts, he is not able to obtain an erection through his fantasies about women. He stroked his wife's breast; he did not respond. He thought of sex with a Nigger girl, the ones he would pick up or arrest, and while "the image of a [B]lack girl caused a distant excitement," his loins longed for something stronger: more erotic, more sexual to ignite his libido.[21]

Jesse then began to think of Niggers. How dangerous they were. Even a Black girl you were fucking could kill you, despite "making believe you made her feel so good." Jesse thought Niggers were ugly, and smelled. He hoped to "never again feel that filthy, kinky, greasy hair under his hand."[22] He hated them. "They were animals, they were no better than animals, what could be done with people like that? Here they had been in a civilized country for years and they still lived like animals. Their houses were dark . . . the smell was enough to make you puke your guts out, and they sat, a whole tribe, pumping out kids, it looked like, every damn five minutes." Jesse's racism took him to a particular scenario where Blacks were surrounding the courthouse to register to vote. The leader of the protest was captured and Jesse's friend; "Big Jim C. and some of the boys really had to whip that nigger's ass today."[23] Because the Black protesters would not disperse, they were targeted for violence. They took the ringleader to the cell, he was bleeding from his ears, a sign of his truculence. They prodded this man, even in his testicles. The amount of violence his body withstood led Jesse to conclude, "This ain't no nigger[;] this is a god-damn bull." As the Black man's body laid almost lifeless on the cold floor of the cell, Jesse remembers he had met this man as a boy. As a boy, he addressed Jesse as "white man," and told him that he would respect his grandmother, Mrs. Julia Blossom. The boy told the white man he would no longer call his grandmother Old Julia. This resistance from a Nigger angered Jesse. He wanted to "pistol whip him until the boy's head burst open like a melon." The singing of Blacks outside the jailhouse protesting the violence of the white police on the Black man overtook Jesse. "He felt an icy fear rise in him and raised him up, and he shouted, he howled, 'You lucky we pump some white blood into you every once in a while—your women.'" This horror, the anger and disgust he felt towards the Nigger made him have another reaction. His fear drained him; "he was abruptly, almost too weak to stand; to his bewilderment, his horror, beneath his own fingers, he felt himself violently stiffen—with no warning at all."[24]

Baldwin draws the reader to the unacknowledged sexual attraction the white man has to violence against Black men. To some Baldwin's story seems merely fiction, but he captures the desire, structurally concealed but present, that inspires white men to want Black men dead. While our accounts of violence in the academy range from marginalization to silencing, sexual violence has been reserved only for the imagining we have of rape. Baldwin suggests this is much too limiting. The white man learns of himself through the death of the Nigger. Just as puberty is the biological development of his sexual capacity, so too does it open his mind to sexual fantasies—one of which is the murder of the Black male-beast and the possession of his big Black cock. Jesse lusts for the sight of the bleeding, almost dead Black male body; it is pornographic, produced by his own hand. His creation. Killing Black men gives white men power to create their fantasies in the world.

Jesse remembers this horrific arousal—the stiffening of his penis from the sight of an almost dead Nigger. He remembers it because he felt it for the first time when his father took him to his first lynching. Jesse remembers that the white mob was in awe of the naked Nigger hanging from the erected foundation: "There was no hair left on the nigger's privates."[25] He remembers the sexual arousal of the crowd—specifically, the arousal he saw in his mother: "He watched his mother's face. Her eyes were very bright, her mouth was open: she was more beautiful than he had ever seen her, and more strange."[26] He, like his mother, was mesmerized by the sight of the suffering, bleeding, naked, hanging Black man. To him, the "gleaming body [was] the most beautiful and terrible object he had ever seen till then." There was an allure to killing and castrating a Nigger that Jesse understood even as a young boy. A friend of his father held the knife that inevitably would be used to castrate the lynched Black man: "Jesse wished that he had been that man." The man with the knife walked up to the hanging Black man; he "took the nigger's privates in his hand, one hand, . . . as if he were weighing them." Even as a boy, Jesse eroticized the Black phallus. Jesse describes the Black man's penis and testes as though they were to be found only in his personal fantasies. To him, "the nigger's privates seemed as remote as meat being weighed on scales; but heavier, too, much heavier." This realization made young Jesse's scrotum tighten. Jesse could think only of its size: it was "huge, huge, much bigger than his father's, flaccid, hairless [penis], the largest thing he had ever seen till then, and the [B]lackest." The white man with the knife, his father's friend, "stretched them, cradled them, caressed them." This was the moment the crowd had gathered to witness. The knife flashed, "first up, then down, cutting the dreadful thing away." The lynched man was now castrated; "The blood came roaring down." The white mob attacked the now dickless and dying Black man; they tore at his body with "their hands, with knives, with rocks, with stones, howling and cursing."[27] Jesse's recollection comes to a close as he takes his father's hand, walking away from the charred body: "The head was caved in, one eye was torn out, one ear was hanging." What was once a Black man was now just a [B]lack charred object, lying "spread-eagled with a wound between what had been his legs."[28]

Jesse feels something rise within him; his libido returned as he "thought of the boy in the cell; . . . the man in the fire; he thought of the knife and grabbed himself and stroked himself and a terrible sound, something between a high laugh and a howl, came out of him." He grabbed his wife, whispering to her, "Come on, sugar, I'm going to do you like a nigger, just like a nigger, come on, sugar, and love me just like you'd love a nigger."[29] Through castration, the white man takes possession of the Black phallus; he dominates the Black man and the mythological power of the Nigger dick. He is able to fuck his wife; he is a man, because his whiteness (civilized, reason, order) can temper the Nigger's (savage) sexual potency. His manhood is thereby defined in overcoming the bestiality he imagines to be symbolized by the Black phallus.

David Marriott understands Baldwin's "Going to Meet the Man" similarly. As an origin story of white masculinity—the generational inheritance of white patriarchy through the castration of the Black male—Marriott observes:

Fucking his (now) nigger-loving wife, savouring the inheritance of that paternal secret, Jesse knows that what he had witnessed was a gift from his father. That gift, the desire and power to castrate—to take and so to take on—the sexuality of [B]lack men, brings them together and forges their futures as white men. Disconcertingly, what sustains Jesse (and his wife) "as he labored and she moaned" are the correspondences between that gift and the terrible, gaping wound.[30]

Marriott makes apparent that Jesse's necrophilia, his sexually murderous lust, "thrives on imitating derogatory images of [B]lack men as either dangerously oversexed and/or emasculated or dead."[31] The white boy is made a man through the destruction of the Black male body, his conquering of the Black male beast. He is made the white man through his castration of the Black man and through the use of the Black phallus as his own. As with Eldridge Cleaver's description of the Omnipotent Administrator, it is the immateriality of the white man—his a-physicality—that creates the drive to dominate and embody the hyper-physicality of the Nigger. This is why he wants to "fuck like a Nigger," to sexually satiate his white wife. As a white man, he is enabled by reason to fuck a white woman like a Nigger—to satisfy what she craves—without raping her. Murder, the death of the Black male body, is the ritual of transference for white men. As with the charred body left in the wake of his first lynching, Jesse believes that he can embody—through castration—the sexual potency of the Black male. This embodiment allows him to overcome his sexual lack, the hereditary inadequacy and flaccidity of his father's white penis. The white man who murders the Black man attempts to be MAN, since he has shown the superiority of being the white mind over the Black male body. Killing Black men is an attempt to reduce the number of Black phalluses that can cause white men anxiety and worry. The death of Black men arrests the yearning white men have for their flesh and phallus. They remove the penis to signify their domination of the Black male body—thus making him a lifeless corpse and not man.

Baldwin's elucidation of the multiple levels of sexual desire and objectification that motivate the murder of, and the pleasure obtained from murdering, Black men destabilizes the very idea of a shared maleness with white men that can be thought of as a history of patriarchy. Baldwin describes white masculinity as dependent on the castration and death of Black men and boys. This speciation between racial males and white men disrupts the unified narratives of privilege and masculinity by differentiating the histories of Black males, their reactions to the sexual violence they survived, from those of white men. Baldwin's insight is restated, and slightly updated to address the intersectional paradigms of our current era, in Darren Hutchinson's work in post-intersectionality. Hutchinson rejects the idea that maleness, or male privilege, can be ascertained through the gender component of intersectional analysis. Such categorical delineations based on gender are untenable be-cause there are "heterosexual stereotypes that inform the 'sexualized racism' endured by all people of color."[32] Under racialized systems of oppression, gen-der was not categorical, but situational. Black males were deemed rapists and killed with this stereotype serving as the justification. Black women did not suffer under such a label because they were, in fact, women and for much of history deemed incapable of rape. Hutchinson points out to intersectional theorists that their categorical accounts of race and gender are far too simplis-tic to actually capture the multiple dynamics and histories involved in Black maleness:

> Lynching, for example, was frequently justified through a racist, sexu-alized rhetoric that constructed [B]lack males as heterosexual threats to white women. Thus, heterosexual status, typically a privileged cat-egory, has served as a source of racial subjugation. This history com-plicates the apparent stability of privileged and subordinate categories; the meanings of these identity categories are, instead, contextual and shifting.[33]

Like Baldwin, Hutchinson understands that all racism is erotic and sexual, which means that there is no one body or history to which gender can solely refer within an intersectional matrix. To simply ignore or decentralize the sexual racism suffered by Black males, to contort their realities into maleness or patriarchy so that the intersectional critique seems urgent, simply contin-ues the sacrifice of Black male life to caricature for political and disciplinary convenience. History simply resists such reductionism, given the actual op-pression and sexual violence that Black males suffer.

When a Black boy is raped, his rape is exceptionally confounding because rape is thought to be the province of the female body and thought not to be possible, much less actual, when related to the male body generally and to the Black male body specifically. Rape is never thought to be a desire inspired by the Black male body. His hyper-masculinity, his savageness, is thought to make the rape of the Black male brute an impossibility. As discussed in Chap-ter 3, the Black male can only *be*—and is only thought to be—the rapist. But exceptionality is not a comment on the oppression of the Black male; it is only a commentary concerning how other interpreters, who are not Black males, see and think about the Black male body. If violence matters, if erasure mat-ters, if the accuracy of understanding the lives of Black men is the aim of study, then we must concede that we are not liberating people in reality when we deny aspects of life that do not align with academic theories. Not assigning gender or sexuality to Black men does not mean they do not suffer from sexual violence; what this refusal to "see" shows is that there are external, disciplinary problems of knowledge that refuse to acknowledge the violence in their lives in pursuit of other, less liberating interests. Erasing the sexual violence against Black men is not only a political blindness; it also has its origins in the categorical arrangement of knowledge that makes sexual violence and rape the province of female vulnerability, not that of males. Black women were raped during slavery, so the sexual order of race and gender even today is thought of as an extension of these antebellum logics. Black men, however, are denied such an account of their racial and sexual vulnerability, even though they are raped, castrated, and anally penetrated according to the same logics. Denying the rape of Black men, their sexual assault at the hands of white men and women, is a product of the heterosexual framing of slavery, a denial that asserts that white men were the rapists and Black women were their only victims. This denial began in our imposing of the categorical arrangements of gender, which fixates on the feminine and neglects the power of anti-Blackness to denature the assumed hierarchies between men and women. Being white allowed white men and women to sexually assault and define Black masculinity in America. The sexual attraction to and sexual abuse of Black men and boys, this unimaginable violence, emerged from a collapsing of gender itself, because the rape of Black men and boys was in excess of the sexuality of the day. It had to remain hidden to protect white manhood and allow white womanhood to remain immaculate. This, however, is a historical problem.

On Thomas Foster's "The Sexual Abuse of Black Men under American Slavery": Engaging Saidiya Hartman's *Scenes of Subjection* on the Basis of the Raping of Black Men during Slavery

Whereas the institution of American slavery is often offered as the origin of the Black female's sexual exploitation, the origin of Black male's oppression during slavery is confined to race. Despite the various examples of (homo) eroticism at play in the murder and rape of Black men in our society, the sexual subjugation and rape of Black males during slavery is denied as a horror that they suffered. Adrienne Davis asserts that "slavery's political economy forced enslaved women to labor in a second way that was not required of any other group. . . . [E]nslaved women, and only enslaved women, were forced to perform sexual and reproductive labor to satisfy the economic, political, and personal interests of white men of the elite class."[34] Even Joy James, who correctly notes that "gender analyses expand critical depictions of the neo-slave narrative and the historic role of Black Americans as commodities or racial text for (white) consumers and activists," considers gender within slavery as the domain of only women: "Considering gender, one sees that racial-sexual violence marks [B]lack women's bodies as spectacle."[35] As with the paradigm first commented on in Angela Davis's *Women, Race and Class*, gender and its subsequent vulnerabilities are assumed to be the province of the female body. Davis understood that "the slave system discouraged male supremacy in Black men . . . [because] the promotion of male supremacy among slaves might have prompted a dangerous rupture in the chain of command." But she fails to extend this account into Black males' sexual vulnerability to white men and women. In other words, the account of slavery offered by Davis conceptualizes Black men as vulnerable to racial violence because of their lack of power within slavery to resist it, but her account does not imagine this same vulnerability to sexual violence within slavery because they are male. There is nothing about the male body she finds particularly or sexually vulnerable to the desires of whites. The Black female body, however, is thought to be perpetually vulnerable to sexual violence. Davis writes, "As females, slave women were inherently vulnerable to all forms of sexual coercion. If the most violent punishments of men consisted in floggings and mutilations, women were flogged and mutilated, as well as raped." For Davis, rape is a technology specific to the female body, the "uncamouflaged expression of the slaveholder's economic mastery and overseer's control over Black women as workers."[36] Male bodies are assumed to be immune from sexual assault and rape at the analytic level, since the category of gender implies that rape is female-specific.

The problem with these accounts of slavery is that they assume slavery, an institution that denatured and distorted the very concept of the human, nonetheless preserved and cherished humanist categories such as race, gender, or worker as useful designations applicable to enslaved Black bodies. Enslaved Blacks were animals that possessed none of the intersectional categories of our day in any meaningful way, especially insofar as one could assert that these categories, if they did apply, could remain ordered on our present notions of heteronormativity.[37] Slavery did not denature the human but leave the precious category of gender untouched. Over the past several decades, Robert Aldrich's *Colonialism and Homosexuality* and Ronald Hyam's *Empire and Sexuality: The British Experience* have shown that homosexuality and the sexual exploitation of "savage males" were well established and extensive under British colonialism. Unfortunately, such knowledge has done little to challenge the heteronormative mythology that makes enslaved women the sole victims of rape, even though America was a British colony when American chattel slavery was instituted.[38] Given the work of historians and literary scholars, it is now known that the rape of Black males by white men and white women during slavery was commonplace. These discoveries, however, have not led to a reorienting of Black feminist historiography or of gender thinking more generally.

What does Frederick Douglass ask the reader to understand when he confronts Edward Covey, the Nigger-breaker, in his narrative? Is his fight with Covey a battle of recognition, or is it Douglass's refusal to be physically and sexually subjugated as a slave? The rush of Covey to strip Douglass naked, the

tiger-like fierceness of tearing his clothes, Covey's wearing out of his switches
on Douglass's body, the eagerness that Covey displays in this first whipping
after telling Douglass to strip naked—what does this mean to our imagination, when our thinking is turned to the sexual violence of an enslaved man?[39]
For years, thinkers have pointed to the sexual implications and homoeroticism present within the conditions of slavery.[40] In reality, the rape of enslaved
men, just like the rape of enslaved women, was used as a routinely present
technology of racial domination.[41] Over the past several years, a multitude of
scholars have sought to characterize the violence of slavery as persisting beyond the legal epochs of racial change throughout America's history. These
scholars, collectively referred to in the literature as Afro-pessimists, argue that
slavery continues to modernize itself as a condition coextensive with Blackness.[42] One of the central features of "wretchedness" and the libidinal vulnerability of Blackness is the sexual violence of rape married to the condition of
enslavement. But enslavement, the unimaginable condition of nonbeing from
which innumerable cruelties on Black bodies grew, is largely a stage of fantasy when used as the foundation of our reconstruction of anti-Blackness.

The ever-growing distance we have from enslavement produces idealizations of this period of history, idealizations demanded to conform to our
predetermined categories of subjectivity. Despite the incoherence involved in
how "the slave" is thought of from within the boundaries of the twenty-first
century, this moment—its cruelty, barbarism, and ontology—is thought to
mirror the categories of subjectivity used to describe our present. Race, class,
and gender are manipulated as if they are the building blocks, the pages of
every story ever created about Black people. Instead of seeing our inquiry into
slavery as a critical mode of presenting our present conceptualization of the
world with categorical rupture(s) and bewilderment, this history, this fading
past, is demanded to be unambiguous and presentable as parallel to our current reality. In this world, gender is assumed to be fixated on one subject—or,
as Greg Thomas argues:

> Histories of gender and slavery focus overwhelming on women, as if
> gender and women are coextensive and men have no gender. This
> observation points to a problem with the conceptualization of sex and
> gender across academic disciplines. For if there is a structural neglect
> of manhood in studies of gender, and if womanhood is misunder-
> stood to be synonymous with gender itself, then this approach signi-
> fies an extension rather than an analysis of gender ideology, which
> traditionally inscribes women as being gendered and men as being
> generic and beyond gender.[43]

Our considerations of what suffering "belongs" to whom obscures rather than
clarifies our attempts to understand the varieties of violence by which Black

bodies have been brutalized throughout history. Our romantic obsession with categorical caricatures blinds us to the ubiquity of anti-Blackness and the extremes of white supremacy.

In Saidiya Hartman's *Scenes of Subjection*, however, the ubiquity of rape during slavery is narrowed to a prerequisite body: that of the Black female. Hartman argues that the brutality, the libidinal economy of slavery is, at its apex—or, more accurately, at its most extreme degree—exercised on the female slave body because of rape.[44] Jared Sexton's "People-of-Color-Blindness: Notes on the Afterlife of Slavery" is an attempt to correct Achille Mbembe's (mis)reading of Hartman in "Necropolitics."[45] According to Sexton, "Mbembe abandons too quickly this meditation on the peculiar institution in pursuit of the proper focus of his theoretical project: the formation of colonial sovereignty." For Sexton, Mbembe overlooks the historical rise of "colonial rule" already established in the legal and political structure of slavery—specifically, "the legal and political status of the captive female that is paradigmatic for the (re)production of enslavement," in which "the normativity of sexual violence . . . establishes an inextricable link between racial formation and sexual subjection." Sexton then offers a normative analysis of the Black female slave that explains "why for Hartman resistance is figured through the [B]lack female's sexual self-defense."[46] Sexton reads Hartman's analysis of slavery as a commentary on the extremity of asymmetrical colonial power; thus, he argues that Mbembe's concern over the terror formation of colonial rule is most accurately expressed by the gendered dimensions of slavery—the libidinal economy of sexual violence, or rape—where gender is the "designation of the absoluteness of power."[47]

While Hartman's work is innovative, offering an analysis that guards against viewing the violence of slavery as "spectacle," it, along with Sexton's reading of it, reifies the idea that rape and sexual assault are the province of enslaved womanhood and uniquely tied to gender:

> Gender, if at all appropriate in this scenario, must be understood as indissociable from violence, the vicious refiguration of rape as mutual and shared desire, the wanton exploitation of the captive body tacitly sanctioned as a legitimate use of property, the disavowal of injury, and the absolute possession of the body and its "issue." In short, [B]lack and female difference is registered by virtue of the extremity of power operating on captive bodies and licensed within the scope of the humane and the tolerable.[48]

Here Hartman asks too much of the gender claim: She insists on the historical coherence of the category, despite its fracturing under the weight of racism, so that it may yield *her* subject. Blackness extended forward, or enslavement in this epoch, was/is the condition of myriad types of violence that remain without boundaries and limited only by the force applied to the body. In many cases, even the death of the slave did not arrest the horrors inflicted on the Black corpse. While Hartman is fruitful in pointing out the routine violence in enslavement—the living of death, so to speak—she attempts to persuade the reader of the horror of slavery through the allure of making the ahistorical moral claim that rape is a weapon against the womanhood-gender of the enslaved female. Hartman asks the reader to judge rape within the parameters of our contemporary moral sentiments of this sexualized violence. She asks us not only to affirm our contemporary sensibilities but also to morally assert the recognition of the enslaved woman's gender as a means by which we problematize allegedly overdetermined racial histories that fail to differentiate the unique violence, the forcible penetration, thought to be possible only because she is, in fact, Black and female. This account of sexuality, the heteronormative thrust, is not imaginative. It exists as a re-collective analogy—an anachronistic projection into the past—that casts the terror and immorality of our present-day thinking about rape backward on the enslaved Black female body. It is this status of gendered, violated woman with which "we" endow her that makes rape and the subsequent violations of the enslaved conceptually possible. In short, we are able to theorize rape and violence during slavery only through the schema made possible by *our* values, which are privileged in this revision.

Historically, rape during slavery was not bound by sexual designation. While Hartman insists that "sexuality formed the nexus in which [B]lack, female, and chattel were inextricably bound and acted to intensify the constraints of slave status by subjecting the body to another order of violations and whims,"[49] history shows that Black "males" were also sexually abused, and the bodies of these men and boys were sodomized throughout the diaspora. James Sweet presents accounts of enslaved men submitting to rape out of fear of death throughout the eighteenth century. For example, he offers the story of "a Mina slave named Luís da Costa, [who] confessed that one day while he and his master were out in the woods, his master forced him to submit to anal sex." His master, Manuel Alvares Cabral, was known to have sodomized six of his former male slaves in 1739.[50] Sweet also notes:

> Perhaps the most violent sexual assaults of slaves occurred in Pará in the late 1750s and early 1760s. Francisco Serrão de Castro, heir to a large sugar *engenho*, was denounced for sodomy and rape by no less than nineteen male slaves, all Africans. Among those who were assaulted were teenage boys and married men. As a result of these sexual attacks, a number of the victims suffered from "swelling and . . . bleeding from their anuses." Francisco Serrão de Castro apparently infected his slaves with a venereal disease that eventually took more than a quarter of his victims to their graves.[51]

Although Hartman correctly points out that "the nonexistence of rape as a category of injury pointed not to the violence of the law but to the enslaved woman as a guilty accomplice and seducer,"[52] she simultaneously ignores that "the violence and coercion that characterized the rape of male slaves were symptoms of a broader pattern of violence aimed at forcing male slaves to submit to their masters' power."[53] No reason or justification was put forth to warrant the sexual assault of the Black male slave; his rape was the totality of violence, the natural extremity of the violence of the day. The rape of the Black male slave had no socially recognized justification; it was an act of white barbarism that did not pretend to maintain the moral superiority of the master. It was simply the complete brutality and the animalistic sexual domination of a Black (male) body throughout.[54] Whereas the Black female body was objectified to endure—to reproduce and be a sexual thing for the repetitive enjoyment of white men—the Black male body offered no reproductive benefit to white men and was sexually objectified to satisfy the sadistic cravings of white men and women. The Black male was not meant to survive the sexual encounter beyond the white man's infatuation, since doing so would be proof of the white man's homosexuality to himself and to a public that viewed homosexuality as a violation of the Puritanical ethos of his day, or beyond the white woman's infatuation, since he offered proof of her infidelity and sexual promiscuity.

Hartman's text, like the other Black feminist historiographies, continues to advance an understanding of rape during slavery as a kind of sexual violence specific to the Black female body. This understanding of rape holds that it is only the practice of rape against Black women and girls that defines the act. In other words, Black female bodies are raped, while Black male bodies are not and, more important, cannot be raped. Consequently, because rape is manifested as heterosexual violence of white males against Black females, the subjective position of the Black female who is raped is taken to be the objective condition constituting rape itself. Such a conflation is not surprising, given that rape historically has been understood as "the carnal knowledge of a woman without her consent, obtained by force, threats, or fraud"; however, such societal and cultural practices do not, in fact, justify determining rape to be only, or predominately, of the heterosexual variety.[55] Stated differently, while it is true that our current cultural and societal norms understand rape as heterosexual violence against women, it does not hold true that this heteronormative sexual arrangement was the organizing principle of sexual violence during slavery—or in the present. Hartman asks readers to believe not only that slavery was a heterosexual institution in which only heterosexual white men imported and owned slaves but also that rape was designed specifically to torture the enslaved female. How can scholars and gender theorists reconcile that enslaved African people who were denied recognition as humans and defined as animals were nonetheless given recognition as gendered, where they were spared certain violence(s) because of an obligation to their manhood or womanhood? Enslaved Blacks were denied manhood and womanhood; they were defined as beasts of burden whose bodies were used at the discretion of whites. Violence against the enslaved took no gendered form. It was unbridled violence against Black bodies where rape was enacted against both sexes.

Vincent Woodard shows the danger of erasing the violence and distortion of Black male bodies during slavery for the heteronormative myths that currently sustain our dominant gender frames. Instead of focusing on the erotic binary of heterosexuality and homosexuality, Woodard conducts a study of homoeroticism—"the same-sex arousal . . . and attention to those political, social, and libidinal forces that shape desire and, ultimately, the homosexual act" in American slave culture.[56] Woodard believes that the obsession whites had with classifying enslaved Blacks as animal-like or child-like demonstrated "indexes of desire—of white people's fixations on and obsessions with [B]lack bodies and sex."[57] Woodard focuses on the consumptive culture cultivated within American slavery:

> Within the culture of consumption, there existed numerous examples of homoerotic affection between [B]lack and white men, sexualized violence, and incest bonds, among other phenomena. Yet such affections were often veiled or hidden within rhetorics of objectification and abjection. For white men, sex with and sexual attraction to [B]lack men was a natural by-product of their physical, emotional, and spiritual hunger for the same.[58]

Whereas Hartman focuses specifically on the sex act to differentiate the gendered or female-specific reality of enslaved women, Woodard focuses on the various aspects of consumption and sex that result not only in the rape of Black men but also in the homoerotic rituals of cannibalism and torture inflicted on Black male bodies. Black male resistance was punished through consumption as well as rape. For example, Nat Turner was literally ingested by whites for daring to challenge the slave system. According to Woodard, "After Turner was captured, he was hung, skinned, and bled and his body was boiled down to grease."[59] For some time afterward, whites in the region consumed his flesh in the form of an elixir appropriately called "Nat's Grease."[60] Largely rooted in the assumption that whites remained a civilized race despite the practices of slavery, and were therefore ineligible for the primitive practices of cannibalism, the consumption of Black males remains a denied practice of American slavery.

Cannibalism (consumption) and the homoerotic dimensions of slavery were not separate practices. "The need to annihilate the threat of one's terror" almost necessitates consumption. *Within* some whites, the need to consume

Black male bodies led to the abjection, the expulsion of the desire. In these whites, this tendency "generated the opposite effect, leading whites to rape, pillage, behead, and castrate [B]lacks."[61] This is not to understate the effect of the need to consume the bodies and flesh of Black males. The popularized history of slavery suggests that the abjection, the murder, the casting away of Blackness was the dominant strategy of white supremacy; it is important to conceptualize the eating of Black males as just as true and actual as the larger historical narrative. The racist sexualization (craving) of Black men is fundamental to grasping the actual horror—the truth found in the fiction—of American slavery. Woodard understood that

> tasting and ingesting Turner in this context of retribution and erotic violation would have represented for white men the ultimate erotic and satiating act. Rather than projecting their desire—through the violation of [B]lack bodies, communities, and homes—white men could, through the oral ingestion of Turner, experience at first hand a taste of the terror, fascination, hatred, and death wish that they felt toward the [B]lack liberator.[62]

Woodard's vision of slavery as a homoerotic institution destabilizes the dominant heteronormative gender accounts that de-emphasize attempts to show how various erotics functioned within empire and colonial institutions distinct from female embodiment. The present-day focus on the penile penetration of the vagina excludes not only accounts of anal penetration but also the various practices of sexual and erotic domination that determined the fates and constituted the trauma experienced by enslaved men as victims of rape.

These distortions occupy a central place in Thomas Foster's intervention into the sexual historiography of slavery. In "The Sexual Abuse of Black Men under American Slavery," Foster explodes the intuitive deployment of gender as synonymous with female that Hartman makes use of in *Scenes of Subjection*. Foster maintains that "the sexual assault of enslaved [B]lack men was a component of slavery and took place in a wide variety of contexts and in a wide range of forms. . . . In addition to the direct physical abuse of men that happened under slavery, this sexual exploitation constituted a type of psychological abuse that was ubiquitous."[63] Foster offers the reader a violent historical incident of rape. In 1787, an enslaved man in Maryland was forced at gunpoint by two white men to rape Elizabeth Amwood. While we have an image and moral set of values that easily map onto the violations that offended and lessened the humanity of Amwood, we lack certain ascriptions of moral violation to the enslaved Black man in this scenario. Foster claims this "lack of explanation" is to be expected, as "the rape of Elizabeth Amwood reveals that [B]lack manhood under slavery was also violated in other ways that are less easily spoken of (then and now), namely, the sexual exploitation of enslaved men."[64]

In alerting us to our *inability to speak or think about* the sexual coercion of Black men (making an enslaved man have sex), our tacit dismissal of the claim and its significance depends on the racist assumptions about predatory Black men who desire to rape or the sexual insatiability of the Black male who always craves sex. Ironically, the abhorrence of the idea that an enslaved Black men wanted to be raped—made to penetrate a woman—would be immediately apparent to the reader if the subject in question was an enslaved Black woman. Our moral sensibilities urge us not to be complicit in believing that the Black female slave, like the Black female of today, could enjoy her own rape, but for the Black male, the idea that he could enjoy being forced to have sex with a woman at gunpoint crosses the reader's mind, if only for a moment. There is a foreignness in our sympathies toward enslaved Black males. Hartman points this out repeatedly in her analysis of how seduction was used by white men to imagine the rape of the enslaved Black female as pleasurable to her, but our viewing of the enslaved Black male suffering from the sexual mythologies of his virility lacks the same perceptiveness. There are simply no conceptual tools available to understand the violence that occurs to enslaved Black men who are made to rape for the sexual enjoyment of white men. Can we be so secure in our beliefs about his desires, his wants, and his enjoyment to exclude him from being a victim of rape and coercion, as well? Does our disciplinary training, the dominant modes of studying race, class, and gender, offer any assuredness of rigorously understanding the enslaved Black male—a body racialized as both rapist and raped?

During slavery, the sexual coercion of Black men and boys was conditioned by white (sexual) desire for Black bodies and white (Puritanical) repulsion toward Blackness/sex itself. Nowhere is this as poignant as in the case of white women raping enslaved Black men. The call to undertake serious study of white women's brutality against enslaved Black women was first made in Sabine Broeck's "Property: [w]hite Gender and Slavery," but few have pursued this line of inquiry regarding Black males.[65] Foster argues that "the traditional denial of white women's sexual agency has contributed to our obscured view of those white women who sexually assaulted and exploited enslaved men."[66] The dominant narrative of slavery makes white men the heterosexual culprits of sexual assault against Black women; however, little to no literature considers the rape of enslaved men and boys by white women. Within the present heteronormative account of rape during slavery, the white woman is erased; she is made into an inactive bystander. In reality, white women were active participants in the rape and sexual abuse of Black men and boys; as Foster notes, "All white women could coerce enslaved [B]lack men given the legal and social setting in which they lived." The rape of enslaved Black men was not about physical strength:

> Women who may have been physically smaller and weaker than their victims [still] wielded a powerful threat. Wives and daughters of

planters who formed these sexual relationships were simply taking advantage of their position within the slave system. Having sex with their white counterparts in the insular world of the white planter class, if exposed, would certainly have risked opprobrium, and even gossip about their public actions might have marred their reputations. Daughters of planters could use enslaved men in domestic settings, however, and retain their virtue and maintain the appearance of passionlessness and virginity while seeking sexual experimentation. In other words, one of the ways that some southern women may have protected their public virtue was by clandestine relations with [B]lack men.[67]

The coercive force white women wielded over Black males during slavery is considered in Harriet Jacobs's *Incidents in the Life of a Slave Girl*. Commenting on the predatory logic of white planters' daughters, Jacobs writes, "They know that the women slaves are subject to their father's authority in all things; and in some cases they exercise the same authority over the men slaves."[68] Jacobs recounts that she saw "the master of such a household whose head was bowed down in shame; for it was known in the neighborhood that his daughter had selected one of the meanest slaves on his plantation to be the father of his first grandchild."[69] His daughter deliberately targeted the most abused and broken enslaved Black male. As Jacobs writes, "She did not make her advances to her equals, nor even to her father's more intelligent servants. She selected the most brutalized, over whom her authority could be exercised with less fear of exposure."[70] It is often suggested that white women were too weak—too feminine—to overpower the Black male brute, but such responses deny the vulnerability enslaved males faced within slavery and in its aftermath. The ever-looming threat of death as punishment for offending the social order empowered white women to act and coerce Black males as they pleased.

Under the cloak of white femininity woven by her actions and claims of vulnerability throughout history, the white woman raped the Black male. The historicity of the white woman exceeds what is traditionally thought of as her confinement to womanhood—that she is a rapist; that she reduced him to his phallus and executed him as her rapist when her transgressions were discovered; that she used her confinement to virtue as the guise for her violence against Black men and boys; that she raped them for pleasure and to satisfy her need for power over the Black male; and that her conquering of the "Mandingo," the undifferentiated (phallic) flesh of the enslaved male, excited her and created the mystique of womanhood—all of this is unknown. This rape of Black males by white women is denied by theory, since theory, founded on the anthropology of the white/European/Western man, aims to protect the innocence of the white women from the horrors her presence has committed within history. The mystique of the feminine is defined by her unimaginable sexual past, the deniability of a sexuality that could spoil her virtue. Instead of exposing this deployment of power, sex, and racial violence, contemporary feminism, even Black feminism, has allowed rape to be understood primarily as heteronormative violence that originates from the male and is perpetrated against the female. Because it is founded on the mythology of white gender relations, this ahistorical account allows women as a notion to remain inculpable for the activity of rape. Although the rhetoric of intersectionality claims to perceive the intersection and overlap of race, class, and gender, gender remains categorically superior and overdetermined by a heteronormative mythology that places the male above the female. This calculus holds manhood to be impervious to female sexuality, incapable of being victim to any violence from women, thereby making white women's rape of Black men impossible. Mythology/theory is different from history, and the question before scholars, and before Black men writ large, is this: How does this history of white women raping Black men and boys reconfigure and destabilize the history of rape, the category of gender that makes such analysis possible, and the arrangement of knowledge that, as Sexton and Hartman have maintained, reveals our subject of postcolonial resistance: the Black female? Does gender theory itself mean that white women are not capable of being rapists? If we admit this sexual power of the white woman, how would it not only complicate the homoeroticism operating in the history of white men raping Black male bodies under slavery but also reconfigure the heteronormative myths that currently make seeing the white woman as a rapist of Black men and boys impossible?

Some authors have argued that gender itself—the category of gender as synonymous with the woman—is the problem. Greg Thomas argues that gender is an obstacle to understanding the full reach and extent of rape as a dominating act of enslavement:

> It is almost impossible to locate a text of slavery which does not construe rape as the bottom line factor that differentiates the experience of slavery along lines of sex, or gender. Allegedly, the female can be violated, and the male cannot. This assumption is unacceptable, if not absurd, because it perversely requires heterosexuality to recognize exploitation and abuse. Not only is sexual violence reduced to whatever qualifies as rape, narrowly construed, but rape is also reduced to penile penetrations of female bodies, perhaps not even those unless they result in pregnancy and offspring.[71]

Why, then, does Hartman choose the body of the Black female slave as the sign of rape? One may not configure sexual violence on the "male" or recognize the Black male slave as gendered, but this recognition does not dispute the historical facts that sexual violence and rape did occur. According to Foster, "The rape of slave men has also gone unacknowledged because of the current and historical tendency to define rape along gendered lines, making both victims and perpetrators reluctant to discuss male rape. The sexual assault of men dangerously points out cracks in the marble base of patriarchy that asserts men as penetrators in opposition to the penetrable, whether homosexuals, children, or adult women."[72] To say that we do not see, or recognize, the violence occurring to this body lacking "gender" is not to say that sexual violence or rape did not actually occur; it is simply to recognize alongside the historical record that the category of gender, as deployed by Hartman, obstructs rather than clarifies the actual relations of sexual violence and Black male bodies by asserting an ahistorical claim as axiomatic rather than actual.

Conclusion

The death of Black men and boys exceeds their representation as simply the dead bodies shown by the media. In our conceptual schema, Black men and boys are little more than the background of our thinking about American racism. Even in death, the Black male is not vulnerable. He is refused center stage. He is negated, reduced to mere numbers argued as taking attention away from more pressing and progressive bodies and identities. While their lives are perpetually extinguished by police, white vigilantes, and the pathology of urban poverty, there is an academic market subsidizing articles and conferences that deny acknowledging Black men and boys as the primary victims of this violence. They have no worth in the actual world, which is demonstrated by their disposability within society, but are found worthy of negation in death. Academic theory demands our disregard of Black male death; it is claimed that the murder of Black males occupies far too much of our thinking. This demand to push theory beyond attending to Black men and boys is thought not only to be progressive but also the only moral outcome. Although they are the greatest victims of violence in America, Black males are condemned for their vulnerability. They are dehumanized first by their actual dying, since it is their "thingification" that spares them regard, and second by the ability of theorists not to "see" them as more than the death that imposes itself on them by making them corpses. The Black male corpse, as the next chapter shows, is thought to be inevitable—the death of the superpredator. But as theorists, we must look beyond the quotidian toward the quintessential. The body of the Black male must become a site of exploration, an investigation conducted not from the standpoint of his suffering but through his existence. The history of Black male death, rape, and lynching is a lens from which to view the actuality of disciplinary categories. It is the test of their veracity—most specifically, that of gender.

If we look beyond the corpse, we notice any number of insidious violence(s) and erotics exerting themselves. The imperative of this conceptual reorientation is to see that the effect of anti-Black racism, what craves Black male death, is not simply hatred but an erotic, a yearning. This not only complicates our understanding of racism as it is; it also demands a reconsideration of the libidinal and sexual drives responsible for activating the phobic responses of white men and women toward Black males. Why does theory "not see" the sexual vulnerability of the Black male? What is it about the Black phallus—its historical vulnerability to excision—that cultivates indifference or, worse yet, an expected apathy? Because Black male death is made generic, non-gendered, it is thought to be ontologically irrelevant. Because it is encapsulated within the category of race and understood as the violence to which all raced bodies are subjected, Black male death fails to designate a specificity within our present theoretical/disciplinary order. The violence Black male bodies experience is thought to be summarized within the intersectional modes of the Black and the female, the Black and the transgendered, the Black and the queer/quare subject. Thus, the histories that show the transfiguration of maleness, in which Black men have been made to be the female or the queer body through the force of white lust, remain completely ignored. Our understanding of the origins of Black male death in white libidinal lust and power as well as Black male death's various manifestations throughout history require a jettisoning on the end of white violence—the charred, castrated corpse or the young dead Black male body. Scholars must identify the motivation that oscillates between the Negrophobic and necrophilic rage of whites to accurately capture the reality of Black males in this country.

In the Fiat of Dreams

*The Delusional Allure of Hope and
the Reality of Anti-Black (Male) Death that
Demands Our Theorization of the Anti-ethical*

But say to a people: "The one virtue is to be white," and the people
rush to the inevitable conclusion, "Kill the 'nigger'!"[1]

O N JUNE 16, 1944, George Stinney Jr., a fourteen-year-old Black boy, was
executed for the murder of two white girls: eleven-year-old Betty June
Binnicker and seven-year-old Mary Emma Thames.[2] Stinney was tried
and convicted of murder with intent to rape. On March 24, 1944, Betty June
and Mary Emma told their families they were going to pick flowers and
would be back in thirty minutes. They rode off together on a single bicycle.
On their way to pick flowers, they passed the Stinney house. George was
playing with his sister Katherine. Betty June said to Katherine, "We're looking for maypops[;] do you know where they are?"[3] Katherine replied, "No,"
and the two girls went on their way. When the two girls did not return to
their families later than night, a townwide search commenced. Their bodies
were found in a shallow ditch the following morning with severe head trauma: "Mary Emma's head was fractured in five different places and the back
of Betty June's skull was smashed." It was said that George and Katherine
Stinney were the last people to see these little white girls alive. George was
immediately thought to be the killer. Katherine recalled, "All I remember is
the people coming to our house and taking my brother. . . . [N]o police officers with hats or anything—these were men in suits or whatever that came."
George was taken to the sheriff's office, where he was interrogated. He was
afforded no counsel or even the comfort of his parents. Within an hour,

Deputy H. S. Newman had announced that the fourteen-year-old boy had confessed to the murders. Newman maintained that George wanted to have sex with Betty June and realized that he had to kill Mary Emma in order to do so.[4] George was to stand trial for the murder of two white girls, a murder allegedly motivated by his will to rape. On April 24, 1944, more than a thousand people packed into the Claredon County Courthouse. It took the all-white jury only ten minutes to convict Stinney of murder and sentence him to death in the electric chair.

A Black boy who weighed not even a hundred pounds and stood under five feet tall was made into a murderous rapist. The young George Stinney Jr. was "so slight that the guards had difficulty strapping him into the chair and attaching the electrodes to his legs." During his execution the mask placed over his face slipped off, "revealing his wide-open, tearful eyes and saliva coming out of his mouth."[5] This young Black boy was the youngest person sentenced to death in the twentieth century. His execution is a stark reminder for those bodies born Black and male that innocence and guilt have little to do with what one actually is. It is the consensus others make about Black men and boys that determines what they are. On December 17, 2014, Stinney's conviction was vacated by a writ of coram nobis, "not on the grounds that the judgment against him was wrong on the merits, but [on the grounds] that the courts have failed in a capital case to discharge their proper functions with due regard to the constitutional safeguards in the administration of justice."[6] The Charleston School of Law and the Stinney family are still fighting the state to declare George Stinney innocent of the crimes of which he was accused and for which he was executed in 1944.[7] As Ed Bell, president of the Charleston School of Law, says, "Some of the things that were presented in court to prove his guilt were later totally debunked. . . . [S]ome of the evidence used is totally false and fabricated and the real evidence to prove someone else did it is there and was available."[8]

It took seventy years to overturn the conviction of a Black boy that was reached in ten minutes, and even then he was not declared innocent of the crimes of which he was accused. The fight for his innocence is still being waged. Can Black men ever be innocent of that which they are accused? Despite the improbability of the crime, the nation was convinced that a Black male child—not an adult but a boy—was both a rapist and a killer. Is this simply the meaning, the definition, of Black maleness? Is it the existential confinement to guilt, of being robbed of innocence, of any sort of character or moral competence, a positional void filled with the negativity (fear, anxiety, and hatred) of others who perceive the Black male body? In a world that denies that Black males are human beings, he became a monster. He needed no provocation; he and other Black males are assumed to be guilty of that which they are accused, regardless of their actual actions.

Guilty and Never Proved Innocent: The Characterological
Deficit of Black Maleness

How many times do we have to observe the phenomenon of Black men and boys be falsely accused of transgressions or crimes before it becomes part of our analytic sensibilities? The murder of George Stinney Jr. was not some relic of Jim Crow–era racism. The motivating disposition toward Stinney remains active even in our own time. It is a very real operating ontology that conveys the meaning of the relationship between Black and male. Stinney's execution, like the unbridled executions and convictions of thousands upon thousands of Black males in America since the nineteenth century, shows that Black males suffer from a specific characterological oppression in which they are thought to lack any capacity for innocence. Even in the twenty-first century, Black males are known to the world as savages, affixed within the American schema as the negation of all that is good, ordered, and civilized. The Black male is nocuous, robbed of any possible character that would make him unlikely to use violence against others. His very nature is thought to be malicious and contrary to civility, so he exists as the physical manifestation of evil—bestial—where any violence imaginable becomes a possible action or atrocity that a Black male would commit.

When Charles Stuart decided to murder his wife and unborn child on October 23, 1989, in Boston, he was presumed innocent because he and his wife were thought to have been shot by a Black man.[9] When Susan Smith killed her two sons on October 24, 1994, by drowning them in a lake, she simply accused a Black man of kidnapping them.[10] The world, just as in the Stuart case, believed that the murderous intent of a Black male was more probable than the murderous actions of whites. Black males—specifically, heterosexual Black males—exist, then, as the depository of others' negativity, the scapegoats for all social and ethical ills in America.

It would be grossly inaccurate to assert that the scapegoating of Black males is prefigured on only the presumed threat that Black men pose to white men as the criminal and to white women as the rapist. The vulnerability of Black males far exceeds the presumed heteronormative racial frames of current theory. The case of James Bain is instructive in this regard. In 1974, Bain, a nineteen-year-old Black boy, was convicted of raping and kidnapping a nine-year-old boy. Bain spent thirty-five years in jail, despite an alibi and blood tests that indicated he did not commit the crime.[11] The strength of the sexual myths surrounding Black males makes any and all crimes, especially sexual violence, likely in the minds of Americans. Black males are deprived of any acknowledged characterological self or societal personality projected and thereby recognized as moral and humane. Consequently, Black males are (socially) constituted by the accusations waged against them. This phenomenon is not only interracial but also intraracial and societal. For example, in

2002 Wanetta Gibson, a Black teenage girl, claimed that fifteen-year-old Brian Banks raped her at Long Beach Polytechnic High School. Gibson's mother then sued the school district for endangering her daughter and reached a $1.5 million settlement.[12] Years later, Wanetta Gibson confessed that Banks had never raped her and that he was simply the most convenient scapegoat for a teenage girl fearful that her mother would find out she was sexually active.[13] But this occurred after Banks had spent five years in jail, ultimately losing his opportunity to play college football and his chance to play for the National Football League. His innocence was denied because he was a Black male. The world believed he was guilty of rape because the world fundamentally believes Black men, more likely than not, are rapists.

Such claims are far from anecdotal. Earlier this year, the Federal Bureau of Investigation admitted that forensic errors in hair analysis for more than two decades before 2000 could have led to hundreds of false convictions in murder and rape cases.[14] False convictions for rape and murder disproportionately affect Black males. Among those freed by post-conviction DNA testing for rape and murder, "many more exonerees were minorities (71%) than is typical even among average populations of rape and murder convicts."[15] Samuel Gross, a lawyer deeply involved with the Innocence Project, has consistently shown that while Black men make up less than one-third of convicted rapists, they represent more than 60 percent of those exonerated. Perhaps the most terrifying fact is that there are "far more false convictions than exonerations. That should come as no surprise. The essential fact about false convictions is that they are generally invisible: if we could spot them, they'd never happen in the first place."[16] What could innocence even mean for Black males in such a world if it flees when confronted by mere accusations? Even when Black men and boys are innocent, the criminal justice systems and juries that convict them ultimately believe they are deviant and more likely than not to be criminals.

Faith's Misgivings: The Pessimistic Foundation of Black Male Realities

For many philosophers and social-political theorists, the eventuation of an egalitarian humanist society is the teleological impetus, the inevitable consequence, of embracing liberalism and integrationist theories of democracy. While these proclamations have been made by Black thinkers for centuries as the promulgations of America's democratic potential, the Black victims of America's fetish for racism, those who are forced to endure the failure of white theory to arrest the racist tyranny, have their deaths, their murders, their deprivation interpreted as caricatures. Their deaths, images of their dead bodies, show the brutality of oppression, which is taken to be academic capital used to drive philosophical engagements with and theorizations about race within the liberal white public. In this illusory world, Black citizens are aspirations—

thought experiments created from one's desire to motivate political theories beyond the excoriation many have toward Blackness. To establish commonality with (white) others, hope is made the end of political theorization, even if it results in political delusion or the complete mischaracterization of the actual world. Black scholars become voyeurs in this regard, gazing forward, hoping that the world will cease to be what it is and transform into a place that recognizes their distance from Blackness and, by effect, their humanity. But what of this world can Black men and boys actually grasp onto?

We often contend that the obstacles to this more perfect world are merely a matter of stereotype, where erroneous generalizations about Black males are applied to particular Black male individuals. This is, however, a gross simplification of the reality under which Black men and boys suffer. The problem confronting Black men and boys is not one of application. The problem— which results in Black male death—is one of definition, in which the nature of Black men is thought to be synonymous with the negativity imposed on them. In a society consumed by its hatred for Black men, there is no resistance to the negation of the Black male's humanity. He possesses no character that stands apart from the imposition of the ideas others thrust on him. Black men and boys are literally perceived as the dangers and fears that others project on them. Unbelievably, this general anxiety felt toward the Black male is suggested to be at the core of his being. Regardless of whether these fears are simply imagined, not at all actual, they operate as the cognitive marker of his perceptibility. Fear distinguishes the Black male body from other, less terrifying bodies. Consequently, the Black male is known by the potential he has to be a rapist, a murderer, or a thief.

The Black male stands alone in his surety of self. He defines himself for himself against a world that condemns him for being. The existential import of this choice cannot be disregarded, since it is the basis of his social self and his attempts to resist the imposition of society. This social self, this humanity, is denied as possible within the larger society. The at-large consensus of others has predetermined his fate, so to speak, making him an outcast even among other Blacks. They are all marked men. Sometimes this is acknowledged with the slightest (head) nod, but it is known and shared among them. He is killed for what he is taken to be in this world, and the struggle with this reality exacts a cost on his mental and physical self. He lives against the will society has for his death. He invents concepts that sustain him. His anger toward the world generates a place of construction where music, writing, and his very being are positioned against the order of society that continues to breed oppression and empire. This aspect of Black male existence is deliberately missed by theory. Instead of condemning the negative mythology surrounding Black males and attempting to dig further into their actual thinking and activity in the world, academic theory revels in the stereotypes and antisocial caricatures concerning them.

For race and gender theorists, the suffering and death of the Black male are not condemned as deprivations of his humanity—his very life—but weighed against other identity politics and often interpreted as a distraction from other subjects. This routinely leads to the decentering of the death of Black men and boys. The Black male's oppression indicates a fundamental indifference the world has toward Black life, a position Black elites and progressives also embrace to gain the recognition and reward of liberal white publics and institutions. At the end of the day, the reality Black men and boys face is ultimately incompatible with the hope—the *faith*—one has for democratic civility and social-class mobility within society.

Racial Misandry and the Subordinate Male Target Hypothesis

It is often difficult to see Black males as vulnerable because of their maleness. Despite works by authors such as Calvin Hernton, David Marriott, and James Baldwin that describe the racism against Black men as a function of their sexual vulnerability to women and other men in a white-supremacist society, our present gender order understands claims of Black male vulnerability to be more akin to a masculinist apologetic than a signifier that directs one to the historical conditions that continue to endanger the lives of Black men and boys. This aversion to Black men that conditions their vulnerability to others is best understood as a particular type of misandry. The education theorist William A. Smith has similarly observed:

> Black misandry is an exaggerated pathological aversion toward Black males that is created and reinforced in societal, institutional, and individual ideologies, practices, and behaviors including scholarly ontologies (or understandings of how things exist), axiologies (or values such as ethics, aesthetics, religion, and spirituality), and epistemologies (or ways of knowing). Like Black misogyny, or aversion toward Black women, Black misandry exists to justify and reproduce the subordination and oppression of Black males while concomitantly erecting edifices of racial and gender inequality.[17]

Racist, or racial, misandry then describes the specificity racism acquires when it is directed toward Black men and boys. Whereas Black male vulnerability expresses the actual disadvantage and violence Black males suffer as both Black and male, racist misandry expresses the vulnerability Black men and boys have to the obsessive hatred society directs toward them. In this sense, racial misandry not only expresses the pathological aversion society holds toward Black males but also names the ontological program that is constantly operating to socialize the public into believing that, given the savage nature of Black men and boys, the various cruelties and stereotypes used to dehumanize them are accurate. Even within the academy, misandry functions to make the sociological condition of Black men and boys synonymous with their being, thereby making it necessary to morally condemn and sanction them to preserve civility and order in society. In other words, the Black male is theorized as deserving and necessitating the repressive forces set against him.

Before James B. Stewart and Joseph W. Scott argued that Black males are the victims of processes that lead to their "temporary and permanent removal . . . from the civilian population through the operation of labor market mechanisms, the educational system, the health care delivery system, the public assistance complex, the subliminal institution of crime and vice, the penal correction system, and the military,"[18] there was very little effort to theorize Black male disadvantage as a function of a *specific maleness* that is vulnerable and targeted by the white patriarchal regime of America. Social dominance theorists, however, have remained fascinated by this phenomenon in patriarchal capitalist societies in which subordinated males seem to be the consistent target of most egregious forms of violence and death. Jim Sidinias and Felicia Pratto argue in *Social Dominance: An Intergroup Theory of Social Hierarchy and Oppression* that modern capitalist societies organize around three primary social-stratification systems: age systems in which adults govern children; gender systems in which males tend to have disproportionate power and status over females; and arbitrary-set systems, which are "socially constructed and highly salient groups based on characteristics such as . . . ethnicity . . . , race, caste, social class, . . . any other socially relevant group distinction that the human imagination is capable of constructing." In these societies, age and gender tend toward fixity because of their biological designations but have some degree of malleability, while arbitrary-set systems are marked by an "unusually high degree of arbitrariness, plasticity, flexibility, and situational and contextual sensitivity in determining which group distinctions are socially salient."[19] Sidinias and Pratto claim that the foundational nature of age and gender stratifications make them "no strangers to very brutal forms of social control,"[20] but it is those defined by their position within socially constructed arbitrary sets who experience the most brutal forms of direct violence, especially when these arbitrary sets are defined by ethnic or racial differences. Whereas age and gender groups designate power within the dominant or superior group, arbitrary-set systems construct the characteristics of the other.

Defined by these arbitrary sets within a patriarchal society, Black men (outgroup males) invoke peculiar psychological responses and perceptions of formidability in white men (ingroup males).[21] When white men see Black men, these Black males are perceived as larger in size and strength in the minds of white men, regardless of their actual physical attributes. Even fictional male figures evoked through racialized names evoke feelings of aggression, fear, and danger in whites. Colin Holbrook, a psychologist looking at racial stereotypes and Black formidability in whites, "consistently found that fictional Black or Hispanic men are envisioned to be physically larger, higher in aggression, and lower in status" than white or Asian males.[22] As one co-author of the study explains:

> Not only did participants envision the characters with [B]lack-sound-ing names as larger, even though the actual average height of [B]lack and white men in the United States is the same, but the researchers also found that size and status were linked in opposite ways depending on the assumed race of the characters. The larger the participants imag-ined the characters with "[B]lack"-sounding names, the lower they en-visioned their financial success, social influence and respect in their community. Conversely, the larger they pictured those with "white"-sounding names, the greater they envisioned their status. . . . In essence, the brain's representational system has a toggle switch, such that size can be used to represent either threat or status. However, apparently because stereotypes of [B]lack men as dangerous are deeply entrenched, it is very difficult for our participants to flip this switch when thinking about [B]lack men. For study participants evaluating [B]lack protago-nists, dangerous equals big and big equals dangerous, period.[23]

Black men are represented fantastically by whites despite their actual physical constitution or social prestige. These perceptions of Black males are a matter not of simply identifying errant stereotypes but of identifying how stereo-types translate into meanings and actions by the whites who perceive Black male bodies. Imagining a Black or Latino male, or hearing a Black or Latino name, can trigger whites' survival instincts. Black men are thought to be for-midable foes to whites, and this position has both physical and social costs. Because racialized men are conceptualized as having lower status than more prestigious, ingroup white males, "it should be acknowledged that prestigious individuals are also inherently capable of inflicting costs on others by virtue of their rank. . . . [R]espected persons can typically damage others' reputa-tions merely by expressing criticism publicly. In this sense, elements of dom-inance are retained in prestige-oriented status, as captured in relatively encompassing constructs of status such as 'power.'"[24] As such, racialized (out-group) maleness has a character that is fundamentally different from that of dominant (ingroup) white men and women.

Racial arbitrary sets actually invert the gender relations of the patriarchal society and generate "the counterintuitive prediction that minority men, not minority women, should be expected to be the primary targets of racial and ethnic prejudice and discrimination."[25] Racialized men, or the subordinate male target, have been shown to experience the most extreme forms of violence and discrimination in patriarchal societies throughout the world. In Western societies in particular, racialized men face harsher discrimination in housing, retail, employment, criminal justice, and education than their racialized female counterparts.[26] This difference is not simply happenstance, since social dominance theorists have shown that the treatment of subordinate males (arbitrary-set distinctions) is common throughout white patriarchal regimes. Contrary to feminist accounts that locate women as the primary targets of aggression in patriarchal societies, this theory, appropriately named the subordinate male target hypothesis, maintains that "discrimination against both dominant and subordinate women is not primarily driven by the desire to harm, destroy, or debilitate them, but to control them. On the other hand, discrimination against outgroup males appears to have a distinctly aggressive and debilitative character."[27] Stated differently, while it is certainly the case that women will be discriminated against and repressed within patriarchal societies to maintain social hierarchies, because they are seen as threats and competition for various resources, racialized subordinated males are marked for extermination.

Traditionally, feminist accounts do not describe women in the dominant group as holding social roles that aim to preserve patriarchal structures through racist acts specifically tied to their femininity. While white males are bioculturally situated as patriarchal and racist, white females are not thought to have the same biocultural dispositions. As initially conceptualized by sex role theory, women, because they were oppressed by patriarchy, were thought to be set against the system as a whole. Social dominance theory, however, suggests that women of the dominant racial class define themselves as vulnerable to outgroup men while simultaneously being more powerful and influential than the lower racialized male group. Consistent with the mythology of the Black male rapist, social dominance theory suggests that, "because women are considered a highly valued resource among men, they are not targeted as members of outgroups for harm or debilitation, but are instead often incorporated into the winning group."[28] Instead of assuming that women of the dominant class are affected by simple ignorance or false consciousness, social dominance theorists assert that women of the dominant group have developed specific sex roles within patriarchal societies that establish superiority over outgroup males: "Whereas prejudice held by men may be driven by aggression against and dominance over men belonging to arbitrary-set groups other than one's own (outgroups), women's prejudice is more likely to be characterized by wariness or fearfulness of such men."[29] As such, women of the dominant group act as triggers, so to speak, of dominant male aggression. These women have specific gender prejudices against subordinate male groups that reify the position of the dominant males. In other words, women of the dominant racial stratification have racist conceptualizations of and motivations against outgroup males that are specific to their gender position. Social dominance theorists understand that arbitrary sets speciate members of society so much so that nothing is shared between outgroup subordinate racial males and the members of the dominant racial group. Racist/racial misandry, then, is the attempt to identify the psychologically and socially induced behaviors and frames that target Black men and boys as subordinate (death-bound) males in American society.

The intersectional responses to subordinate male target theory have continued to assert the superiority of their categorical structures of race, class, and gender as the basis of interpreting other models. In other words, intersectional approaches have continued to define other competing theories and evidence only within their rubrics of singularly disadvantaged and multiply disadvantaged group identities. So while one may show that the categories necessary for intersectional calculi are inaccurate because Black maleness, for example, can also include histories of rape, sexual violence, and disproportionate death and incarceration, a heterosexual Black male is still defined as a single subordinate group within intersectionality because maleness is considered, analytically, to represent privilege.

One justification for maintaining this delineation is offered by Valerie Purdie-Hughes and Richard P. Eibach in the form of intersectional invisibility. By *intersectional invisibility*, Purdie-Hughes and Eibach mean "the general failure to fully recognize people with intersecting identities as members of their constituent groups. Intersectional invisibility also refers to the distortion of the intersectional persons' characteristics in order to fit them into frameworks defined by prototypes of constituent identity groups."[30] Instead of comparing the disadvantage of singularly and multiply subordinated groups, intersectional invisibility asserts that "the forms of oppression that people with intersecting disadvantaged identities experience differ from the forms of oppression that people with a single disadvantaged identity experience."[31]

Intersectional invisibility claims to maintain that the primary struggle of multiple subordinate groups is for recognition, where members of these groups "struggle to have their voices heard and, when heard, understood."[32] But the authors themselves admit that historical, cultural, legal, and political invisibility is rooted not in the sociological disadvantages these groups have to one other, as in social dominance theory, but in the theoretical difference intersectional accounts hold of androcentrism. They maintain that this subordinate male target theory

> naturalizes androcentrism. The oppression of subordinate group men is the product of psychological dispositions that evolved as males competed for resources in the human ancestral environment. By contrast, our model views the oppression of subordinate group men as a reflection of the general tendency in an androcentric society to view all men—both those of dominant groups and those of subordinate groups—as more important than women. It is this marginalization of women in an androcentric society that causes subordinate women to be relatively ignored as direct targets of oppression compared to subordinate men.[33]

It is important to examine the assumptions of this claim. While social dominance theorists assert that the subordinate male target fundamentally differs in kind and social position from the patriarch in patriarchal societies, intersectional theorists prefer to conceptualize subordinate male targets as belonging to the dominant androcentric category because they are male. Differences between male bodies are established only through predetermined categories such as sexuality and class under intersectionality, not through the group's actual subordinate position to other males. Under intersectional invisibility theory, androcentrism is a property allowed to stand in for all maleness. As such, it functions as an analytic formulation whereby the sexual designation of male (the category) is synonymous with androcentrism (the cultural, historical, and sociological superiority of men over women) despite the observable disadvantage that subordinate male groups have to women in the society. The claim that subordinate males are defined as not male, *Man-Nots*, within patriarchal societies is overlooked by Purdie-Hughes and Eibach so they can continue to assert that the possession of a body sexed as male is equivalent to possessing male power. This is an essentialist assertion based on a somatological epistemology thought to articulate a particular history and picture of a social structure that need not actually exist. In reality, the subordinate male's station in patriarchal societies has very little in common with that of dominant males, but conceptually a relationship is established between dominant group males and subordinate males because of their sexual designation rather than their actual condition in a given society or historical context. Such conceptual schemas do not tell us about the disadvantage groups have in relation to one another; instead, these theories tell us that we should predetermine that the defect of maleness is its cost to our perception of femaleness. This theory insists: No matter how great the violence against subordinate males actually is, these males are privileged because they are targeted for the maleness they share with the dominant racial group.

This perspective is undoubtedly related to Purdie-Hughes and Eibach's criticism of the subordinate male target hypothesis as being too dependent on establishing universal empirical claims based on active oppression of subordinate male groups across multiple societies. This empirical focus on subordinated males is androcentric, according to Purdie-Hughes and Eibach, meaning that it makes "male experiences" the standard of oppression, even when comparisons between subordinated males and females show that males experience harsher discrimination, violence, and daily offenses. The authors then conclude that the position of invisibility, even though it protects subordinate women from direct oppression, is a more disadvantaged position because it exists as a sphere of less worth—feminine—within patriarchy, or androcentricity. Purdie-Hughes and Eibach offer this explanation: "From the perspective of intersectional invisibility, subordinate men will more often be the victims of active forms of oppression directed at their groups because of their greater prototypicality compared to subordinate women."[34] Ultimately, intersectional invisibility maintains that while femininity makes women safer than racialized men in patriarchal societies, the deaths of racialized men are less a measure of oppression than of the invisibility of the marginalized groups less targeted by lethal violence.

Intersectional invisibility holds a contradictory view of violence under patriarchy that suggests this: While violence against women in patriarchal societies is evidence of their lower status and domination under patriarchy, the greater levels of violence against racialized men in the same society are not evidence of their dehumanization, but their privilege as men. If one discovers that a subordinate group of men is more disadvantaged generally or in a specific area when compared with a subordinate group of women, does intersectional invisibility demand that the scholar interpret those findings as the result of male superiority rather than subordinate male inferiority? Instead of providing conceptual clarity, intersectional invisibility seems to be dedicated to interpreting the death and disadvantage of subordinate males as a function of male privilege rather than of their actual vulnerability or disadvantage. If the interpretive schema of study (highlighting racialized male disadvantage) is as condemnable as the material consequences, such that the physical death of subordinate males is equal to nonrecognition, what possibility exists for bringing the specific oppression of racialized or outgroup males to the forefront of inquiry within these intersectional models? Is the moral charge to say that Black males, whose disadvantage is so overwhelming that it necessitates both theoretical and political intervention, must not be centered because they are biologically sexed as men and hence androcentric? Intersectional invisibility asserts that scholars must value the unrecognized and imperceptible as equivalent to—and, in some cases, as having more moral import than—the actual deaths before them. It is this predilection for analytic gymnastics among scholars that enables them to decide and weigh, or interpret and negate, the oppression of others so that the subjects the scholars favor are made to matter more than others.

Suicide and the Problem of Black Male Existence: Huey P. Newton and the Consciousness of Nonbeing

Because the death of Black men and boys is not symbolic but actual and real, there is a need to disown the incongruence the Black male causes for liberal academic theory and the problem he presents for Black academics, who rationalize their emergence as fixtures in the middle class as the product of their hard work, intelligence, and integrity while claiming that poor Black men's underclass position is simply evidence of their defects. The effects—the meaning the deaths of Black males convey in various sectors of society—have been deliberately excluded from philosophical analysis. The death of Black men and boys by state violence, white vigilantism, and economic deprivation not only removes this group from being seen in society but also erases them, censors the meaning of their lives for the sake of maintaining ideological coherence. Democracy, hard work, capitalism, education, and civility can work if we simply do not see—ignore and disown—the large numbers of Black males who do not exist in this social register. Despite seeing Black men's demise daily, Americans do not find it shocking. Mainstream media, social media, and daily conversations routinely accept Black males' dying as somewhat inevitable. Pictures, videos, and caricatures of Black male death are passed around with little regard for the expired lives. The spectacularization of the Black male corpse discourages sympathy. Whereas tragedies (such as rape, the murder of white children, mass killings of whites) are censored because they are thought to be too graphic for all Americans (something in need of discernment and discretion), Black male death is not thought too profane or grotesque for the same public. America has been desensitized to the corpse of the Black male. This is what is meant by saying that Black male life has lost its meaning. Insofar as racism has made the Black male disposable, and misandry has made him pathological, there is an acceptance of the idea that he is in need of death—that his dying is necessary for the persistence and thriving of America.

The normalization of the death of Black men, who are seen as problems for society, and of Black boys, who are thought inevitably to grow into criminals beyond their playful adolescent deviance, remains central to the ongoing genocidal program against Black males in this country. The calls for Black life and recognition suppose a civility and respect for middle-class Black life that simply does not apply to poor Blacks and, specifically, poor Black males—hence, their odes to eschatology throughout history. When Michelle Alexander argues that young Black men "are part of a growing under-caste, permanently locked up and locked out of mainstream society,"[35] she is describing a population of Black men who are unfamiliar to white America and much less preferable to the middle-class-aspiring, socially mobile Black classes who see the recognition of Black humanity as the panacea for anti-Black violence. The Black classes proclaiming the value of Black life, those who have self-identified as the avant-garde of twenty-first-century Black politics, remain unmoved by the brutal deaths of Black men and boys. These middle-class Blacks presuppose that a democratic system is at the foundation of this country. While they may acknowledge that violence is systemic, they nonetheless believe it is ameliorable upon acknowledgment. As Dr. Huey P. Newton argues:

> Direct and unconcealed brute force and violence—although clearly persisting in many quarters of society—are today less acceptable to an increasingly sophisticated public, a public significantly remote from the methods of social and economic control common to early Amer-

ica. This is not a statement, however, that there is such increased civility that Americans can no longer tolerate social control of the
country's under classes by force of violence; rather, it is an observation
that Americans today appear to be more inclined to issue endorse-
ment to agents and agencies of control which carry out the task, while
permitting the benefactors of such control to retain a semidignified,
clean-hands image of themselves. This attitude is very largely responsible for the rise of the phenomenon to which systematic attention is
given in the study undertaken here: the rise in the 1960s of control
tactics heavily reliant upon infiltration, deliberate misinformation,
selective harassment, and the use of the legal system to quell broad
based dissent and its leadership.[36]

Black males are decentered in our contemporary political moment, despite
their death at the hands of police, and serve as evidence of the magnitude and
force that the genocidal logics of the state have in the lives of the oppressed.
Because their deaths expose the class privilege of the new Black political activists in relation to the caste position of poor Black males, there is a need for
these new Black bourgeois leaders to morally condemn working-class Black
males. For these activists, the deaths of Black men can be commodified as
evidence of police violence and the prevalence of anti-Black racism in America, but Black male lives must be disregarded as politically worthwhile so that
race, class, and maleness are not centered in emerging movements. Newton
shows that the repressive civility advocated by socially mobile Blacks and liberal whites is not, in fact, nonviolent. It actually owes a great deal to government programs of militarism and lethal force that kill undesirable populations
such as poor and working-class Blacks. The death and incarceration of poor
Black people is de-radicalizing. It lessens their numbers and inspires fear
among them. The logics of these clandestine programs facilitate the support
for bourgeois morality among middle-class Blacks, because they are disassoci-
ated from the violence committed by poor Black males. Because they are
among the groups that are most victimized and killed by police and the state,
poor Black males do not have the luxury of that recognition. Within the logics
of the ongoing intersectional plea for Black life, Black males are merely the
examples of state violence; they are barred from being leaders capable of interpreting the worth of their own lives and the meanings of their deaths. It is
precisely because they are defined by death, viewed only as the corpse, that
they are found condemnable for any attempt to enter the political. Because he
is the contradiction to civility, the Black male is anathema to the bourgeois
conceptual of contemporary Black political life. He is a stark reminder of the
tyranny known as American democracy, an argument the avant-garde can
never make against the liberal order because it desires to be elevated within it.

The barring of Black men and boys from the political and their confinement to the violence of America's racial under-caste is a historical position. It is from this location—their sociological and historical position as Black and male within America—that many Black male thinkers began their analysis and calls for revolutionary consciousness. Newton opened his famous text *Revolutionary Suicide* (1972) with a reflection on the publication of Herbert Hendin's work on Black suicide in *Ebony* magazine.[37] Newton was particularly concerned with Hendin's finding that "the suicide rates among Black men between the ages of nineteen and thirty-five had doubled in the past ten to fifteen years, surpassing the rate of whites in the same age range." As Newton admitted of Hendin's work, "The article had—and still has—a profound effect on me."[38] To contextualize Hendin's findings to the conditions of racism Black Americans experience, as well as to his aspirations for revolutionary structural change, Newton theorized them as an extension of Émile Durkheim's treatise *Suicide: A Study in Sociology* (1897).[39] Newton saw *Suicide* as a resource because it offers an account of how social inequality becomes individual psychopathology. Newton understood that for Durkheim, "all types of suicide are related to social conditions. [Durkheim] maintains that the primary cause of suicide is not individual temperament, but forces in the social environment. In other words, suicide is caused primarily by external factors, not internal ones."[40] Newton posited Black people in America as sane and therefore not victims of neurasthenia.[41] Durkheim posited that suicide arises from the dominance of social states. Individuals can be moved toward suicide through their retreat from society into an excessive individuality, a melancholy state distant from the social, or because of a maladjustment with society, a situation in which their psychical needs exceed their physical means.

This account of anomic suicide, as opposed to the egoistic account of suicide, is of some interest to Newton. Durkheim explains:

> No living being can be happy or even exist unless his needs are sufficiently proportioned to his means. In other words, if his needs require more than can be granted, or even merely something of a different sort, they will be under continual friction and can only function painfully. Movements incapable of production without pain tend not to be reproduced. Unsatisfied tendencies atrophy, and as the impulse to live is merely the result of all the rest, it is bound to weaken as the others relax.[42]

Anomic suicide is a regulative problem found primarily in modern societies. Individuals commit suicide because they have lost the foundation of their sociality; they are deprived of the means to achieve their ideals of the self and psychic necessities. Unlike animals, which depend on purely material conditions to establish equilibrium with their environment, humans crave social improvement and resist the stagnation of their social position. For humans, equilibrium is not determined solely by the body, for "beyond the indispensable minimum which satisfies nature when instinctive, a more awakened reflection suggests better conditions, seemingly desirable ends craving fulfillment."[43] It is this theme that directed Newton's reading of Hendin.

Hendin's *Black Suicide* (1969) established that suicide among Blacks was a psychological effect of racism, especially among urban youth.[44] This phenomenon in the 1960s, like the increases in Black suicide rates in the twenty-first century, disproportionately affected Black males. Despite the significant increase in suicide among young Black males since the 1990s,[45] Daphne Watkins observes that "frequently in the literature on Black men, depression is not reported as a major health concern."[46] Social determinants such as education, unemployment, and systemic discrimination "are precursors for depression in many Black men."[47] The various threats to Black males' lives, their constant vulnerability historically to violence and death, limit the future orientation of many young Black males. As Hendin notes, "Not generally realized, however, is that [B]lack homicide reaches its peak at the same twenty to thirty-five age period as [B]lack suicide."[48] The wretchedness of ghetto life—the systemic racist isolation and poverty many urban Blacks experience—has a formative influence on Black people in the United States.[49]

In the case of the Black male, this effect is accentuated by his alienation from America's social system. Sociologist Anthony Lemelle Jr. observed that Black males' neglect within lower socioeconomic family structures, their inability to graduate from high school, their unemployment, and their high levels of incarceration contribute to their high rates of homicide and their increased rates of suicide from the late 1970s forward.[50] The Black male's proximity to death—not only his fear of dying but also his repetitive encounters with death and personal loss of male family members and peers—conveys a sense of absence and nonexistence. The Black males Hendin interviewed expressed the belief that they had "no future."[51] Violence and despair combine to vacate Black life from the activity of living for males of the subordinate racial group. This perspective manifests not as an individual pathology but as a group condition. For Black men, suicide manifests as an internalization of the conditions Blacks suffer generally. Many Black males think there is no future because their present is defined by such loss. This is not to suggest that Black women, especially those who suffer under the same environmental conditions, do not experience similar levels of rage and despair. Hendin is clear that his case studies reflect this commonality;[52] however, over the past two decades the educational and economic mobility of Black males has worsened such that suicide emerges as a particular worry for this population. As Stewart argued in 1980, "Suicide is among the most efficient ways by which institutional decimation is accomplished and cannot be effectively addressed independent of a systematic attack on the forces which decimate the [B]lack male population."[53]

Revolutionary Suicide was written as an attempt to make sense of the increasing suicide rates among Black males, given the political and economic condition of Black people in the early 1970s. Newton synthesized Hendin's findings and Durkheim's insights to create a theory of reactionary suicide. For Newton, reactionary suicide is "the reaction of a man who takes his own life in response to social conditions that overwhelm him and condemn him to helplessness. The young Black men in [Hendin's] study have been deprived of human dignity, crushed by oppressive forces, and denied their right to live as proud and free human beings." Newton understood that Black maleness had a particular relation to racial oppression, a specific suffering inflicted on the Black man as both Black and male that was conditioned by both his lack of work and his determination as antisocial and deviant. This nexus served as the foundation from which Black male vulnerability springs, where the deprivation of human dignity and the negation of the Black male's humanity converged within his own psyche. The internalization of the external societal rage against him, his interiorizing of the racist misandry used to justify violence against him, ignites his motivation toward suicide. Like Durkheim, Newton is careful not to suggest that it is only poverty or social inequality that drives one's motivation toward suicide. Whereas Durkheim relied on his study of Ireland and Calabria to show that poverty did not cause suicide, Newton offered an existential analysis to differentiate the reactionary nature of oppression from that of poverty. Turning to Dostoevsky's character Marmeladov in *Crime and Punishment*, Newton explains that poverty need not "be a vice," as one may still maintain a "noble soul." The beggar, however, has no such luxury, as he is deprived of dignity and internalizes his diminution within society. It is the beggar's internalization of this societal negation that leaves him "bereft of self-respect, immobilized by fear and despair, [where] he sinks into self-murder."[54] This is the same vulnerability Black males have to racism—the condition Newton describes as reactionary suicide. It is this vacating of self-worth by the society that is thereby internalized by the Black male individual that makes suicide appear as a tenable escape from dehumanization. This is the choice between execution and escape that Black male life finds itself overdetermined by in this society.

The Fiat of Dreams: Anti-ethical Thought and Its Relevance to Futural Subjectivity

What end can hope serve for the oppressed if the ultimate end of racism is death? Can hope even be justified in a white-supremacist society that murders Blacks to maintain its social order? What of the lives lost to this order? Is hope the fitting rationalization of their deaths—is it the value they have, in fact, died for? The death of Black men and boys is not simply about these bodies; rather, their deaths are an indication of the lethality that can be exacted on the whole race. Because the class distance between those who speak of racism and

those who endure it is so vast, there is disregard for the measures the Black
poor indicate. But can deaths in the now, in fact, justify some incremental
change for the better in the future, especially when there are populations con-
sisting mostly of Black males who cannot anticipate tomorrow because of the
violence and death that plague them today? Durkheim argues:

> To pursue a goal which is by definition unattainable is to condemn
> oneself to a state of perpetual unhappiness. Of course, man may hope
> contrary to all reason, and hope has its pleasures even when unrea-
> sonable. It may sustain him for a time; but it cannot survive the re-
> peated disappointments of experience indefinitely. What more can
> the future offer him than the past, since he can never reach a tenable
> condition nor even approach the glimpsed ideal?[55]

Newton acknowledges a similar effect of despair and social degradation on
Black people alongside that of revolutionary suicide. In fact, he goes as far as
to argue that "connected to reactionary suicide, although even more painful
and degrading, is a spiritual death that has been the experience of millions of
Black people in the United States." This spiritual death is a form of fatalism in
which "its victims have ceased to fight the forms of oppression that drink their
blood. The common attitude has long been: What's the use?"[56] "Believing this,
many Blacks have been driven to a death of the spirit rather than the flesh,
lapsing into lives of quiet desperation. Yet all the while, in the heart of every
Black, there is the hope that life will somehow change in the future."[57] This
problem is one of faith, the belief among the oppressed that miracles, the
seemingly random transformation of one's oppressors, should determine one's
relationship with structural violence, institutional racism, and death. Hope, as
the foundation of these ethics where oppression is thought to be mediated
though a rationalized faith in the humanity of one's oppressor, is nihilistic, at
best. Such hope paralyzes the oppressed through an a priori duty to the oppressor. Such a duty confines oppressed people to a faith in the potential of a
not-yet-present white humanity that could learn to respect Black life without
any evidence that this quality can or does exist within the dominant racial
group. In this sense, the potentiality of whiteness—the proleptic call of white
antiracist consciousness—that serves as the basis of our current Black political
theory is nothing more than the fiat of an ahistorical dream.

But this project supposes an erroneous view of the white racist, which oc-
cludes the reality of white supremacy and anti-Black racism. As Robert F. Williams argues, "The racist is a man crazed by hysteria at the idea of coming into
equal contact with Negroes. And this mass mental illness called racism is very
much a part of the 'American way of Life.'"[58] The white racist is not seen as the
delusional individual ostracized from society as a result of his or her abhorrent

social pathologies of racist hate. Rather, the white racist is normal—the extended family, the spouse, the sibling, the friend of the white individual—the very same entities on which the intersubjectivity-intrasubjectivity nexus of the white self is founded. The white (he) experiences no punishment for his longing for Black servitude and his need to exploit and divest the Black worker here and there of (his) wealth. The white (she) has no uneasiness about her raping of, destruction of generations of Black selves—mothers, children, and men— and today usurps the historical imagery of "the Nigger" to politically vacate Blackness and demonize Niggers as beyond political consideration. She rewrites history, pens morality, and embodies the post-racial Civil Rights subject. As such, racism, the milieu of the white racist, is not the exposed pathological existence of the white race. Rather, it is valorized in white individuality, the individuality that conceptualizes white racism as a normative aspiration of what the world should look like and, even more damning, an aspiration that can be supported and propagated in the world. [w]hite racists recognize the deliberateness of the structures, relations, and systems in a white-supremacist society and, like their colonial foreparents, seek to claim them as their own.

Traditionally we have taken ethics to be, as Henry Sidgwick claims, "any rational procedure by which we determine what individual human beings 'ought'—or what is right for them—or to seek to realize by voluntary action."[59] This rational procedure is, however, at odds with the empirical reality with which the ethical deliberation must concern itself. To argue, as is often done, that the government, its citizens, or white people should act justly assumes that the possibility of how they could act defines their moral disposition. If a white person could possibly be not racist, it does not mean that the possibility of not being racist can be taken to mean that white people are not racist. In ethical deliberations dealing with the problem of racism, it is common practice to attribute to historically racist institutions and individuals universal moral qualities that have yet to be demonstrated. This abstraction from reality is what frames our ethical norms and allows us to maintain, despite history and evidence, that racist entities will act justly given the choice. Under such complexities, the only ethical deliberation concerning racism must be anti-ethical, or a judgment refusing to write morality onto immoral entities.

In the poststructuralist era, postcolonial thinking about racism specifically, and difference/otherness generally, has given a peculiar ameliorative function to discourse and the performance of "othered" identities. In this era, the dominant illusion is that discourse itself, an act that requires as its basis the recognition of the other as "similar," is socially transformative—not only with regard to how the white subject assimilates the similitude of the othered but also as an actual activity gauged by the recognition by one white person or by a group of white people in any given scenario—and it is uncritically accepted and encouraged as antiracist politics. In actuality, such discourse appeals, which necessitate—become dependent on—(white) recognition, function very much like the racial stereotype in that the concept of the Black body's being the expression and source of experience and phenomena (existential-phenomenological-theorization) is incarcerated by the conceptualization created by the discursive catalyst yearning to be perceived by the white thing seeing the Black. Such appeals lend potentiality-hope-faith to the already present/demonstrated ignorance-racism-interest of the white individual, who in large part expresses the historical tone/epistemology of his or her racial group's interest. When morality is defined not by the empirical acts that demonstrate immorality, but by the racial character of those in question, our ethics become nothing more than the apologetics of our tyrannical epoch.

Ought implies a projected (futural) act. The word commands a deliberate action to reasonably expect the world to be able to sustain or support. For the oppressed racialized group, the dead Black male, *ought* is not rational but a repressive utterance. For the oppressed racialized thinker, the ethical provocation is an immediate confrontation with the impossibility of actually acting toward values such as freedom, liberty, humanity, and life, since none of these values can be achieved concretely for the Black in a world controlled by and framed by the white. The options for ethical actions are not ethical in and of themselves; they are merely the options the immorality of the racist world will allow. Thus, the oppressed are forced to idealize their ethical positions, eliminating the truth of their reality and peeling away the tyranny of white bodies, so that as the oppressed they can ideally imagine an "if" condition whereby they are allowed to engage racism from the perspective of "If whites were moral and respected the humanity of Blacks, then we could ethically engage in this behavior." Unfortunately, this *ought* constraint only forces Blacks to consciously recognize the futility of ethical engagement, since it is in this *ought* deliberation that they recognize that their cognition of all values is not dependent on their moral aspirations for the world. Instead, their perceptions of the world and its white architects are determined by the will of white supremacy to maintain virtue throughout all ethical calculations. The Black is confronted with a cynical proposition: that the alleged evil that asserts itself as the cause and reason for Black death is ultimately good and needed to sustain the white world before him. In short, Black ethical deliberation is censored so that it can engage moral questions only by asserting that whites are virtuous and hence capable of being ethically persuaded toward right action—hence, all ethical questions about racism, white supremacy, and anti-Blackness are not about how Blacks think about the world but about what possibility the world allows Blacks to contemplate under the idea of ethics. Under this philosophical anthropology, one's Blackness aspires to be part of what the world allows rather than the impossibility he-she *is*.

These ethics, the ethics that result from this vitiated morality, are not arbiters of oppression at all. There is an implicit appeal to a hierarchy of being that is both empirical and universal—all MAN is superior to non-man. Hence, ethics emerges as the product of the overrepresentation of Western man thinking itself—projecting itself—into the future. These ethics, theorized away from the material peculiarity of anti-Blackness not within its corporeal limits, uphold only an overdetermined virtue of whiteness. They hold within them no actual delineation between good and bad, only a Puritanical call to reason to turn its attention toward the other(ed) that is created. This attention, however, relies on the perceptions and caricatures of Black torment that appeal to the whites' self-assuring imagining of themselves, so that even when confronted with racism and their role as whites thinking about Black people incarcerated within a racist society and dying, these whites can claim that their conceptualization of racism itself or (intersectionally) next to other injustices such as poverty, sexism, and homophobia *makes* them (whites) virtuous. It is the process of, the appeal to, "getting whites to recognize" racist oppression that allows Black death to continue unabated, since it is the exact moment that whites are forced to engage racist problems in America, such as the anti-Black violence of American society, that animates aversion of the justice system, the police state, the white citizenry, and the practice of American democracy itself (where the death of Black people/criminals/deviants/thugs remains normal and justified by whites). The white(s) thinking about racism get to impose on Black reality a racist moral maxim—namely, that racism is not death or the end of an ethical calculus or a moral evaluation itself but, ultimately, a call for all moral and liberal people in America to condemn racism as a practice. This call is not paramount; however, it is weighed next to the other democratic values that preserve this great white society: security, safety, individuality, property, profit, and freedom—that is, the very values that have justified the doom of Black bodies when concretized in the white-supremacist republic known as America. At best, these appeals encourage reformism.

Black male death places Black men and boys within a horizon of finality. They are confined to the present by the denial of futurity. Death is the border of this time—a medium of what *is known* that Black males share. The conditions of violence, their murder at the hands of all people in society, articulate the unbridled inhumanity of the Black male's peculiar oppression. To *see* these logics operating not only within but as the foundation of the liberal democracy, serving as the stage for Black lives to be recognized, is the benefit of studying the condition of Black men and boys. It is their submergence within the most wretched conditions created for their slow extermination that offers a purview of the ontology deployed against all oppressed groups in modern society. This insight is often disregarded as hopeless, as unjustified pessimism or melancholia about the world, because Black male consciousness of the world is not articulated within the grammar or orders of futural subjects. Reason, ethics, and love have little effect in a world engineered to kill all those who oppose its power. These are the possessions of those who murder Black men. The murders of Niggers are virtuous; they are just. The Black male is the injustice—the evil—that stands against their civil virtues. Death invalidates the persuasiveness of morality, the embodied virtue, of democratic citizens, because there will always be those who did not survive to enjoy the embrace of the transformed public. Their corpses are forgotten so that those who live can enjoy the illusion of futurity. There are no futural selves for Blacks, only those contingently placed farther away from violence than others. This is the insight of the Black male—his relentless assault on the logics embodied by modern capitalist and patriarchal societies driving the oppressed toward self-murder.

Anti-ethics is necessary to demystify the present concept of MAN. It is an attempt to expose the assumed ethical orientation of reason as an essential anthropological quality of the human—the futural self—as an illusion and a stratagem. It is precisely this alleged pessimism that allows a fundamental and axiomatic rupture between the humanity of Blacks and the assertion that white existence is, in fact, the substance of the human. To accept the oppressor as is, the white life made manifest within empire, is to transform the white bourgeois concept of the human as a godlike sovereign citizen to contingent, mortal, and other-able. The Black male, as an anti-futural entity, resists the class mobility and assimilation that make specific classes of the oppressed imitate and seek to stand alongside the oppressor. The Black male is the polar opposite of white civilization. His intimacy with death has bred a different eschatological calculus that enables him to struggle against oppression, to live within tyranny, despite the seeming permanence of the repressive conditions.

The realities of poverty, death, execution, and erasure under which Black males languish are usually cast aside as too pessimistic to serve as the basis of theory. Their pessimism illuminates the mechanisms and structures of doom. The dismissal of their reality—Black males' vulnerability in the world—is reflective of the bourgeois orientation of theory, its need to reflect a world of progress and possibility within the political and ideological programs of the status quo, no matter the costs. Because theory is a means of recognition, utilized by various classes to mark their aspired positionality and allegiance with academic complexes, the degree to which optimism is centered in discourse reveals the distance the thinker has from the deaths of those observed. There is no proximity to the oppressor the Black male can enjoy without threat of injury, so any theoretical account of the Black male based on his actual condition nurtures realism as to the nature and complexities of white supremacy as well as a refusal of recognition and mobility within structures such as the academy that work to exclude him.

In this sense, anti-ethics shares a great deal with Newton's original formulation of revolutionary suicide. The futural self is the essence of the privileged subject in Newton's thinking. The revolutionary emerging from oppression cannot expect to live. George Jackson similarly maintained, "If revolution is tied to dependence on the inscrutabilities of long range politics, it cannot be made relevant to the person who expects to die tomorrow."[60] The future is embodied by whites; it is what makes their genders complementary and reproductive, and necessary to civilization and the continuation of white humanity. In this way, whiteness anticipates time—its future. Society, empire, is built with the expectation that whites will thrive and inhabit it. Oppression nourishes the dominant class because it sustains the hierarchies justifying their claim to civility and the length of their lives. The colonial victim, however, is "born to a premature death."[61] At the heart of Newton's conceptualization of Black maleness is an eschatological mandate holding that "it is better to oppose the forces that drive me to self-murder than endure them."[62] As premature death is seemingly inevitable for the Black male, hope is rearticulated as the activity of acting against the intolerable conditions set before him. For the Black male, death is possibility. It offers an end to the tragedy, a life beyond the confines, what DuBois celebrated as escape from this world for his son. Newton is reacting against passivity—the idea that Black men should not resist and reject the moral order established by their oppressor. To not act against, to remain passive and non-actional, encourages death, just as acting, resisting, moving toward revolution implies "repression, counter-terrorism . . . prison, and funerals."[63] To act against the world that condemns the life of Blacks is to accept death as a consequence—a more just death.

Newton and many of the Black men who converse with revolution understood that the enduring social death of Black male life may be a physical existence, but it is not actual living. The anti-ethical stance of Black males frames the rejection of the futural self as impossibility, a sensibility that emerges from the liminality of the perilous existence Black males face. Death complicates the *now*. It emphasizes the complexity of the present. Drawing from the work of Albert Camus, Newton explains that the truly revolutionary orientation understands that "real generosity toward the future lies in giving all to the present."[64] This was not only a personal commitment but also an organizational doctrine. As Newton explains, "The Black Panther Party embraces this principle. By giving all to the present, we reject fear, despair, and defeat."[65] It is the adamancy through which the Black male confronts the *now* that defines his resistance against the repressive forces at the foundation of racism and patriarchy. To coherently explain his condition and the distance he has from society, there must be new theories that can account for what we know historically and empirically about the Black male and his conceptualization of life within this narrow of time.

Sylvia Wynter's "No Humans Involved" and the Problem of "Thought" When the Nigger Is Written about but His Death Is Avoided

More than two decades ago, in the article "No Humans Involved," Sylvia Wynter exposed the complacency of the academic enterprise in the social reification, rather than the refutation, of the onto-anthropological nomenclature of Western biologism taken to "be" MAN and the violence this exclusionary anthropology has on the Black man in America. Wynter used the Rodney King verdict as her case study. The force of her analysis surrounding the violence against King is not simply the infusion of social (non-ideal) context or horror into the vacuous albatross of disciplinary knowledge, or an attempt to remind us to think more critically about what we claim to "know" or define what we claim to possess in "knowing" as "knowledge"; rather, Wynter demands that we reject the biologized conception of humanity we claim has the faculty of knowing and the concomitant apotheosis of disciplinary/conceptual/theoretical knowledge that valorizes Western man as the revelatory vessel of colonial history to the exclusion of Black people—the Non-Humans. The Non-Human/the No Human/the Man-Not does not refer to a slurring of Black men that can be thought of as "speaking badly" of poor, young, Black men. It is not a stereotype in the sense that it can be rationally engaged; rather, to speak of Black men's engagement with the Los Angeles Police Department in the case of Rodney King, or the police state more generally, is to articulate the meaning Black maleness has in the grammar of racism, its discursive logics, that legitimates and subtly produces the logics of (genocide)/violence. For Wynter, this term held in focus the dehumanizing intent of police engagement with Black men, since "these young men had to be first classified and thereby treated differently from all other North Americans."[66]

Rejecting such ontology is not simply the work of discussions over and writings about the degraded anthropos of modernity. This is not a dialogic resolution of "death" symbolically, where dead Black bodies become textualized/re-cast(e) in academic literature. Black death is the silencing of, the extinguishing of, lives that demonstrates the contradiction of anti-Blackness within empire—or, rather, the white-supremacist republic parading the mask of democracy, which displays the deaths of Black men and boys for social order and political subservience. For Black men specifically, the denial of their humanity, of being a human, while being epidermalized as "the Nigger" is catalytic—it brings with it the basis for Black death, while remaining seemingly invisible in the various facets of Black social life. Here Black academics point to political progress, mutual dialogue, and class mobility (economic difference from Black death) as justifications for their racial diagnosis. In this view, Black death/physical death/murder is external, and not endemic, to a "normative/civilized/educated" Black existence; it is a phenomenon that appears among "problem people," not educated, hardworking Blacks.

Wynter urges the reader to consider the relationship among the paradigms of dehumanization that resulted in the genocide of Armenians by Turkish Pan-Nationalists and the Holocaust inflicted on Jews by the Germans and the language used to describe, through taxonomy, Black men as a species deserving death. To classify the deaths of Black men as "No Humans Involved" is to reify the sociogenic principle behind anti-Blackness. As Wynter says, "The social effects of this acronym [N.H.I.], while not overtly genocidal, are clearly serving to achieve parallel results: the incarceration and elimination of young Black males by ostensibly normal and everyday means."[67] Wynter's analysis of anti-Black death makes the Black male the conceptual paradigm of inquiry, the lens through which this kind of death is best viewed and the body that should be grasped by the imagination to fully comprehend the ontology and consequence of the violence that perpetuates this anti-Black horror. Destroying the Black male body, murdering the Black life that demanded to be more than the petrified phantasm of the white imagination, extinguishes the idea of the Black human that the white-supremacist world demands cannot exist. Killing Black men who dare to speak against and live beyond their place erases them from the world, making an example, and leaving only their melaninated corpses as a deterrent against future revolts against white knowledge/order.

The Black man is not a normative subject; there is no "should" question that does not imply his death. He is not capable of being captured by thought; nor is he able to be seen in society. Huey P. Newton's "Fear and Doubt" points out the problem posed to the thinker aiming to describe and animate the Black man as a political subject capable of political life and social participation. Newton maintains that "society responds to [the lower-socioeconomic Black man] as a thing, a beast, a nonentity, something to be ignored or stepped on. He is asked to respect laws that do not respect him. He is asked to digest a code of ethics that acts upon him but not for him."[68] The consequence of this "nonbeing" is dire, as there are no historical patterns of rationality or ethicality that project Black male existence into futurity—that normative plane of academic thought. What would a world of living Black male subjects look like? Can this white-supremacist society support the existence of such a thought experiment? Would not the existence of thinking Black men, freed to act without death as the consequence of their freedom, be a contradiction of terms, the end of the thought experiment? Would the entities that constitute "our thought" cease to exist in the reality of living, free Black men, able to act against the social reality that serves as the background of our conceptual reality?

The lack of a normative positionality of poor Black male subjectivity is a problem of empathy just as much as it is a problem of conceptualization. The Black intellectual cannot "feel," much less "see," the Black male as a subject thrust into, or on, futurity. He cannot be thought as acting—an actional man, transformative, thinking human—much less one who lives, and expects life. Zygmunt Bauman expresses a similar concern regarding the conceptually othered/new poor resulting from the rise of the global capitalist structure, which supports and enables the institutional validation of the knowledge produced by universities as useful and the products/students as labor. Although he is not speaking specifically to anti-Black racism, Bauman remarks that "today's intellectuals, while they feel and express their pity [for poverty], refrain from proposing to marry their thought with this particular variety of human suffering."[69] Bauman interestingly describes this as a consequence of rationality and the cemented dispositions of subjectivity. Bauman continues:

> All in all, pity takes the place of compassion: the new poor need help on humane grounds; they are unfit for grooming as the future remakers of the world. With historiosophical indifference comes disenchantment with poverty. Being poor once again seems unromantic. It contains no mission, it does not gestate future glory. Psychologically, if not logically nor historically, it appears residual, marginal, alien.[70]

Bauman's explanation of poverty mirrors the concerns for the poor Black male raised by Newton as a problem of thought—or, rather, as the problem of being unable to be thought as a living, vibrant human being. Being poor, Black, and male resists conception. Wynter's call to rewrite knowledge depends on the abandonment of the categories and institutions that prop up and support the world as we know it. Our partiality to maintaining the world and the entities in it "as we know it" is the central obstacle to relativizing Western man.

Wynter demands a reformulation of our popular academic understandings that account for how we explain discourse as actively cultural. This reformulation is not "critical" in the traditional sense from which discourse/ language/knowledge is legitimated or semiotically relevant in specific social/ cultural/historical contexts. But language is cultural in that discourse births, gives legitimacy to, institutions and symbiotically regenerates sociocultural environments that reconfirm the problem of white knowledge internalized by the "learned Negro." Like Carter G. Woodson in *The Mis-education of the Negro*, Wynter highlights the dangers of asserting power/recognition/knowledge, all constructs emanating from the concept of MAN birthed within the matrix of white supremacy, as inapplicable to Blackness generally, and to Black male life more specifically. In "Beyond the Categories of the Master Conception" (1992), written the same year as "No Humans Involved," Wynter argues:

> To be effective systems of power must be discursively legitimated. This is not to say that power is originally a set of institutional structures that are subsequently legitimated. On the contrary, it is to suggest the equiprimordiality of structure and cultural conceptions in the genesis of power. These cultural conceptions, encoded in language and other signifying systems, shape the development of political structures and are also shaped by them. The cultural aspects of power are as original as the structural aspects; each serves as a code for the

other's development. It is from these elementary cultural conceptions that complex legitimating discourses are constructed.[71]

The presenting of the biological sign for male totalizes our understanding and discourse. He is male and thereby like Western man, because such categorization functions specifically within our grammar and the symbolic order that sustains such relations as our reality. This is how meaning is established and resonates in the world.

Such is the case with the categories imposed on our study of Black maleness: They are culturally, politically, and institutionally legitimated first. Gender is imposed on the Black male as part of a predetermined set of structures and cultural assumptions about maleness. This narrative of domination asserts the Black male to be a burgeoning patriarch, despite his historical inability to be the white type of male capable of political, economic, and structural domination, and despite his vulnerability to anti-Black death. This repetitive reality, which has continued throughout the centuries, has had no substantive effect on the manner by which Black maleness is spoken about within disciplines. To motivate the consideration and inclusion of femininity, masculinity is thought to be all-powerful and as such "written about" in complete hierarchal opposition to femininity. While not historically captured by this generalization, Black masculinity is spoken about within a totalizing schema asserting that, although Black men have been particularly erased from and neglected by history and denied political power and recognition, the partial historical survey of Black men available affirms Black masculinity as the dominating ethos of the Black male. Because the Black male is thought of as a "problem subject," no reflective redemption can be spoken of within this gendered schema. He is always already a potential brute capable of exactly the murder and violence anti-Blackness asserts is part of his character. These barbaric caricatures of Black maleness are historically salient in the minds of scholars and policy makers precisely because they are thought of as the same figures throughout the centuries—the rapists and killers of women. While dismissed in name as racist, the sanctions used to police and terrorize Black maleness are thought to be absolutely necessary, given the (gender) predilection Black men are asserted to have toward women. Contrary to the intersectional dividing up of the subject, the gender category involving Black maleness is part of the Black man's entrapment within the anti-Black matrix of his existence; it cannot be extricated from the systems of power that give shape to the language used to speak of and describe gender as if it exists in a neutral and pure form. Thus, the observer, the intellectual, is determined/recognized/rewarded in large part by this activity of description itself.

Bauman reminds us that "the line dividing 'intellectuals' and 'non-intellectuals' is drawn and redrawn by decisions to join in a particular mode of activity,"[72] so the grammar act—the signifying system deployed as Wynter suggests—must remain conceptualized as culturally reifying and compatible with the actual institutions representing the structures that house the tools of study. The Black academic bourgeoisie learn to use these categories to save themselves from death, categories that allow us to cling to life/recognition/ solidarity with the worker, or the woman, or the progressive, that breathe life into the *thingified* sociogenic product of anti-Black racism that is anthropologically participating in and, by consequence, beyond—or "seen as more than"—the inanimate properties of the Black thing. In "No Humans Involved," Wynter concretizes what this relationship between "discursive legitimacy" and "power" means for the unhumanized in what she calls the "historical-racial schema [that] predefines his body as an impurity to be cured, a lack, a defect, to be amended into the 'true' being of whiteness."[73] Our conceptual schema as being American is, in fact, a distancing from the jobless Black man who is targeted for death. Wynter's analysis reiterates the economic analysis of Brown and the larger ontological point made by Newton in "Fear and Doubt":

> It is this category of the jobless young [B]lack males who have been made to pay the "sacrificial costs" (in the terminology of Rene Girard's *The Scapegoat*, 1986) for the relatively improved conditions since the 1960s that have impelled many [B]lack Americans out of the ghettos and into the suburbs; that made possible therefore the universal acclamation for the Cosby-Huxtable TV family who proved that some [B]lack Americans could aspire to and even be drawn inside the sanctified category of Americanness in its present form.[74]

This ascendency of specific classes of Black Americans—those Black Americans who aspire to be seen as different from those "Not Humans" or those "Niggers"—has been achieved through neglecting the death of Black men and boys and embracing Negrophobia. The manifestation of Negrophobic sentiment in the writing and scholarship of Black intellectuals is institutionally rewarded and marks the difference between the plain Black folk and the Black intellectual, specifically with regard to how Black intellectuals use intersectional categories to distance themselves and caricature those *other* Blacks. A problem emerges in how we assign, describe, and evaluate the conditions of Black people. The Black male is constrained into categories that are suitable for expressing academic analysis but inadequate for expressing his actual being, academic categories that continue to ignore the limitations and moralities that are privileged in the study of "him" in these sorts of conditions. In short, our blindness, our indifference to Black male death, our seeking recognition of "life" through our descriptions of him as barbarous, only fuels the necromantic rage of white supremacism—the sexual racism, the desire for the Black body, and the intellectual obsession with speaking of him as corpse. Our attention to the empirical reality of Black men and boys suffering sexual racism proves that sexual violence is not married to the narrowing category of gender, which is summarily denied to this group.

The task is not to fold the Black male into the gender category as an attempt to resuscitate his being. To study the Black male is not to write him into recognition but, rather, to reject such an urge. The Black male is not simply an unrecognized identity; he is an existence that resists, reformulates, recasts, and endures, though currently unknown as such, throughout time. As such, his being must be accounted for with *new theory* that goes beyond the simple classifications of gender and race that presume caricature. He must be the subject of genre studies. Similarly, for Wynter, the Black male is not only the "N.H.I." but also "Baldwin's 'captive population,' [Frantz] Fanon's *les damnes*,"[75] constrained/castrated within the existing taxonomies/categories built on the assumptions of a white Western man. His inclinations are limited by how we describe and, by effect, know and mean the Black male. Drawing on Asmaron Legesse's *Gada: Three Approaches to the Study of African Society*, Wynter argues that the Black male is, in fact, condemned by the sociogenic principle of his negation—the Man-Not. Black manhood is created as the inadequate, the degraded and fleeting, the ever-dying body. Legesse argues that this rule-governed negation of the subject,[76] or group of subjects, is the province of the liminal, not because these subjects lack recognition by the structure but because the structure depends on their marginality—or, in the case of the Black male, his death—to legitimize itself. Legesse emphasizes this point, stating, "The liminal person is not irrelevant to the structured community surrounding him. On the contrary, he is its conceptual antithesis and therefore very relevant to its continued existence. It is by reference to him that the structured community defines and understands itself."[77] The liminal, then, is a condition of study, a foundation from which new grammars and cultural systems can be formulated. This is why Wynter concludes "No Humans Involved" with a reminder to the reader that "the starving 'fellah,' (or the jobless inner city N.H.I., the global new poor, or *les damnes*), Fanon pointed out, does not have to inquire into the truth. They are the truth. It is we who institute this 'truth.' We must now undo their narratively condemned status."[78] Wynter's recognition of the Black male as *the truth* cultivates the liminal being as a "genre study of death and dying," a study of the creative potential of the particular type of being not allowed, a kind of sociogenic inadequacy created as the farthest distance from the white Western human form.

It is from our exploration of the cosmologies and political incongruence of Black maleness—its not-ness—that we better understand the categorical architecture of subjectivity and the faults that justify the logics from which Black male relation in the world is thought. Legesse suggests that it is from this exploration of contradiction, rooted not simply in experience but also in the consequence of liminal existence, that "the liminal person remind[s] us that we need not forever remain prisoners of our prescriptions. He generates conscious change by exposing all the injustices inherent in structure, by creating a real contradiction between structure and anti-structure, social order and man-made anarchy."[79] In sharp contrast to the contemporary configurations of race and gender, which seek to dismiss the idea of the Black male as a necessitating thought, Wynter's work suggests that his study rather than his apotheosis as subject par excellence is necessary to dissolve the mythologies that dictate our encounters with the material world and his actual death. The Black man exists as a kind of human being, a new human possible, who creates, negates, and reflectively interprets the world around him. He creates art and experiences tragedy. He is resistant just as he is frail. He is the *possible* that emerges from the inadequate ethno-class of Western man—what we now mistake as the human.

Conclusion

In thinking about Blackness, the Black scholar removes Black existence from the horrors of America, preferring to think of Blackness as unrealized possibility. This is a conceptual failing of Black scholarship that Frank Wilderson describes as "people consciously or unconsciously peel[ing] away from the strength and the terror of their evidence in order to propose some kind of coherent, hopeful solution to things."[80] It is in this act—the cessation of inquiry whereby the epistemic is collapsed into the political/ontological—that the dereliction of Black thought, its predilection toward becoming a racial normative, is apparent.[81] Much like the dilemmas found in dealing with Black death and confronting the genocidal tendencies that haunt the lives of Black men articulated in Wynter's "No Humans Involved," there is a need to sanitize, make tolerable, *academify* Black (male) existence so that it becomes not nihilistic and fatalist but a live thought experiment that is revised around improvement and optimism—a discursive design that offers the white listener, reader, or colleague entrance into the possibility of being an antiracist, compassionate white reformist invited by the graciousness of the Black theorist. The Black scholar is rewarded for such hypothetical ventures that co-sign the disdain whites have for Black men as violent, antisocial, dysfunctional, and so on. Black males are the depositories of the negativity traditionally associated with Blackness that makes transcendence socially, politically, and conceptually possible for other Black bodies. Hating them solidifies the class position and indicates the class aspirations of other Blacks.

There is an eerie connection between the deaths of Black males in society and the erasure of Black male life in the realm of theory. In reality, Black males are genre-ed as nonhuman and animalistic in the minds of whites, but our theories relish assigning the death of Black males to the generic description of racism, a notion not thoroughly analyzed in identity scholarship and unable to adequately capture the specific kind of oppression and violence that defines Black male existence. Because this racist societal architecture is de-emphasized, academic discourse(s) of race/class/gender—presupposing the infinite power of all male bodies—prefigures a conceptual calculus dedicated to eradicating the vulnerability of Black men because they are men. The Black male is thought to be a mimetic (white) patriarch, an untenable theoretical position, given the empirical evidence of Black male disadvantage, that serves only to affirm the disposition that *his* death is the only way to remedy the dangers *he* poses to society.

Conclusion

Not MAN but Not Some Nothing

Affirming Who I Cannot Be through
a Genre Study of Black Male Death and Dying

I thought I knew him: When I met myself, I saw him, but as I was educated, I was taught not to see but imagine, and through imagining fear, what I thought I knew but could no longer recognize. Theory did this. . . . I taught me who I/He/It could not be and was for its sake, not his.

W HAT DOES IT MEAN to think of the Black male—to pull the meaning of his existence away from his body to be used by thought? How possible is it for him to be thought of, studied, or engaged beyond the historical caricaturization(s) that relegate him to the Macho, the criminal, the liar, the rapist, the murderer, the thug, the deadbeat father, the abuser, the misogynist, the beast, the beast cub, the super-predator, or the devil? Is he nothing more than an unactualized (hu)man, a fatally flawed thing, struggling not against the murderous logics that rationalize his death but against the savageness assigned to him that continues to justify treating him as a nonhuman entity? The Black male is unthought. He is an intuitive problem, an analytic failing designated by the negative ascriptions of Blackness and maleness. He is a being who is described and defined by his menace, with little need to be understood as a living and complex human being subject to external and environmental forces and vulnerable to the mental anguish or depression of his death, imprisonment, and abuse within the present order of American society. Because he is *the Nigger*, possessing only the nature of a savage *thing*, driven almost solely by his animal intuitions and lust for violence, he is said to have no sociological, historical, or economic causes for his behavior. He is

only an unyielding victim of his nature. This account of Black manhood is a
caricature. It does not represent Black men and boys as reflective and impres-
sionable human beings; it offers thinkers a display of a Black entity that demands no recognition or consideration beyond the fear he inspires or the
problems he presents to society. Despite the language of intersectionality and
antiessentialism, and the emphasis on progressivism and pluralization, this
caricature is the foundation of various disciplinary theories concerning Black
males.

Many of the tropes surrounding Black masculinity rely for effect on a savage heterosexualism. For example, the long-standing myth of the Black rapist
depends entirely on an insatiable and violent lust by Black men for women.
While such mythology is usually cast as a historical relic in our contemporary
conversations about Black masculinity, there are very real murders of Black
men by police and white vigilantes that justify a closer look at the specific
motivations behind Black male death. The execution of Jonathan Ferrell by
police for seeking help from a white woman named Sarah McCartney immediately comes to mind. McCartney's 911 call and tears urging the police to
"help her" conveyed a very real cultural cue that required lethal force to put
down the Black male beast who, McCartney claims, "was trying to kick down
her door."[1] However, despite such vulnerability, which rears itself even in the
logic of mass shootings such as that by Dylann Roof, in which a white-supremacist shooter announced, "You rape our women, and you're taking over our
country. And you have to go,"[2] Black maleness is continually denied consideration as sexually vulnerable and a stigma operating to justify the murder of all
Blacks. Despite its societal impact, Black maleness is theorized as Black masculinity and thereby relegated to an isolated function. It is distanced from its
empirical consequence in such a way that it can be justifiably rendered insig-
nificant as a field of study in the academy, especially when dealing with the
experiences and impositions imposed on the heterosexual Black male body.

In many ways, the theoretical articulations of masculinity—specifically,
our understandings of Black masculinity—are offered only as the cause of
every historical ill, such that femininity, since it is thought to be the opposite
of masculinity, becomes the almost intuitive solution. Such oppositional appeals to the feminine are just as illusory as the disowning of the masculine.
Just as white masculinity and femininity were symbiotic relations that reified
similar values, political goals, and aspirations specifically on matters of race,
so, too, did Black masculinity and femininity overlap historically, endorsing
the same values, political goals, and aspirations. This is not to say that there
are no differences within these groups based on economic position, region,
religion, and the like but to acknowledge explicitly that the assumed differences in the values and politics between genders currently attributed to being
a man versus being a woman have little historical evidence. As shown throughout Chapter 1, many of the ideas that are used to condemn nineteenth-

century Black males as sexist and decadent, such as their emphasis on Black women focusing on the home and being good mothers, not only were explicitly endorsed by nineteenth-century Black women, as well, but also were the basis of educated/bourgeois Black women's altruism toward the lower classes. Yet such nuance, while apparent in history, is lacking in our theoretical accounts of Black men throughout the centuries.

Nuance, the attention to detail and contextual distinction, is absent from many theoretical accounts of Black gender relations because history is replaced by symbols that come to represent fixed ontological dispositions. The historical character of Black men exhibited throughout the centuries is elided for popular mythologies that hold heterosexual Black males to be rapists, Machos, bucks, or criminals. The actual vulnerabilities and thinking of Black men from the mid-1900s are ignored altogether for narratives linking late nineteenth-century Black intellectuals to mid-twentieth-century Black Civil Rights activists. Black male patriarchy is thought to be evidenced by the nationalism of race men of the late 1800s and evolves from their nineteenth-century ethnological thinking to the Black Power Movement of the 1970s. Jim Crowism and the specific violence, both physical and sexual, endured by Black men and boys for the better part of a century are completely ignored in favor of an abridged account of Black masculinity that is defined by the interest specific classes have in propagating the myth of Black men as savages. Under this historiography, Black Nationalism was not a reaction Black men had as humans to their unbridled murder at the hands of whites, their rape by white men or women, or their economic oppression. It was only their pursuit of power so that they could take their place alongside white males. They are thought only to be violent—the largest killers of themselves and abusive to all those around them.

Black males are not thought of as sociological beings that have existential relevance for theory. Because theory is the abstraction from the empirical— the attempt to establish the idea as causally related to actual phenomena— there is the risk that theory will remain disconnected from the world and from the relations the selves in that world share. Sometimes the idea becomes self-justifying and thought of as determining the phenomena from which it was initially derived. This is the problem with Black masculinity. It is an idea that obscures how Black males actually live and die in the world. In other words, theory never posits that Black men behave violently or criminally because they are victims of poverty, prior physical or sexual abuse, or mental anguish caused by racism and their specific sexual vulnerability to both men and women. Gender theorists are never asked to imagine the conditions that determine choice, or their lack thereof. Regardless of the social phenomenon one attends, theory asserts that Black men's higher rates of homicide, domestic abuse, and crime and even their political attitudes are the consequence of their obsession over their lack of power and patriarchy. This answer, which relies on essentialist and biological notions of maleness thought to have been rejected decades ago, remains unchallenged in its contemporary iterations. In our present moment, these essentialist identity accounts of social phenomena remain safe behind theoretical labels thought to disown the dangers of such categorical mistakes. Stated differently, because poststructuralism and intersectionality are thought to be, and are popularized as, antiessentialist paradigms, there has been a reluctance to identify essentialist notions that are still operating within these theories. Across disciplines, Black males' behavior, politics, and aspirations are explained by their cultural appropriations of white violence and their desire for white masculinity. Their violence is rooted in a theoretically justified circularity: Black men are violent because Black men *are* violent, a premise that is rarely questioned and often is taken as truth. The reality is that any question that approaches a serious inquiry into Black male vulnerability is more than a scholarly exercise seeking to present evidence to the contrary of the stereotypes of the Black male in society and the dogmas that guide the interpretation of his existence throughout the centuries. To study the Black male as historically vulnerable for being Black and male due to his criminalization and the denial of his victimization (sexually and economically) is to assert a position that contravenes the assumed meaning of gender itself. Studying Black men and boys as constituted by a historically relevant but academically denied sexual vulnerability unsettles the disciplinary boundaries of gender that are being used as intuitive indicators of the female and undermines the reasons used to justify the present academic order of public intellectuals and pundits.

These theories diminish the actual vulnerabilities of Black males by over-determining Black male life via the stereotypes of the Black male's aspiration to dominate and his alleged danger to others. By holding that Black males are dangerous, lusting after the power to dominate others, gender theory and popular intellectual works actually deny the intrinsic value of Black male life and assert that all social problems endured by or involving Black men—whether their deaths at the hands of white police or vigilantes or the violence in their communities or homes—actually emanate from their nature. This violent (Black) masculinity is thought to be irredeemable through its own faculties. In other words, Black masculinity is permanently stained, a defect akin to original sin. Contemporary gender theorists maintain that the only hope for Black men and boys lies in reformulating Black masculinity toward a Black feminist ethics. Although this claim is largely accepted by the culture of disciplines throughout the university, it has never been substantiated with any actual proof; instead, it is insisted on as if it is the only proper moral conclusion, given the direction of gender theory in the university. Why is it necessary to understand Black masculinity as problematic, redeemable only by the externalized politics of other groups, rather than through the study of Black males' actual lives and realities? What makes Black manhood such a problem that it cannot be studied but only condemned and reconstructed from the position of moral condemnation? Violence does not stain femininity regardless of its prevalence or cruelty, but individual Black men constitute evidence of an all-encompassing personality that determines the ends of Black males from birth. Denied individuation, Black men and boys are all thought to manifest this curse.

Beyond Caricature: An Assessment of Black Masculinity in the Lives of Black Men and Boys under Our Present Order

James Baldwin once remarked, "I am not a Nigger, I's a man, but if you think I am a Nigger, it means you need it. Why? That's the question you have got to ask yourself."[3] Does the university, its disciplines, its gender theory, truly believe the Black male is a Nigger—a violent super-predator lacking morality, compassion, or reason? Baldwin's question forces scholars of Black manhood and boyhood to demand an answer from theory itself—an answer for what appears to be a symbiotic bond between the racist ideology of American society and theories of gender in the academy. Why does academic theory need the Nigger to hold itself, its histories, together? Would patriarchy be less of a historical phenomenon if it did not include the journey of the Black male from slavery to citizen? Does gender theory need a Black male caricature thought to be apathetic about, if not fundamentally opposed to, Black women's issues—anti-woman? What is it about theory that it depends on a Black male that is violent, dangerous, and immoral to motivate its analysis of patriarchy? Such questions emerge not because they are at all natural to the existence of the Black male in America but as a response to the interpretive paradigms elevated to fact about his existence within theories that concern him. The Black male is ultimately the depository of all social ills. He is thought to be the origin of all of the domestic abuse, violence, homicide, homophobia, and rape in the Black community. As scholars, we might ask why all of the sociological, economic, psychological, and medical traumas that we know as linked to these maladies disappear simply from conceptualizing Black men. And more important, what sort of evidence, or principle of discernment, allows all of these sociological phenomena to be posited as facts and analysis in journals, conferences, and blogs as fundamentally tied to the Black male's ontology and sexual biology?

Black masculinity has become the name of these analytic truths in many regards. To say a racial account is "masculinist" or that a phenomenon originates from Black masculinity is to suggest that the maleness operating in the construction is condemnable. This ontology of Black masculinity is deathly allergic to empiricism; thus, it avoids historical, psychological, and sociological accounts of Black male life in America. Often sustaining its force through the adamance by which it is asserted, the conviction that Black masculinity is the evil birthed by the Black male's attempt to grasp his rights in America and gain political power has become the plot undergirding his journey toward freedom. As an interpretive lens, this account allows Black males to be dismissed as potential leaders, political actors, or thinkers, since all thoughts and ends they produce share the same defects. This essentialism holds that Black masculinity is predestined to crave domination and power over others, despite its actual societal vulnerabilities. Concerning Black masculinity, our current order simply asserts teleology to be the defining aspect of ontology. The presumed purpose or end of Black males, what we think of when we speak of Black masculinity, is domination and the subjugation of women, so it is assumed that all acts of Black males aim toward this end. This perspective has now become accepted as the product of theoretical innovation and continues to overshadow evidence of the actual values expressed by Black males throughout the centuries. In this case, Ockham's law of parsimony reduces Black males to the racist platitudes of our day while demanding that the most obvious social problems Black men exhibit be considered a manifestation of something more ontological. The inability of scholars to make distinctions between the theoretical attributes associated with Black masculinity—its end and very being—and the actual existence, lives, and death of Black men and boys is evidence of how stereotype is allowed to become theory.

It is far too common for contemporary feminist analyses of Black masculinity to simply retreat into racial stereotypes that apply the logics of power and domination to the fundamental character of every Black male in society. Black males such as Ray Rice, convicted of domestic abuse, or Adrian Peterson, punished for disciplining his child, are simply examples of how the masculine desire to dominate women and children is imposed without context or empirical substantiation.[4] Rice's domestic assault was depicted as the fulfillment of a male birthright thought to unite all men in America, despite racism and their economic distance at the expense of women and every other group. Michelangelo Signorile holds that Ray Rice's assault of Janay Rice convincingly proves there is no real need for particular distinctions in "masculinity," since "masculine identity as defined for generations . . . is so culturally powerful that it cuts across class and race boundaries—bonding men of all kinds together."[5] Similarly, Peterson's whipping of his child, whether one agrees with corporal punishment or not, is depicted as an exclusively male phenomenon used by Peterson to teach his son "a lesson in patriarchy—that a man's power comes from the control and degradation of weaker others."[6] Despite the prevalence of whipping throughout lower socioeconomic communities generally, and within Black communities specifically, it is only when Black men whip children that the act becomes patriarchal and dominating.

For context, when Peterson whipped his son with a switch for pushing his brother, he was charged with felony child abuse, but when Toya Graham was recorded on video assaulting her sixteen-year-old son, cursing at him, hitting him in the head and face, and pushing him, she was called a hero and mom of the year.[7] Contrary to the focus on Black males' use of corporal punishment, multiple studies confirm that Black women of lower and middle socioeconomic status believe in the use of corporal punishment on children as a normal form of discipline.[8] In fact, qualitative studies have shown that Black mothers view the ability to physically discipline a child as their mother-right, while "children's grandmothers, aunts, uncles, and biological fathers had to earn the privilege of disciplining through prior acts that earned mothers' trust that the individuals really cared about their children."[9] Here again, despite actual fact or accountability to the complexity of corporal punishment in working-class communities, the Black male is used as a scapegoat to link the use of spanking to abuse and parental negligence to the racist trope of Black patriarchal violence and domination, a theory that simply does not hold for Black parents and their rearing of their children.[10]

As discussed in Chapter 3, none of these "theories of masculinity" take into account the sociological, cultural, and economic conditions that facilitated the violence between Ray and Janay Rice. There is no thought about the factors that contribute to the escalation of domestic violence, such as alcohol use or bidirectionality of violence, as was displayed between the Rices. Ray Rice is a Black man; Janay Rice is a Black woman; therefore, he aims to dominate her. Such simplistic renderings, which simply apply predetermined categories to individuals, have become the pillar of gender analysis when dealing with Black males. The economic, cultural, and psychological motivations that condition such responses are disregarded in favor of an overarching narrative of the Black male as a violent patriarch, a cog in a conceptual scheme that reduces Black male life to the examples, or proof, of a predetermined abstraction. Far too often, this fatalism concerning Black men and boys is defended as theory. Despite the disavowal by the creator of the Duluth model, which insists that men abuse women because they are men who seek power over others, the ideological function of the position is so solidified culturally that its application, even erroneously, is thought of as proper gender analysis.

It was not so long ago that Judith Butler warned feminism about simply picking and choosing incidents as proof of a universal theory of patriarchy. Butler maintained that "the urgency of feminism to establish a universal status for patriarchy in order to strengthen the appearance of feminism's own claims to be representative has occasionally motivated the shortcut to a categorical or fictive universality of the structure of domination, held to produce women's common subjugated experience."[11] Despite the theorizations around performativity, the idea that man is defined as the external negation of the female and thereby concretizes gender based on this biological difference remains affixed in many accounts of Black masculinity. In the same way that Oyèrónké Oyewùmì warns us that the biologization of the woman is used to explain the cultural and social inequality of the female sex, we can also see that the sexual confinement of a body to that of male remains conceptually predetermined by the assumed biologism of white-Western-imperial masculinity that insists on patriarchal violence to enforce the social order.

Oyewùmì's understanding of the gaze as "an invitation to differentiate" is relevant here.[12] Black males are not studied because they are intuitively grasped as problems. Maurice O. Wallace describes this concern as the "reckless racial eyeballing" of Black male embodiment.[13] When imposed on the Black male body, the gaze of others tends toward monocularity—meaning that one's sight can fixate itself on only one aspect of that which is seen. In the case of the Black male, this perception leads toward negativity and the accentuation of colonial phallic myths to explain his relation to the *other*. The phobias perceived—the inhumanity and savageness of Black males—presume the genital-sexual-Nigger as its origin. Wallace thus restates Oyewùmì's problem of the body as that of representation, or how that which is *seen* by the observer is perceived through fixed/overdetermined aspects of the object itself. Wallace thus concludes, "For the Black male there is a need for the end of monocularity," which is his "metaphor for a single mode of colonial supervision maintained in the evil eye of objectification."[14] The Black male is known by, trapped within, a pathological epistemology that intuitively assigns all forms of evil to him as if these attributes are, in fact, knowledge about him.

Gender, then, becomes a placeholder for the assumed sexual dominance of man over woman rather than a contextual rendering of various differences and the consequences of those differences on bodies and historical relations between those bodies. Gender theory, then, fulfills its aim insofar as it announces the "woman" as the substantive product of gender and masculinity as its negating apparatus. In short, gender theory is offered not as an explication of the various expressions of male and female bodies in relation to their particular society or culture but as the construction of a theorizable subject: the woman and that which must be conceptually suppressed because it negates her, the man. The cultural theorist and ethnomusicologist Miles White makes a similar point, saying, "While it is also the case that women's studies and gender studies began largely as a way to include women's excluded histories, gender studies cannot or should not preclude the study of men if only to interrogate the presumptions of male privilege."[15] This assertion becomes even more problematic when we think of the peculiar position of Black males in American society. Ronald Jackson stresses that under our present regime of gender theory—specifically, the assumptions of feminism—Black men are thought to be purely negative and antagonistic entities, despite the presence of viable, healthy, and actual Black masculinities:

> Feminist thinkers, who encapsulate and hold liable negative masculine tendencies for the American fixation on power, competition, greed,

control, and institutionalized exclusion, have inspired a large segment of critical masculinity scholarship. Consequently, the versions of masculinity that are described are often culturally generic, fragmented, and aloof. There are very few gender studies that depict masculinities as positive, healthy, mature, productive, and balanced identities, but these masculinities do exist. The gender descriptors "masculinity" or "masculinist" usually refer to antagonistic, puerile, insecure, very unaware, and chaotic male identities. It is true that masculine, like feminine, persons enact a wide range of behaviors on a daily basis, from dysfunctional to quite functional. So, theorizing masculinities, in terms of a gendered continuum ranging from healthy to unhealthy and positive to negative self-definitions, is both necessary and revolutionary. As mentioned previously, the everyday existence of healthy and productive human beings is not so new, which means that there has been slippage in some gender theories with respect to how they account for healthy masculinities.[16]

Because Black masculinity—the category itself—represents an infinite monolith, the endless nocuous potentials and despotic possibilities of the Black male that drive him to conquer those weaker than he, any attempt to think of Black masculinity as healthy or nonviolent is formulated as Black men embracing something like the feminine, or the "not masculine." The ontology of Black masculinity is thought of as pure negativity, so thinking that uses such a concept demands that the thinker externalize any positive or desirable characteristics of Black males as their rejection of masculinity rather than as the substance of a Black masculinity itself. Since we define Black masculinity as condemnable, anything that we find worthwhile does not belong to the actualization of something in Black males; instead, it is something they embrace as outside themselves. In this way, progressive pro-woman Black masculinities are thought to originate in thinking that problematizes Black masculinity, not the awareness and thought of Black males' consciousness about the world surrounding them.

Gender theories asserting that masculinity is synonymous with patriarchy obfuscate attempts to theoretically engage Black manhood and boyhood as it exists in the world, outside the presumed relation of white gender(ed) domination and racism. Despite poststructural and intersectional gender theories that claim to recognize the difference between Black men and boys' material actualities and (white) patriarchy, Black men and boys remain confined to biological fixations that make their sexual designation synonymous with their gendered aspiration for power over others. We have arrived at a time of theory in which Black males are thought to be privileged even as they are the overwhelming victims of various systems and bodies in society. Even in their victimization—their unjust incarceration, death, poverty, and absence in institutions of higher education—Black males are thought to be a threat to themselves and society. While the amelioration of these conditions is claimed to be part of antiracist advocacy, the stigma associated with an ontological view of Black masculinity would still hold that achieving this goal, saving their lives, would ultimately allow them to harm other men, women, and children in their communities. In this way, the oppression of Black men serves a prophylactic function in the minds of theorists who hold the ontological view of Black masculinity, because if Black males were free, they would seek only to harm or dominate all others they would engage.

As Rinaldo Walcott observes, "The representation of [B]lack masculinity as in need of repair and rescue is not merely internal to the U.S. conversation, it leaks across borders. In the context of neoliberalism's production of 'wasted populations' in a 'lawlikely' fashion, [B]lack masculinity has globally come under new kinds of cultural policing."[17] This policing of Black masculinity exists appositionally between the force of the prison and the legitimizing rationalizations of such force originating in the academy. Drawing from Stuart Hall's analysis of the managerialism within academic neoliberalism,[18] Walcott continues:

> Conversations concerning [B]lack manhood are premised on neoliberalism's new managerial regime in which [B]lack masculinities are understood to be underperforming, in need of programs of efficiency and better management. Such is particularly so for poor, redundant, and "wasted" masculinities that appear to have nothing to contribute to the global engines of capitalism. In this instance managerialism as both discourse and practice seeks to control and conduct how these wasted persons, often reduced only to a body, might be understood in light of the numerous contradictions that plague the wealthy West.[19]

The discursive production and reproduction of Black masculinity legitimized under the guise of theoretical innovation within and across disciplines still hold to the racial stereotypes that flourish throughout society. The view that Black males are aggressive, dangerous to women, and prone to violence is the same one that police, courts, and vigilantes use to excuse the violence leveraged against these disposable entities—to keep them in their place. In the university, however, holding such views is absolved of racism when presented as *Black masculinity*. Because Black masculinity exists as theory, the construct that names the character of the bodies and predilections of the heterosexual Black male is thought of not as racism or misandry against this disadvantaged group but, rather, as progressivism. It is often accepted as a necessary corrective not only to Black males' presence in the university but also in terms of threats they pose to society more generally.

Advocated as gender progressivism, Black masculinity is problematized not only conceptually but also corporeally, thereby re-creating the disappearance of work with which Black males are currently confronted. Within the academic enterprise, scholars market themselves as managers of this population and their work as the inoculation against their spread. Departments and hiring committees routinely rationalize not hiring Black men using this logic of diversity—or, more accurately, the logic of the presumed threat Black male hires pose to women and other groups. It is in this moment that managers are called on to rationalize their discrimination through an appeal to theory. Black male privilege now becomes a rationale that discourages remedying Black male under-representation by focusing on Black males' undesirability, a trope deployed by liberals as a way to justify discriminating against Black men. In fact, cohorts of scholars are identified as marketable precisely by the extent to which they argue Black masculinity must be avoided. Such a stance identifies not only the labor of this academic class but also their bodies as distant and unsympathetic to the empirical realities and disciplinary erasure of Black men and boys. These are progressive scholars, or scholars who are able to increase their worth within the university by supporting theories of Black masculinity that legitimize and justify the fears society has of Black men and boys more generally.

Although intersectional methodology claims not only to be aware of the unique position of Black males but also analytically competent in the fundamental difference that race, class, and gender establish between Black maleness and what historically has been understood as white male patriarchy, contemporary gender conceptualizations of Black masculinity within these theories still insist that all maleness is committed to attaining patriarchy, regardless of race or class location. In this schema, race merely expresses the degree to which one manifests the power or privileges of white masculinity and patriarchy writ large. It does not describe Black males' cultural or material distance from the historical power and antagonistic will of white males. In other words, race serves to indicate the degree to which one may express the capacity of patriarchy/maleness, but it does not mark the modal limit of patriarchy itself. Whereas that which is "female" is thought to be conceptually and biologically distinct from patriarchy, despite being formulated, historically situated, and geographically located in many cases at the helm of empire, colonialism, militarism, corporatism, and classism, the sexual designation of "female," meaning "not male," intuitively marks a modal boundary that indicates "the absence of patriarchy." This (intersectional-categorical) modality conceptualizes Black masculinity as "othered-within" (white) masculinity-patriarchy-man, whereas that which is female is "othered without" and thereby separated and distanced from man-patriarchy altogether.

Intersectionality's Black Male Problem: Dominance Theory as Intersectional Anthropology

Intersectionality is thought to be the most visible and promising theoretical innovation of Black feminism of the twentieth and twenty-first centuries. At a theoretical level, it is argued that intersectionality can be applied to any number of subjects (Black men, Black queer/quare identity, women of color throughout the world, disability, and so on). This theoretical novelty is commonly tied to Kimberlé Crenshaw's first exploration of the idea in "Demarginalizing the Intersection of Race and Sex: A Black Feminist Critique of Antidiscrimination Doctrine, Feminist Theory, and Antiracist Politics."[20] In the article, Crenshaw is specifically concerned with Black women's experience of discrimination. She argues, "Black women sometimes experience discrimination in ways similar to white women's experiences; sometimes they share very similar experiences with Black men. Yet often they experience double-discrimination—the combined effects of practices which discriminate on the basis of race, and on the basis of sex. And sometimes, they experience discrimination as Black women—not the sum of race and sex discrimination, but as Black women."[21] In her subsequent article "Mapping the Margins: Intersectionality, Identity Politics, and Violence against Women of Color," written two years after her introduction of "intersectionality" as an analytic concept, she attempts to expand intersectionality as a method particular to Black women to one peculiar to the experiences and history of women of color generally regarding access to domestic violence resources. Whereas "Demarginalizing the Intersection of Race and Sex" argued for an experiential-epistemological foundation of race/sex in the body of the Black woman as a protected class within the law, "Mapping the Margins" maintained that Crenshaw's "focus on the intersections of race and gender only highlights the need to account for multiple grounds of identity when considering how the social world is constructed."[22] In an effort to establish a grounding for intersectionality, Crenshaw articulates two aspects of her theory: a structural intersectionality that considers the material effects of various social stratifications, which for her thinking about domestic violence were poverty and women of color's access to shelters, and a political intersectionality that "highlights the fact that women of color are situated within at least two subordinated groups that frequently pursue conflicting political agendas."[23] Crenshaw maintains that the need to split one's political energies between two sometimes opposing groups is a dimension of intersectional disempowerment that men of color and white women seldom confront."[24]

The exact disadvantages men of color—specifically, heterosexual Black males—confront seems largely absent in intersectionality theory. Some intersectionality thinkers assert that Black males have privilege and advantages over Black women because they are male; others suggest that while Black men are shown to be the greatest victims of incarceration and police brutality, the attention to their suffering excludes the suffering of Black women, as well as that of Black gay and lesbian groups. Devon Carbado observes, "Heterosexual Black men occupy a privileged victim status in antiracist discourse."[25] For heterosexual Black males, intersectionality insists that both Black male advantage and disadvantage over other groups is male privilege. On the one hand, a heterosexual Black man's advantages over Black women or Black gay men and lesbians in terms of income could be evidence of his patriarchal privilege as a straight Black man, while on the other hand, his relative disadvantage to white men and women, and sometimes Black women, regarding unemployment, incarceration, and homicide is that same patriarchal privilege because he draws attention away from other victimizations. In the latter case, Carbado frames this as a problem of focus: "[As a] result of this focus on Black men, without a similar focus on Black women, Black men are perceived to be significantly more vulnerable and significantly more 'endangered' than Black women."[26] How can Black male vulnerability be adequately engaged theoretically under such a paradigm, when every insistence of Black men's disparate suffering and victimization is morally condemnable as the erasure of another group, even in cases such as police brutality and incarceration, where Black men are, in actual fact, overwhelming the greatest casualties of these encounters? Throughout various publications, scholars use intersectionality to suggest that Black males share the same proclivities as white males, or patriarchs,[27] even in their disadvantage to this dominant group.

Crenshaw's development of intersectionality was inspired in part by the dominance theory of female subordination offered by Catharine MacKinnon.[28] The law, like the society it reflects, establishes patterns of inferiority and power asymmetry between men and women. Women are dominated as women. This is not simply an essentialist argument for MacKinnon, since she believes that what makes the particular subject vulnerable is shared sexual vulnerability to male dominance:

> When the Reconstruction Amendments "gave Blacks the vote," and Black women still could not vote, weren't they kept from voting "as women"? When African-American women are raped two times as often as white women, aren't they raped as women? That does not mean that their race is irrelevant and it does not mean that their injuries can be understood outside a racial context. Rather, it means that "sex" is made up of the reality of the experiences of all women, including theirs. It is a composite unit rather than a divided unitary whole, such that each woman, in her way, is all women.[29]

Crenshaw recognizes that such politicized accounts of sameness that rely on the vulnerability of "the woman," especially in the case of rape and domestic abuse, can obscure other subject realities, such as that of male victims or same-sex relationships. She seems aware that "theories of women's subordination as well as the interventions that such theories anticipate will obviously exclude subjects whose contexts are not anticipated, accommodated, or recognized."[30] However, she seems hesitant to think of these relations of women beyond the events missed that delineate Black women from white. She resists the more radical decentering of gender as a marker of white anthropology, because the idea of woman carries a notable political currency. While Crenshaw has acknowledged the nonuniversality of categories such as woman, she fails to inquire into the limits that such a category imposes on the normative operation of man within the theory.

Under the intersectional frame, to say that the female is subordinated on the basis of sex presumes the sameness of men, because the Black male, like the white male, does not suffer from sexual subordination. The recognition of multiple subordinations brings with it the assertion of multiple causes for said subordination. At the level of identity, the Black male, in his exception as male, is found to enjoy the privilege of not being "sexed" and therefore not vulnerable like the female. But this conclusion results from a rendering of the very subjects, and their histories, Crenshaw has acknowledged are excluded in politicized calls to sameness. The centering of the Black woman as sexually vulnerable, the symbolic representation of race and sex, and the violence of rape and domestic abuse, by consequence, exclude Black males from being seen as vulnerable. The centering of the Black female subject implies that, because of his maleness, the Black male is always dominant because of patriarchy, not vulnerable to it. Crenshaw's system thereby links the exclusion of Black women from antiracist movements to the same operating patriarchal norms of the larger society. The subordinated male, then, is hegemonic because he strives for recognition as subordinated at the expense of the Black female, yet such designations do not apply in the case of sexual violence such as rape because, for Crenshaw, male dominance is enforced with the erasure of Black women from antiracism, while there is no female dominance operating in the erasure of Black men as sexual victims. Under this paradigm, an implicit biologism is operating at the level of theory that defines Black maleness as not sexed and hence normative alongside the structural operation of patriarchy, while the Black woman as sexed and raced nuances the substance of the woman.

There is an eerie continuity between the pre-intersectional feminist analysis of Black males and the intersectional era that many scholars now suggest benefits from the cultural and conceptual insights of the theory. Despite the decades between MacKinnon's thinking about Black men and Crenshaw's, it seems that intersectionality has done little to complicate how Black men are seen politically and economically when related to Black women. In 1979, MacKinnon argued, "When [B]lack women enter the labor market of the dominant society, they succeed to the secondary place of white females (remaining, in addition, under the disabilities of [B]lacks), while [B]lack men succeed at least to some of the power of the male role. Indeed, many of the demands of the [B]lack civil rights movement in the 1960s centered upon just such a recovery of manhood."[31] Where would MacKinnon get such an idea in 1979? She offered no footnote to substantiate empirically her assertion that that Black men's biological (sex) maleness was enough to confer concrete economic and political benefits in the workplace. Although she was writing only a few years after the creation of affirmative action and a little more than a decade after the Civil Rights Act was passed, she asserted that Black men had already achieved and solidified male privilege. While MacKinnon did offer the prefatory disclaimer that "racism does not allow [B]lack men to share white men's dominance of economic resources,"[32] she also asserted that maleness was recognized and advantaged in the workplace. In fact, she went as far as to suggest that because of race, Black men enjoyed the benefit of dissuading white women from claiming sexual harassment in the workplace: "Some white women confide that they have consciously resisted reporting severe sexual harassment by [B]lack men authorities because they feel the response would be supportive for racist reasons." MacKinnon argued, "Although racism is deeply involved in sexual harassment, the element common to these incidents is that the perpetrators are male, the victims female."[33] Despite racism, MacKinnon asserted that, in economic and political matters, the access to manhood Black men had recently gained because of Civil Rights meant that power primarily revolved around the male-female axis; it transformed a Jim Crow context in which white women viewed accusing Black men of rape as a racial obligation into a post–Civil Rights context in which, because of gender, white women became hesitant to accuse Black men of harassment.

For MacKinnon, gender expresses the hierarchical distance between the male sex and the female sex: "Gender emerges as the congealed form of the sexualization of inequality between men and women. So long as this is socially the case, the feelings or acts or desires of particular individuals notwithstanding, gender inequality will divide their society into two communities of interest."[34] Instead of describing habits of performance or the consequences of sexual differentiation between bodies, gender becomes the consequence of male power over the female. It emerges as that which names this particular asymmetry. MacKinnon goes as far as to suggest that gender inequality is sustained by the sexual pleasure the male gains from the subjugation of the female. This view holds that "aggression against those with less power is experienced as sexual pleasure" for the masculine gender, while the female is defined by submissiveness.[35] Race and the brute reality of racism do little to alter the function of gender within this schema.

Intersectionality and Hegemonic Masculinity

While contemporary intersectionality theorists argue that the theory can and, in fact, does apply to Black males, there has been no critical interrogation of the role dominance theory plays in explaining or defining heterosexual Black male behavior under intersectionality. For example, Frank Rudy Cooper's "Against Bipolar Black Masculinity: Intersectionality, Assimilation, Identity Performance, and Hierarchy" asserts that the analysis of Black male bipolarity (the oscillation between the Good Black and Bad Black male image) "is an intersectional phenomenon because it is the product of the combination of narratives about [B]lackness in general and narratives about [B]lack masculinity in particular."[36] At the same time, however, he asserts that heterosexual Black men, good and bad, are seduced "into taking pleasure in the present hierarchies"[37] Despite their material location, in prison or in the boardroom, "heterosexual [B]lack men are taught to emulate the economically-empowered heterosexual white men who set the norms in this culture."[38] Using Michael Kimmel's essay "Masculinity as Homophobia," Cooper interprets Raewyn Connell's theory of hegemonic masculinity to conclude:

> The predominant account of normative United States masculinity describes it as fundamentally based on a fear of being associated with denigrated others. To be a full man, one must distinguish oneself from femininity. One accomplishes that by distancing himself from the qualities associated with women and from women themselves. Instead, one treats women as possessions to be displayed as evidence of one's manhood. Similarly, one must distance oneself from gay men. This is the attempted repudiation of the presence of feminine qualities in men.[39]

Kimmel cites Connell's *Gender and Power* to explain hegemonic masculinity as "the image of masculinity of those men who hold power."[40] According to Kimmel, "We equate manhood with being strong, successful, capable, reliable, in control."[41] In fact, it is these definitions of manhood that are used to "maintain the power that some men have over other men and that men have over women." As discussed previously, these notions simply do not apply to racially subordinated males who are targeted by white patriarchy. As decades of data have suggested, Black men and boys simply do not see masculinity either as the ideal for which one should strive or as synonymous with Black manhood.

Cooper argues that heterosexual Black men seek to emulate this normative white masculinity, making them "feel compelled to prove their manhood through acts that distance them from marginalized others." Perhaps most interesting, he maintains that intersectional disadvantage does not change the impulse of the heterosexual male. Despite their condition or circumstances, "heterosexual [B]lack men will seek to offset their feelings of powerlessness by subordinating others."[42] This explanation highlights the difference between the application of a theory and anthropological assumptions behind a theory. Cooper argues that intersectionality helps us understand the identity-level tensions and conflicts between Black men being designated as good or bad in a white-supremacist society, but behind the analysis of identity is an assumption about the nature of heterosexual Black men. Cooper's claim does not emerge from any historical or empirical study of heterosexual Black males, but from the familiarity this narrative has among gender theorists—his repetition of the consensus concerning Black males held by his audience. Cooper only cites the anecdotal analysis bell hooks offers of Black males' political aspirations after emancipation. While hooks admits that newly freed Black men and women were both struggling with the contradictions of gender in which Black women demanded that Black men protect and provide for them, it is only Black men, in their struggle to fulfill this role and be recognized as men, who are deemed patriarchs.[43] Like Michele Wallace, hooks is unable to conceptualize (non-feminist-inspired) Black masculinities, especially after racial integration.[44] She assumes that the history of Black gender relations can be told as one that conceptualizes Black womanhood as participating in sexism but is much less innocuous in its reproduction of patriarchy than Black males, while the political struggles of Black men are primarily mimetic and motivated by their desire to dominate others. Since hooks provides no citations to substantiate her interpretation of (heterosexual) Black men's 150-year struggle for freedom in this country, the reader is expected to accept Cooper's understanding of the Black male personality based solely on the authoritative force of bell hooks's pronouncement. Regardless of their location, heterosexual Black men, because they are male, are thought always to aspire to the characteristics of white (bourgeois) masculinity. Even in those cases where the Black male is shown to be materially oppressed, Cooper asserts, Black males will subordinate others to compensate for the power they lack.

In all cases, the fundamental nature of the Black male, whether he has power or not, is to dominate other men and women. Intersectionality theorists have been able to consistently conflate the question of whether the method can be applied to heterosexual Black males with the assumptions the method holds about heterosexual Black males. Similar criticisms against Crenshaw's intersectional view of masculinity have previously been made. The legal theorist Angela Harris, for example, has explained that "the fact that men are divided by race, ethnicity, religion, class, and sexual orientation means that there is not just one kind of masculinity."[45] Harris's point demands a conceptualizing of differing ends and desires of these multiple masculinities, something that is currently ignored by scholars' *applying* intersectionality to Black males. In the work of intersectionality theorists such as Cooper, *all* masculinity tends toward domination and subjugation. This is an *essential* nature found in the category of male.

Since slavery, there has been a well-documented history of gratuitous violence in white patriarchal societies against males of the subordinate racial group that has prevented the participation and integration of those males into mainstream society. Anthony J. Lemelle Jr.'s *Black Masculinity and Sexual Politics* argues that an anti-Black male ontology justifying the exacting of brutality and murder against Black males as a group has always been central to the anti-Black racist program of America, so much so that Black males have never been considered (or defined as males such that they could be) viable partners in the (white) patriarchal endeavor. Black male experience is a condition of victimization by white patriarchy, not the basis of emulation of it. Lemelle argues for an understanding of Black maleness, the experience of the subordinate position, as an anthropological and historical condition created by the political, legal, and economic institutions of the United States to define Black males as savage and position these bodies in relation to juridical structures and institutions that hasten death as a display of white male power and white racial order. American society was organized around the subjugation of subordinate racialized males. Lemelle argues that Black male subjugation is prior to Black men's experiencing of it. It is a structural dynamic built into white patriarchal societies that

> precede[d] the full development of a dominant culture that functioned to gag the legitimate aspirations of the [B]lack internally colonized—the West could not have thought of [B]lacks as patriarchal equals given the function of race in its historical system of norms and roles. . . . [T]he [B]lack subalterns were educated in self-hate under the logic of white citizenship theory by the dominant political class, the co-opted leadership from among the [B]lack masses, as well as privileged stratified fractions of other tormented aggregates that were hierarchically organized in U.S. cultural imperialism. In other words, the organization of imperialism through colonial-like technologies does not develop at a certain phase of [B]lack male experience. The colonial-like technologies are, to the contrary, organizationally first in time to assist in the assurance that [B]lack males are a "criminal," or at least a "deviant," class of "citizen." The ideologies supporting this organization offer a rationale for treating [B]lack males differently.[46]

Lemelle offers a penetrating analysis that highlights the gap that exists between Black male victimization and the alleged socialization of Black males into patriarchy. The Black male is not born with the expectation that he will elevate to the ranks of white males; rather, he is socialized under a racial order that denies that the racialized/subordinate/Black male can expect any class mobility. He is defined as deviant and criminal precisely because this position as antithetical and dangerous to the order of civil society makes him discernable. The tremendous amount of violence committed against him as a Black male is normalized and often challenged by academics and policymakers as irrelevant. It is this normality of his death, the negotiation of what his life could have meant when compared with other human lives, that indicates that he is beyond the specter of humanity. The fact that this violence is normalized, even when it fundamentally exceeds the level of brutality against any other human beings or citizens in the same society, is evidence of the dehumanized station Black men and boys are determined by in this country. As Lemelle correctly insists, "The cultural domination of [B]lack males means that power relationships prevent understanding gender as a straightforward cultural reality where it either signifies female or male statuses. There are, in fact, equivocal gender statuses and consequently various masculinities."[47] Under intersectionality, the disadvantages of Black men are conceptualized as consequences of the racial category, not the gendered subordinate male category, since "male" is thought of only as a designation of privilege. If gender is not categorical, meaning that it cannot be understood as tending to one sort of experience or structural position, what is the basis for the assumption that because someone is "male," he aspires to hegemonic masculinity? Why is gender not, as in the case of the subordinate male, the basis of anti-patriarchal culture and positionality? In other words, where does this impetus to pursue patriarchy come from if the biological and cultural bases of gender are distorted?

Some authors argue that intersectionality is more nuanced than this, but their defense of intersectionality's ability to analyze Black males remains confined to the question of application, not anthropology. Carbado, for instance, argues that "Black women do not experience double jeopardy in every context . . . [and] there are contexts in which Black men do."[48] By emphasizing the applicability of intersectionality to various groups and the possibility for multiple configurations to emerge, Carbado leads the reader to believe that the method is open-ended. Through an intersectional analysis of Henry Louis Gates's arrest by James Crowley and the murder of Trayvon Martin, Carbado attempts to identify (mark away from color or gender blindness) the role that *normative masculinity* plays in both encounters. On the one hand, Professor Gates expected his respectable masculinity as a noted celebrity intellectual to counteract, if not negate outright, the racist stereotypes held by Officer Crowley. When Crowley engaged Gates and Gates did not back down or comply, Carbado suggests, citing Cooper's work on hegemonic manhood, "Gates was drawing on his surplus masculinity."[49] This disobedience was so great that it constituted a "masculinity challenge" to Crowley and led in consequence to Gates's arrest.[50] While both Carbado and Cooper are claiming to offer an intersectional analysis of Black males, it is important to realize that their work attempts to extend hegemonic masculinity theory to Black men, not theorize about Black men as subjugated masculinities with completely different trajectories and motivations from those of white men, as even Connell herself maintains.[51] Similarly, but on the complete opposite end of the spectrum, Trayvon Martin was possibly killed because the Black masculinity he presented (hoodied) connoted danger and violence to his killer, George Zimmerman. Carbado uses Martin's death to show how "the representational currency of Black men, even Black boys, turns on their racial respectability and gender normativity" but ignores causes unrelated to one's perceivable identity, such as homoeroticism, psychological disorders, and homicidal rage.[52] Under these previous accounts, identity sets the stage for all other dispositions.

Even when Black males occupy inferior social positions, and lag behind their white and female counterparts by multiple measures of a population's health and prosperity, intersectional analyses such as Paul Butler's "Black Male Exceptionalism" urge us to de-emphasize their actual deprivation. This line of thinking holds that the Black male must not be centered in any study or discussion as part of an effort to avoid perpetuating patriarchy. Take note of the essentialism. "Black men are still men," says Butler. "They don't have access to all the 'benefits' of the patriarchy, but they have some of them. To the extent that Black male exceptionalism allocates gender-based benefits, there is the danger that it reinforces gender-based hierarchy. In a patriarchal system, empowering men poses potential dangers."[53] If we are concerned with hierarchies, then as observers we should be able to point to specific inequities between groups that will be exacerbated by this attention. In other words, if Black men are not "white men," and thereby disadvantaged, are we to assume disadvantage exists only next to white men? If not, we should certainly be able to test, observe, or measure the inequities between Black men and white women, or Black men and Black women, or Black men and other ethnic women to see which inequities are exacerbated because of their maleness. Why must specific actions seeking to address Black male disadvantage be morally condemned as perpetuating patriarchy when such remedies are needed precisely because there is a very real political, economic, and structural distance between patriarchs and Black males?

Surprisingly, Butler only sees Black men as worthy of this kind of analysis. We do not hear similar arguments objecting to programs for white women on the basis that their racial identity and centuries of racial (gender) privilege perpetuate white supremacy or the race hierarchy. Similarly, we do not hear objections to equal pay initiatives for women generally, even though Black men hold less wealth and income than white women and less education, social mobility, and income (in some instances) when compared with (educated or employed) Black women. None of these ongoing discourses or initiatives exacerbate inequalities between white or Black women and Black men, so why the dismissal when Black males are the focus? How do Black men, gain power over white men and women and Black women when, as a group, Black men are struggling simply to achieve equity with them? Butler demands that scholars, theorists, and students endorse the idea that Black men, simply by being male, benefit from white patriarchy, despite the sociological and historical position of Black men that makes them economically and politically vulnerable to patriarchy.

Could programs that focus on young Black boys and not women and girls be based on a simple verifiable premise holding that while "issues related to both genders are important . . . boys and young men of color are consistently at the highest risk for the poorest life outcomes (e.g., incarceration, shorter life expectancy, poverty)"?[54] The resistance Butler shows toward acknowledging Black male vulnerability is permitted throughout disciplines because such condemnations toward the recognition of Black male suffering parallel the efforts of a status quo that already denies the violent conditions and death under which Black men and boys suffer more generally as males. Denying the specific disadvantages of Black men and boys is proof of the position Black males occupy as *already dehumanized—disposable*—and allows for outrage and condemnation of the efforts to have their deaths and plights recognized publicly. No other group of people could be so easily dismissed and condemned as "privileged," given the horrors that confront them. Their *humanity* would resist it. This calculus depends on analytic assumptions about the place of Black males in relation to other racial groups that are asserted prima facie, before the conditions of Black males are assessed and ascertained. This approach demands that Black men who are empirically demonstrated to be poor, uneducated, unemployed, and vulnerable to homicide at the hands of every other racial group (whites and other Black men and women) should be thought of as all-powerful and privileged over women, specifically Black women, not because they actually are but because they are biologically male.

While popular, the identity politics behind Butler's analysis, which holds that Black males have some structural privilege, do little to arrest the actual deaths of Black males in America, eradicate Black male poverty and unemployment, or advance our understandings of the causes underlying the murder of Black males at the hands of an increasingly militarized police state. The disciplinary division asserted between Black men and boys and every other raced, gendered, and classed subject, which is presumed to be "more oppressed" purely from an arithmetic of race, class, and gender location, prevents a serious study of the relationship between the historical and political causes of the seemingly endless violence against Black men and boys. Our intersectional conceptualizations of gender progressivism are blind to the sexualized and specific dimensions of Black male death, unduly emphasizing only the categories of our chosen subject rather than the dynamics responsible for the events we observe. In failing to address the deeper causes responsible for the death of so many Black men, often at the hands of those seemingly charged with their protection, we fail to address America's long-standing predilection toward killing Black males that is not easily reduced to the fact of racism.

Intersectional Essentialism

Social processes are complex and varied even within the same locales. History shows that no one category is absolutely synonymous with any dynamic of power. In some cases, it could very well be that women have been disadvantaged politically, economically, or otherwise compared with men, but in some cases, Black men, for example, could suffer economic and political disadvantage compared with white or Black women. These asymmetries, however, are not given the status of overarching "historical dynamics" or made synonymous with intersectional categories such as "maleness," because maleness is synonymous with patriarchy—an overarching dynamic that is associated with and fills in the meaning of gender for the thinker. The category of maleness used by theory ultimately revolves around white maleness and patriarchy, a dynamic that most nonwhite men historically not only have been denied but also have been victimized by for centuries. If the category of maleness was defined on the particular history of Black men, then one might say that their rape by white men and white women; lynching at the hands of white women as a way to secure white female political freedom; and historical disadvantage compared with Black women in education, employment, and incarceration would invert the idea of male superiority to the female. In this way, intersectionality depends on this sort of hierarchal imposition to legitimize the force of its categories, such as race, class, and gender.

To account for social groups, identity theorists must suggest that certain oppressions and hierarchies are unchanging throughout history. Individuals who identify as Black are located within history as historically disadvantaged by white superiority, just as women are located by their identity as disadvantaged by their gender by patriarchy, and the poor are thought to be inferior to the rich. What intersectionality therefore suggests is not an "analytic sensibility" that is capable of endless complexity and conceptual distension but, rather, the capturing of myriad historical time periods and sociological differences intuitively through the mere "seeing" of the body possessed by the subject thought of as the way to place both the perceived and unperceivable phenomena operating in the social world under the hierarchal modalities of race, class, and gender.[55] These modalities are asserted to exist and manifest themselves as obviously perceived categories, rather than how complexities actual are, can and have changed, or may, in fact, be changing literally before one's very eyes throughout society.

Intersectionality presumes that the thinker can intuit social dynamics and know the relative position of subjects within society simply through an account of the categories used to describe their biological bodies. In the case of sexual violence such as domestic abuse and rape and even the economic asymmetries between Black males and white men and women (and, in many cases, Black women), there is no awareness of such vulnerability within the intersectional ordering of "Black maleness," since maleness is assumed to connote a privilege built into social organizations, institutions, and individual disposition. This allows intersectionality theorists to assert that bodies outside the chosen configuration of privilege are less powerful and disadvantaged, regardless of their actual position in society. In the case of Black femaleness, intersectionality affixes both knowledge and moral innocence to Black women's experience. This worry is not altogether new. Two decades ago, Peter Kwan argued:

> Scholars who wrote about intersectionality responded to marginalization by creating new marginal categories that, by their very nature, themselves encourage the idea of categorical hegemony . . . by focusing, for example, on the particularities of [B]lack women's experience[;] intersectionality stands in danger of pushing to its margins issues of class, religion, and able-bodiedness, as well as issues of sexual orientation. Thus, without a more developed theory of how to "factor in" these issues, as Crenshaw predicted, intersectionality stands in danger of perpetuating the very dangers to which it alerted with regard to male dominance in racial discourses, and white supremacy in feminist discourses.[56]

Kwan understood that behind the theoretical language and attempts to attribute universality to the categorical combinations of intersectionality lurked a chosen subject, an essential—pure and moral—subject.

How does intersectional analysis begin? Whose histories are used to stand in for *the history* of class, race, and gender used in an intersectional analysis? Who chooses these categories above all others? Which category defines or limits the others? For example, Black men have conceptually thought of work—or, more accurately, the denial of work to them—as linked to their race and sex. As Black men, they were deprived of the status of the worker. Under intersectionality, such a concern would be designated under class. Without an understanding of Black male history and the specific relationship Black males have had to the idea of the worker, how does one decide which category actually refers to a specific social phenomenon? Is it intuitive? Do we pick the category we feel applies? How can these questions be answered unless there is a subject, an ideal intersection that gives coherence to the randomness of human reality? In other words, the substance and meanings of the categories deployed in an intersectional analysis will be those used to justify the particular history and marginalization of the subject chosen to represent the intersectional mode. If I chose Black males, the world would look very different from how it would look if I chose Black women or racialized migrant workers. The fundamental configuration of the category itself based on the identity chosen demonstrates that the result of intersectionality is not objective—able to render a repeatable analysis of social or structural organization. It is existential in that it produces possible viewpoints of social organization from the perspectives of the subject chosen. The danger of this method is that all other histories and complexities will, at best, be de-emphasized or altogether condemned as part of the erasure of the intersectional subject centered at the intersection of the race, class, gender, and such matrices.

Unlike other theories that respond to criticism in defense of the original position, Crenshaw has never responded to post-intersectionality theorists' critiques of intersectionality. Confirming Kwan's worry, championing the study of "the Black woman," centering her experience in all conversations about race or gender, became a valued ideological statement where simply uttering the words *race*, *class*, and *gender* indicated the progressivism and rightness of the speaker and made critique impossible (since attacking intersectionality is attacking the subject placed at its center). Ignoring the external critiques leveled by post-intersectionalists allowed intersectionality theorists to co-opt the works of other scholars under their guise of internal criticism. In this way, serious methodological holes in intersectionality could be addressed by fellow intersectionalists not as refutations of intersectionality as a theory or as evidence of the efficacy of alternative systems of thought but, rather, as scholarship and queries aimed at the continual development of intersectionality itself. Athena Mutua characterizes this tendency among intersectional thorists by saying, "Through the process of a multitude of scholars explaining, interpreting, and using intersectionality, the theory was broadened, turning many of the critiques into mere expansions and elaborations of the theory, a theory that Crenshaw herself initially saw as transitional."[57] Extending her criticism of intersectionality to the categories claimed to constitute intersectional relations, Mutua insists that Darren Hutchinson's insights in "Identity Crisis: Intersectionality, Multidimensionality, and the Development of an Adequate Theory of Subordination" have not been fully appreciated by intersectionality theorists.

Whereas intersectionality offers the Black female subject a world to herself full of her own history, her own political drives and aspirations—her reality free from the contamination of others and the errors of her time—the (heterosexual) Black male is robbed of any complexity and presented as a lesser white man. He has no specific history, no specific will separate from that demonstrated by white men to which he is said to aspire. Intersectionality presents him as simply mimetic and lacking. As noted in Chapter 4, Hutchinson suggests that intersectionality assumes a far too static concept of disadvantage and privilege by its categories to offer an effective and historically accurate analysis of oppression. His theory of multidimensionality aims to complicate "the very notions of privilege and subordination" deployed by Crenshaw's theory by focusing on the presumed advantages of heterosexuality, homosexuality, and multiple identities.[58] Similarly, Mutua has argued that the categorical assertion of Black men's advantage over Black women necessitated by Crenshaw's system is an assumption found to be inaccurate when subjected to empirical scrutiny:

> When intersectionality was applied to [B]lack men, it was initially interpreted to suggest that "[B]lack men were privileged by gender and subordinated by race"; that is, [B]lack men sat at the intersection of the subordinating and oppressive system of race ([B]lack) and the privileged system of gender (men). Intuitively this notion seemed correct. It also seemed to support the dominant social and academic practice of examining the oppressive conditions that [B]lack men faced from a racial perspective. Yet the interpretation of [B]lack men as privileged by gender and oppressed by race appeared incorrect in our observations of racial profiling. . . . [W]hile this interpretation of intersectionality seemed to capture some of the differentials between women and men in the [B]lack community, as in wage differentials for example, it did not capture the harsher treatment [B]lack men seemed to face, not only in the context of anonymous public space that often characterized racial profiling but also in terms of higher rates of hyper incarceration, death by homicide and certain diseases, suicide rates, and high unemployment as compared to [B]lack women. These conditions almost seemed to negate the idea that [B]lack men had any male privilege at all as posited by feminist theorizing.[59]

Mutua realized that intersectionality demonstrates a resistance toward seeing Black males as gendered and vulnerable and that new terminology was needed to capture the gendered disadvantage of Black maleness's multidimensionality. She concludes, "What [B]lack men were experiencing was not sexism, a term that over a long history seemed to me to reference the discrimination and oppression of women, but rather, was gendered racism."[60] This term, however, presents problems for intersectionality theory because, when it is applied to racialized males, it complicates privilege and disassociates it from the category of male. As Mutua reports, "Our studies indicated that the assumed privileged gender position of men, in the context of people of color, was not always accurate because being gendered men could sometimes be a source of oppression."[61] Like Jim Sidinias and other social dominance theorists, Mutua realized that the distinctions between Black (racialized) males and white males is not merely a difference of race, but, as Hutchinson announced, a difference of a sexual (masculine) kind.

An evaluation of the categorical assumptions behind intersectional thinking has yet to be seriously engaged in our analyses of Black males, due in no small part to the lack of scholarship specifically applying intersectionality to Black males since its inception in the late 1980s. However, as this book demonstrates, there is a certain amount of incompatibility between the evidence that serves as the basis of a theory for Black male vulnerability and intersectionality. Black men need nuanced theories and accounts of their social and existential position instead of analytic statements asserting that power, domination, and privilege are attached to their maleness. Intersectionality does not offer Black males this specificity; it reduces Black men and boys to reflections of decades-old dominance theory and conceptualizes them as unidimensional subjects who are hegemonic, mimetic, and invulnerable. There is simply no way to write about the vulnerability of the Black male under intersectionality without that act—announcing his structural and corporeal disadvantage as Black and male—being seen as an exercise of advantage and power over women, specifically Black women. Under such a paradigm, the Black male will always be marked by exception—that is, "Black men are oppressed, but . . ." The Black male is never understood as the center of history and the conditions that uniquely affect him. His rape, his death, his poverty, his marginality—the material facts of his existence—will remain negotiated and negated by the overarching ideological interests of those unwilling to accept the actual condition and disadvantage of Black men and boys.

Toward a Genre Study that Considers the Black Male a Complex and Vulnerable Human

There can never be a détente between the geographies of Western thought and those who inhabit the territories of Blackness. Just as there is no thought that simply fiats the complete dismantlement of Western man, we cannot presume that the reification of categories such as gender, and life, on Black male bodies and their recognition will move us conceptually beyond the actual violence under which these bodies suffer. Western humanity, the humanity politically asserted on the death of Black men and boys, will always remain anti-Black by its nature. The most immediate task before the Black thinker is to construct new concepts that can support the meanings of the actualities set before him in our own realities; in those instances in which our language, the grammar of our world, cannot support the weight of the Black thinker's reality, those structures and their cultural representations must be dissolved. Black men and boys cannot continue to exist as caricatures, with their humanity weighed against the mythologies holding them to be rapists, criminals, and aspiring patriarchs who aim to rule both women and society. These ideas are not paradigms of analysis; they are racist caricatures that claim theoretical relevance by the extent to which they make the sociological the ontological. These caricatures are accepted not because they express some truth about how to understand Black males but because they express *how society insists Black males already are*. Ironically, the very theories that are proposed as useful analytic interventions for the analysis of Black masculinity presuppose the very stereotypes by which Black males are defined in society. The conceptualization of Black masculinity offered by such theories are so overbearing that even armed political strategies made necessary by the terrorism of the state aimed to protect Black men, Black women, and Black children against the Ku Klux Klan or tyrannical cops are posited as attempts to gain patriarchal power. The history of Black men and boys itself is revised and amended for the coherence of gender within disciplinary thought. These narratives have little to do with the actual character Black men have demonstrated throughout history or the attitudes and values of Black men and boys today.

In a very real sense, the understanding one has of Black men is not drawn from a historical survey of their actions or an understanding of their positionality throughout the centuries. Instead, our understanding of the Black male is constructed on the interests a particular class of scholars—Black and white, male and female—have in exploiting the shared fear of his existence for their own advancement within the academy. Our present academic and popular cultural considerations of Black males are not formulated on any real understanding of their plight with incarceration, poverty, or domestic and sexual abuse at the hands of male and female caregivers. Our present theory insists that the ambiguous perceptions others have of Black males in their personal lives and in society are, in fact, true and should rise to the level of theory. Conceptually, Black masculinity is personified as the aversion an individual feels toward Black men and boys. Despite mountains of historical research and sociological data attesting to the fact that the Black Macho is a myth, the actual vulnerability and historical suffering of Black men and boys continue to be reduced to the impression Michele Wallace, a twenty-seven-year-old Black feminist, had about Black Panthers she saw on television. The caricature of the Black Macho is given disciplinary legitimacy under the name of theory and historical substantiation as an accurate ontology. It is a conceptualization of Black males that continues to operate within the reasoning of contemporary political movements such as Black Lives Matter, as well as the moralization of politics within the Black intelligentsia.[62] It is in this way that such theories remain racist and misandrist and that racial chauvinism operates unquestioned in various scholarly productions. Suspicion of Black men and boys and condemnation of their presence in the academy and theory is taken as praiseworthy. Scholars celebrate any and all commentaries that portray Black male theorists and activists simply as sexist and patriarchal, particularly supporting perspectives that hold heterosexual Black males to be dangerous to women. Instead of displacing gender essentialism, this academic milieu reifies and nurtures theories of Black masculinity that presume defects in Black males as a matter of fact.

The entrance of Black males into theory (the thought of scholars) as defect is not as simple as misperception or stereotype. The distortion of the Black male and the caricatures of him that populate the pages of books and articles, lecture halls, and discourse, on the one hand, are necessitated by the peculiar fear that inspires myths shared by the university and society. On the other hand, however, the Black male's misrepresentation is produced disciplinarily and marketed intergenerationally. The expanding attention to gender has not freed Black males from history's sexual stereotypes; it has only solidified them. For many theorists, the Black man represents the untamed savagery of white masculinity. Thought is attributed to white men as a way for them to be regarded as aware of power—as able to turn their reason into a faculty of transformation, despite their historical crimes against humanity. The Black male is robbed of this reflexivity, regardless of his battles against white/Western man. Because he is thought to be pre-rational/savage, he lacks the same features as the white male in theory. Black men are often taken to be purely sensuous creatures whose thinking about the world is thought to be little more than an extension of their corporeal selves. The Black man is thought of as the untamed violence of the white man, the depository of all negativity, evil.

It is because the Black male is an affront to virtue and self-improvement that life is divorced from him. Black men and boys are theorized only as the antecedents to their own deaths. Their violence ignites the violence against them. As such, they are always imagined with a certain wrongness as Black males—an original sin of sorts—that explains through a subtle circularity the reason for their failures. The Black male has been formulated by disciplines through anecdotal examples that not only represent him at his worst but also deliberately erase him from history such that his efforts and vulnerabilities remain unknown. Unlike his white male counterpart, he is judged purely by the standard of the politics in our present moment.

Whereas white men are theorists, worthwhile despite their personal convictions, the Black male can never be forgiven or redeemed by his theoretical insights into a social problem. Historical Black male figures are forever stained by their faults or lack of progressivism (their failure to disown themselves as male). All disagreements—political and personal—that they have had with any woman, white or Black, are proof of their sexism. Even in the cases of intellectual disagreement such as that between the providential imperialism of Anna Julia Cooper and the Pan-Africanism of W.E.B. DuBois, the stake in the intellectual commitment is reduced to DuBois's sexism—his failure to agree with a woman of his time—rather than his admonishment of her Christian imperialism or class politics. Black males, whether historical or contemporary figures, are judged on the basis of one standard: Do they agree with the women of their time? There is little investigation into the cause or experience that may breed intellectual and political differences between Black males and females; there is only the assertion that any disagreement with the "politics" of the Black female subject—even when such thinking is decadent and imperialist—is proof of *the Black male's* patriarchy and *his* inhumanity.

Black male thinkers deserve closer examination. These figures deserve theories that formulate their existence as more than the negativity and fears they inspire in humanity. The Black male is neither perfect nor eternally (ontologically) flawed; he is a living and reflective being. He is not the discard of history or thought and thus should not be relegated to entering the perception of others solely as defect. Black males, like other reflective beings, have offered the world a specific example of corporeal existence and aspiration. While they have lacked the power to determine the abstract and categorical ideas used to capture the world, they have nonetheless expanded the realm of the living through their deaths. Their murder and exclusion from the social and their condemnation within the conceptual show to all those who are looking the unimaginable extent of oppression. It is the Black male's continued will to *be* despite the violence placed on him in theory and in practice that shows us the extent to which white supremacism polices and confines Black existence generally. The Black male has continued to create and exhibit endless possibilities, despite the genocidal logics that operate through force—and, as Sylvia Wynter and Huey P. Newton remind us, theory—to extinguish him. Studying him, understanding the life that precedes his death, offers opportunities to learn from him. Resisting the urge to confine the Black male to mimicry would allow us to see how Black men and boys demonstrate unique perceptions into the undisclosed consequences of the world obscured by identity politics and academic theory. The study of his life is, in fact, a revelation of the conditions to the reality mystified by the illusions of theory.

Black Male Studies as a Liberatory Knowledge Schema

Black male existence and the force a Black male's being has on the world around him (the imprint of his being in the world, history, art, thought, and so on) are not only the negations of the established taxonomies used by theory to describe humanity; they are also the evidence that the disciplinary theories in vogue today are simply inapplicable to Black male life. As Legesse notes, "Liminality is the repository of the creative potential underlying human society."[63] The Black male does not simply pose a problem for the gender category; he exposes the erroneous, analogous reasoning behind the constant misapplication and misapprehension of anti-Black violence and liberatory responses to it. He is the possibility of thinking beyond the arrangement of gender and power, which now codify and weigh down theory. He is a bridge between the reality of the world and failure of theory/thought/reason to capture the world due to its own obsession. He is a break in the presumption of progress, whether political or philosophical. The Black male, understanding his history and vulnerability, is first and foremost a problem of (Black) study, not as a project of substitution (whereby we attempt to substitute one more perfect Black subject for another), but as a project of how we think about "our thinking" concerning Black men and boys. The murders and sexual assaults perpetrated against Black men are not fanciful. They are not imagined, but we have no signs that convey the veracity and force of their meaning. Creating such signs—to create substance and meaning to Black male life theoretically—requires the uncompromising rejection of all previous paradigms. To understand Black males beyond their corpses, we must reformulate the assumptions and narratives that make the current reality of gender, masculinity, and mythologies concerning Black males cohere. To be seen as he truly is, the Black male must be configured within a new history that tells of his complexity, his embracing of the mother right, his anti-imperialism, his anticolonialism, his Black socialism, his Pan-Africanism—simply put, his struggles to realize himself within his own experiences, meanings, and formulations. He must be thought of as a traveler toward liberation, not simply as a mimetic trope. He must be thought of as reflective and deliberate but flawed—as a kind of human, not perfect, but not condemnable. He is not the perfect subject but a worthwhile subject/*subject* of study and theory.

Contrary to the enthroned dogmas of disciplinarity and the stereotypes of society, Black males are, in fact, the concretization of alternative forms of being. They continue to survive and invent. They embody a kind of manhood that challenges and redefines the economic and colonial schema that many forms of feminism and gender progressivism still hold dear. Their study can actually show us how to escape the perils of patriarchy, as well as rid us of the desire to elevate within the higher ranks of hegemonic-imperial masculinity through political ideology and capital. The Black male—as a liminal being—resists simple mimicry. Structurally, he is often denied entrance into the dominant cultural generators of American society. It is this antisociality, the buried history of abuse and activity against the hegemonic foundations of society, that demonstrates a fundamentally different order of knowing—a register that presumes not somatic resonance but phenomenological and cultural coherence. If it is to be believed, as is often asserted in the twenty-first century, that the location from which one theorizes is central to the insights one has of the world, then would it not hold that Black males—those subjects who have been defined by societal exclusion through incarceration, poverty, unwantedness, demonization, and death—could possess different experiences that identify the border to a different register of knowledge?

The Black male suffers as an impossibility within the binary logics of theory. His existence to the world has been defined as the rapist while he has been the unseen rape victim. He is both the murderer and the corpse. He lives in exile from society but manages to formulate a basis of life and creation within the between-ness of the super-predator, the perpetrator of violence, and the perpetual victim of death. He is simultaneously in the minds of others but is existentially neither. He is not-MAN, but he demonstrates himself as something more than the representations offered by the West's imagination. Because he is unacknowledged and denied, he perceives the world from an undisclosed place where thinking is needed but that theory/thought/reason has not yet corrupted. He just has not had the opportunity to speak or describe the world in his own terms. His existence fractures gender because of its expansion of the historical scope of racism while nuancing the seemingly endless relations sexuality displays within oppression. The Black male is the reminder of the limitations of the categorical frames and ontological assertions that theory has used to attempt to capture phenomena in the world. He shows that the definitions of masculinity are not only ever changing but also fundamentally contradictory when placed in relation to other entities.

Sometimes theory forgets there is flesh in the world. For all the arguments against gender as the colonial apparatus it is, our rejection of such an idea must be accompanied by an account of the sexed flesh that Frantz Fanon describes as "a terrifying penis."[64] To ground the study of Blackness beyond the conceptual limits of gender, our thinking must have explanatory power in the world. For all of its theoretical flair, Blackness is still concretized in flesh, and that flesh is differentiated by sex. The inability of the Black male to impose himself on the world as he is makes him vulnerable to the imagination of others. In others' minds, his recognition creates anxiety. Fanon explains that for white men, the Black man represents a raw sexual instinct, "unpunished rapes,"[65] whereas for the white woman he is "the keeper of the impalpable gate that opens into the realm of orgies, of bacchanals, of delirious sexual sensations."[66] These ideas are integrally mixed with how Black males are engaged in abstract processes of judgment, be they in society or in the academy. To suggest that we need not focus on the multiple dynamics of Black males' sexual degradation that serve as catalysts for the fear and aversion manifested against Black men and boys in society because they are an exhausting subject is an act of cowardice that elevates the theorists above the murderous conditions that take the lives of the people they claim to respect in scholarship and honor by thought.

This book has sought to explore one historical process of Black sexual differentiation in the zone of nonbeing, the difference marked by male(d) Black flesh and the phobias this subsequently produced. Future Black manhood scholars must confront an uncomfortable truth: the Black male remains un-thought but overdetermined. Theory disowns his vulnerability; he is little more than the societal stereotypes and myths of maleficence renamed for academic purposes. The world of violence the Black male suffers under is unthinkable. Since the acceptance of his reality destroys ours, he is caricaturized for convenience, and it is this mockery that has been used as the basis of theory. He lacks signification in the language of gender and is erased as a subject/*subject* of interest in regard to race. This ignoring (decentering, as it is called) is taught by scholars and students alike as the natural progression of compassion cultivated by the journey toward diversity of thought. We are made to believe, and rewarded for believing, that his erasure from thought is the moral result of reason turned to our sociohistorical reality, and it is this act (of erasure) that is key to revealing/creating new and more complex subjects. The un-thought Black male being is sold to us as simply being the product of our new ethics, as ethical thought itself. His life and the complexities within must be vacated categorically so that his absence creates space for the conceptualization of other subjects. Perhaps such a world—or, rather, in the configuration of this world where ethics can be used to describe the process of thinking of the Black male child as the cub of the Black male beast and where the death of Black men and boys is not able to be thought of as aberrational—is not a world for Black people at all. Black male studies begins with this premise—this epoché: *this* declaring of Black male life as worthy of study that arrests/suspends the caricatures of current research described under the rubric of Black masculinity. Black male studies refuses the pathologization of Black men and boys as theoretical advance and proposes the empirically informed accounts of Black male life—its indisputable value—as the basis to condemn and object to Black male death.

Epilogue

Black, Male, and (Forced to Remain) Silent

*Censorship and the Subject/*Subject *Dilemma*
in Disciplinary Conceptualizations of the Black Male

WHILE BLACK MEN AND BOYS continue to be criminalized and die at the hands of the state and white vigilantes, disciplinary morality asserts that scholars should resist the urge to account for these deaths theoretically through any serious philosophical or conceptual study. Black male scholars throughout the academy have noted the resistance of journals and various disciplines to seriously consider Black male vulnerability beyond Black feminism or other paradigms that assume that Black males are culturally maladjusted and pathologically violent. To study Black men and boys outside their descriptions as problems is taken to be heresy; any study of Black male vulnerability is taken to be at odds with, and thereby an erasure of, Black female suffering and, more generally, theoretically irrelevant, despite Black males' actual social condition. Conferences are reluctant to accept papers; editors discourage submitting such work for review; and there is vitriol toward the authors of such works that allows booing, ridicule, and intimidation throughout the academy. In my discipline of philosophy, one text has yet to be written that specifically analyzes the life and experience of Black men and boys in America. The at-large morality, in fact, demands that one never be written, because Black males are not thought to be the right subject to/ *subject* of study.

For example, when the editors of an anthology analyzing anti-Blackness solicited "Eschatological Dilemmas" (Chapter 4) as a contribution, they condemned and then dismissed my focus on Black male death and rape. They suggested that my work would have been "easily publishable" had it been submitted as an article to a journal.[1] But for the anthology, it was said that analyzing the historical and sociological realities of Black males would have unjustifiably privileged them as subjects of study and disrupted the overall tone of the volume. One e-mail stated, "[The other editor] believes [the essay] comes across as preferring Black men. I think it is a bit fuzzy; [it] could be stated more clearly[,] particularly because I think some readers would find any essay on [B]lack men suspect from the start (the 'oh here we go' syndrome). Obviously, this would be something we would want to stay clear of, that is, privileging [B]lack men."[2] Notice the conflation: Arguing for the study of the Black male—or, in this case, the Black male corpse—is taken to mean privileging Black males. Contending that Black men and boys are *subjects worthy of study* is such an affront under the gender morality of our day that such works demand the activism of scholars to prevent such writing from seeing the light of day. This censorship of scholarship dealing with Black men and boys both demonstrates and reinforces the unquestioned racist misandry at work within disciplines. While white male and female authors are thought to serve as theoretical guides for various racial projects, regardless of their personal and historical racism, and they can even become sociologically interesting when they realize and own their white privilege, Black males, who remain oppressed and largely absent from the academy as students and professors, are considered pariahs when they are centered as victims.

While journals, college lectures, and books remain dedicated to and composed of endless engagements with white men who supported slavery and believed in Black inferiority, as well as white women who conspired alongside the mythology of the Black rapist and held Black people to be of a savage kind, it is only the writing about Black men and boys that is censored and deliberately prevented from being conceptually engaged. Denying Black men and other scholars who interpret Black masculinity outside feminist paradigms access to journals, book contracts, and specializations or employment dedicated to theorizing about Black manhood originates in a dangerous chauvinism that is used to rationalize pathologized accounts of the Black male as undoubtedly true and beyond contestation. The Black male shall not speak—he is silenced not simply by disciplines, but also by the at-large morality of the scholars who constitute them. It is not that Black men and boys do not actually and in reality suffer the greatest societal disadvantage for being Black and male; it is that the intersectional calculus that dominates the interpretation of Black masculinity denies Black male disadvantage even when it is empirically demonstrated. In short, under our current disciplinary regime Black men cannot be recognized as the most disadvantaged, not because facts demonstrate otherwise, but because theory denies that such recognition is possible because their sex is male. They are simply the wrong subjects to center as the origin of theory.

Since no counter-evidence or explorations are allowed to challenge the rampant dogmas about Black masculinity, disciplines from philosophy to gender studies are allowed to maintain ahistorical mythologies and self-referential theories about Black males without accounting for the disadvantage Black male existence has in the world materially or verifying the alleged privilege Black males enjoy within America's social organizations—its economy, prison industry, institutions of higher education, and so forth. While these inaccuracies themselves should give any serious thinker pause, the most dehumanizing aspect of this paradigm is the assumption that the reporting of Black male death is no different from writing about Black male life. Saying that Black men and boys die does little to capture the causes that extinguish their lives. This reporting requires no academic engagement; it simply requires interpretation of the Black male lives lost. Often these deaths are not thought to be of the kinds important enough to learn more about. Black male deaths are normalized. We already know they happen constantly in our society, so they need not be analyzed. Because Black males are known to die, we need not make them a subject of study. There is no need to divert theoretical resources to the facticity of their demise. Attempting to do so, to study Black males as affected by particular ecological or ideological forces, is reduced to the "Oh, here we go again" syndrome. This is the pathological power of the corpse maintained by Black and white scholars alike, where the overrepresentation of everything Black and male in the dead body is presented as evidence of the Black male's social savagery and disciplinary irrelevance.

Since 2002, homicide has been the leading cause of death of Black males age fifteen to thirty-four.[3] Those Black males who seemingly escape the finality of *death* live to suffer from mass incarceration, poverty, and unemployment and often seek escape through suicide.[4] Although these realities have endured for several decades, many gender theorists insist that the deaths of Black men need not be accounted for beyond the phenomenon of racism that affects all Black people equally. In our current political-disciplinary milieu, patriarchy is thought to direct its violence primarily toward women through misogyny, despite the historical and sociological findings that show Western patriarchy to be a structural system that directs its most lethal violence against racialized (outgroup) males while preserving the lives of females through paternalism.[5]

As a *subject* of study, the Black male is persona non grata. Young racialized males repeatedly have been shown to be at the "greatest risk for witnessing and becoming victim to violence,"[6] factors that make them more likely than other groups in similar environments to suffer anxiety, depression, or aggression as a response.[7] The vulnerability of this group is often ignored by race scholars and gender theorists because of the overwhelming societal stigmas attached to Black males. As the Social Policy Report "The Development of Boys and Young Men of Color" recently explained, the vulnerability of young men of color to death and violence "often goes unnoticed or is dismissed because their victimization is seen as caused by their own criminal behavior and violence."[8] Because Black men and boys are often represented as dangerous and violent in society, they are brought into theory similarly. Said differently, Black males are dismissed as victims of violence because they are conceptualized tautologically—as the cause of the violence and death in the communities that have the effect of causing their violent deaths in these communities.

Discouraging theoretical works written solely for the study of Black males allows for an implicit, but permissible, censorship of discussions and writings that direct attention toward Black male vulnerability, be it political, sexual, or economic. This censorship not only discourages new thinking about Black males but also denies that there is a need for new theories beyond the generic language of intersectionality to speak to the death, poverty, and societal dislocation that disproportionately affect Black males. In short, Black men are the only group in academia that is morally condemned and institutionally excised for attempting to build theories on the experiences and oppression of their own group. Black men are demanded to interpret themselves through the lens of others—coerced into explaining their existence through the theories and biases of white, bourgeois, and (various) feminist lenses. This inability to theorize racialized male experience freely discourages research into dilemmas peculiar to Black males and ultimately coerces Black men into accepting their erasure as a matter of theoretical advancement. This silence takes advantage of the deaths that cause Black men to be underrepresented throughout society and the racism that makes it unlikely that they will graduate from high school or college and ultimately *be* present and considered in the academy.[9] In other words, the deaths and incarceration of Black males in society create the shortage of the actual bodies needed to constitute a demographic as students or professors capable of being represented or recognized as needing to be theoretically accounted for within disciplines.

This book presents an analysis of racism and patriarchy as it has historically affected Black males. It endeavors to show how Black males, as subordinate racialized males, are victimized by the sexual impositions of this white-supremacist society. Insofar as the categorizations of Black males are ideological (as in the mythologies of the Black rapist and the Black criminal) and structurally enforced (as in mass incarceration and policing), various groups and individuals who are not Black and male can perpetuate and structurally benefit from what I have termed *racist misandry*—that is, the peculiar brand of sexual racism against Black men and boys. This book dares to theorize Black males as victims and, in some cases, as more disadvantaged than their female counterparts. The evidence showing the Black male's victimization through rape and other sexual violence, as well as homoeroticism, will be regarded with suspicion, not because such claims are not true, but because such contentions deeply challenge what many students, scholars, and theorists intuitively take to be true about how maleness is situated within the gender concept itself. I can only hope that careful readers will be prompted to place their beliefs in proximity to the evidence presented.

No matter the evidence, some will condemn this book because it cares for—and centers—Black men and boys. Theory insists that they are not the right *bodies*, not the right story. I deliberately defy this always present but often unannounced norm. This book argues that it is (racial) chauvinism that tells scholars, students, and the public that Black men and boys are not worthy of study, that they have no perspective worth considering as intrinsically valid and true about the world, but it is (racist) misandry, the visceral hatred this society has for the Black male, that celebrates his death, finds humor in his rape, and exhibits indifference to his suffering. It is this same hatred of Black men and boys that allows scholars to deny the suffering of the Black male because they prefer other lives to his.

In this regard, I understand that this book may not be written for this time, for those politics, or for those scholars, because this book is written to serve as a basis for a new kind of study that engages Black males beyond the threats they are assumed to be and the phobias imposed on them. This book not only endeavors to think differently about Black men and boys; it endeavors to establish a genuine theoretical orientation to their study and, thus, to escape—to reach beyond—the thinking and thinkers of this time.

Acknowledgments

I WAS INSPIRED to write this manuscript to correct what I saw as a lack of historically informed and sociologically relevant accounts of Black men and boys in liberal arts fields beholden only to theory. Undertaking such a work was called perilous by some and courageous by others. What emerged as the final manuscript was the product of comments, discussions, and debates across the country over theory, history, and the ability or inability of theory to account for the realities offered by empirical data. These conversations rarely reached a consensus, but they allowed me to enrich the manuscript in infinitely fruitful ways.

I will forever be grateful for the support of my colleagues Linda Radzik and Bob Shandley in the publication of this work. Linda's commentary and pensiveness helped me tailor the text to a larger audience than I thought possible. Bob's cutthroat inspiration echoed in the weeks preceding the completion of the text. Amir Jaima, Jessica Otto, Colleen Murphy, T. Hasan Johnson, Randal Jelks, Jonathan Lee, Fred Hord, and Melvin Rogers gave of their time and minds to offer close readings and comments on earlier drafts or versions of the chapters. Others, such as Joe Feagin, Violet Johnson, Kenneth Nunn, Floyd W. Hayes, John Drabinski, Richard Delgado, Jean Stefancic, James Haile, Dwayne Tunstall, Lisa Corrigan, Naomi Zack, and LaRose Parris, provided invaluable commentary. Evelyn Simien, a fellow Lake Charlesian, took time out from her schedule not only to discuss her findings on Black males' gender-progressive attitudes but also to make recommendations regarding publishers and venues. I also thank Joan Vidal and the staff at Temple University Press.

Multiple organizations supported this project, facilitating invited panels or presentations of my research on Black males. I thank Jane Gordon and the Caribbean Philosophy Association, Philosophy Born of Struggle, and Darryl Scott and the Association for the Study of African American Life and History for allowing the Alain Locke Seminar to be the first to share the discovery of Eldridge Cleaver's lost manuscript *The Book of Lives*, and the African American Professional Organization at Texas A&M University. *Our Common Ground*, with Janice Graham; Rob Redding's *Talking Tough with Tommy* on Sirius XM; and Gus Renegade's *C.O.W.S.* have provided venues and an audience for my work.

I must also acknowledge the voices that motivated me to undertake a theoretical treatise on Black males. I thank all the Black men and boys who through e-mails and private messages rallied me to write without apology. My exchanges with scholars in education such as Fred Bonner, Donna Ford, and William A. Smith were invaluable. The Black Masculinity group—Ryon Cobb, Darrius Hills, Joshua Lazard, Farris Muhammed, and Ronald Neal—kept me grounded. Rondee Gaines, Rachel Hastings, and Ebony Utley demanded that my words say more than I thought possible.

In addition, I thank my graduate students. Patrick Anderson's reading and editing of an earlier version of the manuscript was immeasurably helpful. Rocio Alvarez's, Dalitso Ruwe's, and Andrew Soto's readings of and responses to various sections of the manuscript informed and colored my research and the final product.

My wife—my beautiful wife—Gwenetta Curry has listened to me read section after section and allowed me to ask her time and time again, "Does this sound like me?" She also read innumerable passages without complaint. To Gwenetta and my daughters I owe the drive to persist.

Finally, I thank the Black men in philosophy who have survived the onslaught of white supremacy and racial misandry and who have served as my inspiration and as mentors and friends: the late Derrick Bell, Dr. Leonard Harris, Dr. Bill Lawson, Dr. Al Mosley, and Dr. Lucius Outlaw.

To those who have offered their input who are not mentioned here, I extend my heartfelt gratitude for countless comments that have both impacted me and improved the text.

Notes

INTRODUCTION

1. Campbell Robinson, "Black Man's Body Found Hanging from Tree in Mississippi," *New York Times*, March 19, 2015, http://www.nytimes.com/2015/03/20/us/black-mans-body-found-hanging-from-tree-in-mississippi.html.

2. Todd C. Frankel, "FBI Investigates Suspicious Death of North Carolina Teen Lennon Lacy," *Washington Post*, December 19, 2014, http://www.washingtonpost.com/national/fbi-investigates-suspicious-death-of-north-carolina-teen-lennon-lacy/2014/12/19/02499522-8609-11e4-a702-fa31ff4ae98e_story.html.

3. Shaun King, "Video Shows Police Tasing a Bloody Restrained Matthew Ajibade in the Testicles before His Death," DailyKos.com, October 13, 2015, http://www.dailykos.com/story/2015/10/13/1431428/-Bloody-strapped-to-chair-video-shows-police-tasering-Matthew-Ajibade-in-the-testicles-before-death?detail=emailclassic.

4. Heather Catallo, "Allen Park Police Sued after Man Says He Underwent an Illegal Body Cavity Search," Wxyz.com, September 16, 2016, http://www.wxyz.com/news/monday-at-11-disturbing-video-captures-dehumanizing-jailhouse-incident.

5. Josiah Hesse, "Convicted of Rape Based on a Dream, Man Relishes Freedom after 28 Years," TheGuardian.com, December 24, 2015, https://www.theguardian.com/us-news/2015/dec/24/clarence-moses-el-free-denver-rape-case.

6. Jeff Hearn, "Is Masculinity Dead? A Critique of the Concept of Masculinity/Masculinities," in *Understanding Masculinities: Social Relations and Cultural Arenas*, ed. Mairtin Mac an Ghaill (Buckingham, UK: Open University Press, 1996), 202–217; Michael Flood, "Between Men and Masculinity: An Assessment of the Term Masculinity in Recent Scholarship on Men," in *Manning the Next Millennium*, ed. Sharyn Pearce and Vivienne Muller (Bentley, Australia: Black Swan, 2002), 203–213.

7. Mike Donaldson, "What Is Hegemonic Masculinity," *Theory and Society* 22, no. 5 (1993): 643–657; Jeff Hearn, "From Hegemonic Masculinity to the Hegemony of Men," *Feminist Theory* 5, no. 1 (2004): 49–72.

8. James W. Messerschmidt, "Engendering Gendered Knowledge: Assessing the Academic Appropriation of Hegemonic Masculinity," *Men and Masculinities* 15.1 (2012): 56–76, 73.

9. Ann-Dorte Christensen and Sune Qvotrup Jensen, "Combining Hegemonic Masculinity and Intersectionality," *Norma* 9, no. 1 (2014): 71.

10. Arthur F. Saint-Aubin, "Testeria: The Dis-ease of Black Men in [w]hite Supremacist, Patriarchal Culture," *Callaloo* 17, no. 4 (1994): 1056.

11. Andrea G. Hunter and James Earl Davis, "Hidden Voices of Black Men: The Meaning, Structure, and Complexity of Manhood," *Journal of Black Studies* 25, no. 1 (1994): 21.

12. Calvin C. Hernton, *Sex and Racism in America* (New York: Doubleday, 1965), xiii.

13. Saint-Aubin, "Testeria," 1057.

14. Ibid., 1058.

15. Saint-Aubin, "Testeria," 1066.

16. Oyèrónké Oyewúmì, "Visualizing the Body: Western Theories and African Subjects," in *The Invention of Women: Making an African Sense of Western Gender Discourses* (Minneapolis: University of Minnesota Press, 1997), 1–20.

17. Maria Lugones, "Toward a Decolonial Feminism," *Hypatia* 25, no. 4 (2010): 743.

18. Ibid., 744.

19. Sylvia Wynter, "Afterword: Beyond Miranda's Meanings: Un/silencing the Demonic Ground of Caliban's Woman," in *Out of Kumbla: Caribbean Women and Literature*, ed. Carolyn Boyce Davies and Elaine Savory Fido (Trenton, NJ: African World Press, 1994), 358.

20. In an "Interview in Proudflesh," in *Proudflesh* 4 (2006): 24, Wynter continues: "For example, in our order, which is a bourgeois order of kind, a bourgeois order of the human, the woman was supposed to be the housewife and the man was supposed to be the breadwinner. Each was as locked into their roles. By making the feminist movement into a bourgeois movement, what they've done is to fight to be equal breadwinners. This means that the breadwinning man and the breadwinning woman become a new class, so that the woman who remains in her role becomes a part of a subordinated class."

21. See Becky Bratu, "After Zimmerman's Website Raises more than $200,000, Prosecution Asks Judge to Raise Bond," MSNBC.com, April 27, 2012, http://usnews.nbcnews.com/ _news/2012/04/27/11427416-after-zimmermans-website-raises-more-than-200000-pros ecution-asks-judge-to-raise-bond. See also Natalie DiBlasio, "Cash Raised for Mo. Cop Surpasses Brown Donations," USAToday.com, August 24, 2014, http://www.usatoday.com/ story/news/nation/2014/08/23/support-darren-wilson-rally/14495459.

22. Michele Wallace, *The Black Macho and the Myth of the Superwoman* (New York: Dial, 1979), 73.

23. Ibid., 73.

24. Ibid., 79.

25. Ibid.

26. Ibid., 79.

27. Aaronette M. White, *Ain't I a Feminist? African American Men Speak Out on Fatherhood, Friendship, Forgiveness, and Freedom* (New York: State University of New York Press, 2008), xv.

28. Gary Lemon's memoir *Black Male Outsider: Teaching as a Pro-Feminist Man* (Albany: State of New York University Press, 2008) suggests that Black male gender progressivism begins with the question "Why would a Black man advocate for change that would deny him his patriarchal piece of the pie?" posed by Aaronette White in *Ain't I a Feminist?* Lemon writes, "It is a question with personal and political resonance for every [B]lack man in a culture of male supremacy, where all men (in spite of race, ethnicity, and/or class) ben-

efit from being a 'man'": Lemon, *Black Male Outsider*, 14. We find a similar call in David Ikard's *Breaking the Silence: Toward a Black Male Feminist Criticism* (Baton Rouge: Louisiana State University Press, 2007), 1–28, which makes a distinction between patriarchy as a system and practices of inequality but nonetheless asserts that Black males are patriarchs by definition.

29. Raewyn Connell, *Masculinities* (Berkeley: University of California Press, 2005 [1995]).

30. Sojourner Truth, "Address to the First Annual Meeting of the American Equal Rights Association, 1867," in *The Concise History of Woman Suffrage: Selections from "History of Woman Suffrage"* (Urbana: University of Illinois Press, 2005), 235–236.

31. Paula Giddings, "The Lessons of History Will Shape the 1980s—*Black Macho and the Myth of the Superwoman* Won't," *Encore America and Worldwide News* 8 (1979): 51.

32. Ibid.

33. Wallace, *The Black Macho and the Myth of the Superwoman*, 7.

34. The rumor began in the late 1970s with the publication of *The Black Macho and the Myth of the Superwoman*. Wallace argues that "Ruby Doris Smith Robinson . . . participated in and perhaps led a sit in earlier that year in SNCC offices protesting the relegation of women to typing and clerical work. She is said to have written a paper on the position of [B]lack women in SNCC. The paper was lost and no one is quite certain of its content . . . but it prompted Stokely Carmichael to respond, 'The only position of women in SNCC is prone'": Wallace, *The Black Macho and the Myth of the Superwoman*, 6–7. From this quote Wallace extrapolates: "With freedom presumably on the horizon, [B]lack men needed a movement that made the division of power between men and women clearer, that would settle once and for all the nagging questions [B]lack women were beginning to ask: 'Where do we fit in? What are you going to do about us? It was the restless throng of ambitious [B]lack female civil rights workers—as much as any failure of the Civil Rights Movement—that provoked Stokely Carmichael to cry 'Black Power'": ibid, 7. Peniel Joseph notes that the quote "shorn of context . . . damaged his personal reputation, cost him political credibility in feminist circles, and unfairly minimized SNCC's democratic culture": Peniel Joseph, *Stokely: A Life* (New York: Basic Civatas, 2014), 80.

35. Mary King, *Freedom Song: A Personal Story of the 1960s Civil Rights Movement* (New York: William Morrow, 1987), 446.

36. Ibid., 452.

37. Ibid.

38. Ibid.

39. Ibid.

40. Casey Hayden, "In the Attics of My Mind," in *Hands on the Freedom Plow: Personal Accounts by Women in SNCC*, ed. Faith S. Holbert, Martha Prescod, Norman Noonan, Judy Richardson, Betty Garman Robinson, Jean Smith Young, and Dorothy M. Zellner (Urbana: University of Illinois Press, 2010), 385.

41. Michele Wallace, "How I Saw It Then, How I See It Now," in *The Black Macho and the Myth of the Superwoman* (New York: Verso, 1990), xx.

42. Ibid., xix.

43. Raewyn Connell, *Ruling Class, Ruling Culture* (London: Cambridge University Press, 1977).

44. Raewyn Connell, *Gender and Power: Society, the Person, and Sexual Politics* (Redwood City, CA: Stanford University Press, 1987), 183.

45. Ibid., 186.

46. Ibid., 153–154.

47. Ibid., 184.

48. Ibid.

49. Connell defines emphasized femininity as "defined around compliance with this subordination and is oriented to accommodating the interests and desires of men": Connell, *Gender and Power*, 183.

50. Raewyn Connell, *Masculinities* (Berkeley: University of California Press, 1995), 68.

51. Ibid.

52. Connell, *Gender and Power*, 197.

53. Raewyn Connell, *Gender* (Cambridge: Polity, 2009), 84.

54. Raewyn Connell and James W. Messerschmidt, "Hegemonic Masculinity: Rethinking the Concept," *Gender and Society* 19 (2005): 847.

55. Ibid., 848.

56. Raewyn Connell, "Margin Becoming Centre: For a World-Centred Rethinking of Masculinities," *Norma* 9, no. 4 (2014): 217–231.

57. Robert Staples, "The Myth of Black Macho: A Response to Angry Black Feminists," *Black Scholar* 10, nos. 6–7 (1979): 24–33.

58. Connell actually says, "Economics and ideology were equally emphasized in Robert Staples's *Black Masculinity*, a pioneering study of ethnic difference. Staples connected the social situation of [B]lack men within American racism to the dynamic of colonialism in the third world, an insight which has rarely been followed up": Connell, *Masculinities* (1995), 36.

59. Messerschmidt, "Engendering Gendered Knowledge," 56–76.

60. Angela Davis, "Reflections on the Black Woman's Role in the Community of Slaves," *Black Scholar* 3, no. 4 (1971): 7, 15.

61. Gloria Joseph, "The Incompatible Ménage a Trois: Marxism, Feminism, and Racism," in *Women and Revolution: A Discussion of the Unhappy Marriage of Marxism and Feminism*, ed. Lydia Sargent (Cambridge, MA: South End, 1981), 94–95.

62. Raewyn W. Connell, Dean Ashenden, Sandra Kessler, and Gary Dowsett, *Making the Difference: Schools, Families, and Social Division* (Sydney: George Allen and Unwin, 1982).

63. Lawrence E. Gary, ed., *Black Men* (Beverly Hills, CA: Sage, 1981).

64. Ibid., 10.

65. Ibid., 11.

66. Ibid.

67. Robert Staples, *Black Masculinity: The Black Male's Role in American Society* (San Francisco: Black Scholar Press, 1982), 135.

68. Ibid., 7.

69. See Robert Staples, "Masculinity and Race: The Dual Dilemma of Black Men," *Journal of Social Issues* 34, no. 1 (1978): 169–183.

70. Ibid., 135.

71. Staples, *Black Masculinity*, 14.

72. Ibid., 13–16.

73. Jo Jones and William D. Mosher, "Fathers' Involvement with Their Children: United States, 2006–2010," *National Health Statistics Reports* 71 (2013): 1–22.

74. Serie McDougal and Clarence George, "I Wanted to Return the Favor: The Experiences and Perspectives of Black Social Fathers," *Journal of Black Studies* 47, no. 6 (2016): 524–549.

75. Anthony Lemelle Jr. and Juan Battle, "Black Masculinity Matters in Attitudes toward Gay Males," *Journal of Homosexuality* 47, no. 1 (2004): 46; Charles Negy and Russell, "A Comparison of African American and [w]hite College Students' Affective and Attitudinal Reactions to Lesbian, Gay, and Bisexual Individuals: An Exploratory Study," *Journal of Sex Research* 42, no. 4 (2005): 291–298.

76. Clyde Franklin, *The Changing Definition of Masculinity* (New York: Plenum, 1984), 53–54.

77. Andrea G. Hunter and James Earl Davis, "Constructing Gender: An Exploration of Afro-American Men's Conceptualization of Manhood," *Gender and Society* 6, no. 3 (1992): 475.

78. Nathan Hare and Julia Hare, *Bringing the Black Boy to Manhood: The Passage* (San Francisco: Black Think Tank, 1985), 20.

79. Hunter and Davis, "Constructing Gender,"471.

80. Ibid., 475.

81. Noel A. Cazenave, "A Woman's Place: The Attitudes of Middle-Class Black Men," *Phylon* 44, no. 1 (1983): 21.

82. Ruby Lee Gooley, "The Role of Black Women in Social Change," *Western Journal of Black Studies* 13, no. 4 (1989): 169.

83. Kathleen M. Blee and Ann R. Tickamyer, "Racial Differences in Men's Attitudes about Women's Gender Roles," *Journal of Marriage and Family* 57 (1995): 29.

84. Andrea G. Hunter and Sherrill L. Sellers, "Feminist Attitudes among African American Women and Men," *Gender and Society* 12, no. 1 (1998): 97.

85. Ibid., 82.

86. Ibid., 94.

87. Ibid., 95.

88. Evelyn Simien, *Black Feminist Voices in Politics* (New York: State University of New York Press, 2006), 54.

89. Ibid., 55–56.

90. Evelyn Simien, "A Black Gender Gap? Continuity and Change in Attitudes to Black Feminism," in *African American Perspectives on Political Science*, ed. Rich Wilbur (Philadelphia: Temple University Press, 2007), 146.

91. Patricia Hill Collins, "Defining Black Feminist Thought," in *The Second Wave: A Reader in Feminist Theory*, vol. 1, ed. Linda J. Nicholson (New York: Routledge, 1997), 243.

92. Catherine Harnois, "Race, Gender, and the Black Women's Standpoint," *Sociological Forum* 25, no. 1 (2010): 82–84.

93. Catherine Harnois, "Complexity within and Similarity across: Interpreting Black Men's Support of Gender Justice, amidst Cultural Representations that Suggest Otherwise," in *Hyper Sexual, Hyper Masculine? Gender, Race and Sexuality in the Identities of Contemporary Black Men*, ed. Brittany C. Slatton and Kemesha Spates (Burlington, UK: Ashgate, 2014), 85–102.

94. Lugones, "Toward a Decolonial Feminism," 744.

95. Darieck Scott, *Extravagant Abjection: Blackness, Power, and Sexuality in the African American Literary Imagination* (New York: New York University Press, 2010), 19.

96. Ibid., 19.

97. Abdul JanMohamed, "Sexuality on/of the Racial Border: Foucault, Wright, and the Articulation of 'Racialized Sexuality'," in *Discourses of Sexuality: From Aristotle to AIDS*, ed. Donna Stanton (Ann Arbor: University of Michigan Press, 1992), 94–116, 96.

98. Abdul JanMohamed, *The Death-Bound-Subject: Richard Wright's Archaeology of Death* (Durham, NC: Duke University Press, 2005), 10.

99. Hortense Spillers, "Mama's Baby, Papa's Maybe: An American Grammar Book," *Diacritics* 17, no. 2 (1987): 67.

100. Ibid., 8–10.

101. Ibid., 249.

102. Greg Thomas, *The Sexual Demon of Colonial Power: Pan-African Embodiment and Erotic Schemes of Empire* (Bloomington: Indiana University Press, 2007), 42.

103. William Styron, *The Confessions of Nat Turner* (New York: Random House, 1967).

104. Eldridge Cleaver, "Bitches," in *The Book of Lives*, n.d., Eldridge Cleaver Collection, 1959–1981, Cushing Library, Texas A&M University, College Station, series 13, box 2, folder 26, 1.

105. Tyrone C. Howard, *Black Male(d): Peril and Promise in the Education of African American Males* (New York: Teachers College Press, 2014).

106. Carla R. Monroe, "African-American Boys and the Discipline Gap: Balancing Educators Uneven Hand," *Educational Horizons* 84, no. 2 (2006): 102–111.

107. Sandra I. Ross and Jeffrey M. Jackson, "Teacher's Expectations for Black Males' and Black Females' Academic Achievement," *Personality and Social Psychology Bulletin* 17, no. 1 (1991): 78–82; Valora Washington, "Racial Differences in Teacher Perceptions of First and Fourth Grade Pupils on Selected Characteristics," *Journal of Negro Education* 51, no. 1 (1982): 60–72; Seth Gershenson, Stephen B. Holt, and Nicholas Pagageorge, "Who Believes in Me? The Effect of Student-Teacher Demographic Match on Teacher Expectations," Upjohn Institute Working Paper no. 15-231, W. E. Upjohn Institute for Employment Research, Kalamazoo, MI, 2015).

108. Scott Graves, "Are We Neglecting African American Males: Parental Involvement Differences between African American Males and Females during Elementary School," *Journal of African American Studies* 14 (2010): 263–276; Stephanie J. Rowley, Latisha Ross, Fantasy T. Lozada, Amber Williams, Adrian Gale, Beth Kurtz-Costes, "Framing Black Boys: Parent, Teacher, and Student Narrative of the Academic Lives of Black Boys," *Advances in Child Development and Behavior* 47 (2014): 301–332.

109. National Center for Education Statistics, "The Condition of Education 2012," U.S. Department of Education, Washington, DC, 2012, https://nces.ed.gov/fastfacts/display.asp?id=72.

110. John W. Curtis, *The Employment Status of Instructional Staff Members in Higher Education, Fall 2011* (Washington, DC: American Association of University Professors, 2014), 54–55.

111. Anne MacDaniel, "The Black Gender Gap in Educational Attainment: Historical Trends and Racial Comparisons," *Demography* 48 (2011): 891.

112. Rhonda V. Sharpe and Omari H. Swinton, "Beyond Anecdotes: A Quantitative Examination of Black Women in Academe," *Review of Black Political Economy* 39 (2012): 344.

113. Ibid., 352.

114. Richard R. Verdugo and Ronald D. Henderson, "The Demography of African American Males in Higher Education," *Diversity in Higher Education* 6 (2009): 67–82. See also Rhonda V. Sharpe and William Darity, "Where Are All the Brothers? Alternatives to Four-Year Colleges for Black Males," *Diversity in Higher Education* 6 (2009): 135–153; James R. Dunn, "The Shortage of Black Male Students in the College Classroom: Consequences and Causes," *Western Journal of Black Studies* 12 (1988): 73–76.

115. W.E.B. Du Bois, "Boys and Girls," *The Crisis* 34, no. 6 (1927): 69.

116. Wilma J. Henry, Dyonne M. Butler, and Nicole M. West, "Things Are Not as Rosy as They Seem: Psychosocial Issues of Contemporary Black College Women," *Journal of College Student Retention* 13, no. 2 (2011): 137–153; "College Degree Awards: The Ominous Gender Gap in African American Education," *Journal of Blacks in Higher Education* 23 (1999): 6–9.

117. Heather C. West, *Prison Inmates at Midyear 2009* (Washington, DC: U.S. Department of Justice, 2010), 20.

118. E. Ann Carson, "Prisoners in 2014," U.S. Bureau of Justice Statistics, Washington, DC, 2015, http://www.bjs.gov/content/pub/pdf/p14.pdf, 15.

119. Derek Neal and Armin Rick, "The Prison Boom and the Lack of Black Progress after Smith and Welch," National Bureau of Economic Research Working Paper no. 20283, 2014, 42.

120. Evelyn Patterson and Christopher Wildeman, "Mass Imprisonment and the Life Course Revisited: Cumulative Years Spent Imprisoned and Marked for Working-Age Black and [w]hite Men," *Social Science Research* 53 (2015): 335.

121. Becky Pettit, *Invisible Men: Mass Incarceration and the Myth of Black Progress* (New York: Russell Sage Foundation, 2012), 18.

122. Evelyn Patterson, "Incarcerating Death: Mortality in the U.S. State Correctional Facilities, 1985–1998," *Demography* 47 (2010): 587–607.

123. Lara Stemple, Andrew Flores, and Ilan Meyer, "Sexual Victimization Perpetrated by Women: Federal Data Reveal Surprising Prevalence," *Aggression and Violent Behavior* (2016): 2.

124. FBI Uniform Crime Report, "Rape," Crime in the United States 2013, https://www.fbi.gov/about-us/cjis/ucr/crime-in-the-u.s/2013/crime-in-the-u.s.-2013/violent-crime/rape.

125. Lara Stemple and Ilan Meyer, "The Sexual Victimization of Men in America: New Data Challenge Old Assumptions," *American Journal of Public Health* 104, no. 6 (2014): e21.

126. Karen Weiss, "Male Sexual Victimization: Examining Men's Experience of Rape and Sexual Assault," *Men and Masculinities* 12, no. 3 (2010): 275–298.

127. Stemple and Meyer, "The Sexual Victimization of Men in America," e21.

128. Ibid., e23.

129. Kim Shayo Buchanan, "Engendering Rape," *UCLA Law Review* 59 (2012): 1633.

130. See M. Dyan McGuire, "The Empirical and Legal Realities Surrounding Staff Perpetrated Sexual Abuse of Inmates," *Criminal Law Bulletin* 46, no. 3 (2010): 428–451.

131. Buchanan, "Engendering Rape," 1668.

132. Frantz Fanon, *Black Skin, [w]hite Masks* (New York: Grove, 1967), 156.

133. Ibid., 157.

134. Ibid., 159.

135. Dexter Rogers, "Death in Mississippi: Lynching or Suicide?" HuffingtonPost.com, February 28, 2011, http://www.huffingtonpost.com/dexter-rogers/frederick-jermaine-carter_b_827970.html.

136. Desire Thompson, "Black Man Sues NYPD after Spending Six Weeks in Jail for Wearing a Hoodie," NewsOne.com, October 21, 2015, http://newsone.com/3218096/black-man-arrested-jail-for-wearing-hoodie-sues-nypd/.

137. Laura Bult, Rocco Parascandola, and Nancy Dillon, "Transit Cop Who Busted Innocent Subway Rider for Stealing Backpack Has Been Accused before of False Arrest," NYDailyNews.com, October 21, 2015, http://www.nydailynews.com/new-york/nyc-transit-faces-claim-false-arrest-article-1.2404953.

138. Eyder Peralta, "Kalief Browder, Jailed for Years without Trial, Kills Himself," NPR.org, June 8, 2015, http://www.npr.org/sections/thetwo-way/2015/06/08/412842780/kalief-browder-jailed-for-years-at-rikers-island-without-trial-commits-suicide.

139. Jennifer Gonnerman, "Kalief Browder: 1993–2015," NewYorker.com, June 7, 2015, http://www.newyorker.com/news/news-desk/kalief-browder-1993-2015.

140. Justin Wolfers, David Leonhardt, and Keven Quealy, "1.5 Million Missing Black Men," NYTimes.com, April 20, 2015, http://www.nytimes.com/interactive/2015/04/20/upshot/missing-black-men.html.

141. David A. Love, "America's 1.5 Million Missing Black Men Is Nothing Short of Genocide," TheGrio.com, April 24, 2015, http://thegrio.com/2015/04/24/million-missing-black-men-genocide.

142. Alexia Cooper and Erica L. Smith, *Homicide Trends in the United States, 1980–2008* (Washington, DC: U.S. Bureau of Justice Statistics, 2011), 14, http://bjs.gov/content/pub/pdf/htus8008.pdf. See also Erica L. Smith and Alexia Cooper, *Homicide in the U.S. Known to Law Enforcement, 2011* (Washington, DC: U.S. Bureau of Justice Statistics, 2013), http://www.bjs.gov/content/pub/pdf/hus11.pdf, 1–17.

143. Jeffrey A. Bridge, Lindsey Asti, Lisa M. Horowitz, Joel B. Greenhouse, Cynthia A. Fontanella, Ariella H. Sheftall, Kelly J. Kelleher, and John V. Campo, "Suicide Trends among Elementary School-Aged Children in the United States from 1993 to 2012," *JAMA Pediatrics* 169, no. 7 (2015): 673–677.

144. Earlise Ward and Maigenete Mengesha, "Depression in African American Men: A Review of What We Know and Where We Need to Go from Here," *American Journal of Orthopsychiatry* 83, nos. 2–3 (2013): 386–397.

CHAPTER 1

1. X-Ray, quoted in *The Colored American* (Washington, DC), 1899.

2. Oyèrónké Oyewúmì, "Visualizing the Body: Western Theories and African Subjects," in *The Invention of Women: Making an African Sense of Western Gender Discourses* (Minneapolis: University of Minnesota Press, 1997), 1–20.

3. See J. Lorand Matory, "Sexual Secrets: Candomblé, Brazil, and the Multiple Intimacies of the African Diaspora," in *Off Stage/On Display: Intimacy and Ethnography in the Age of Public Culture*, ed. Andrew Shyrock (Stanford, CA: Stanford University Press, 2004), 157–190; Agnes Atia Apusigah, "Is Gender Yet Another Colonial Project: A Critique of Oyèrónké Oyewúmì's Proposal," *Quest* 20 (2008): 23–44.

4. Oyewúmì, "Visualizing the Body," 5.

5. Ibid., 8.

6. Melissa N. Stein, *Measuring Manhood: Race and the Science of Masculinity, 1830–1934* (Minneapolis: University of Minnesota Press, 2015), 89–96.

7. Barry Alain Shain, *The Myth of American Individualism: The Protestant Origins of American Political Thought* (Princeton, NJ: Princeton University Press, 1994), 294.

8. G.W.F. Hegel, *The Philosophy of History* (New York: Prometheus, 1991), 111.

9. Ibid., 113.

10. Ibid., 117.

11. Teshale Tibebu, *Hegel and the Third World* (Syracuse, NY: Syracuse University Press, 2010), esp. chaps. 4, 6.

12. Thomas Jefferson, "Notes on Virginia: Query 14," in *Jefferson: Political Writings*, ed. Joyce Appleby and Terence Ball (Cambridge: Cambridge University Press, 2004), 476.

13. George M. Stroud, *A Sketch of the Laws Relating to Slavery in the Several States of the United States* (Philadelphia: Henry Longstreth, 1856), 147.

14. Willie Lee Rose, "The Domestication of Domestic Slavery" in *Slavery and Freedom*, ed. William H. Freehling (New York: Oxford University Press, 1982), 21.

15. Ibid., 24–25.

16. J. H. Van Evrie, "Introduction," in *The Dred Scott Decision*, vol. 2 (New York: Van Evrie, Horton, 1859), iv.

17. Angela Y. Davis, *Women, Race, and Class* (New York: Vintage, 1983), 7.

18. Rose, "The Domestication of Domestic Slavery," 29.

19. C. G. Memminger, *Lecture Delivered before the Young Men's Library Association of Augusta, April 10, 1951* (Charleston, S.C.: Library Association of Augusta, 1851), 14–15.

20. Ann Firor Scott, *The Southern Lady: From Pedestal to Politics, 1830–1930* (Chicago: University of Chicago Press, 1970), 14, 19.

21. Ibid., 8.

22. Ibid., 37.

23. Horace Mann, *A Few Thoughts on the Powers and Duties of Woman: Two Lectures* (Syracuse, NY: Hall, Mills, 1853), 125.

24. Mary P. Ryan, *The Empire of the Mother: American Writing about Domesticity, 1830–1860* (Binghamton, NY: Harrington Park Press, 1982), 97.

25. Ibid., 112.

26. Ibid., 113.

27. Ibid., 18.

28. Amy Kaplan, "Manifest Domesticity," *American Literature* 70, no. 3 (1998): 583.

29. Ibid. Kaplan continues, "Isolating the empire of the mother from other imperial endeavors, however, runs two risks: first, it may reproduce in women's studies the insularity of an American studies that imagines the nation as a fixed, monolithic, and self-enclosed geographic and cultural whole; second, the legacy of separate spheres that sees women as morally superior to men can lead to the current moralistic strain in feminist criticism, which has shifted from celebrating the liberatory qualities of white women's writing to condemning their racism": ibid.

30. Ibid., 581.

31. Amy S. Greensberg, *Manifest Manhood and the Antebellum American Empire* (New York: Cambridge University Press, 2005), 270.

32. Kaplan, "Manifest Domesticity," 583.

33. Ibid., 586.

34. Margaret D. Jacobs, *[w]hite Mother to a Dark Race: Settler Colonialism, Maternalism, and the Removal of Indigenous Children in the American West and Australia, 1880–1940* (Lincoln: University of Nebraska Press, 2009), 22.

35. Terry A. Barnhart, "Toward a Science of Man: European Influences on the Archaeology of Ephraim George Squier," in *New Perspectives on the Origins of Americanist Archaeology*, ed. David Browman and Stephen Williams (Tuscaloosa: University of Alabama Press, 2002), 87–116.

36. A. H. Keane, *Ethnology: Fundamental Ethnical Problems; the Primary Ethnical Groups* (Cambridge: Cambridge University Press, 1909), 2.

37. Wilhelm Dilthey, *Introduction to the Human Sciences*, vol. 1, ed. Rudolph A. Makreel and Frithjof Rodi (Princeton, NJ: Princeton University Press, 1989), 91–92.

38. Arthur de Gobineau, *The Inequality of the Human Races* (New York: G. P. Putnam's Sons, 1915), 88.

39. Ibid., 40.

40. Ibid., 89.

41. Ibid., 182.

42. Jules Michelet, *Woman (La Femme)* (New York: Carleton, 1867), 133.

43. Anne McClintock, *Imperial Leather: Race, Gender, and Sexuality in the Colonial Contest* (New York: Routledge, 1995), 55–56.

44. James Hunt, *The Negro's Place in Nature* (London: Trubner, 1863), 39.

45. Robert Dunn, "Civilisation and Cerebral Development: Some Observations on the Influence of Civilisation upon the Development of the Brain in the Different Races of Man," *Transactions of the Ethnological Society of London* (1866): 25.

46. Stein, *Measuring Manhood*, 107.

47. J. H. Van Evrie, *The Negroes and Negro Slavery: The First in an Inferior Race* (New York: Van Evire and Horton, 1863), 102.

48. Ibid., 102–103.

49. Stein, *Measuring Manhood*, 94.

50. Ibid., 107.

51. Hunter McGuire and G. Frank Lydston, *Sexual Crimes among the Southern Negroes* (Louisville, KY: Renz and Henry, 1893), 17.

52. F. E. Daniel, "The Cause and Prevention of Rape," *Texas Medical Journal* 19, no.11 (1904): 459.

53. William Lee Howard, "The Negro as a Distinct Ethnic Factor in Civilization," *Medicine* 9 (1903): 424.

54. See F. E. Daniel, "Castration of Sexual Perverts," *Texas Medical Journal* 27, no. 10 (1912): 369–385; G. Frank Lydston, "Castration Instead of Lynching," *Atlanta Journal-Record of Medicine* 8 (1906): 456–458.

55. Louise Newman, *[w]hite Women's Rights: The Racial Origins of Feminism in the United States* (New York: Oxford University Press, 1999), 161.

56. Gail Bederman, *Manliness and Civilization: A Cultural History of Gender and Race in the U.S., 1880–1917* (Chicago: University of Chicago Press, 1995), 28.

57. Newman, *[w]hite Women's Rights*, 161.

58. G. Stanley Hall, *Adolescence: Its Psychology and Its Relations to Physiology, Anthropology, Sociology, Sex, Crime, Religion and Education*, vols. 1–2 (New York: D. Appleton, 1904). For an explanation of recapitulation theory, see Robert E. Grinder, "The Concept of Adolescence in the Genetic Psychology of G. Stanley Hall," *Child Development* 40, no. 2 (1969): 355–369. For an explanation of recapitulation and progressive era education reforms and assumptions, see Thomas D. Fallace, *Race and the Origins of Progressive Education, 1880–1929* (New York: Teachers College Press, 2015).

59. Ann L. Stoler, *Carnal Knowledge and Imperial Power: Race and the Intimate in Colonial Rule* (Berkeley: University of California Press, 2002), 57.

60. See Allison Sneider, *Suffragists in an Imperial Age: U.S. Expansion and the Imperial Age, 1870–1920* (Oxford: Oxford University Press, 2008); Jacobs, *[w]hite Mother to a Darker Race*.

61. Newman, *[w]hite Women's Rights*, 14.

62. Abouali Farmanfarmaian, "Did You Measure Up? The Role of Race in the Gulf War," in *Collateral Damage: The New World Order at Home and Abroad*, ed. Cynthia Peters (Boston: South End, 1992), 119.

63. Newman, *[w]hite Women's Rights*, 14.

64. Grace Elizabeth Hale, *Making [w]hiteness: The Culture of Segregation in the South, 1890–1940* (New York: Vintage, 1998), 74.

65. Crystal Feimster, *Southern Horrors: Women and the Politics of Rape and Lynching* (Cambridge, MA: Harvard University Press, 2009), 64.

66. Ibid., 65.

67. Rebecca Felton, "Women on the Farm," *Atlanta Journal*, August 12, 1897.

68. Charlotte Gilman, *Women and Economics: A Study of the Economic Relation between Men and Women as a Factor of Social Evolution* (Boston: Small, Maynard, 1898).

69. Ibid., 60.

70. Ibid., iii.

71. Ibid., iv.

72. Bederman, *Manliness and Civilization*, 142.

73. Jane Addams, "Respect for Law," *Independent*, January 3, 1901.

74. Archibald H. Grimke, "The Sex Question and Segregation," in *The American Negro Academy Occasional Papers*, nos. 1–22 (New York: Arno, 1969), 20–21.

75. Ibid., 21.

76. Beverly Guy-Sheftall, *Daughters of Sorrow: Attitudes toward Black Women, 1880–1920* (New York: Carlson, 1990), 2.

77. Ibid., 3.

78. Ibid., 4.

79. Lawrence J. Friedman, *The [w]hite Savage: Racial Fantasies in the Postbellum South* (Englewood Cliffs, NJ: Prentice-Hall, 1970), 142.

80. Ibid., 160.

81. Ibid., 172–173.

82. bell hooks, *Black Looks: Race and Representation* (Boston: South End, 1992), 92.

83. Hazel Carby, *Race Men* (Cambridge, MA: Harvard University Press, 1998), 10.

84. Newman, *[w]hite Women's Rights*, 9.

85. Anna Julia Cooper, "Womanhood," in *The Voice of Anna Julia Cooper*, ed. Charles Lemert and Esme Bhan (Lahham, MD: Rowman and Littlefield, 1998), 63.

86. Ibid., 53.

87. Ibid., 54.

88. Ibid., 55.

89. Ibid., 59.

90. Ibid.

91. Alexander Crummell, "The Black Woman of the South: Her Neglects and Her Needs," in *Africa and America: Addresses and Discourses* (Springfield, MA: Willey, 1891), 79.

92. Cooper, "Womanhood," 59.

93. Lucy Laney, "Address before the Woman's Meeting," in *Social and Physical Condition of Negroes in Cities* (Atlanta: Atlanta University Press, 1897), 57.

94. Paula Giddings, *When and Where I Enter: The Impact of Black Women on Race and Sex in America* (New York: Perennial, 2001), 99.

95. Michele Mitchell, *Righteous Propagation: African Americans and the Politics of Racial Destiny after Reconstruction* (Chapel Hill: University of North Carolina Press, 2004), 12.

96. Cooper, "Womanhood," 61.

97. Ibid., 63.

98. Ibid., 64.

99. Ibid., 61.

100. Glenda Gilmore, *Gender and Jim Crow: Women and the Politics of [w]hite Supremacy in North Carolina, 1896–1920* (Chapel Hill: University of North Carolina Press, 1996), 44.

101. Feimster, *Southern Horrors*, 106.

102. Gilmore, *Gender and Jim Crow*, 44.

103. Newman, *[w]hite Women's Rights*, 9.

104. Cooper, "Womanhood," 60.

105. Historians such as Crystal Feimster have already made this connection: see Feimster, *Southern Horrors*, 104–105.

106. Crummell, "The Black Woman in the South," 68.

107. Ibid., 65–66.

108. Ibid., 76.

109. Ibid., 81.

110. Cooper, "Womanhood," 56.

111. Mitchell, *Righteous Propagation*, 84.

112. Gilmore, *Gender and Jim Crow*, 75.

113. Newman, *[w]hite Women's Rights*, 9.

114. Kevin K. Gaines, *Uplifting the Race: Black Leadership, Politics, and Culture in the Twentieth Century* (Chapel Hill: University of North Carolina Press, 1996), 14.

115. Ibid., 4.

116. See Vivian M. May and Anna Julia Cooper, *Visionary Black Feminist: A Critical Introduction* (New York: Routledge, 2012), 21; Guy-Sheftall, *Daughters of Sorrow*, 161–162.

117. Tommy J. Curry, "The Fortune of Wells: Ida B. Wells-Barnett's Use of T. Thomas Fortune's Philosophy of Social Agitation as a Prolegomenon to Militant Civil Rights Activism," *Transactions of the Charles S. Pierce Society* 48, no. 8 (2012): 456–482; Tommy J. Curry, "It's for the Kids: The Sociological Significance of W.E.B. DuBois's Brownie Books and its Philosophical Relevance for our Understanding of Gender in the Ethnological Age," *Graduate Faculty Philosophy Journal* 36, no. 1 (2015): 1–31; Adelaide Cromwell Hill and Martin Kilson, eds., *Apropos of Africa: Sentiments of Negro American Leaders on Africa from the 1800s to the 1900s* (London: Frank Cass, 1969), 175–177.

118. Rosalyn Terborg-Penn, "Black Male Perspectives on the Nineteenth-Century Woman," in *The Afro-American Woman: Struggles and Images* (Baltimore: Black Classic Press, 1978), 42.

119. Giddings, *When and Where I Enter*, 51.

120. Elsa Barkley Brown, "Negotiating and Transforming the Public Sphere: African American Political Life in the Transition from Slavery to Freedom," *Public Culture* 7, no. 1 (1994): 106–146.

121. Mrs. N. F. [Gertrude] Mossell, *The Work of the Afro-American Woman* (Philadelphia: Geo. S. Ferguson, 1908), 5.

122. Martha S. Jones, *All Bound Up Together: The Woman Question in African American Public Culture, 1830–1900* (Chapel Hill: University of North Carolina Press, 2007), 11. Jones insists:

> The men in this story are as complex as the women with whom they were allied. Some "women's rights men" were converted to the rights of women by moral suasion before the Civil War. Their words and deeds followed from a transformation that had already taken place in their hearts and minds. Others did so less out of personal conviction than from a sense that to call for women's rights would mark them, and perhaps more significantly, their institutions as advanced and civilized. From this perspective, to recognize the rights of women was one means by which [B]lack institutions distinguished themselves as forward-thinking, if not as superior to white-run institutions. Few, if any, did so out of baldly strategic or cynical thinking. Why not? The price to be paid by any African American who openly advocated the rights of women was high. . . . Mindful of the cruel parodies to which they would likely be subjected, those African Americans who spoke of women's rights opened the door to a form of public ridicule that few would invite lightly.

123. Joane Nagel, "Masculinity and Nationalism: Gender and Sexuality in the Making of Nations," *Ethnic and Racial Studies* 21, no. 2 (1998): 242–269.

124. Farmanfarmaian, "Did You Measure Up?"

125. Rudyard Kipling, "The [w]hite Man's Burden: The United States and the Philippine Islands, 1899," in *Rudyard Kipling's Verse: Definitive Edition* (Garden City, NY: Doubleday, 1940), 321–323.

126. Patrick Brantlinger, "Kipling's 'The [w]hite Man's Burden' and Its Afterlives," *English Literature in Transition, 1880–1920* 50, no. 2 (2007): 172–192.

127. Gretchen Murphy, *Shadowing the [w]hite Man's Burden: U.S. Imperialism and the Problem of the Color Line* (New York: New York University Press, 2010).

128. Willard B. Gatewood Jr., *Black Americans and the [w]hite Man's Burden, 1898–1903* (Champaign: University of Illinois Press, 1975).

129. Dr. J. H. Magee was the president of the Illinois Colored Historical Society. He died on May 29, 1912, from heart failure at age seventy. See "Death of J. H. Magee," *Journal of Illinois State Historical Society* 5 (1912): 316–317.

130. H. T. Johnson, "The Black Man's Burden," in Willard B. Gatewood, Jr., *Black Americans and the [w]hite Man's Burden, 1898–1903* (Urbana: University of Illinois Press, 1975), 183.

131. Ibid., 184.

132. J. Dallas Bowser, "Take Up the Black Man's Burden," *Colored American*, April 8, 1899, http://www.overalltech.net/huff/YBurden.htm.

133. Hubert Harrison, "The Black Man's Burden," in *A Hubert Harrison Reader*, ed. Jeffrey B. Perry (Middleton, CT: Wesleyan University Press, 2001), 63.

134. Ibid., 65.

135. Ibid., 69.

136. Ibid., 71.

137. Edward Blyden, *African Life and Customs* (Baltimore: Black Classic Press, 1994 [1908]), 8–9.

138. Jean Finot, *Race Prejudice*, trans. Florence Wade-Evans (New York: E. P. Dutton, 1906), 308.

139. Blyden, *African Life and Customs*, 37.

140. W.E.B. DuBois, *The Negro* (New York: Holt, 1915).

141. W.E.B. DuBois, *Darkwater: Voices from within the Veil* (Mineola, NY: Dover, 1999), 112.

142. See J. J. Bachofen, *Myth, Religion, and Mother-Right*, trans. Ralph Manheim (Princeton, NJ: Princeton University Press, 1973).

143. DuBois, *Darkwater*, 112.

144. Ibid., 114.

145. Curry, "It's for the Kids."

146. W.E.B. DuBois, *The Negro* (Mineola, NY: Dover, 2001), 138.

147. Robert F. Williams, *Negroes with Guns*, ed. Marc Schleifer (New York: Marzani and Munsell, 1962), 68.

148. Freedom Archives, "Self-Respect, Self-Defense and Self-Determination," Vimeo.com, February 24, 2014, https://vimeo.com/87520418.

CHAPTER 2

1. Eldridge Cleaver, *Soul on Ice* (New York: Dell, 1968), 18.

2. Walter C. Rucker, "Eldridge Cleaver," in *Encyclopedia of African American History*, ed. Leslie M. Alexander and Walter C. Rucker Jr. (Santa Barbara: ABC-CLIO, 2010), 706.

3. Cleaver, *Soul on Ice*, 16.

4. Huey P. Newton, "Eldridge Cleaver: He Is No James Baldwin," in *The Huey P. Newton Reader*, ed. David Hillard and Donald Weise (New York: Seven Stories, 2002), 287.

5. Huey P. Newton argues, "I see now that Eldridge was not dedicated to helping Black people but was in search of a strong manhood symbol. This was a common misperception at the time—that the Party was searching for badges of masculinity. In fact, the reverse is true: the Party acted as it did because we were men. Many failed to perceive the difference.

As for Eldridge, at that stage of his life he was probing for his own manhood": Huey P. Newton, *Revolutionary Suicide* (New York: Penguin, 2009), 142.

6. See Newton, "Eldridge Cleaver," 287–288.

7. Ibid., 288.

8. Susan Brownmiller, *Against Our Will: Men, Women and Rape* (New York: Fawcett Columbine, 1975), 248–249.

9. Michele Wallace, *Black Macho and the Myth of the Superwoman* (New York: Warner, 1980), 67.

10. Ibid., 68.

11. Ibid., 10.

12. Ibid., 24.

13. Ibid., 25.

14. Ibid.

15. Ibid., 27.

16. Ibid.

17. Ibid., 36.

18. Ibid., 37.

19. Ibid.

20. Ibid.

21. Ibid., 66.

22. Ibid., 67.

23. Ibid., 68.

24. Duchess Harris argues, "Despite the publication of many reviews and critical essays on [Michele]Wallace and [Ntozake] Shange, no Black male intellectual was ready to stand up for these Black feminists and say that there is at least something redeeming in them and their work. In addition, almost half of the women scholars reviewing their work went against Wallace and Shange in a way that suggests they had internalized the negative sentiments against these two Black feminist writers": Duchess Harris, *Black Feminist Politics from Kennedy to Clinton* (New York: Palgrave Macmillan, 2009), 44. This statement makes an uncomfortable point about Black Macho ideology: It simply cannot be wrong whether the detractor is a Black man or a Black woman. Despite Harris's acknowledgment of the new introduction to *The Black Macho*, published in 1990—in which Wallace admits her mistakes and says that "Black Macho" was not the reason Black Power failed and that she had no hard data to support its very existence—Harris still maintains that "[*The*] *Black Macho* remains a well-articulated account of the betrayal and frustration that was felt by many women in the Black Power Movement at the time": Harris, *Black Feminist Politics*, 46. What intellectual defense do Black males have if Wallace herself admits the construct is not true empirically but scholars and laypeople alike simply assert that the Black Macho does exist and apply it to a whole group of Black men and boys? In this way, the Black Macho idea operates more as a stereotype than an analytic to understand Black males.

Marlon Riggs articulates a very similar point, saying, "By the tenets of [B]lack macho, true masculinity admits little or no space for self-interrogation or multiple subjectivities around race. Black Macho prescribes an inflexible ideal: Strong Black men—'Afrocentric' Black men—don't flinch, don't weaken, don't take blame or shit, take charge, step to when challenged, and defend themselves without pause for self-doubt. Against this warrior model of masculinity, Black Macho counterpoises the emasculated Other: the Other as punk, sissy, Negro Faggot, a status with which any man, not just those who are, in fact, gay, can be branded should he deviate from rigidly prescribed codes of hypermasculine conduct"; Marlon Riggs, "Black Macho Revisited: Reflections of a SNAP! Queen," in *Black*

Men on Race, Gender, and Sexuality, ed. Devon Carbado (New York: New York University Press, 1999), 311.

25. Jared Sexton, "Race, Sexuality, and Political Struggle: Reading *Soul on Ice*," *Social Justice* 30, no. 2 (2003): 30.

26. Ibid. See also Paula Giddings, "The Lessons of History Will Shape the 1980s—*Black Macho and the Myth of the Superwoman* Won't," *Encore American and Worldwide News*, 2007, 50–51; Alison Edwards, *Rape, Racism and the [w]hite Women's Movement* (Chicago: Sojourner Truth Organization, 1979); M. Ron Karenga, "On Wallace's Myth: Wading through Troubled Waters," *Black Scholar* 10, nos. 8–9 (1979): 36–38.

27. Wallace argues, "My critique of the Black Power Movement was based upon a limited perception of it taken primarily from the mainstream media; through my reading of literature written by white writers such as Norman Mailer and Tom Wolfe; and, more importantly, by [B]lack writers such as Richard Wright, Ralph Ellison, James Baldwin, Amiri Baraka and Eldridge Cleaver": Michele Wallace, "How I Saw It Then, How I See It Now," in *Black Macho and the Myth of the Superwoman* (New York: Verso, 1990), xxi.

28. Ibid., xxxv.

29. Ibid., xxiv–xxv.

30. In her newest introduction to *The Black Macho*, Wallace discloses even more of her personal history and frame of looking at Black life during the 1970s. Wallace begins, "At the time I wrote *Black Macho*, I had only a Bachelors in English from the City College of New York": Michele Wallace, "New Introduction to *Black Macho and The Myth of the Superwoman*," Academia.edu, January 4, 2014, https://www.academia.edu/s/66809b0112, 2–3. She reminds the reader, "My ambition until then had been to be a novelist. I was, in fact, at that very time working on the third or fourth draft of a novel for which I had a contract. My education at [the City University of New York], which had been largely focused on literature and creative writing, had done fairly well by me, but it hadn't given me that sense of the place of the analysis of intellectual and cultural history, which was from that day to this the most important key to my future life of the mind that I would ever obtain": ibid., 4.

Despite Wallace's previous and, now, most recent disclosure of her ahistoricism and the creative license she took in formulating the Black Macho thesis, there remains little concession among gender scholars that the constructs she evokes to explain Black male political life simply do not exist. Even when Wallace continues to distance herself from the actual writing of the text and her vulnerability in the editorial process to an anti-Black, anti-feminist editor, accounts of the book have taken no serious look at the racist sexualization of Black men and women accepted by Wallace at that time. It is not as if these ideas were hidden. Wallace has actually said, "Although I haven't looked at it in years (it is still too painful), there is a substantially edited original manuscript of *Black Macho* in the state in which it first went to the publisher's typist available to researchers as part of my papers at the [New York Public Library's Schomburg Center for Research in Black Culture]. In order to speed my book to publication, I incorporated almost all of my editor's suggestions because it never occurred to me that she wasn't the final word on all things having to do with my book, even though she was a rabid anti-feminist and probably hated [B]lack women": ibid., 21–22.

31. Wallace, "How I Saw It Then, How I See It Now," xxi.

32. Faith Ringgold, *A Letter to My Daughter, Michele Wallace, in Response to Her Book, "Black Macho and the Myth of the Superwoman"* (North Charleston: Createspace Independent Publishing, 2015), 3.

33. Ibid., 7.

34. Ibid.

35. Ibid.

36. Michele Wallace, "Some Things Never Change, Some Things Always Do," Amazon
.com, http://www.amazon.com/Letter-Daughter-Michele-response-Superwoman/dp/15175726
65/ref=sr_1_5?ie=UTF8&qid=1453015110&sr=8-5&keywords=a+letter+to+my +daughter.

37. See Vincent Woodard, *The Delectable Negro: Human Consumption and Homoeroticism within U.S. Slave Culture* (New York: New York University Press, 2014), 203.

38. Ibid., 22.

39. Ibid.

40. Eldridge Cleaver, "Little Jesus," in *The Book of Lives*, n.d., Eldridge Cleaver Collection, 1959–1981, Cushing Library, Texas A&M University, series 13, box 2, folder 26, 4.

41. Ibid., 1.

42. Ibid., 3.

43. Ibid.

44. Ibid.

45. Ibid.

46. Cleaver, *Soul on Ice*, 136.

47. Cleaver, "Little Jesus," 5.

48. Ibid.

49. Ibid., 10

50. Cleaver, "Little Jesus," 11.

51. Ibid.

52. Cleaver, *Soul on Ice*, 5.

53. Cleaver, "Little Jesus," 11–12.

54. Ibid., 12.

55. Ibid.

56. Ibid.

57. Ibid., 13.

58. Ibid.

59. Ibid.

60. Cleaver, *Soul on Ice*, 7.

61. Cleaver, "Little Jesus," 13.

62. Ibid., 18.

63. Eleanor Novek, "State Property and Friends: Black Men's Performances of Masculinity and Race in Prison," in *Communicating Marginalized Masculinities: Identity Politics in TV,
Film, and New Media*, ed. Ronald L. Jackson and Jamie E. Moshin (New York: Routledge,
2013), 218–232.

64. Cleaver, *Soul on Ice*, 164.

65. Cleaver, "Ahmen's Jacket," in *The Book of Lives*, 1.

66. Ibid.

67. Ibid.

68. Cleaver, *Soul on Ice*, 20.

69. Maxwell Geismar, "Introduction," in Cleaver, *Soul on Ice*, xi–xv, xi.

70. Frantz Fanon, *Black Skin, [w]hite Masks* (New York: Grove, 1967), 156.

71. Ibid., 154.

72. Ibid.

73. Ibid., 180.

74. Ibid., 181.

75. Ibid., 134.

76. Ibid., 182.

77. Ibid., 78.

78. Mumia Abu-Jamal, "Caged and Celibate," in *Prison Masculinities*, ed. Don Sobo, Terry A. Kupers, and Willie London (Philadelphia: Temple University Press, 2001), 140.

79. Ibid.

80. Cleaver, "Bitches," in *The Book of Lives*, 4.

81. Fanon, *Black Skin, [w]hite Masks*, 154.

82. Ibid.

83. Anthony Lemelle Jr., "The Political Sociology of Black Masculinity and Tropes of Domination," *Journal of African American Men* 1, no. 2 (1995): 96.

84. Eldridge Cleaver, *Target Zero: A Life in Writing*, ed. Kathleen Cleaver (New York: Palgrave Macmillan, 2006), 61.

85. Ibid.

86. Cleaver, *Soul on Ice*, 184.

87. Ibid., 185.

88. Thomas Foster, "The Sexual Abuse of Black Men under American Slavery," *Journal of the History of Sexuality* 20, no. 3 (2011): 450.

89. Ibid., 461.

90. Martha Hodes, *[w]hite Women, Black Men: Illicit Sex in the 19th-Century South* (New Haven, CT: Yale University Press, 1997), 202.

91. Ibid., 202.

92. Crystal M. Feimster, *Southern Horrors: Women and the Politics of Rape and Lynching* (Cambridge, MA: Harvard University Press, 2009), 155.

93. Kathleen Blee, *Women of the Klan: Racism and Gender in the 1920s* (Berkeley: University of California Press, 2009).

94. Danielle McGuire, *At the Dark End of the Street: Black Women, Rape, and Resistance—a New History of the Civil Rights Movement from Rosa Parks to the Rise of Black Power* (New York: Vintage, 2010), 58.

95. Ibid., 58–59.

96. Ibid., 59.

97. *McQuirter v. State*, 63 So.2d 388 (1953).

98. I. Bennett Capers, "The Unintentional Rapist," *Washington University Law Review* 87, no. 6 (2010): 1348–1349.

99. Alvin Pouissant, "Sex and the Black Male," *Ebony*, August 1972, 114–120; Anne Valk and Leslie Brown, *Living with Jim Crow: African American Women and Memories of the Segregated South* (New York: Palgrave Macmillan, 2010), 54.

100. Richard Wright, *[w]hite Man, Listen! Lectures in Europe, 1950–1956* (New York: Harper Perennial, 1957), 4.

101. Fanon, *Black Skin, [w]hite Masks*, 157.

102. Ibid., 156.

103. Calvin C. Hernton, *Sex and Racism in America* (New York: Doubleday, 1965), 59.

104. Ibid., 60. It is no secret that many of these authors presumed a racial heteronormativity as the basis of their theorizations. In a somewhat ironic turn, Wallace's pointing out of these issues remained committed to a strong homophobic sentiment throughout. This is why Cheryl Clarke's "The Failure to Transform: Homophobia in the Black Community," in *Home Girls: A Black Feminist Anthology*, ed. Barbara Smith (New York: Kitchen Table-Women of Color Press, 1983), 197–298, is a noteworthy intervention into the debates of the late 1960s and 1970s, warning of the problem with the ideology of Black men and Black feminists following Wallace's prescriptions. Clarke maintains, "Black bourgeois female intellectuals practice homophobia by omission more often than rabid homophobia. Wallace's *Black Macho and the Myth of the Superwoman* is a most obvious example. This

brave and scathing analysis of the sexual politics of the [B]lack political community after 1965 fails to treat the issues of gay liberation, [B]lack lesbianism, or homophobia vis-à-vis the [B]lack liberation or the women's liberation movement": ibid., 203. This erasure is not as innocent as one may think. Clarke is very attentive to Wallace's representations of homosexuality and her exploitation of it in *The Black Macho*, arguing:

> For the sake of her own argument re the [B]lack macho neurosis, Wallace exploits the popular conception of male homosexuality as passivity, the willingness to be fucked (preferably by a white man, according to Cleaver). It is then seen as antithetical to the concept of [B]lack macho, the object of which is to do the fucking. Wallace does not debunk this stereotype of male homosexuality. In her less effective essay, "The Myth of the Superwoman," Wallace omits any mention of [B]lack lesbians. In 1979, when asked at a public lecture at Rutgers University in New Jersey why the book had not addressed the issues of homosexuality and homophobia, the author responded that she was not an "expert" on either issue. But Wallace, by her own admission, was also not an "expert" on the issues she *did* address in her book. (Ibid., 204)

Clarke seems to be unimpressed with Wallace's apologetic suggesting she is not an expert on homosexuality, since she admitted she was not an expert on Black heterosexuality, either.

105. Cleaver, *Soul on Ice*, 13.

106. Ibid., 14.

107. Ibid.

108. Ibid., 15.

109. Ibid.

110. Ibid., 17.

111. Ibid., 14.

112. Cleaver, "Bitches," 5.

113. Cleaver, *Soul on Ice*, 10.

114. Brownmiller, *Against Our Will*, 247.

115. Angela Davis, *Women, Race, and Class* (New York: Vintage, 1981), 178.

116. Davis argues, "Susan Brownmiller's discussion on rape and racism evinces an unthinking partisanship which borders on racism. In pretending to defend the cause of all women, she sometimes boxes herself into the position of defending the particular cause of white women, regardless of its implications": Davis, *Women, Race, and Class*, 198.

117. Stephen J. Whitfield, *A Death in the Delta: The Story of Emmett Till* (Baltimore: John Hopkins University Press, 1991), 17.

118. Simeon Wright, *Simeon's Story: An Eyewitness Account of Emmett Till* (Chicago: Lawrence Hill Books, 2010), 51.

119. Timothy B. Tyson, *The Blood of Emmett Till* (New York: Simon and Schuster, 2017), 4.

120. Quoted in ibid., 4–5.

121. Ibid., 6.

122. Wright, *Simeon's Story*, 8–9.

CHAPTER 3

1. Elaine Brown, *The Condemnation of Little B* (Boston: Beacon, 2002), 336.

2. E. Franklin Frazier, "The Failure of the Negro Intellectual," in *The Death of [w]hite Sociology: Essays on Race and Culture* (Baltimore: Black Classics, 1973), 65.

3. Ibid., 59.

4. Frazier is commenting on a propping up of Black intellectuals by a philanthropic white class. He argues:

> Sometimes I think that the failure of the American Negro intellectual to grasp the nature and the significance of these experiences is due to the fact that he continues to be an unconscious victim of these experiences. After an African intellectual met a group of Negro intellectuals, he told me that they were really men who were asleep.
>
> All of this only tends to underline the fact that educated Negroes or Negro intellectuals have failed to achieve any intellectual freedom. In fact, with the few exceptions of literary men, it appears that the Negro intellectual is unconscious of the extent to which his thinking is restricted to sterile repetition of the safe and conventional ideas current in American society.
>
> This is attributable in part, of course, to the conditions under which an educated and intellectual class emerged in the American society. This class emerged as the result of white American philanthropy. Although the situation has changed and the Negro intellectuals are supported through other means, they are still largely dependent upon the white community. There is no basis of economic support for them within the Negro community. And where there is economic support within the Negro community it demands conformity to conservative and conventional ideas. (Frazier, "The Failure of the Negro Intellectual," 58–59)

See also Fabio Rojas, *From Black Power to Black Studies: How a Radical Social Movement Became an Academic Discipline* (Baltimore: John Hopkins University Press, 2010).

5. David Schwartzman, *Black Unemployment: Part of Unskilled Unemployment* (Westport, CT: Greenwood, 1997).

6. Amadu J. Kaba's work on the economic gains of Black women and the economic state of Black America is expansive: see Amadu Jacky Kaba, "Race, Gender and Progress: Are Black American Women the New Model Minority?" *Journal of African American Studies* 12, no. 4 (2008): 309–335; Amadu Jacky Kaba, "Black Females as Geniuses," *Journal of African American Studies* 15, no.1 (2011): 120–124; Amadu Jacky Kaba, "The Gradual Shift of Wealth and Power from African American Males to African American Females," *Journal of African American Studies* 9, no. 3 (2005): 33–44; Amadu J. Kaba and Deborah E. Ward, "The Gradual Progress of Black Women in Political Representation," *Review of Black Political Economy* 36, no.1 (2009): 29–50.

7. James B. Stewart and Joseph W. Scott, "The Institutional Decimation of Black American Males," *Western Journal of Black Studies* 2, no. 2 (1978): 82–92.

8. Peter Edelman, Harry J. Holzer, and Paul Offner, *Reconnecting Disadvantaged Young Men* (Washington, DC: Urban Institute Press, 2006), 2.

9. Harry J. Holzer, Steven Raphael, and Michael A. Stoll, "How Do Employer Perceptions of Crime and Incarceration Affect the Employment Prospects of Less-Educated Young Black Men?" in *Black Males Left Behind*, ed. Ronald B. Mincy (Washington DC: Urban Institute Press, 2006), 67. See also Andrew Penner and Aliya Saperstein, "Engendering Racial Perceptions: An Intersectional Analysis of How Social Status Shapes Race," *Gender and Society* 27, no. 3 (2013): 319–344.

10. Devah Pager, "The Mark of a Criminal Record," *Focus* 23, no. 2 (2004): 44–46.

11. Roland Fryer and Stephen Levitt, "The Causes and Consequences of Distinctively Black Names," *Quarterly Journal of Economics* 119, no. 3 (2004): 767–805; Stevie Watson, Osei Appiah, and Corliss G. Thornton, "The Effect of Name on Pre-interview Impressions

and Occupational Stereotypes: The Case of Black Sales Job Applicants," *Journal of Applied Social Psychology* 41, no. 10 (2011): 2405–2420.

12. See Devah Pager, *Marked: Race, Crime, and Finding Work in an Era of Mass Incarceration* (Chicago: University of Chicago Press, 2007), esp. 88–116.

13. Major G. Coleman, "Job Skill and Black Male Wage Discrimination," *Social Science Quarterly* 84, no. 4 (2003): 892–905.

14. Gregory Acs, "Downward Mobility from the Middle Class: Waking Up from the American Dream," *Pew Report*, September 2011, 1–29.

15. See Catharine MacKinnon, *Sexual Harassment of Working Women: A Case of Sexual Discrimination* (New Haven, CT: Yale University Press, 1979), 176–177.

16. Mark A. Fossett, M. Therese Seibert, and Cynthia M. Cready, "Ecological and Structural Determinates of Declining Labor Force Participation of African American Men," in *Continuities in Sociological Human Ecology*, ed. Michael Micklin and Dudley L. Poston (New York: Springer Science, 1998), 157–194.

17. Cynthia F. Esptein, "Positive Effects of the Multiple Negative: Explaining the Success of Black Professional Women," *American Journal of Sociology* 78 (1973): 912–935.

18. Robert W. Livingston, Ashley S. Rosette, and Ella F. Washington, "Can an Agentic Black Woman Get Ahead? The Impact of Race and Interpersonal Dominance on Perceptions of Female Leaders," *Psychological Science* 23, no. 4 (2012): 354–358.

19. Robert W. Livingston and Nicholas A. Pearce, "The Teddy Bear Effect: Does Having a Baby-Face Benefit Chief Executive Officers?" *Psychological Science* 20, no. 10 (2009): 1229–1236.

20. Melissa Chan, "Inmate Found Dead inside Virginia Jail Cell after Alleged Theft of $5 Worth of Groceries," *New York Daily News*, August 25, 2015, http://www.nydailynews.com/news/national/inmate-found-dead-jail-cell-alleged-5-theft-article-1.2340813.

21. Michelle Alexander, *The New Jim Crow: Mass Incarceration in the Age of Colorblindness* (New York: New Press, 2010), 11.

22. Michelle Alexander, "The Zimmerman Mind-Set: Why Black Men Are the Permanent Underclass," *Time*, July 29, 2013.

23. Pager, *Marked*, 3.

24. Victor Rios, *Punished: Policing the Lives of Black and Latino Boys* (New York: New York University Press, 2011), 45.

25. Becky Pettit, *Invisible Men: Mass Incarceration and the Myth of Black Progress* (New York: Russell Sage Foundation, 2012), 3.

26. Emily Wang, Jenerius A. Aminawung, Christopher Wildeman, Joseph S. Ross, and Harlan M. Krumholz, "High Incarceration Rates among Black Men Enrolled in Clinical Studies May Compromise Ability to Identify Disparities," *Health Affairs* 33, no. 5 (2014): 852.

27. Toby S. Jenkins, "Mr. Nigger: The Challenges of Educating Black Males within American Society," *Journal of Black Studies* 37, no. 1 (2006): 127–155.

28. Cynthia Tucker, "Black Crime Problem Muddled by Racism, Denial," *Baltimore Sun Times*, December 15, 2003, http://articles.baltimoresun.com/2003-12-15/news/0312150177_1_black-men-lionel-tate-michael-lewis.

29. Brown, *The Condemnation of Little B*, 25.

30. Ibid., 29.

31. "Keeping Kids from Killing," *Atlanta Journal Constitution*, January 31, 1997, A10.

32. Melissa Harris Barlow, "Race and the Problem of Crime in 'Time' and 'Newsweek' Cover Stories, 1946 to 1995," *Social Justice* 25 (1998): 177.

33. Ibid., 178.

34. John DiIulio Jr., "The Coming of the Super-predators," *Weekly Standard*, November 27, 1995, http://cooley.libarts.wsu.edu/schwartj/criminology/dilulio.pdf.

35. Ibid.

36. John DiIulio Jr., "My Black Crime Problem, and Ours," *City Journal*, Spring 1996, http://www.city-journal.org/html/6_2_my_black.html.

37. Quoted in Vincent Schiraldi, "Will the Real John DiIulio Please Stand Up," *Washington Post*, February 5, 2001, http://www.highbeam.com/doc/1P2-411813.html.

38. Angela Davis, "Rape, Racism, and the Capitalist Setting," *Black Scholar* 9, no. 7 (1978): 24–30

39. DiIulio, "The Coming of the Super-Predators."

40. William J. Bennett, John DiIulio Jr., and John P. Walters, *Body Count: Moral Poverty and How to Win America's War against Crime and Drugs* (New York: Simon and Schuster, 1996), 27.

41. See Elizabeth Becker, "As Ex-Theorist on Young 'Superpredators,' Bush Aide Has Regrets," *New York Times*, February 9, 2001, http://www.nytimes.com/2001/02/09/us/as-ex-theorist-on-young-superpredators-bush-aide-has-regrets.html. The myth pops up every now and again: see Brian Johnson, "Return of the Super-predators," *Jackson Free Press*, August 30, 2006, http://www.jacksonfreepress.com/news/2006/aug/30/return-of-the-super-predators.

42. Lawrence A. Greenfield, Michael R. Rand, Diane Craven, Patsy A. Klaus, Craig A. Perkins, Cheryl Ringel, Greg Warchol, Cathy Maston, and James Alan Fox, *Violence by Intimates: Analysis of Data on Crimes by Current or Former Spouses, Boyfriends, and Girlfriends* (Washington, DC: U.S. Bureau of Justice Statistics, 1998), http://bjs.gov/content/pub/pdf/vi.pdf.

43. Ibid., 10.

44. Ibid., 8.

45. Callie Marie Rennison and Sarah Welchans, *Intimate Partner Violence* (Washington, DC: U.S. Bureau of Justice Statistics, 2000), 4.

46. Michele C. Black, Kathleen C. Basile, Matthew J. Breiding, Sharon G. Smith, Mikel L. Walters, Melissa T. Merrick, Jieru Chen, and Mark R. Stevens, *The National Intimate Partner and Sexual Violence Survey: 2010 Summary Report* (Atlanta: National Center for Injury Prevention and Control, 2011), 40.

47. Ibid., 14.

48. bell hooks, *Feminism Is for Everybody: Passionate Politics* (Cambridge, MA: South End, 2000), 61. It is important to recognize that bell hooks does not include female abuse of men in her analysis of domestic violence. She says, "Initially feminist focus on domestic violence highlighted male violence against women, but as the movement progressed evidence showed that there was also domestic violence present in same-sex relations, that women in relationships with women were and are oftentimes the victims of abuse, that children were also victims of adult patriarchal violence enacted by women and men."

49. For example, Gemma Tang Nain argues that Black men's patriarchy is evidenced by their lack of vulnerability to domestic violence: Gemma Tang Nain, "Black Women, Sexism, Racism: Black or Anti-racist Feminism," *Feminist Review* 37 (1991): 11–12.

50. Ellen Pence and Michael Paymar, *Education Groups for Men Who Batter: The Duluth Model* (New York: Springer, 1993), 1.

51. Ibid., 5.

52. Donald G. Dutton, *Rethinking Domestic Violence* (Vancouver: University of British Columbia Press, 2006), 181.

53. Kenneth Corvo, Donald Dutton, and Wan-Yi Chen, "Do Duluth Model Interventions with Perpetrators of Domestic Violence Violate Mental Health Professional Ethics?" *Ethics and Behavior* 19, no. 4 (2009): 325. It is relevant to point out that individuals with alcohol or drug addiction, mental health issues, and behavioral disorders are thought to be "inappropriate" for the education groups: see Pence and Paymar, *Education Groups for Men Who Batter*, 23–24.

54. See Miriam K. Ehrensaft, Terrie E. Moffitt, and Avshalom Caspi, "Is Domestic Violence Followed by an Increased Risk of Psychiatric Disorders among Women but Not Among Men? A Longitudinal Cohort Study," *American Journal of Psychiatry* 163 (2006): 885–982; Miriam K. Ehrensaft, Patricia Cohen, Jocelyn Brown, Elizabeth Smailes, Henian Chen, and Jeffrey Johnson, "Intergenerational Transmission of Partner Violence: A Twenty-Year Prospective Study," *Journal of Consulting and Clinical Psychology* 71, no. 4 (2003): 741–753.

55. See Denise Hines, "Intimate Terrorism by Women towards Men: Does It Exist?" *Journal of Aggression, Conflict and Peace Research* 2, no. 3 (2010): 36–56; Denise Hines and Emily Douglas, "Predicting Potentially Life-Threatening Partner Violence by Women toward Men: A Preliminary Analysis," *Violence and Victims* 28, no. 5 (2013): 751–771; Denise Hines and Emily Douglas, "Alcohol and Drug Abuse in Men Who Sustain Intimate Partner Violence," *Aggressive Behavior* 38 (2012): 31–46. Other authors have also argued that despite the overwhelming evidence of female perpetration of domestic violence, it is ignored even when exceeding or being equal to male violence, see John Archer, "Sex Differences in Aggression between Heterosexual Partners: A Meta-Analytic Review," *Psychological Bulletin* 5 (2000): 651–680. Murray Straus, for instance, has argued that ideological bias has led to the deliberate concealment and denial of female perpetrators of IPV: see Murray Straus, "Why the Overwhelming Evidence on Partner Physical Violence Has Not Been Perceived and Is Often Denied," *Journal of Aggression, Maltreatment and Trauma* 18 (2009): 552–571.

56. Ellen L. Pence, "Some Thoughts on Philosophy," in *Coordinating Community Responses to Domestic Violence: Lessons from Duluth and Beyond*, ed. Melanie F. Shepard and Ellen L. Pence (Thousand Oaks, CA: Sage, 1999), 28.

57. Ibid., 29.

58. Ibid.

59. Ibid.

60. Ibid., 33.

61. As mentioned earlier, Kimberlé Crenshaw uses the work of Susan Schecter as evidence of the link among patriarchy, sexism, and domestic abuse. Schecter was not only a colleague of Ellen Pence but also a supporter of the Duluth paradigm who used the reports, as well as interviews from Pence, as evidence of the patriarchal thesis: see Kimberlé Crenshaw, "Mapping the Margins: Intersectionality, Identity Politics, and Violence against Women of Color," *Stanford Law Review* 43, no. 6 (1991): 1241–1299; Susan Schecter, *Women and Male Violence: The Visions and Struggles of the Battered Women's Movement* (Cambridge, MA: South End, 1982), 176–177; Jeffrey L. Edelson, "What's Pence's Line?" *Violence against Women* 16, no. 9 (2010): 981–984.

62. Carolyn West, "Partner Abuse in Ethnic Minority and Gay, Lesbian, Bisexual, and Transgender Populations," *Partner Abuse* 3, no. 3 (2012): 336.

63. Ibid.

64. R. L. McNeely and Jose Torres, "Reflections on Racial Differences in Perceptions of Intimate Partner Violence: Black Women Have to Be Strong," *Social Justice in Context* 4, no. 1 (2009): 129–136.

65. West, "Partner Abuse in Ethnic Minority and Gay, Lesbian, Bisexual, and Transgender Populations," 342.

66. Niki Palmetto, Leslie L. Davidson, Vicki Breitbart, and Vaughn I. Rickert, "Predictors of Physical Intimate Partner Violence in the Lives of Young Women: Victimization, Perpetration, and Bidirectional Violence," *Violence and Victims* 28, no. 1 (2013): 103–121.

67. It is important to note that while authors such as Carolyn West acknowledge the mutuality of violence among Black men and women, she maintains that the consequence of the violence is asymmetrical. For West,

> Mutuality of violence does not mean that women's and men's violent acts are equal. While both partners may use violence, when taken in context it is evident that the frequency and severity of their assaults are seldom equal. These relationships may be better characterized as bidirectional asymmetric violence. The following scenario is offered to illustrate this point: A wife shoves and scratches her husband. He then punches her in the face and breaks her nose. In other words, although this scenario is an example of bidirectional IPV in that both partners are violent, the outcome is asymmetrical because the wife sustained the most serious injury." (Carolyn West, "Sorry, We Have to Take You In: Black Battered Women Arrested for Intimate Partner Violence," *Journal of Aggression, Maltreatment, and Trauma* 15, nos. 3–4 [2007]: 99)

68. Raul Caetano, Suhasini Ramisetty-Mikler, and Craig A. Field, "Unidirectional and Bidirectional Intimate Partner Violence among [w]hite, Black, and Hispanic Couples in the United States," *Violence and Victims* 20, no. 4 (2005): 401.

69. Eric H. Holder Jr., "Attorney General Eric Holder Speaks at Domestic Violence Awareness Month Event," October 19, 2009, https://www.justice.gov/opa/speech/attorney-general-eric-holder-speaks-domestic-violence-awareness-month-event.

70. Several high-profile articles in the domestic violence literature cite this statistic: see Carolyn West, "Black Women and Intimate Partner Violence: New Directions in Research," *Journal of Interpersonal Violence* 19, no. 12 (2004): 1489; Kathleen Malley-Morrison, Denise A. Hines, Doe West, Jesse J. Tauriac, and Mizuho Arai, "Domestic Violence in Ethnocultural Minority Groups," in *Family Interventions in Domestic Violence*, ed. John Hamel and Tonia L. Nicholls (New York: Springer, 2007), 325; Jacquelyn C. Campbell, Daniel Webster, Jane Koziol-McLain, Carolyn Rebecca Block, Doris Campbell, Mary Ann Curry, Faye Gary, Judith McFarlane, Carolyn Sachs, Phyllis Sharps, Yvonne Ulrich, and Susan A. Wilt, "Assessing Risk Factors for Intimate Partner Homicide," *NIJ Journal* 250 (2003): 18.

71. Glenn Kessler, "Fact Checker: Holder's 2009 Claim that Intimate-Partner Homicide Is the Leading Cause of Death for African American Women," WashingtonPost.com, December 18, 2013, https://www.washingtonpost.com/news/fact-checker/wp/2013/12/18/holders-2009-claim-that-intimate-partner-homicide-is-the-leading-cause-of-death-for-african-american-women/?postshare=9491470635302968&tid=ss_fb.

72. Campbell, "Assessing Risk Factors for Intimate Partner Homicide," 18.

73. Holder, "Attorney Gender Eric Holder Speaks at Domestic Violence Awareness Month Event."

74. Centers for Disease Control and Prevention, "Leading Cause of Death by Age Group, Black Females—United States, 1998, 1999, 2001, 2002, 2004–2013," CDC.gov, http://www.cdc.gov/women/lcod. For ages of first marriage, see Casey E. Copen, Kimberly Daniels, Jonathan Vespa, and William D. Mosher, "First Marriages in the United States: Data from the 2006–2010 National Survey of Family Growth," *National Health Statistics Report* 49 (2012): 12.

75. David L. Fortes, "Male Victims of Domestic Violence," in Hamel and Nicholls, *Family Interventions in Domestic Violence*, 303–318.

76. West argues, "In all cases, psychological aggression is most frequently reported. Regarding physical abuse, mutual or bidirectional violence is most common with both men and women participating in the abuse. When physical abuse occurred, it typically took the form of minor aggression, such as throwing objects, pushing, slapping, and shoving. When unidirectional aggression was considered, it was somewhat more likely to be female perpetrated, particularly among African American couples": West, "Partner Abuse in Ethnic Minority and Gay, Lesbian, Bisexual and Transgender Populations," 350.

77. Laurie Hannah, "Maryland Woman Arrested for Pouring Hot Grits on Sleeping Man, Beating Him with Baseball Bat," NYDailyNews.com, August 14, 2015, http://www.nydailynews.com/news/national/woman-arrested-pouring-hot-grits-sleeping-man-article-1.2325544; "Woman Arrested for Allegedly Pouring Hot Grits on Man," TheGrio.com, August 15, 2015, http://thegrio.com/2015/08/14/woman-hot-grits-baseball-bat-attack.

78. Don Parker, "White House Staffer Fires Glock Handgun," KeyeTV.com, August 10, 2015, http://www.keyetv.com/news/features/top-stories/stories/White-House-staffer-fires-Glock-handgun-at-her-boyfriend-a-Capitol-Police-officer-183390.shtml; Myriah Towner, "Obama Aide Banned from the White House after She Shoots at Her Cop Boyfriend with His Own Gun in Argument over Affair," Dailymail.co.uk, August 10, 2015, http://www.dailymail.co.uk/news/article-3192914/White-House-staffer-Barvetta-Singletary-arrested-firing-boyfriend-gun.html.

79. Elizabeth Vanmetre, "Ray J's girlfriend, Princess Love, Arrested after Allegedly Beating Him," NYDaily.com, February 16, 2015, http://www.nydailynews.com/entertainment/gossip/ray-girlfriend-arrested-beating-report-article-1.2117680.

80. Mitchell Northam, "Woman Throws Bleach on Boyfriend, Sets Him on Fire in Salisbury," Delmarvanow.com, September 29, 2015, http://www.delmarvanow.com/story/news/local/maryland/2015/09/29/salisbury-bleach-fire/73026860.

81. Jennifer Langhinrichsen-Rohling, "Rates of Bidirectional versus Unidirectional Intimate Partner Violence across Samples, Sexual Orientations, and Race/Ethnicities: A Comprehensive Review," *Partner Abuse* 3, no. 2 (2012): 223.

82. Denise A. Hines and Kathleen Malley-Morrison, "Psychological Effects of Partner Abuse against Men: A Neglected Research Area," *Psychology of Men and Masculinity* 2, no. 2 (2001): 75–85; Michelle Carney, Fred Buttill, and Don Dutton, "Women Who Perpetrate Intimate Partner Violence: A Review of the Literature with Recommendations for Treatment," *Aggression and Violent Behavior* 12, no.1 (2007): 108–115; Alfred DeMaris, "Male versus Female Initiation of Aggression: The Case of Courtship Violence," in *Intimate Violence: Interdisciplinary Perspectives*, ed. Emilio Viano (Oxford: Taylor and Francis, 1992), 111–120.

83. R. L. McNeely and Gloria Robinson-Simpson, "The Truth about Domestic Violence: A Falsely Framed Issue," *Social Work* 32 (1987): 485–490.

84. Malley-Morrison, "Domestic Violence in Ethnocultural Minority Groups," 325.

85. Ibid.

86. Hines and Malley-Morrison, "Psychological Effects of Partner Abuse against Men," 79–81.

87. John Hamel, "Domestic Violence: A Gender Inclusive Concept," in Hamel and Nicholls, *Family Interventions in Domestic Violence*, 15–16.

88. West, "Partner Abuse in Ethnic Minority and Gay, Lesbian, Bisexual and Transgender Populations," 349.

89. Ronald E. Hall, "The Feminization of Social Welfare: Implications of Cultural Tradition vis-à-vis Male Victims of Domestic Violence," *Journal of Sociology and Social Welfare* 39, no. 3 (2012): 7–27.

90. Physical and sexual abuse are generally not discussed in Black communities, despite their prevalence: see Kathryn J. Lindholm and Richard Wiley, "Ethnic Differences in Child Abuse and Sexual Abuse," *Hispanic Journal of Behavioral Sciences* 8, no. 2 (1986): 111–125; Robert L. Hampton, ed., *Black Family Violence: Current Research and Theory* (Lanham, MD: Lexington Books, 1991), esp. chap. 2.

91. Nikitta A. Foston, "Behind the Pain Nobody Talks About: Sexual Abuse of Black Boys," *Ebony* 58, no. 8 (2003): 126.

92. Ibid., 128.

93. Federal Bureau of Investigation, *Rape*, Uniform Crime Report: Crime in the United States (Washington, DC, 2013), https://www.fbi.gov/about-us/cjis/ucr/crime-in-the-u.s/2013/crime-in-the-u.s.-2013/violent-crime/rape/rapemain_final.pdf.

94. Oronde Miller, Frank Farrow, Judith Meltzer, and Susan Notkin, "Improving Outcomes for African American Males Involved with Child Welfare Systems," *Center for the Study of Social Policy* (2014): 1–24.

95. Mariagiovanna Baccara, Leonardo Felli, Allan Collard-Wexler, and Leeat Yariv, "Gender and Racial Biases: Evidence from Child Adoption," CESifo Working Paper no. 2921, Ifo Institute, Center for Economic Studies, Munich, 2010, 24.

96. Natalie N. Alund, "Richmond: Woman Charged in Teen's Murder Apparently Had Child with Him," Contracostatimes.com, April 17, 2014, http://www.contracostatimes.com/news/ci_25586860/richmond-woman-charged-teens-murder-apparently-had-child.

97. Foston, "Behind the Pain Nobody Talks About," 130. Often female perpetrators of sexual assault and rape are seen as less culpable than male perpetrators: see Michelle Davies, Paul Pollard, and John Archer, "Effects of Perpetrator Gender and Victim Sexuality on Blame toward Male Victims of Sexual Assault," *Journal of Social Psychology* 146, no. 3 (2006): 275–291.

98. Within Black feminist literature, the sexual abuse of Black boys is mentioned in passing, rarely occupying more than a few paragraphs and usually interpreted as the basis of future male sexual dysfunction and abuse of women. In *Gender Talk*, the sexual abuse of Black males is confined to homosexual abuse: see Johnnetta B. Cole and Beverly Guy-Sheftall, *Gender Talk: The Struggle for Women's Equality in African American Communities* (New York: Random House, 2003), 145–146.

99. Shirley Salmon-Davis and Larry E. Davis, "Group Work with Sexually Abused African American Boys," in *Working with African American Males: A Guide to Practice*, ed. Larry Davis (Thousand Oaks, CA: Sage, 1999), 15.

100. Ibid., 18–19.

101. Ibid.

102. Diana O. Eromosele, "The Diverse Ways They Each Coped with Abuse," TheRoot.com, April 19, 2015, http://www.theroot.com/articles/history/2014/04/famous_black_men_who_were_sexually_abused_as_kids_and_why_some_didn_t_know.html.

103. "Sexual Abuse Often Taboo for Black Boys," NPR.com, July 13, 2009, http://www.npr.org/templates/story/story.php?storyId=106538016.

104. Lily Rothman, "Chris Brown Was Raped. Does It Matter If He Doesn't Think So?" Time.com, October 09, 2013, http://entertainment.time.com/2013/10/09/chris-brown-was-raped-does-it-matter-if-he-doesnt-think-so.

105. Myriam S. Denov, "The Myth of Innocence: Sexual Scripts and the Recognition of Child Sexual Abuse by Female Perpetrators," *Journal of Sex Research* 40, no. 3 (2003): 303–314.

106. Men generally are refused services and treatment for sexual abuse and rape: see Denise A. Donnelly, "Honey, We Don't Do Men: Gender Stereotypes and the Provision of

Services to Sexually Assaulted Males," *Journal of Interpersonal Violence* 11, no. 3 (1996): 441–448; Michelle Davies, "Male Sexual Assault Victims: A Selective Review of the Literature and Implications for Support Services," *Aggression and Violent Behavior* 7 (2002): 203–214; Guy Holmes, Liz Offen, and Glenn Waller, "See No Evil, Hear No Evil, Speak No Evil," *Clinical Psychology Review* 17, no. 1 (1997): 69–88.

107. Lauren E. Duncan and Linda M. Williams, "Gender Role Socialization and Male-on-Male versus Female-on-Male Child Sexual Abuse," *Sex Roles* 39, no. 8 (1998): 765–785.

108. Bryana H. French, Jasmine Tilgham, and Dominique A. Malebranche, "Sexual Coercion Context and Psychosocial Correlates among Diverse Males," *Psychology of Men and Masculinity* 16, no. 1 (2015): 42–53.

109. Elaine Brown, "Proud Flesh Interview: Elaine Brown," *Proud Flesh* 1, no. 2 (2003): 1–14.

110. Brown, *The Condemnation of Little B*, 211. For a sociological analysis of Brown's description, see Benjamin P. Bowser, *The Black Middle Class: Social Mobility and Vulnerability* (Boulder, CO: Lynne Reiner, 2006).

111. Ibid., 238.

112. Ibid., 211–212.

113. Ibid., 212.

114. W.E.B. DuBois, "Socialism and the American Negro," in *Against Racism: Unpublished Essays, Papers, Addresses, 1887–1961*, ed. Herbert Aptheker (Amherst: University of Massachusetts Press, 1985), 304.

115. Frazier, "The Failure of the Negro Intellectual," 57.

116. Ibid., 58.

117. Geoffrey Canada, *Reaching up for Manhood: Transforming the Lives of Boys in America* (Boston: Beacon, 1998), xiii.

118. Our present configurations of race, class, and gender exclude material accounts of the role that criminogenic accounts of Black males have on the lives of Black people generally and how this affects Black women specifically. The death of Rekia Boyd, for instance, was the consequence of the shooting at a Black man named Antonio Cross by an off-duty cop (Dante Servin): see Erin Meyer, "Rekia Boyd's Friend Sues Chicago Cop Who Killed Unarmed Woman," DNAinfoChicago.com, March 21, 2013, http://www.dnainfo.com/chicago/20130321/ chicago/rekia-boyds-friend-sues-chicago-cop-who-killed-unarmed-woman. The force used to apprehend Chauncey Owens similarly caused the death of Aiyana Stanley-Jones: see Diane Bukowski, "Owens Never Said Aiyana Jones's Dad Gave Him the Gun Used in Teen's Killing," VoiceofDetroit.net, May 23, 2011, http://voiceofdetroit.net/2011/05/23/owens-never-said-aiyana-jones%E2%80%99-dad-gave-him-gun-used-in-teen%E2%80%99s-killing.

119. The consequences of Black male unemployment and racism are largely framed as secondary moral concerns in conversations about Black men. The concept of Black male privilege operates to de-emphasize the empirical condition of Black men next to other groups. Whereas simple comparisons of disparity would allow ample clarity and attention to all groups involved, many gender scholars insist that Black men, because of their maleness, not only are privileged by their gender but also can make no claims to the contrary without risking moral condemnation: see Mark Anthony Neal, *New Black Man* (New York: Routledge, 2015), 152.

120. Angela Harris, "Gender, Violence, Race, and Criminal Justice," *Stanford Law Review* 52 (2000): 779.

121. Ibid., 797.

122. Wesley Lowery, "How Many Police Shootings a Year? No One Knows?" Wash-

ingtonPost.com, September 8, 2014, https://www.washingtonpost.com/news/post-nation/wp/2014/09/08/how-many-police-shootings-a-year-no-one-knows.

123. Arlene Eisen, *Operation Ghetto Storm: 2012 Annual Report on the Extrajudicial Killings of 313 Black People by Police, Security Guards and Vigilantes*, Malcolm X Grassroots Movement, 2013, http://www.operationghettostorm.org/uploads/1/9/1/1/19110795/new_all_14_11_04.pdf, 28.

124. "304 Black Lives Lost to Police Violence in 2014," EmpathyEducates.org, http://empathyeducates.org/Journeys-to-and-through/mapping-police-violence.

125. "Police Shootings," WashingtonPost.com, http://www.washingtonpost.com/graphics/national/police-shootings. *The Guardian* offers slightly different numbers. In 2015, 306 Blacks were shot by police, of whom 294 were Black men: see "The Counted: People Killed by Police in the U.S.," TheGuardian.com, June 1, 2015, http://www.theguardian.com/us-news/ng-interactive/2015/jun/01/the-counted-police-killings-us-database.

126. "Fatal Force," WashingtonPost.com, https://www.washingtonpost.com/graphics/national/police-shootings-2016.

127. Javier M. Rodriguez, Arline T. Geronimus, John Bound, and Danny Dorling, "Black Lives Matter: Differential Mortality and the Racial Composition of the U.S. Electorate," *Social Science and Medicine* 136–137 (2015): 193–199.

128. Phillip Attiba Goff, Matthew Christian Jackson, Brooke Alison Lewis Di Leone, Carmen Marie Culotta, and Natalie Ann DiTomasso, "The Essence of Innocence: Consequences of Dehumanizing Black Children," *Journal of Personality and Social Psychology* 106, no. 4 (2014): 540.

129. Phillip Attiba Goff, Jennifer L. Eberhardt, Melissa J. Williams, and Matthew Christian Jackson, "Not Yet Human: Implicit Knowledge, Historical Dehumanization, and Contemporary Consequences," *Journal of Personality and Social Psychology* 94, no. 2 (2008): 292–306.

130. Adam Waytz, Kelly M. Hoffman, and Sophie Trawalter, "A Superhumanization Bias in [w]hites' Perceptions of Blacks," *Social Psychological and Personality Science* 6, no. 3 (2015): 352–359.

131. See Tommy J. Curry, "Michael Brown and the Need for a Genre Study of Black Male Death and Dying," *Theory and Event* 17, no. 3 (2014): 1.

CHAPTER 4

1. W.E.B. DuBois, *The Souls of Black Folk* (New Haven, CT: Oxford University Press, 2015), 157.

2. Ibid.

3. Ibid., 160.

4. Aubrey Wilean "Police Begin Probe of Teenager's Arrest," Philly.com, January 18, 2014, http://www.philly.com/philly/news/20140118_Police_begin_probe_of_teenager_s_arrest.html.

5. Kristen Gwynne, "How 'Stop and Frisk' Is Too Often a Sexual Assault by Cops on Teenagers in Targeted New York City Neighborhoods," Alternet.com, January 21, 2013, http://www.alternet.org/civil-liberties/how-stop-and-frisk-too-often-sexual-assault-cops-teenagers-targeted-nyc.

6. Joseph Fried, "In Surprise, Witness Says Officer Bragged about Louima Torture," *New York Times*, May 20, 1999, http://www.nytimes.com/1999/05/20/nyregion/in-surprise-witness-says-officer-bragged-about-louima-torture.html; Mike McAlary, "They Saw Loui-

ma's Terror," *New York Daily News*, September 5, 1997, http://www.nydailynews.com/news/crime/louima-terror-article-1.238610.

7. Carlyle Van Thompson, *Eating the Black Body: Miscegenation as Sexual Consumption in African American Literature and Culture* (New York: Peter Lang, 2006), 149.

8. Ibid., 150.

9. Ibid.

10. John Garcia, "Man Wins Four Million Dollar Lawsuit against Chicago Cops," "ABCLocalgo.com, October 7, 2007, http://abclocal.go.com/wls/story?section=news/national_world&id=5711052.

11. Alex Kane, "Chicago Police Accused of Using Gun to Sodomize Innocent Man," Alternet.com, June 24, 2013, http://www.alternet.org/news-amp-politics/chicago-police-officer-allegedly-abused-and-sodomized-innocent-man.

12. Ely Portillo and Cleve R. Wootson Jr., "What Video Shows Is at Dispute in Jonathan Ferrell Shooting Case," *Charlotte Observer*, September 18, 2013, http://www.charlotteobserver.com/2013/09/18/4323491/cmpd-chief-contradicts-lawyers.html#.Uty1qRDnbIU.

13. Angela Watkins, "Officer May Be Liable for Tasering Teen's Scrotum," Courthouse News Service, October 22, 2013, http://www.courthousenews.com/2013/10/22/62249.htm.

14. John Marzulli, "NYPD Cop Accused of Stomping, Crushing, Brooklyn Man's Privates," NYDailyNews.com, December 22, 2015, http://www.nydailynews.com/new-york/brooklyn/accused-stomping-crushing-brooklyn-man-privates-article-1.2473420. See also Stephen A. Crockett Jr., "New York City Man Loses Testicle after Police Allegedly Stomp His Groin during Arrest," TheRoot.com, December 22, 2015, http://www.theroot.com/articles/news/2015/12/ny_man_loses_testicle_after_police_allegedly_stomp_his_groin_during_arrest.html.

15. "Rachel Jeantel Tells Piers She and Trayvon Feared Zimmerman Might Be Gay Rapist," YouTube video, at :30, posted by MichaelSavage4Prez, July 16, 2013, http://www.youtube.com/watch?v=loEROU1XA5E.

16. "U.S. Teens 'Had Three-Way Sex on Corpses of Men They Lured to Their House, Strangled to Death and Hog-Tied,'" MailOnline.com, February 26, 2013, http://www.dailymail.co.uk/news/article-2284890/Joliet-murders-Teens-3-way-sex-bodies-men-strangled.html.

17. Maxim Alter, "Bond Set at $1 M[illion] for Two Accused of Sexually Assaulting, Beating Teen to Death after Robbery," Wpco.com, December 3, 2013. http://www.wcpo.com/news/local-news/warren-county/franklin/dione-payne-case-bond-set-at-1m-for-two-accused-of-beating-teen-to-death-after-robbery. See also Amanda Lee Myers, "Ohio Man Pleads Guilty in Teen's Beating Death," *Washington Times*, May 8, 2014, http://www.washingtontontimes.com/news/2014/may/8/attorney-plea-deal-expected-in-ohio-teens-death.

18. Amanda Seitz, "Verdict Reached in Teen Beating Death Trial," Dayton Daily News, July 31, 2014. http://www.daytondailynews.com/news/news/jury-left-to-deliberate-in-di one-payne-murder-tria/ngrzC/.

19. James Baldwin, "The Black Boy Looks at the [w]hite Boy," in *Nobody Knows My Name* (New York: Dial, 1961), 217.

20. Oyèrónké Oyewúmì, *The Invention of Woman: Making African Sense of Western Gender Discourses* (Minneapolis: University of Minnesota Press, 1997), 1–2.

21. James Baldwin, "Going to Meet the Man," in *Baldwin: Early Novels and Stories* (New York: Library of America, 1998), 933.

22. Ibid.

23. Ibid., 934–935.

24. Ibid., 936.

25. Ibid., 948.

26. Ibid., 948–949.

27. Ibid., 949.

28. Ibid., 950.

29. Ibid.

30. David Marriott, *On Black Men* (New York: Columbia University Press, 2000), 18–19.

31. Ibid., 19.

32. Darren Hutchinson, "Identity Crisis: Intersectionality, Multidimensionality, and the Development of an Adequate Theory of Subordination," *Michigan Journal of Race and Law* 6 (2001): 312.

33. Ibid.

34. Adrienne Davis, "The Sexual Economy of American Slavery," in *Sister Circle: Black Women and Work*, ed. Sharon Harley (Piscataway, NJ: Rutgers University Press, 2002), 107.

35. Joy James, "Black Revolutionary Icons and Neo-Slave Narratives," *Social Identities* 5, no. 2 (1999): 137.

36. Angela Davis, *Women, Race, and Class* (New York: Vintage Books, 1983), 7.

37. For a discussion of the anachronism of gender as a category on colonized peoples, see Maria Lugones, "Toward a Decolonial Feminism," *Hypatia* 25, no. 4 (2010): 742–759. For a similar discussion of Marxism and the designation of the worker, see Frank Wilderson, *Red, [w]hite and Black: Cinema and the Structure of U.S. Antagonisms* (Durham, NC: Duke University Press, 2010); Jared Sexton, "Racial Profiling and the Societies of Control," in *Warfare in the American Homeland: Policing and Prison in a Penal Democracy*, ed. Joy James (Durham, NC: Duke University Press, 2007), 197–218.

38. Richard Aldrich, *Colonialism and Homosexuality* (New York: Routledge, 2003); Ronald Hyam, *Empire and Sexuality: The British Experience* (New York: Manchester University Press, 1990).

39. Frederick Douglass, "Narrative of the Life of Frederick Douglass," in *The Classic Slave Narratives*, ed. Henry Louis Gates Jr. (New York: Mentor, 1987), 291.

40. Connie A. Miller Sr., *Frederick Douglass: American Hero and International Icon of the 19th Century* (Bloomington, IN: Xlibris, 2008), 43; Thomas Loebel, *The Letter and Spirit of 19th-Century Literature: Justice, Politics, and Theology* (Montreal: McGill-Queen's University Press, 2005), 202–203; Maurice O. Wallace, *Constructing the Black Masculine: Identity and Ideality in African American Men's Literature and Culture, 1775–1995* (Durham, NC: Duke University Press, 2002), 86–87.

41. James Hoke Sweet, *Recreating Africa: Culture, Kinship and Religion in the African-Portuguese World, 1441–1770* (Chapel Hill: University of North Carolina Press, 2003), 74.

42. See Frank Wilderson, *Incognegro: A Memoir of Exile and Apartheid* (Cambridge, MA: South End, 2008); Jared Sexton, "The Social Life of Social Death: On Afro-Pessimism and Black Optimism," *InTensions Journal* 5 (2011): 1–41; Fred Moten, "Blackness and Nothingness: Mysticism in the Flesh," *South Atlantic Quarterly* 112, no. 4 (2013): 737–780.

43. Greg Thomas, *The Sexual Demon of Colonial Power: Pan-African Embodiment and Erotic Schemes of Empire* (Bloomington: Indiana University Press, 2007), 45.

44. Saidiya Hartman, *Scenes of Subjection: Terror, Slavery, and Self-Making in Nineteenth-Century America* (New York: Oxford University Press, 1997), 79–112.

45. Jared Sexton, "People-of-Color-Blindness: Notes on the Afterlife of Slavery," *Social Text* 28, no. 2 (2010): 31–56; Achille Mbembe, "Necropolitics," *Public Culture* 15, no. 1 (2003): 11–40.

46. Sexton, "People-of-Color-Blindness," 32.

47. Hartman, *Scenes of Subjection*, 86.

48. Ibid.

49. Ibid., 87.

50. Sweet, *Recreating Africa*, 74.

51. Ibid.

52. Hartman, *Scenes of Subjection*, 87.

53. Sweet, *Recreating Africa*, 74.

54. Douglass argues, "Slavery has its own standards of morality, humility, justice, and Christianity. Tried by that standard, it is a system of the greatest kindness to the slave—sanctioned by the purest morality—in perfect agreement with justice—and of course not inconsistent with Christianity. But, tried by another it is doomed to condemnation. The naked relation of master and slave is one of those monsters of darkness, to whom the light of truth is death": Frederick Douglass, "Letter to William Lloyd Garrison," *The Liberator*, February 27, 1846. Throughout this letter he remarks on both his time with Covey and the Christianity of this Nigger-breaker.

55. The definition of rape changed in the United States on January 1, 2013: see Federal Bureau of Investigation, *Rape Addendum*, Uniform Crime Report: Crime in the United States (Washington, DC, 2013), http://www.fbi.gov/about-us/cjis/ucr/crime-in-the-u.s/2013/crime-in-the-u.s.-2013/rape-addendum/rape_addendum_final.pdf. The legacy definition of rape is "carnal knowledge of a female forcibly and against her will." The revised definition is "penetration, no matter how slight, of the vagina or anus with any body part or object, or oral penetration by a sex organ of another person, without the consent of the victim."

56. Vincent Woodard, *The Delectable Negro: Human Consumption and Homoeroticism within U.S. Slave Culture* (New York: New York University Press, 2014), 14.

57. Ibid., 9.

58. Ibid.

59. Ibid., 91.

60. Ibid., 92.

61. Ibid., 93.

62. Ibid.

63. Thomas Foster, "The Sexual Abuse of Black Men under American Slavery," *Journal of the History of Sexuality* 20, no. 3 (2011): 464.

64. Ibid., 446.

65. Sabine Broeck, "Property: [w]hite Gender and Slavery," *Gender Forum* 14 (2006), http://www.genderforum.org/issues/raceing-questions-iii/property.

66. Foster, "The Sexual Abuse of Black Men under American Slavery," 458.

67. Ibid., 461–462.

68. Harriet Jacobs, *Incidents in the Life of a Slave Girl* (New York: Penguin, 2000), 57.

69. Ibid.

70. Ibid., 57–58.

71. Thomas, *The Sexual Demon of Colonial Power*, 46.

72. Foster, "The Sexual Abuse of Black Men under American Slavery," 448.

CHAPTER 5

1. W.E.B. DuBois, *Darkwater: Voices from within the Veil* (Mineola, NY: Dover, 1999), 20.

2. Bill Chapell, "South Carolina Judge Says 1944 Execution of 14-Year-Old Boy Was Wrong," December 17, 2014, http://www.npr.org/sections/thetwo-way/2014/12/17/371534533/s-c-judge-says-boy-14-shouldn-t-have-been-executed.

3. Mark R. Jones, *South Carolina Killers: Crimes of Passion* (Charleston: History Press, 2007), 39–40.

4. Ibid., 40.

5. Steven Hawkins, "Sentencing Children to Death," in *States of Confinement: Policing, Detention, and Prisons*, ed. Joy James (New York: St. Martin's Press, 2000), 24.

6. Carmen Tevis Mullen, *State of South Carolina v. George Stinney Jr.*, 14th Circuit Court, 2014, 28.

7. Deanna Pan, "New Development Coming in the Case of African-American Boy, 14, Executed in Death of 2 [w]hite Girls," August 25, 2016, http://www.postandcourier .com/20160825/160829583/new-development-coming-in-case-of-african-american-boy-14-executed-in-death-of-2-white-girls.

8. Alexis Simmons, "Attorneys Look to File Civil Rights Suit with Help of Law Students in George Stinney Jr. Case," August 26, 2016, http://www.live5news.com/story/32852048/ attorneys-looking-to-file-civil-rights-suit-with-help-of-law-students-in-george-stinney-jr-case.

9. Hilary Sargent, "Extremely Handsome Charles Stuart Charmed Us All, Says Nurse Who Treated Him," October 24, 2014, http://www.boston.com/news/local/massachusetts/ 2014/10/23/operating-room-nurse-charles-stuart-was-extremely-handsome-charmed-all/ 9XRWeu6sYh3VzUQIDs1riO/story.html?p1=related_article_page; Roberto Scales and Hilary Sargent, "The Charles Stuart Murders and the Racist Branding Boston Just Can't Seem to Shake," October 22, 2014, http://www.boston.com/news/local/massachusetts/2014/10/22/ the-charles-stuart-murder-and-the-racist-branding-boston-just-can-seem-shake/RJpeN kL6EQbi8JCAMgfQPN/story.html.

10. Don Terry, "A Woman's False Accusations Pains Many Blacks," November 6, 1994, http://www.nytimes.com/1994/11/06/us/a-woman-s-false-accusation-pains-many-blacks .html.

11. Rene Stutzman, "Stolen Lives: James Bain Spent Thirty-Five Years in Prison for a Rape He Did Not Commit," October 23, 2010, http://articles.orlandosentinel.com/2010-10-23/news/os-innocence-bain-20101023_1_james-bain-dna-tests-wrongful-convic tions.

12. Gary Myers, "Brian Banks Spent Five Years in Prison after Being Falsely Accused of Rape, but Now He Finally Has a Career in NFL," January 25, 2015, http://www.nydai lynews.com/sports/football/wrongfully-imprisoned-banks-career-nfl-article-1.2090727.

13. Ashley Powers, "A Ten Year Nightmare over Rape Conviction Is Over," May 25, 2012, http://articles.latimes.com/2012/may/25/local/la-me-rape-dismiss-20120525.

14. Spencer S. Hsu, "FBI Admits Flaws in Hair Analysis over Decades," April 18, 2015, https://www.washingtonpost.com/local/crime/fbi-overstated-forensic-hair-matches-in-nearly-all-criminal-trials-for-decades/2015/04/18/39c8d8c6-e515-11e4-b510-962fcfabc310_ story.html.

15. Brandon Garrett, "Judging Innocence," *Columbia Law Review* 108 (2008): 66.

16. Samuel R. Gross and Michael Shaffer, "Exonerations in the United States, 1989–2012," National Registry of Exonerations, Ann Arbor, MI, 2012, https://www.law.umich .edu/special/exoneration/Documents/exonerations_us_1989_2012_full_report.pdf, 3.

17. William A. Smith, "Toward an Understanding of Misandric Microaggressions and Racial Battle Fatigue among African Americans in Historically [w]hite Institutions," in *The State of the African-American Male*, ed. Eboni M. Zamani-Gallaher and Vernon C. Polite (East Lansing: Michigan State University, 2012), 267.

18. James B. Stewart and Joseph W. Scott, "The Institutional Decimation of Black American Males," *Western Journal of Black Studies* 2, no. 2 (1978): 82–92.

19. Jim Sidanius and Felicia Pratto, *Social Dominance: An Intergroup Theory of Social Hierarchy and Oppression* (New York: Cambridge University Press, 1999), 33.

20. Ibid., 34.

21. Melissa McDonald, Carlos D. Navarrete, and Mark Van Vugt, "Evolution and the Psychology of Inter-Group Conflict: The Male Warrior Hypothesis," *Philosophical Transactions of the Royal Society* 367 (2012): 671–672.

22. Colin Holbrook, Daniel Fessler, and Carlos David Navarrete, "Looming Large: Racial Stereotypes Illuminate Dual Adaptations for Representing Threat versus Prestige as Physical Size," *Evolution and Human Behavior* 37 (2016): 67–78.

23. Alison Hewitt, "A Black Sounding Name Makes People Imagine a Larger More Dangerous Person, UCLA Study Shows," October 7, 2015, http://newsroom.ucla.edu/releases/a-black-sounding-name-makes-people-imagine-a-larger-more-dangerous-person-ucla-study-shows.

24. Holbrook, Fessler, and Navarrette, "Looming Large," 76.

25. Melissa McDonald, Carlos D. Navarrete, and Jim Sidanius, "Developing a Theory of Gendered Prejudice: An Evolutionary and Social Dominance Perspective," in *Social Cognition, Social Identity, and Intergroup Relations*, ed. Roderick Kramer, Geoffrey Leonardelli, and Robert Livingston (New York: Psychology Press, 2011), 190.

26. See Sidanius and Pratto, *Social Dominance*, esp. chaps. 5–8.

27. Ibid., 298.

28. McDonald, Navarrete, and Sidanius, "Developing a Theory of Gendered Prejudice," 212.

29. Ibid., 191.

30. Valerie Purdie-Vaughns and Richard P. Eibach, "Intersectional Invisibility: The Distinctive Advantages and Disadvantages of Multiple Subordinate-Group Identities," *Sex Roles* 59, no. 5 (2008): 381.

31. Ibid., 380.

32. Ibid., 383.

33. Ibid.

34. Ibid.

35. Michelle Alexander, *The New Jim Crow: Mass Incarceration in the Age of Colorblindness* (New York: New Press, 2010), 7.

36. Huey P. Newton, "War against the Panthers: A Study of Repression in America," Ph.D. diss., University of California, Santa Cruz, 1980.

37. Lacy Banks, "Black Suicide," *Ebony* 25, no. 7 (1970): 76–84.

38. Huey P. Newton, *Revolutionary Suicide* (New York: Penguin, 2009), 1.

39. Émile Durkheim, *Suicide: A Study in Sociology* (London: Routledge Classics, 2005).

40. Newton, *Revolutionary Suicide*, 2.

41. See Durkheim, *Suicide*, 1–29, esp. 14–17.

42. Ibid., 207.

43. Ibid., 208.

44. Herbert Hendin, *Black Suicide* (New York: Basic, 1969), 3.

45. Jeffrey A. Bridge, Lindsey Asti, and Lisa M. Horowitz., "Suicide Trends among Elementary School-Aged Children in the United States from 1993 to 2012," *JAMA Pediatrics* 169, no. 7 (2015): 673–677.

46. Daphne C. Watkins, B. Lee Green, Brian M. Rivers, and Kyrel L. Rowell, "Depression and Black Men: Implications for Future Research," *Journal of Men's Health and Gender* 3, no. 3 (2013): 227–235.

47. Daphne C. Watkins and Harold W. Neighbors, "Social Determinants of Depression and the Black Male Experience," in *Social Determinants of Health Among African-American Men*, ed. Henrie M. Treadwell, Clare Xanthos, and Kisha B. Holden (San Francisco: Jossey-Bass, 2013), 39–62.

48. Hendin, *Black Suicide*, 3.

49. Ibid., 7.

50. Anthony Lemelle Jr., "Betcha Cain't Reason with 'Em: Bad Black Boys in America," in *Black Male Adolescents: Parenting and Education in Community Context*, ed. Benjamin Bowser (Lanham, MD: University of America Press), 1994, 91–128.

51. Hendin, *Black Suicide*, 11.

52. Ibid., 44.

53. James B. Stewart, "The Political Economy of Black Male Suicide," *Journal of Black Studies* 11, no. 2 (1980): 260.

54. Newton, *Revolutionary Suicide*, 2.

55. Durkheim, *Suicide*, 209.

56. Newton, *Revolutionary Suicide*, 2.

57. Ibid., 3.

58. Robert F. Williams, *Negroes with Guns* (New York: Marzani and Munsell, 1962), 110–111.

59. Henry Sidgwick, *The Method of Ethics* (Indianapolis: Hackett, 1981), 1.

60. George Jackson, *Blood in My Eye* (Baltimore: Black Classic Press, 1990), 10.

61. Ibid., 7.

62. Newton, *Revolutionary Suicide*, 3.

63. Ibid., 41.

64. Ibid., 358.

65. Ibid.

66. Sylvia Wynter, "No Humans Involved: An Open Letter to My Colleagues," *Voices of the African Diaspora* 8, no. 2 (1992): 13.

67. Ibid., 14.

68. Huey P. Newton, "Fear and Doubt," in *Essays from the Minister of Defense* (N.p.: Black Panther Party), 15–18, 17.

69. Zygmunt Bauman, *Legislators and Interpreters: On Modernity, Post-modernity, and Intellectuals* (Cambridge: Polity, 1989), 179.

70. Ibid.

71. Sylvia Wynter, "Beyond the Categories of the Master Conception," in *C.L.R. James's Caribbean*, ed. Henry Buhle and Paul Buhle (Durham, NC: Duke University Press, 1992), 65.

72. Bauman, *Legislators and Interpreters*, 2.

73. Sylvia Wynter, "Towards the Sociogenic Principle: Fanon, Identity, and the Puzzle of Conscious Experience, and What It Is Like to Be 'Black,'" in *National Identities and Sociopolitical Changes in Latin America*, ed. Antonio Gomez-Moriana and Mercedes Duran-Cogan (New York: Routledge, 2001), 30–66.

74. Wynter, "No Humans Involved," 14.

75. Ibid., 65.

76. Ibid., 66.

77. Asmarom Legesse, *Gada: Three Approaches to the Study of African Society* (New York: Free Press, 1973), 115.

78. Wynter, "No Humans Involved," 16.

79. Legesse, *Gada*, 271.

80. Saidiya V. Hartman and Frank B. Wilderson III, "The Position of Unthought," *Qui Parle* 13, no. 2 (2003): 183.

81. See Tommy J. Curry, "On Derelict and Method: The Methodological Crisis of Africana Philosophy's Study of African Descended People under an Integrationist Milieu," *Radical Philosophy Review* 14, no. 2 (2011): 139–164.

CONCLUSION

Note: The chapter-opening verse is mine.

1. See Trymaine Lee, "The 911 Call that Led to Johnathan Ferrell's Death," September 17, 2013, http://www.msnbc.com/msnbc/the-911-call-led-jonathan-ferrells.

2. See Erik Ortiz and F. Brinley Burton, "Charleston Church Shooting: Suspect Dylann Roof Captured in North Carolina," June 18, 2015, http://www.nbcnews.com/storyline/charleston-church-shooting/charleston-church-shooting-suspect-dylann-roof-captured-north-carolina-n377546.

3. James Baldwin, "A Conversation with James Baldwin by Kenneth Clark," in *Conversations with James Baldwin*, ed. Fred J. Stanley and Louis H. Pratt (Jackson: University of Mississippi Press, 1989), 45.

4. Wendy Christensen, "The NFL, the Military, and the Problem with Masculine Institutions," *Pacific Standard*, September 22, 2014, https://psmag.com/the-nfl-the-military-and-the-problem-with-masculine-institutions-1a30bb1095ac#.kyoqfdj5l.

5. Michelangelo Signorile, "Is America's Crisis of Masculinity Playing Out in Its Favorite Sport?" *Daily Dot*, September 17, 2015, http://www.dailydot.com/via/nfl-ray-rice-domestic-violence-masculinity-crisis.

6. Khadijah Costley White, "Adrian Peterson Is Not a Racial Symbol," *The Atlantic*, September 15, 2014.

7. Stacey Patton, "Why Is America Celebrating the Beating on a Black Child," April 29, 2015, https://www.washingtonpost.com/posteverything/wp/2015/04/29/why-is-america-celebrating-the-beating-of-a-black-child.

8. Ellen E. Pinderhughes, Kenneth A. Dodge, John E. Bates, Gregory S. Pettit, and Arnaldo Zelli, "Discipline Responses: Influences of Parent's Socioeconomic Status, Ethnicity, Beliefs about Parenting, Stress, and Cognitive-Emotional Processes," *Journal of Family Psychology* 14, no. 3 (2000): 380–400; Murray Straus and Julie H. Stewart, "Corporal Punishment by American Parents: National Data on Prevalence, Chronicity, Severity, and Duration, in Relation to Child and Family Characteristics," *Clinical Child and Family Psychology Review* 2, no. 2 (1999): 55–70.

9. Jean M. Ipsa and Linda Halgunseth, "Talking about Corporal Punishment: Nine Low Income African American Mothers Talk Punishment," *Early Childhood Research Quarterly* 19 (2004): 477.

10. Arthur Waley, "Sociocultural Differences in the Developmental Consequences of the Use of Physical Discipline during Childhood for African Americans," *Cultural Diversity and Ethnic Minority Psychology* 6, no. 1 (2000): 5–12.

11. Judith Butler, *Gender Trouble* (New York: Routledge, 1999), 5.

12. Ibid., 2.

13. Maurice O. Wallace, *Constructing the Black Masculine: Identity and Ideality in African American Men's Literature and Culture 1775–1995* (Durham, NC: Duke University Press, 2002), 8.

14. Ibid., 177.

15. Miles White, *From Jim Crow to Jay-Z: Race, Rape, and the Performance of Masculinity* (Urbana: University of Illinois Press, 2011), 2.

16. Ronald Jackson, *Scripting the Black Masculine Body: Identity, Discourse, and Racial Politics in Popular Media* (Albany: State University of New York Press, 2006), 129.

17. Rinaldo Walcott, "Reconstructing Manhood; or, The Drag of Black Masculinity," *Small Axe* 28 (2009): 76.

18. Stuart Hall introduces his idea of managerialism on the economic and class func-

tion of knowledge production itself. He is clear that "the idea of the university as an 'open' institution, 'freely' in pursuit of knowledge, was, of course, never quite the case. It has always been a bit of a myth. That accompanies the elitism of academic life, the closure around the profession, and the hidden assumptions about who can benefit from it and who can't, and so on": Stuart Hall, "Universities, Intellectuals and Multitudes," in *The Utopian Pedagogy: Radical Experiments against Neoliberal Globalization*, ed. Richard Day and Greig De Peuter (Toronto: University of Toronto Press, 2007), 110. Quite in line with my thinking about Black manhood is the question of who benefits from re-creating, in the university and among theory, the same racist notions about Black males that we see in society. How is it that the stereotypes of a racist society so easily become theory within disciplines?

19. Ibid., 79.

20. Kimberlé Crenshaw, "Demarginalizing the Intersection of Race and Sex: A Black Feminist Critique of Antidiscrimination Doctrine, Feminist Theory, and Antiracist Politics," *University of Chicago Legal Forum* 140 (1989): 139–168.

21. Ibid., 149.

22. Kimberlé Crenshaw, "Mapping the Margins: Intersectionality, Identity Politics, and Violence against Women of Color," *Stanford Law Review* 43, no. 6 (1991): 1241–1299. It is important to note that Crenshaw represents the "social world" as a political world necessitating coalitional activism and strategy. Drawing from Mari Matsuda's "Beside My Sister, Facing the Enemy: Legal Theory Out of Coalition," oppression and multiple subordinations means there are several inescapable needs: a need for unity and a need to focus on multiple oppressions highlighted by overlapping identities, as well as the acknowledgment that "racism is best understood and fought with knowledge gained from the broader anti-subordination struggle"—a call for the end to the reign of the race man: Mari Matsuda, "Beside My Sister, Facing the Enemy: Legal Theory Out of Coalition," *Stanford Law Review* 43 (1990–1991): 1190–1191. Matsuda sees intersectionality as incompatible with the Black male political leadership of the past and seems to interpret previous civil and human rights struggles led by Black males as essentially about race and race only. This sort of reductionism considers all previous attempts at liberation by Black men ineffective and theoretically inadequate, not because they did not focus on particular structures such as economic or legal systems that did not *affect* all Black and oppressed people, but because these Black male thinkers did not include all of the possible identities thought to be relevant to true coalitional struggle. Matsuda argues, "Even if one wanted to live as the old prototype "race man," it is simply not possible to struggle against racism alone and ever hope to end racism": Matsuda, "Beside My Sister, Facing the Enemy," 1191. Matsuda implies that the race man was problematic because he focused only on race and thereby was exclusively dedicated to his own racial interests. It must be said, however, that Matsuda, like other intersectional theorists, is ignoring Black male contributions to economics, sexuality, power, militarism, and religion because some of the strategies they have embraced have fallen outside the reformist rubric of multicultural coalition building.

23. Crenshaw, "Mapping the Margins," 1251–1252.

24. Ibid., 1252.

25. Devon Carbado, "Introduction: When and Where Black Men Enter," in *Black Men on Race and Gender* (New York: New York University Press, 1999), 4.

26. Ibid.

27. Devon Carbado, "Straight Out of the Closet," *Berkeley Women's Journal* 15 (2000): 76–124.

28. See Kimberlé Crenshaw, "Close Encounters of Three Kinds: On Teaching Dominance Feminism and Intersectionality," *Tulsa Law Review* 46, no. 1 (2010): 151–189, esp. 158–160.

29. Catharine A. MacKinnon, "From Practice to Theory, or What Is a [w]hite Woman Anyway?" *Yale Journal of Law and Feminism* 13 (1991): 20.

30. Crenshaw, "Close Encounters of Three Kinds."

31. Catharine A. MacKinnon, *Sexual Harassment of Working Women: A Case of Sexual Discrimination* (New Haven, CT: Yale University Press, 1979), 176–177.

32. Ibid., 176.

33. Ibid., 31.

34. Catharine MacKinnon, *Feminism Unmodified* (Cambridge, MA: Harvard University Press, 1987), 6.

35. Ibid., 7.

36. Frank Rudy Cooper, "Against Bipolar Black Masculinity: Intersectionality, Assimilation, Identity Performance, and Hierarchy," *University of California Davis Law Review* 39 (2005): 858.

37. Ibid., 897.

38. Ibid., 896.

39. Ibid., 899.

40. Michael Kimmel, "Masculinity as Homophobia: Fear, Shame, and Silence in the Construction of Gender Identity," in *The Gender of Desire: Essays on Male Sexuality* (New York: State University of New York Press, 2005), 30.

41. Ibid.

42. Cooper, "Against Bipolar Black Masculinity," 899.

43. bell hooks, *We Reel Cool: Black Men and Masculinity* (New York: Routledge, 2004), 7.

44. Ibid., 9–10.

45. Angela Harris, "Gender, Violence, Race, and Criminal Justice," *Stanford Law Review* 52 (2000): 777–807, 782. Harris takes care to distinguish between the idea of multiple masculinities and intersectionality; she says, "This view of the relationship between gender, race, class, and sexuality thus differs from the 'intersectionality' metaphor used by many critical race feminists."

46. Anthony Lemelle Jr., *Black Masculinity and Sexual Politics* (New York: Routledge, 2010), 133.

47. Ibid., 74.

48. Devon Carbado, "Colorblind Intersectionality," *Signs* 38, no. 4 (2013): 814.

49. Ibid., 840.

50. Ibid.

51. See Frank Rudy Cooper, "Who's the Man? Masculinities Studies, Terry Stops, and Police Training," *Columbia Journal of Gender and Law* 18, no. 3 (2009): 671–742; Frank Rudy Cooper, "Masculinities, Post-racialism, and the Gates Controversy: The False Equivalence between Officer and Citizen," *Nevada Law Journal* 11 (2010): 1–43.

52. Carbado, "Colorblind Intersectionality," 841.

53. Paul Butler, "Black Male Exceptionalism: The Problems and Potential of Black Male Focused Interventions," *DuBois Review* 12, no. 2 (2013): 503.

54. Oscar A. Barbin, Velma McBride Murry, Patrick Tolan, Sandra Graham, and the Boys of Color Research Collaborative, "Development of Boys and Young Men of Color: Implications of Developmental Science for My Brother's Keeper Initiative," *Social Policy Report* 29, no. 3 (2016): 2.

55. Sumi Cho, Kimberlé Crenshaw, and Leslie McCall concur that intersectionality is

best framed as an analytic sensibility. If intersectionality is an analytic disposition, a way of thinking about and conducting analyses, then what makes an analysis intersectional is not its use of the term "intersectionality," nor its being situated in a familiar genealogy, nor its drawing on lists of standard citations. Rather, what makes an analysis intersectional—whatever terms it deploys, whatever its iteration, whatever its field or discipline—is its adoption of an intersectional way of thinking about the problem of sameness and difference and its relation to power. This framing—conceiving of categories not as distinct but as always permeated by other categories, fluid and changing, always in the process of creating and being created by dynamics of power—emphasizes what intersectionality does rather than what intersectionality is. (Sumi Cho, Kimberlé Crenshaw, and Leslie McCall, "Toward a Field of Intersectionality Studies: Theory, Applications, and Praxis," *Signs* 38, no. 4 [2013]: 795)

56. Peter Kwan, "Jeffrey Dahmer and the Cosynthesis of Categories," *Hastings Law Review* 48 (1997): 1276.

57. Althea Mutua, "Multidimensionality Is to Masculinities What Intersectionality Is to Feminism," *Nevada Law Review* 13 (2013): 355.

58. Darren Hutchinson, "Identity Crisis: Intersectionality, Multidimensionality, and the Development of an Adequate Theory of Subordination," *Michigan Journal of Race and Law* 6, no. 2 (2001): 312.

59. Mutua, "Multidimensionality Is to Masculinities What Intersectionality Is to Feminism," 345–346.

60. Ibid., 346.

61. Ibid., 346–347.

62. It is important to note that Black historians have long problematized the narrative of Civil Rights and that offered by popular Black feminist historiography. Paula Giddings argues that Black men and Black women have always engaged in complementarian politics. Her essay "The Lessons of History Will Shape the 1980s—*Black Macho and the Myth of the Superwoman* Won't" (*Encore American and Worldwide News*, 1970, 50–51), is in line with current Black Power studies scholarship such as Linda Lumsden's "Good Mothers with Guns: Framing Black Womanhood in the *Black Panther*, 1968–1980" (*Journalism and Mass Communication Quarterly* 86, no. 4 [2009]: 900–922), which shows that the Black Civil Rights and Black Power movements not only were inclusive but also allowed the only outlet of the time for Black women to challenge sexism within a revolutionary movement.

There is a long history of Black women in the Black Power Movement questioning the efficacy and reality of the gender division in the Black Power Movement. Kathleen Cleaver, for instance, argues:

It seems to me that part of the genesis of the gender question, and this is only an opinion, lies in the way it deflects attention from confronting the revolutionary critique our organization made of the larger society, and turns it inward to look at what type of dynamics and social conflicts characterized the organization. To me this discussion holds far less appeal than that which engages the means we devised to struggle against the oppressive dynamics and social conflicts the larger society imposed on us. Not many answers to the gender question take into account what I've experienced. What I've read or heard as answers generally seem to respond to a particular model of academic inquiry that leaves out what I believe is central: How do you empower an oppressed and impoverished people who are struggling against racism, militarism, terrorism, and sexism too? I mean how do you do that? That's the real question. (Kathleen Cleaver, "Women, Power, Revolution," in *Liberation, Imagination, and the Black Panther Party* [New York: Routledge, 2001], 124)

63. Asmarom Legesse, *Gada: Three Approaches to the Study of African Society* (New York: Free Press, 1973), 249.

64. Frantz Fanon, *Black Skin, [w]hite Masks* (New York: Grove, 1967), 177.

65. Ibid., 165.

66. Ibid., 177.

EPILOGUE

1. E-mail message to Tommy J. Curry from the editor, February 7, 2014.

2. Ibid. See Tommy J. Curry, "Eschatological Dilemmas: The Problem of Studying the Black Male Only as the Deaths that Result from Anti-Black Racism," in *I Am Because We Are*, 2d ed. (Amherst: University of Massachusetts Press, 2016), 479–499.

3. Centers for Disease Control, "Leading Causes of Death by Age Group, Black Males—United States, 2002–2013," http://www.cdc.gov/men/lcod.

4. Black men and boys are at the bottom of every demographic of study. For the relationship between Black male incarceration and societal viability, see James B. Stewart and Joseph W. Scott, "The Institutional Decimation of Black American Males," *Western Journal of Black Studies* 2, no. 2 (1978): 82–92. For a discussion of how stereotypes about Black males being criminals and being dishonest affect employment, see Ronald B. Mincy, ed., *Black Males Left Behind* (Washington, DC: Urban Institute Press, 2006). For a discussion of how Black male incarceration and unemployment show not only that Black males have lower incomes than their female and racial counterparts but also how incarceration creates sample biases across all datasets used to understand Black men and boys, see Becky Pettit, *Invisible Men: Mass Incarceration and the Myth of Black Progress* (New York: Russell Sage Foundation, 2012). For Black male vulnerability to domestic abuse, see Carolyn M. West, "Partner Abuse in Ethnic Minority and Gay, Lesbian, Bisexual, and Transgender Populations," *Partner Abuse* 3, no. 3 (2012): 336–357.

5. See Jim Sidanius and Rosemary C. Veniegas, "Gender and Race: The Interactive Nature of Disadvantage," in *Reducing Prejudice and Discrimination*, ed. Stuart Oskamp (New York: Psychology Press, 2008), 47–69; Mary Jackman, *The Velvet Glove: Paternalism and Conflict in Gender, Class, and Race Relations* (Berkeley: University of California Press, 1994).

6. Deborah Gorman-Smith and Patrick Tolan, "The Role of Exposure to Community Violence and Developmental Problems among Inner-City Youth," *Development and Psychopathology* 10 (1998): 104.

7. Ibid., 101–116.

8. Oscar A. Barbin, Velma McBride Murry, Patrick Tolan, Sandra Graham, and the Boys of Color Research Collaborative, "Development of Boys and Young Men of Color: Implications of Developmental Science for My Brother's Keeper Initiative," *Social Policy Report* 29, no. 3 (2016):14.

9. Historically, Black men have been the most disadvantaged in education: see Anne McDaniel, Thomas A. DiPrete, Claudia Buchmann, and Uri Shwed, "The Black Gender Gap in Educational Attainment: Historical Trends and Racial Comparisons," *Demography* 48 (2011): 889–914.

Index

Fear, 3, 4, 7, 21, 87, 212, 253n104; of Black
  male bodies, 169; Negrophobia and, 128,
  131, 138; phobogenic object and, 88–89. *See
  also* Negrophobia
"Fear and Doubt" (Newton), 189, 192
Federal Bureau of Investigation (FBI), 32, 168
Felton, Rebecca Latimer, 56–57
Female-to-male partner violence (FMPV), 120
Feminine, Black males as, 54–55
Feminism, 12, 204–205, 250n24; ethnology of,
  with primal rape, 55–59; with gender and
  biological body, 40; ideology, 23; intersec-
  tionality and, 141; patriarchy and, 47
Feminists, 2–3, 23, 24, 142, 238n28, 250n24
Ferrell, Jonathan, 144, 198
Finot, Jean, 70
Flores, Andrew, 32
FMPV (Female-to-male partner violence), 120
Forks, Terrance, 124
Foster, Thomas, 93–94, 159–161, 163
Foster care, adoption rates in, 124
Foston, Nikitta, 124
Franklin, Claude, 21–22
Frazier, E. Franklin, 104, 105, 127, 128–129,
  255n4
*Freedom Song: A Personal Story of the 1960s
  Civil Rights Movement* (Mary King), 13
Freud, Sigmund, 16–17
Friedman, Lawrence, 59–60
Fucking: E. Cleaver, on, 91–92, 101; white men
  and, 147, 150. *See also* Phallus
Futural subjectivity, anti-ethical thought and,
  181–187

*Gada: Three Approaches to the Study of
  African Society* (Legesse), 193
Gaffney, Melinda, 124
Gaines, Kevin K., 66
Gary, Lawrence, E., 19, 20
Gates, Henry Louis, 215
Geismar, Maxwell, 88
Gender, 6–7, 24; with abuse, symmetrical
  rates of, 118; Black male death and, 142;
  Black males and, 19–25, 106, 191; Black
  males as de-gendered, 6, 50, 57; Black masculinity and, 205; Black Power Movement
  and, 273n62; with biological body, 40–41;
  education and, 29–30; Man-Not with colonial notions of, 25–26; patriarchy and, 41,
  63–64, 68, 142; race and, 5, 22–23, 40–42,
  50–51, 54–55, 62, 151; with rape, 155–157,
  162; rethinking connotations of, 135, 204;
  roles, 61, 238n20; sex and, 154, 211; sexism
  with, 14–15; slavery and, 18, 45, 160; social

dominance theory and, 173–175; stereo-
  types, 32, 33, 54; systems, 171; violence and,
  132, 259n67; women and, 5–6, 32
Gender and Power (Connell), 16, 17, 212
Genitals. *See* Phallus
Genocide, 7, 189, 225; of Armenians, 188;
  against Black men and boys, 37, 131, 133,
  142, 177–178, 194
Genre: gender and, 6–7; study with Black
  male vulnerability, 222–225
Gibson, Wanetta, 168
Giddings, Paula, 12, 78, 273n62
Gilman, Charlotte, 55, 57
Gilmore, Glenda, 64–65
Glover, Eric, 145
Gobineau, Arthur de, 49–50
Goff, Phillip A., 133, 134
"Going to Meet the Man" (Baldwin), 147–149
"Good Mothers with Guns: Framing Black
  Womanhood in the *Black Panther,* 1968–
  1980" (Lumsden), 273n62
Gooley, Ruby Lee, 22
Graham, Toya, 202–203
Gramsci, Antonio, 15–16
Grant, Oscar, 7
Green, Corey, 144
Greensberg, Amy, 48
Grimke, Archibald H., 58
Guy-Sheftall, Beverly, 59–60, 63

Hale, Grace Elizabeth, 56
Hall, Granville Stanley, 54
Hall, Stuart, 206, 270–271n18
Hare, Nathan, and Julia Hare (*Bringing the
  Black Boy to Manhood*), 22
Harnois, Catherine, 24
Harris, Angela, 132, 213, 272n45
Harrison, Hubert, 69–70
Hartman, Saidiya: on rape as torture, 157; on
  rape during slavery, 155–160, 162–163
Hawkins, Williametta, 95–96
Hayden, Casey, 13
Hegel, G.W.F., 43
Hegemonic masculinity theory: with Black
  males, reality of, 10–15; intersectionality
  and, 211–217; problems with, 15–19
Hendin, Herbert, 179, 180
Henry, Wilma, 30
Hernton, Calvin, 4, 98, 170
Hines, Denise, 118
Hispanics, 120, 123, 172
Historiography. *See* Man-Not, historiography
  of
Hodes, Martha, 94

Tommy J. Curry is a Professor of Philosophy and holds a Personal Chair (Distinguished Professorship) of Africana Philosophy and Black Male Studies at the University of Edinburgh. He is the past president of Philosophy Born of Struggle, and the recipient of the USC Shoah Foundation 2016–2017 A.I. and Manet Schepps Foundation Teaching Fellowship. He is the author of *Another White Man's Burden: Josiah Royce's Quest for a Philosophy of Racial Empire* and the editor of *The Philosophical Treatise of William H. Ferris: Selected Readings from* The African Abroad or, His Evolution in Western Civilization.

Made in the USA
Monee, IL
09 July 2021